Time, History and International Law

Time, History and International Law

Edited by

Matthew Craven
Malgosia Fitzmaurice
and
Maria Vogiatzi

MARTINUS NIJHOFF PUBLISHERS
LEIDEN • BOSTON
2011

This book is printed on acid-free paper.

Library of Congress Control Number: 2007270973

This paperback was originally published in hardback under ISBN 978 90 04 15481 0 as volume 58 in the series *Developments in International Law*.

ISBN 978 90 04 20677 9

CONTENTS

ACKNOWLEDGEMENTS

We would like to express out gratitude to Professor William Wilson, Head of the Department of Law of Queen Mary University of London and Professor Philip Ogden, Senior Vice-Principal of Queen Mary University of London for their generosity and assistance in organising the Conference, which resulted in this book of essays.

We would like also to thank Mr. Sébastien Jodoin-Pilon and Mr. Christiano Sávio Barros Figueirôa, interns at the British Institute of International and Comparative Law, for their assistance in the preparation of this book.

Matthew Craven
Malgosia Fitzmaurice
Maria Vogiatzi

INTRODUCTION: INTERNATIONAL LAW AND ITS HISTORIES

Matt Craven*

Introduction

In an article written in the second volume of the American Journal of International Law in 1908, Lassa Oppenheim was to reflect upon the various tasks that he believed needed to be undertaken in the development of the 'science of international law',[1] foremost amongst which was the 'exposition of existing recognized rules of international law'.[2] He was to maintain, however, that in order to satisfactorily fulfil that task, scholars necessarily had to have 'a knowledge of the history of the rules concerned'.[3] But on this score there was much to be done:

> '[I]n spite of the vast importance of this task it has as yet hardly been undertaken; the history of international law is certainly the most neglected province of it. Apart from a few points which are dealt with in monographs, the history of international law is virgin land which awaits its cultivators. Whatever may be the merits of the histories and historical sketches which we possess, they are in the main mere compilations. The master-historian of international law has still to come.'[4]

The main task, as he saw it, of the 'expected master-builder' was the elaboration of a history of dogmatics ('Dogmengeschichte') the purpose of which would be to explain from where each rule of international law originated, how it developed and how it gradually became recognized in practice. This was, however, only part of the picture as the history of dogmatics would merely supply the 'building materials' of a broader 'history of international law' understood as a 'branch of the history of Western cilivization'. The historian of international law would also be expected to recount the 'ultimate victory of international law over international anarchy' and 'bring to light the part certain states have played in the victorious development of certain rules'. In the process they would have to expose 'the economic, political, humanitarian, religious, and other interests which have helped to establish the present rules of international law'.[5] The task, in other words, would be both celebratory

---

* Professor of International Law, School of Oriental and African Studies, University of London.
[1] Oppenheim, 'The Science of International Law: Its Task and Method', 2 *American Journal of International Law* (1908) 313.
[2] *Ibid*, 314.
[3] *Ibid*, 316.
[4] *Id.*
[5] *Ibid*, 317.

and instructive, it would not only stand as testament to what had come about (the disciplining of politics through law), but also provide a means whereby international lawyers could work with more precision and knowledge, and with a clearer sense of their social role. It would involve both an engagement with the genealogy of specific rules (assisting thereby in the precise delineation of those rules, their limits and exceptions), and the articulation of a grand historical narrative that placed the evolution of international law alongside the evolution of international society. This was not, furthermore, merely a historical endeavour, but would be such as to make clear where the future lay: in the development of a powerful international organization governed by international law.

Oppenheim would be surprised, and perhaps somewhat disconcerted, to learn that a century later no one had answered his call. Histories of international law have certainly been written[6] but none so comprehensive as to combine a full history of doctrinal development with an account of the place of international law within a broader history of Western civilization.[7] The moment for such an undertaking, furthermore, appears to have passed. Two intervening World Wars put firmly in doubt Oppenheim's momentary celebration of the triumph of international law over 'anarchy' or lawlessness, and decolonisation only rendered more problematic his idea of a history of the discipline written in terms of European civilization.[8] More fundamentally, however, the task for which he saw such a history to be written – the furtherance of the 'science of international law' – bespoke of a commitment to a positivist conception of law which, almost from the moment it was articulated, was seen to be incapable of fulfilling its own promises.[9]

Even if the type of history Oppenheim advocated is unlikely now to be undertaken, his observation that the history of international law is the 'most neglected' aspect of the field,[10] is one that can surely no longer be maintained. In recent years, there has been an extraordinary outpouring of articles and monographs written on the history of the discipline (or history and the discipline).[11] Indeed quite apart from the emergence of new specialist journals on the topic, or journals such as the

---

[6] See e.g., R. Redslob, *Histoires des grands principes du droit des gens depuis l'antiquité jusqu'à la veille de la gande guerre* (1923); J.H.W. Verzijl, *International law in Historical Perspective* (1979); A. Nussbaum, *A Concise History of the Law of Nations* (1954); M. Koskenniemi, *The Gentle Civilizer of Nations: The Rise and Fall of International Law 1870–1960* (2002).

[7] For an attempt of something of this kind see E. Carr, *The Twenty Years' Crisis 1919–1939* (1939); W. Grewe, *The Epochs of International Law* (Trans M. Byers, 2000).

[8] But see: A Anghie, *Imperialism, Sovereignty and the Making of International Law* (2005).

[9] For an account of Oppenheim's positivism as that of a 'Noble Lie' see Perreau-Saussine, 'A Case Study on Jurisprudence as a Source of International Law: Oppenheim's Influence' in this volume, 91. See also, Kennedy, 'International Law and the Nineteenth Century: History of an Illusion', 17 *Quinnipiac Law Review* (1997) 99.

[10] A view echoed in Grewe, *supra* note 7, 1.

[11] See generally Hueck, 'The Discipline of the History of International Law', 3 *Journal of the History of International Law* (2001) 194.

European Journal of International Law which, as a matter of editorial policy, have dedicated special issues to prominent international lawyers from the past (e.g. Scelle, Verdross, Anzilotti), one also finds other prominent journals devoting a significant portion of their space to such issues. One example suffices. In the 2002 edition of the British Yearbook of International Law – a journal whose engagement with history has characteristically been confined to the obituary – one finds articles on the Grotian tradition,[12] the work of the Advisory Committee of Jurists in 1920,[13] the Prize Court in the 1914–18 War,[14] the terrorism and International Criminal Court Conventions of 1937,[15] a history of Britain's engagement with the Genocide Convention[16] and an account of Thomas Baty's life and work in Japan.[17] In total, three quarters of the Yearbook's pages are filled with such historical renditions and, when compared to the output of the journal a decade earlier, the current propensity to look backwards rather than forwards is clearly evident.

The Turn to History

This immediately prompts the question: why this recent engagement with history? Why now? Presumably there is something more at work here than merely a millennial retrospection. Presumably also, this is not merely a manifestation of what Bloom called the 'anxiety of influence' – a sense of dispirited 'belatedness' that instils in the author (or in his case the poet) a belief that novelty and innovation are no longer possible, but yet drives them to look back and reinterpret the past for purposes of finding imaginative space for their own creative work.[18] Even if such a psychological drive were to be identified, it still doesn't answer the question as to why history appears to have become important at this particular juncture.

In his contribution to this volume, Lesaffer suggests that the sudden boom in the historiography of international law is, in fact, 'easily explained'.[19] He suggests that

---

[12] Lesaffer, 'The Grotian Tradition Revisited: Change and Continuity in the History of International Law', 73 *British Yearbook of International Law* (2002) 103.

[13] Spiermann, 'Who Attempts too Much does Nothing Well: The 1920 Advisory Committee of Jurists and the Statute of the Permanent Court of International Justice', 73 *British Yearbook of International Law* (2002) 187.

[14] Foxton, 'International Law in Domestic Courts: Some Lessons from the Prize Court in the Great War', 73 *British Yearbook of International Law* (2002) 261.

[15] Marston, 'Early Attempts to Suppress Terrorism: The Terrorism and International Criminal Court Conventions of 1937' 73 *British Yearbook of International Law* (2002) 293.

[16] Simpson, 'Britain and the Genocide Convention', 73 *British Yearbook of International Law* (2002) 5.

[17] Murase, 'Thomas Baty in Japan: Seeing Through the Twilight' 73 *British Yearbook of International Law* (2002) 315.

[18] H. Bloom, *The Anxiety of Influence: A Theory of Poetry* (1973).

[19] Lesaffer, 'International Law and its History: The Story of an Unrequited Love', in this volume, 27.

at all critical moments in the history of international relations, all moments of momentous political change (whether that be the revolutionary era ushered in after 1795, or the aftermath of World conflict in 1919 or 1945) scholars have typically turned back to revisit the discipline's past as part of an 'enquiry into the foundations of the law of nations'.[20] The present climate, marked by the end of the Cold War and the new 'War on Terror', is of similar character and it is the pervasive sense of uncertainty or turmoil that has, once again, propelled scholars into historical reflection as a way of locating some secure foothold for an understanding of those contemporary dilemmas.

Elsewhere, Koskenniemi offers a similar explanation.[21] For him, the period up until 1990 at least, the increasing specialisation of international law in the fields of human rights, trade and the environment left little room for historical reflection: '[f]or a functionally oriented generation, the past offered mainly problems, and few solutions'.[22] After 1989, however, he identifies two possible reasons for the developing interest in international law's history: one being associated with the possible resumption of the liberal internationalist project of the early 20th Century following the end of the cold war, the other identifying that juncture as an inaugural one – giving rise to a total break with an outmoded diplomatic system which had hitherto 'obstructed progressive social transformation'.[23] Each of these conceptions of the 'new era', in Koskenniemi's view, provided reason for return to the past – either to rediscover or 'dust off' debates which had been shelved in the 1930s for their redeployment in the present context, or to provide a historical setting for the emergence and identification of an altogether different type of international law.

Whilst both Koskenniemi and Lesaffer foreground the end of the Cold War as a moment of significance for purposes of explaining the historical turn, where they might be thought to differ is in their tone. For Koskenniemi, it is a matter of a newly-found optimism in the possibilities for the progressive development of international law; for Lesaffer, by contrast, the contemporary era seems to be one marked by anxiety and discomfort – a sense that we are now occupying a moment of transition, but with little sense of what the future might hold. Each of these 'moods' are well reflected in recent literature concerning international law. On the one hand, a sense of optimism appears to be expressed both in the emergence of new discourses

---

[20] *Ibid*, 29.

[21] Koskenniemi, 'Why History of International Law Today?', 4 *Rechtsgeschichte* (2004) 61.

[22] *Ibid*, 64–5.

[23] For an example see Marston, *supra* note 15, 313, in which following an account of the Terrorism and International Criminal Court Conventions of 1937, he observes that the UK's potential participation foundered upon the perception of the law officers that Parliament was unlikely to tolerate amendments to national criminal law insofar as they would have extra-territorial effect. In noting that the UK is now party to the European Convention on the Suppression of Terrorism 1977 and that the Terrorism Act 2000 created several extra-terrirorial crimes, he concludes that '[t]hese considerations are no longer constraining'.

predicated upon the evolution of international law (the right to democratic governance for example[24]) and in the revitalisation of projects from earlier eras (humanitarian intervention[25] and international criminal law[26] perhaps). On the other hand, a sense of anxiety may also be perceived in recent works concerning the rise of unilateralism,[27] the persistence of hegemonic influence[28] and a re-emergence of the rhetoric of 'Great Powers'.[29]

Whether the contemporaneous mood is one of anxiety or optimism is perhaps not that significant, but it is evident that such moods may well affect how the history of international law is conceived. On the one hand, a spirit of confidence would appear to encourage the view that the past is firmly behind us (no longer exercising a stranglehold over the present), and that historical reflection may be useful as a way of 'situating' the present or enlivening contemporaneous debates, but that in other regards it is pretty much a dispensable part of international legal practice. A sense of 'novelty', in other words, might allow an exploratory space for new endeavours unburdened by the restraints of a 'traditional' international law that insisted upon respect for sovereignty or domestic jurisdiction – all is to be invented anew. On the other hand, however, a spirit of anxiety may either lead to a sense that something important has been left behind (and hence the need to look back to rediscover it),[30] or a sense that contemporaneous discourse remains shackled in the discipline's history such that the only way to move on (or 'out' or 'away') is to look back.[31] Here an engagement with a history of the discipline becomes a more urgent and important enterprise.

---

[24] See e.g., G. Fox and B. Roth, *Democratic Governance and International Law* (2000).

[25] N. Wheeler, *Saving Strangers: Humanitarian Intervention and International Society* (2000); S. Chesterman, *Just War or Just Peace* (2001).

[26] E.g., K. Kittichaisaree, *International Criminal Law* (2001); W. Schabas, *Genocide in International Law: the Crime of Crimes* (2000).

[27] E.g, Farer, 'Beyond the Charter Frame: Unilateralism or Condominium?', 96 *American Journal of International Law* (2002) 359; Franck and Yuhan, 'The United States and the International Criminal Court: Unilateralism Rampant', 35 *New York University Journal of International law and Politcs* (2002–3) 519.

[28] M. Byers and G. Nolte (eds), *Hegemony and the Foundations of International Law* (2003); N. Krisch, 'International Law in times of Hegemony: Unequal Power and the Shaping of the International Legal Order', 16 *European Journal of International Law* (2005) 369.

[29] G. Simpson, *Great Powers and Outlaw States* (2004).

[30] Cf. P. Sands, *Lawless World: America and the Making and Breaking of Global Rules* (Penguin, 2005).

[31] For authors who emphasise historical research as an imaginative resource see e.g., Berman, 'Between "Alliance" and "Localisation": Nationalism and the New Oscillationism', 26 *New York University Journal of International Law and Politics* (1993–94) 449, 451–2. ('The ultimate goal of my inquiry is to provide historical and theoretical context for critically evaluating current debates about the appropriate international response to nationalist conflicts... This historical approach explores the deep legal and cultural assumptions that underlie seemingly technical doctrinal argumentation and seeks to initiate reflection on the persuasive power and tenacious persistence of certain policy alternatives. Technical legal debates concerning widenened U.N. competence under the Charter appear rather differently when one realizes that they replicate strikingly similar arguments concerning the scope of the League competence under the Covenant.'). Koskenniemi, *supra* note 6, 5 ('I hope that

The Telling of Histories

Whichever way one looks at the issue, there is clearly a range of different ways in which an international lawyer might engage with the history of international law, and a range of question that might arise therefrom: some histories might be written as 'upper-case' Histories – histories written for purposes of discovering meaningful trajectories and teleologies within the discipline – histories of progressive development, codification and institutional design. Others may, more narrowly, concern themselves with intellectual lineage – the persona, their obsessions and anxieties, their works and 'contributions'.[32] Yet other histories may be written about institutions – the Permanent Court of International Justice,[33] the League of Nations,[34] the European Convention on Human Rights,[35] – or particular ideas such as war,[36] conquest[37], diplomatic immunity,[38] or title to territory.[39] All, no doubt, will have an intellectual framework that locates the past in the present either in terms of a diachronic narrative of progress or change, or synchronically (by way of the identification within present rules, past practice or judicial precedent). In the latter sense, of course, the appreciation that history forms part of the discipline is such as to make us all 'historians' – whether we are so consciously or not.[40] International lawyers (perhaps lawyers more generally) all trade in history, all engage with events and situations arising in particular historical junctures and a consistent feature of that engagement is not merely

---

these essays provide a historical contrast to the state of the discipline today by highlighting the ways in which international lawyers in the past forty years have failed to use the imaginative opportunities that were available to them, and open horizons beyond academic and political instrumentalization, in favour of worn-out internationalist causes that form the mainstay of today's commitment to international law.... The limits of our imagination are a product of a history that *might have gone another way*.)

[32] E.g. Koskenniemi, *supra* note 6.

[33] O. Spiermann, *International Legal Argument in the Permanent Court of International Justice: The Rise of the International Judiciary* (2005).

[34] F. Northedge, *The League of Nations: Its Life and Times 1920–1946* (1986).

[35] B. Simpson, *Human Rights and the End of Empire: Britain and the Genesis of the European Convention* (2001).

[36] S. Neff, *War and the Law of Nations* (2005).

[37] S. Korman, *The Right of Conquest: The Acquisition of Territory by Force in International Law and Practice* (1996).

[38] L . Frey and M. Frey, *The History of Diplomatic Immunity* (1999).

[39] See e.g., J. Castellino and S. Allen, *Title to Territory in International Law: A Temporal Analysis* (2003).

[40] One finds recognition of this in diverse places. See e.g. I. Brownlie, *Principles of Public International Law* (5th ed. 1998) 126 ('In one sense at least law is history, and the lawyer's appreciation of the meaning of rules relating to acquisition of territory, and of the manner of their application in particular cases, will be rendered more keen by a knowledge of the historical development of the law.') Also, D. Kennedy, 'The Disciplines of International Law', 12 *Leiden Journal of International Law* (1999) 88 ('an argument about a rule or principle, or institutional technique in international law is almost always also an argument about history – that the particular norm proffered has a provenance as law rather than politics, has become general rather than specific, has come through history to stand outside history.')

a concern to translate what we know of the past into 'history', but to trans.
of 'history' into law.

Broadly speaking, it is possible to identify at least three different ways in w..cn the relationship between international law and 'history' may be conceived.[41] The first most common idea, and the one to which Oppenheim referred in the passage cited above is: that of a *history of international law*, or a history of parts thereof – a history mapped out in terms of its trajectory or teleology; a history written in narrative form that provides a story about its origins, development, progress or renewal. The second, and equally obvious, representation is that of *history in international law* – of the place that historical events or persona occupy within substantive discussions of law, and of the role they play in arguments about law itself. Any reference to 'state practice', to the writings of authoritative publicists or judicial opinion is a reference to history and, even if resort to those sources is unabashedly instrumental in the sense that it is directed towards the identification of relevant norms or rules of international law, it is clearly an inseparable part of legal activity. The third, and final, way in which that relationship may be understood is in terms of *international law in history* – of understanding how international law, or international lawyers have been engaged, or involved themselves, in the creation of a history that in some senses stands outside the history of international law itself. Here the concern is to identify international law's relationship to the wider world of politics, economics, or sociology against which it is deployed, or within which it is inserted.[42]

It is evident enough that any particular text will tend not to distinguish these three types of historical account, and in most cases will seek to conjoin two or more within the framework of a single project. A history of international law will presumably contain something about the role international law may have played more generally in international relations, and perhaps something about the part that (historical) practice may play in the various constructions of sources doctrine. Similarly an analysis of history in international law will not merely content itself with a discussion, for example, of the contemporaneous significance of the *Lotus case* in the development of rules of jurisdiction, but would necessarily engage, at the same time, with the general development of international law and its place in international relations. That each type of engagement with history and international law will interweave various different types of historical narrative is not such as to obviate analysis by reference to these categories – which remain, for the most part, useful

---

[41] Kennedy, *ibid*, 88–98 (in which he identifies international lawyers as using history in two different types of argument – one as a question of provenance; one as a question of progress).

[42] Cf. Allott, 'International Law and the Idea of History', 1 *Journal of the History of International Law* (1999) 1 in which he describes international law as having its own history which is both 'intrinsic and extrinsic'. Its intrinsic history is the history of its structures and systems, its legal substance and its philosophy. Its extrinsic history is the history of its relationship to 'all other social phenomena, other social structures and systems'.

categories of analysis – rather it points to the typically multi-layered nature of inter-national lawyers' engagement with the past.

The History of International Law

A history of international law, if it is to be written in singular terms ('a' history, as opposed to a plurality of histories of the various 'people and their projects' who are regarded, or regard themselves as part of that history[43]), makes an unflinching demand for the elaboration of some grand narrative – a narrative that somehow cap-tures 'international law' on broad canvass as a singular idea or set of ideas tied together in some coherent manner. At the time at which Oppenheim was writing, few would have had any doubts as to the subject or nature of that history. Yet to think about international law as having *a* history is to make all sorts of assumptions as to the iden-tity of the participants in that history (sovereign states? legal advisors? international organisations?), the sense of what interests international law serves to preserve (the 'rule of law'? 'peace and security'? 'human dignity'?) and how that history might relate to our contemporary understanding of international law. To write *a* history (or more emphatically *the* history[44]) of international law necessarily involves, in other words, setting out in advance the parameters of the discipline (in terms of its subjects and sources, its actors and modes of engagement) and the narration of a story in which the identity of the discipline itself is held relatively constant and in which varied and opposing voices are, for purposes of the narrative itself, silenced or pushed to one side.

As Lesaffer notes the unifying gesture that is signalled by the idea of 'a' history of international law necessarily reduces the historiography of the law of nations in both time and space. The association of international law with the emergence of the mod-ern 'sovereign state', for example, is such as to locate it within a temporal frame that begins, on most accounts, with the Treaties of Westphalia of 1648. For all the signifi-cance of the Westphalian treaties, it is hard not to regard 1648 as anything other than an arbitrary date the choice of which not only ignores the possibility that 'systems' of international law might have existed at earlier points in time[45] but also is such as to render any such history principally European or 'Northern' in character – pushing to the margins the experience of African, Asian or South American societies.[46] Lesaffer argues, in contrast, that 'the modern law of nations in its relation to the sovereign

---

[43] Kennedy, *supra* note 41, 83.

[44] It has frequently been observed that the translation of Grewe's *Epochen der Völkerrechtsgeschichte* was erroneously retitled in its English version bearing the definitive article '*The Epochs of International Law*'. This, despite Grewe's insistence that he was not actually writing *the* his-tory of international law or describing *the* epochs.

[45] See, D. Bederman, *International Law in Antiquity* (2001).

[46] For an early critique of the Europeanization of international law in the 19th Century see C. Alexandrowicz, *An Introduction to the History of the Law of Nations in the East Indies* (1967).

state should not define "international law" in its historical setting'.[47] Rather, it should be studied in its multiple guises in all historical periods.[48]

One of the central reasons Lesaffer identifies for the limited nature of international legal histories, in this regard, is their overtly pragmatic in orientation:

> 'Today as in the past, the popular view among international lawyers is still to a large extent based on broad and vague assumptions that rather bear witness to present-day concerns than to historical reality.'

This, he suggests, is particularly redolent in case of 'evolutionary' histories that seek to present the history of international law as a smooth process of progress and development (or 'renewal and restatement' to use Berman's felicitous phrase). For Lesaffer, this is most egregiously represented in the form of genealogical historicising that seeks to trace contemporaneous ideas back in time:

> 'This genealogic history from present to past leads to anachronistic interpretations of historical phenomena, clouds historical realities that bear no fruit in our own times and gives no information about the historical context of the phenomenon one claims to recognise. It describes history in terms of similarities and differences from the present, and not in terms of what it was. It tries to understand the past for what it brought about and not for what it meant to the people living it.'[49]

Thus to hold the trial of Peter von Hagenbach of 1474 to be the very first war crimes trial is to draw a unsustainably simplistic parallel between the nature and meaning of that trial in the context of 15th Century society, and the ideas and implications associated with the trial of war criminals occurring in the 20th/21st Centuries.

Lesaffer's critique of 'evolutionary' histories is one that chimes with 'new stream' approaches to international law which treat with considerable suspicion the idea that the history of international law may be presented in terms of an enlightenment narrative of progress.[50] Berman, for example, in advancing his version of a 'genealogical' approach to international legal history (informed by the work of Foucault amongst

---

[47] Lesaffer, *supra* note 19, 32.

[48] *Id.*

[49] *Ibid*, 34. He notes that few (with the exception of work such as Bederman's *International Law in Antiquity*) have attempted to look at the past for its own sake.

[50] See Cass, 'Navigating the Mainstream: Recent Critical Scholarship in International Law', 65 *Nordic Journal of International Law* (1996) 341, 354–9. She identifies four reasons for the discomfort: first that the narrative is simply wrong or distorts a far more complex and ambivalent story; secondly that it inhibits proper engagement with contemporary problems; thirdly that it wrongly assumes that the mysticism and universalising ideologies of the past have been effectively displaced; and finally that it buries the colonial heritage that lies at the heart of many doctrinal developments.

others[51]) rejects the account of international legal history presented as an ever-advancing dialectic of restatement and renewal (periodic restatements carrying forward the tradition of modern international law; periodic calls for renewal reframing the tradition 'in light of the policy innovation and situational flexibility, in the light of every-new versions of modernity').[52] Rather, and in his terms, the genealogist views international legal history 'as pockmarked by a series of catastrophes and mutations, as rocked by the countless forms of colonial conquest and anti-colonial resistance'.[53] Where the renewer-restater sees continuity, progress and inclusion (in the abolition of slavery, the prohibition on the use of force, decolonisation, and institution-building for example), the genealogist sees change, regress and exclusion (the continuance of slavery, the authorisation of violence, and the continuity of colonial relations). In contrast to the renewer-restater who sees the advancement of international law in terms of its normative excision of politics or its systemic unity, Berman the genealogist celebrates the idea of international law as being 'normatively impure, culturally heterogenous, and historically contingent'.[54] This is not, he argues, a matter of anxiety or despair for it is precisely because of 'international law's *lack of coherence*' because also of 'the instability of its transitory configurations of rules and players', that he is able to identify it as 'a hopeful enterprise.'[55]

Certain elements of Berman's genealogical approach to international legal history are to be found in Simpson's contribution to this book.[56] To begin with, the subject of his article – Piracy – is one that might have been addressed by way of a narrative about the emergence of the idea of universal jurisdiction in international law: about the historic prosecution of pirates, about the recognition given to that jurisdiction in article 15 High Seas Convention 1958 and subsequently in article 101 of the 1982 Convention on the Law of the Sea, and about the relationship between such initiatives and the development of universal jurisdiction in relation to other international crimes (war crimes, crimes against humanity). Although he begins by nodding in the direction of such a narrative (noting, for example, that 'piracy is regularly invoked as the first international crime, or the first offence to give rise to universal jurisdiction or the precursor to contemporary offences against the dignity of mankind'[57]) he tells a

---

[51] See, Foucault, 'Nietzsche, Genealogy and History', in P. Rabinov (ed.), *The Foucault Reader* (1986) 76. One should note, here, the different meaning ascribed to genealogical legal history by Lesaffer, on the one hand, and Foucault/Berman on the other. Whilst Lesaffer associates 'genealogical history' as one concerned with the search for origins, Foucault sees genealogy as explicitly 'opposed' to such an endeavour (*ibid*, 77).

[52] Berman, 'In the Wake of Empire', 14 *American University International Law Review* (1998–99) 1523.

[53] *Id.*

[54] *Ibid*, 1524.

[55] *Id.*

[56] G. Simpson, 'Piracy and the Origins of Enmity', in this volume, 219.

[57] *Id.*

quite different story – a story about pirates occupying a borderland between 'respectability and deviance', about the ambivalent status of the pirate (neither enemy nor criminal, neither within yet not outside the law, neither driven by private gain nor possessed of a political project) and, ultimately about the centrality of the metaphor of the pirate, with all its *aporias*, in contemporaneous debates about terrorism. In the return of the pirate figure in contemporary literature (in the form of the 'enemy of humankind'[58]) he thus sees as a return to ambiguity

> 'because the identity and identification of pirates has always raised difficult questions about war and peace, about sovereigns and non-sovereigns, and about policing and warfare. Pirates turn out to be not enemies of humankind but humankind in its plural guises.'[59]

The sort of history written by Simpson in these pages is thus not a history that has a beginning, middle and end, nor history of events and 'state practice' (as might be marked, perhaps, by the conclusion of treaties relating to piracy or in the identification of a sequence of seminal cases). Nor, furthermore, is it a structural history (of movements and ideologies, of cause and effect) even if in his discussion of Carl Schmitt he seems to affirm the idea that 'new international law' is being constructed in a 'post-duellist' international order marked by police action against outlaws and pirates rather than wars between sovereign states.[60] As in his book *Great Powers*,[61] the story is one of rehearsal or repetition in which old narratives and ideas are seen to be constantly repackaged and redeployed (the pirate, outlaw or terrorist), and in which background constants (the ideas of humanitarianism, social solidarity or imperialism for example) assume far greater importance than the particularities of the social contexts in which those ideas are discussed. He thus able, and in fact more than willing, to discuss the decision of the English High Court in the *Republic of Bolivia case* (of 1909) and its distinction between plunder for personal gain and for political change, alongside the work of Michael Riesman almost a century later – assuming in the process the terms of their generic engagement with international law and legal doctrine to be largely the same.

This is not necessarily a point of criticism (although it will be noted later that at least one school of historiography would find it problematic), but rather an observation about the nature of his historical reflection. For Simpson, the history of international law (understood primarily as a rhetoric about identities such as Great Powers, outlaw states, colonisers, slavers, pirates and the like) is not 'merely' history – a past to be told and then displaced by a discussion of 'current problems' or contemporaneous concerns – but rather a past marked by ambiguity and ambivalence, rhetorical excess

---

[58] *Ibid*, 225.
[59] *Ibid*, 230.
[60] *Ibid*, 224.
[61] *Supra* note 29.

and definitional undecidability, that finds continuing expression in contemporary legal and political discourse.[62] In this regard, at least, Simpson is decidedly not engaging in the type of historical enquiry that Lesaffer recommends in his contribution[63] and may be seen to pose the question (in his methodology if not otherwise) as to whether there is a history of international law that can be meaningfully disinterred without being framed within contemporary linguistic categories.

In his introduction to the *Gentle Civilizer of Nations*, Koskenniemi echoes the authors here in dismissing the possibility of narrating a grand, monological, history of international law.[64] Any such an endeavour, he remarks, would be 'burdened with contestable assumptions about what was central and what peripheral, what valuable and what harmful in the past, and [would necessarily fail] to address the question of narrative perspective'.[65] For him, the alternative might have been to 'abstract the larger context altogether and to write biographies of individual lawyers' in the style of La Pradelle or Serra. But here again the project would appear to be problematic, not only by reason of the supposition that the history to be told is a 'projection of a few great minds', but also because it would fail to 'account for the external pressures to which the doctrines of those men sought to provide responses'.[66] He thus settles on an explicitly 'non-rigorous' and 'experimental' method that intertwines biographical and contextual (epochal) elements as part of a narrative history of the profession and its ideas (or what he calls its 'sensibility').[67]

There are several obvious tensions within Koskenniemi's overt method[68] – for one thing he never quite escapes his own critique – he still seems largely to present his subject (international law?) in a way that equates it with the ideas and thoughts of a group of predominantly European international lawyers, and he still uses as his context, an account of history that would not be too far removed from that supplied by

---

[62] For a review of Simpson's work which appears to miss almost all of these points see, Sellers, 99 *American Journal of International Law* (2005) 949.

[63] Lesaffer, for example, insists upon an appreciation of context, and is critical of excessive reliance upon doctrine rather than practice, *supra* note 19, 27.

[64] His target, in that respect appears to be accounts such as those of Grewe, *supra* note 7. For a critique of 'monological' historicism see Greenblatt, 'Introduction', to 'The Forms of Power and the Power of Forms in the Renaissance', 15 *Genre* (1982) 5, in which he suggests that such accounts usually reduce historical periods to a single homogenous tradition which are then related as facts rather than the product of the historian's imagination. He suggests, alternatively, that historical practice should be considered as presenting two kinds of dialogue: one within the past, the other *with* it. Not only thus, should the heterogeneity of the past be recognised, but also the constructive role of the historian in representing that past.

[65] *Supra* note 6, 5–6.

[66] *Ibid*, 8.

[67] For similar 'experimental' works of historiography see P. Cohen, *History in Three Keys: The Boxers as Event, Experience and Myth* (1997); O. Figes, *A People's Tragedy* (1996).

[68] For an intelligent review that examines Koskenniemi's historiography see Galindo, 'Martti Koskenniemi and the Historiographical Turn in International Law', 16 *European Journal of International Law* (2005) 539.

Grewe. His techniques of evasion – concentrating upon the 'sensibilities' of the profession rather than a description of the practice of 'international law', and adjusting the temporal horizons of the contemporary era so it starts in 1870 rather than 1919 or 1945 – do not, in themselves, really avoid the impression that here again one is faced with an essentially 'Whiggish' story of great men and their deeds. But at the same time, Koskenniemi does introduce in his work a far more nuanced appreciation of the social context in which prominent international legal scholars develop their ideas or 'sensibilities' concerning international law, and clearly adopts a position which denies any real sense of progress.

Two contributions to this volume develop the kind of biographical/contextual legal history that Koskenniemi sketches out, but do so in respect of particular authors and schools of thought that are otherwise left out of Koskenniemi's broad narrative. Lobban directly situates his argument about the changing sensibilities international lawyers in the late 19th Century within the framework of Koskenniemi's narrative in the *Gentle Civilizer*, but focuses specifically upon English jurists (such as Montague Bernard, John Westlake, and T.E. Holland) rather than the predominantly Continental lawyers to whom Koskenniemi refers (von Martens, Klüber, Asser and Bluntschli).[69] For Lobban the mentality, or professional outlook, of international lawyers in England in the 19th Century changed quite radically from a time in which they represented, as members of the Doctors Commons, a closed professional elite of civilian lawyers concerned with abstract rules of natural justice (represented by figures such as Stowell and Phillimore), to a more pragmatic, politically-attuned, college of scholars based in the Universities of Oxford, Cambridge and London (including Mountague Bernard, Holland, Whewell, Maine, Westlake and Oppenheim). The institutionalisation of international law as a subject of scholarly activity within the academy thus occurred at the same time as (and perhaps was related to) the rejection of rationalist, *a priori*, natural law approaches to international law, and their replacement by a species of legal reasoning that was overtly empirical in orientation and far more closely attuned to the politics of public opinion and the pragmatics of statecraft. This is represented, as Lobban observes, in the debates surrounding the Royal Commission on Fugitive Slaves[70] and the case of *R v. Keyn*.[71] The story then told is one of the subsequent engagement on the part of this new breed of scholar-practitioner with the 'vulgar Austinian' critique of international law (in which John Austin is read as relegating international law to the status of mere 'positive international morality'). For the most part, Lobban's article is one concerned with exposing how and why English international lawyers came to obsess about the work of Austin in the late 19th Century (partly because of what

---

[69] M. Lobban, 'English Approaches to International Law in the Nineteenth Century', in this volume, 65.

[70] Royal Commission on Fugitive Slaves, Parliamentary Papers 1876 [C 1516-I] XXVIII 285.

[71] (1876) 2 Ex. D. 173.

Austin's imperative approach to law offered in terms of providing an anti-speculative foundation for international law), but it also represents an account of what may be taken to be the peculiarities of a burgeoning 'English tradition' of international law.[72]

Perreau-Saussine develops some of the themes laid out by Lobban.[73] Her chapter is overtly concerned with seeking to understand the influence of Lassa Oppenheim's *Treatise* upon successive generations of scholars within England. What becomes fully apparent, however, in her initial account of the editorship (moving from Oppenheim, to Roxburgh, to McNair, to Lauterpacht and finally to Jennings and Watts) is the sense of how the *Treatise* itself seemed to assume canonical (or even totemic) significance for international lawyers within England. Each of the editors was to assume a position of considerable prominence within English academia, and frequently combined this with a high-profile career as a practitioner or legal advisor. Each also appears to have acquired the responsibility of editorship as protégée to the incumbent scholar-editor (in a chain of 'filial piety' as Perreau-Saussine puts it).[74] The significance of the *Treatise*, however, as Perreau-Saussine argues is not merely to be found in the way that the passing of the editorship to the new 'disciples' seemed to ensure the maintenance of a particular 'faith' or set of beliefs about international law – successive editors after all subtly modified key elements of Oppenheim's liberal internationalist vision of international law. Rather, it is to be found in what remained consistent in the *Treatise* through the various editions – a consistency, as Perrau-Saussine suggests, which manifests itself both in its surface style and structure (its systemic orientation, methodological completeness and clarity) and in an underlying commitment to the idea of legal positivism as a technique for the promotion of key political and moral values. In this respect, the *Treatise* seems to mark out most clearly the nature of what was to become a peculiarly English tradition of international law – a tradition which, one supposes, also left its marks on the discipline more generally through the various professional interventions of its adherents.

Perrau-Saussine's analysis of Oppenheim's *Treatise* seems to return the historian of international law back to doctrine rather than practice,[75] back to canonical texts rather than official deliberation, back to cultural particularity rather than universalising assumptions as to the nature or character of international law. But one also senses that the history that can be told through such narratives is also a dense one: a sustained engagement with the process of cultural production and re-production of a canonical text may tell us a great deal more about the assumptions and predispositions of

---

[72] For two of the few accounts of this tradition see D. Johnson, 'The English Tradition in International Law', 11 *International and Comparative Law Quarterly* (1962) 416; J. Crawford, 'Public International Law in Twentieth-Century England', in J. Beatson and R. Zimmerman (eds.), *Jurists Uprooted: German Speaking Émigré Lawyers in Twentieth-Century Britain* (2004) 681.

[73] Perreau-Saussine, *supra* note 9.

[74] *Ibid*, 93.

[75] For criticism of the reliance upon doctrine in historical research see Lesaffer, *supra* note 19, p??

successive generations of international lawyers, and about the sense of a tradition being generated and maintained, than might be garnered for example through an examination of the diverse works of the individual authors themselves, or through accounts of particular subject areas of international law that fail to acknowledge the anthropological embeddedness of the authors or actors themselves. What one gains, at the very least, from such work is the sense of how varied histories of international law might be, and how particular and contingent the position of authors within those stories.

History Within International Law

Even those who either avoid, or see no need for, the writing of grand narrative histories of international law as part of their engagement with the discipline, will inevitably have to marshal and deploy historical material. Whether, for example, as a matter of determining the content of customary international law through an analysis of past and contemporary state practice,[76] interrogating the precedential value of judicial decisions, construing international agreements by reference to the *travaux preparatoires*, or identifying the applicable law or the 'critical date' in the context of dispute resolution, some engagement with history, or more narrowly, the history of the discipline is inevitable.[77] Even for those suspicious of the precedential value of past decision-making or of originalist modes of construction,[78] the past will still represent a repertory of possible 'approaches' to, or 'solutions' for, contemporary problems.

As the various contributions to this book suggest, however, there is considerable unease amongst those who take legal history seriously about the perceived failure on the part of international lawyers to deal with historical material in a rigorous manner. Bederman identifies five different types of defect that he associates with 'law office history' or more specifically 'foreign office international legal history'.[79] These include:

> '(1) a lack of analytic rigor in historical investigations, (2) selective use of historical materials, (3) sloppy or strategic methodologies in the review of historic sources, (4) overt or implicit instrumentalism in the selection of historic data and/or the conclusions drawn from such material, and (5) an unwillingness or inability to reconcile conflicting sources, or an inability to accept ambiguity or incompleteness in the historic record.'[80]

---

[76] See e.g., Carty, 'Distance and Contemporaneity in Exploring the Practice of States: the British Archives in Relation to the 1957 Oman and Muscat Incident', in this volume, 231.

[77] For a thorough examination of the role that 'time' plays in decision-making, see Higgins, 'Time and the Law: International Perspectives on an Old Problem', 46 *International and Comparative Law Quarterly* (1997) 501.

[78] As Kennedy suggests there might appear to be something of a transatlantic divide on this issue – international lawyers in the United States being less convinced of the significance of the pedigree of legal rules than those in Europe or elsewhere. He also suggests, however, that this divide is largely superficial, supra note 41, 91.

[79] D. Bederman, 'Foreign Office International Legal History', in this volume, 43.

[80] *Ibid.*, 46.

The central complaint, thus, is one of the abuse of the historical record for purposes of sustaining an argumentative position – a point which he demonstrates in his examination of *Sosa v. Alvarez-Machain* in the United States and the *Kasikili/Sedudu Island case* before the International Court of Justice (ICJ). He urges, in his conclusion, that international lawyers should be prepared to accept that the historic record may, on many occasions, be simply incomplete, ambiguous or contradictory,[81] and that due consideration should be given to proper methods of historiography. Lesaffer similarly complains about the instrumental nature of much historical enquiry (characterised, as suggested above, by what he terms 'genealogical enquiry') and observes that the problem is not merely the thinness of the historical accounts that are engendered therein, or the 'abuse' of the past, but the tendency to read back from present to past – to think of the past only in terms of what it may tell us about the present, or to present historical material in terms of some smooth evolution from past to present.[82] For him, the past should really be understood in its 'own terms' and by reference to its own standards – recalling implicitly Ranke's demand that historians should tell it 'how it actually happened' (*'wie es eigentlich gewesen ist'*).

As both Lesaffer and Bederman implicitly accept, international lawyers – whether as scholars searching for rules of customary law in state practice, or as practitioners fighting their corner in a dispute – will approach historical material with a view to garner from it some insight or rule of contemporaneous relevance. The primary concern, in such cases, is not to understand the past in its own terms with all its complexities, ambivalence, or ambiguity, but rather to identify within it, a thin tradition of thought and practice that is in some way normative. An evident consequence of this approach is that the telling of history is skewed from the outset. As Kennedy puts it, successive moments or events from the past are deliberately sieved or compressed to generate 'a list of factors and a holding'[83] rather than to relate the experience or lives of those involved. It is not uncommon to find in discourses concerning humanitarian intervention, for example, a brief historical account of 'state practice' (Bangladesh, Uganda, Kampuchea, Iraq, Sierra Leone and Kosovo perhaps) which will identify the 'key events' and the positions adopted by 'relevant actors' (States and international organisations for the most part) followed by a conclusion that purports to lay down when, if at all, intervention on such a basis might be regarded as legitimate.[84] This tends to involve distinguishing between those factors that form part of the normative proposition (such as, perhaps, the severity of the humanitarian crisis and the inability of the UN Security Council to take action) and those which,

---

[81] One may recall Oakshott's description of writing history as an act of restoration in which we discover from fragments of evidence 'what may be inferred from them about a past which has not survived' in M. Oakshott *On History and Other Essays* (1983) 52.

[82] Lesaffer, *supra* note 19, 34.

[83] Kennedy, Disciplines, *supra* note 41, 82.

[84] See e.g., T. Franck, *Recourse to Force: State Action against Threats and Armed Attacks* (2002) 135–173.

whilst historically significant, do not (such as might relate, for example, to the origination of the crisis, the relationship between intervener and intervened, the experience of those facing intervention, or the perceptions of other non-State actors). The excision of these latter contextual factors from the elaboration of the rule is clearly necessary in order for the rule itself to have normative bite (the more factors or conditions included within any particular rule, the fewer the cases in which the rule is likely to have effect), and the extent to which they may figure in any narrative account of the 'practice' itself, will tend to depend upon the intuition as to whether such factors may have some subsequent significance for purposes of distinguishing between the rule and its exception.

Apart from the limited nature of such accounts in terms of the history they purport to narrate, the practice of relating history in this way makes all sorts of assumptions about the past and its relevance to contemporary decision-making. As Kennedy observes:

> 'The rhetorical gestures and motives of scholars and statesmen are extremely hard to compare across time as applications of similar ideas or contributions to a single institutional project. Moreover, it is unlikely that historical actors were primarily concerned, or even noticed, the relationship between their actions and a transcendent historical development of something which would later come to be summarized as 'international law'. The complexity of the historical record – different ideas about what 'law' was, different attitudes about 'sovereignty' and 'war' and 'right' – tend to disappear when one looks at historical events for evidence of what 'the law' about some transhistorical phenomenon like 'conquest' or 'sovereign immunity' has been.'[85]

The caution, then, that the search for law appears to suppose the pre-existence of the law being sought, is one which not only exposes the methodological frailty of the endeavour but also its overtly polemical character.

Kennedy's critique of international lawyers' reading of the past – and particularly their assumption that ideas such as sovereignty, jurisdiction or custom can be taken to be historically stable notions and hence provide a basis for transhistorical analysis – is one that corresponds with elements of the 'Cambridge school's' approach to the history of ideas. As Skinner and others have consistently maintained,[86] the social and cultural context in which political, philosophical or legal ideas come to be inscribed in textual form is critically important for an understanding of what those ideas actually meant to those using them. It is thus only through a critical examination of the linguistic practices and tradition in which a writer was working that one would be able to ascribe particular meaning to the vague phrase or abstract concept articulated in her work. If this was the case, furthermore, one could no

---

[85] Kennedy, *supra* note 41.

[86] See generally, Skinner, 'Meaning and Understanding in the History of Ideas', 8 *History and Theory* (1969) 3; Tuck, 'History of Political Thought' in P. Burke (ed.), *New Perspectives on Writing History* (2001) 218.

longer automatically hold onto the idea that the subject of one's discussion – the idea of sovereignty or the concept of intervention for example – remained an independent and invariable constant nor really to the idea that international law exists as a single phenomenon existing within history.[87]

One initial response to this may be to point out that international lawyers do not necessarily insist upon the stability of concepts within their discipline. The idea of territory, for example, is one which is generally understood to have changed quite radically over the course of the 18th–20th Centuries. Brownlie, for example, describes the 'historical development of the law' in the following terms:

> 'In the Middle Ages the ideas of state and kingship prevalent in Europe tended to place the ruler in the position of a private owner, since feudal law, as the applicable "public law", conferred ultimate title on the ruler, and the legal doctrine of the day employed analogies of Roman private law in the sphere of property to describe the sovereign's power. The growth of absolutism in the sixteenth and seventeenth centuries confirmed the trend. A treaty ceding territory had the appearance of a sale of land by a private owner, and sales of territory did in fact occur. In the eighteenth and nineteenth centuries the significance of private law notions declined. In the field of theory sovereignty was recognized as an abstraction and thus the ruler was a bearer and agent of a legal capacity which belonged to the state.'[88]

There is a movement, here, recorded in Brownlie's account, that sees an essentially patrimonial conception of territory being replaced by one that understood territory primarily in terms of 'jurisdiction' (as realm of competence delineating the space within which governmental agencies may legitimately act), and this itself, was related to changing conceptions of sovereignty on the one hand, and the relative significance of private law analogies in international legal reasoning on the other. Even if generic labels such as 'territory' 'sovereignty' or 'jurisdiction' remain the same, there is acute awareness that the content and meaning of such terms has not, and will not, remain entirely static. [89]

One may wonder, however, why this kind of admission is not more perplexing for international lawyers. If it is the case that 'territory' or 'sovereignty' now mean something quite different from the meaning attributed to them a century or more ago, then what is the relationship between the past and present of those ideas, and why, more importantly, might that history be worthy of being narrated in the manner described? In one sense, it may be taken merely as a warning against the incautious evocation of historical source material: one has to be clear, for example, about the problems of drawing upon historical precedents for purposes of describing the legal

---

[87] Skinner, *ibid*, 30 ('to suggest . . . that a knowledge of the social context is a necessary condition for an understanding of the classic texts is equivalent to denying that they do contain any elements of timeless and perennial interest, and is thus equivalent to removing the whole point of studying what they said.')

[88] Brownlie, *supra* note 40, 126.

[89] See further A. Carty, The Decay of *International Law* (1986) 43–60.

consequences associated with the cession of territory when those consequences seem to depend upon how 'territory' itself is understood.[90] In another sense, however, it also seems to be a matter of conveying a sense of progress: it is a way of describing how international law has divested itself of the authoritarian or imperialist impulses associated with the 'power of the sovereign', and how it now remains open to a more democratic agenda, or perhaps an agenda concerned with 'empowering the self'.[91] But of course, this is to return once again to the problem of 'old historicism' and the dubious postulate that one can confidently map out the history of international law (or anything else for that matter) in terms of a teleology of 'progress'.[92]

The one particular context in which present (putatively democratic) and past (putatively colonial or imperial) visions of international law appear to collide is in case of disputes over historic titles. In such cases, reliance upon Huber's doctrine of 'Inter-Temporal Law' would appear to require deference to an understanding of history 'as it was':

> 'a judicial fact must be appreciated in the light of the law contemporary with it, and not of the law in force at the time such dispute in regard to it arises or falls to be settled'.[93]

Whilst Huber subsequently qualified this initial proposition with the proviso that this only pertained for purposes of the 'creation' of rights rather than their 'continued manifestation', it has generally been taken as meaning that historic titles based on annexation, for example, cannot be called into question simply because annexation is no longer a legitimate means of acquiring title to territory. Precisely this kind of argument was rejected by the ICJ in the *Cameroons/Nigeria case* in which it held that the cession of the Bakassi peninsular to Germany in 1913 was effective notwithstanding the fact that it appeared to breach the terms of the earlier protectorate agreement between Great Britain and the 'Kings and Chiefs of Old Calabar'. The Court concluded, in face of Nigeria's assertions to the contrary, that the 'Treaty of Protection' was, in light of general European practice in Sub-Saharan Africa, not an agreement that recognised or preserved the sovereignty of the Kings and Chiefs of Old Calabar:

> 'many factors point to the 1884 Treaty signed with the Kings and Chiefs of Old Calabar as not establishing an international protectorate. It was one of a multitude in a region where the local Rulers were not regarded as States. Indeed, apart from the parallel declarations of various lesser Chiefs agreeing to be bound by the 1884 Treaty, there is not even convincing evidence of a central federal power. There appears in Old Calabar rather to have been individual townships, headed by Chiefs, who regarded themselves as owing a general allegiance to more important Kings and Chiefs. Further,

---

[90] It is evident, for example, that the changing understanding of 'territory' and hence the implications of its 'cession' had particular relevance for purposes of questions of nationality. See generally P. Weis, *Nationality and Statelessness in International Law* (2nd ed. 1979).

[91] See, T. Franck, *The Empowered Self: Law and Society in the Age of Individualism* (2001).

[92] Such historiography was decisively undermined by Karl Popper in *The Poverty of Historicism* (1957).

[93] *Island of Palmas Case* II UNRIAA (1949) 845.

from the outset Britain regarded itself as administering the territories comprised in the 1884 Treaty, and not just protecting them.'[94]

As a consequence, Britain was taken to have acquired sovereignty over Old Calabar and was competent to subsequently dispose of that territory by agreement with Germany.

Whilst overtly representing a clear example of the application of the doctrine of inter-temporal law, the case of Old Calabar also exposes the limits of this kind of historical enquiry. In essence the Court saw itself as being asked to deliberate upon the significance of a treaty concluded between Britain and the Kings and Chiefs of Old Calabar, not by reference to the standards of treaty interpretation today, but by those pertaining in the 1880s.[95] It thus had to place itself in the mindset of some actor or agent at that time, and the critical choice, of course, was whether it would be that of a legal advisor located within Britain or elsewhere in Europe, or that of the King and Chiefs themselves. Working from the apparent assumption that international law was largely Eurocentric in outlook, and actively facilitated the process of colonisation rather than resisted it, the Court seemed to conclude that relevant actors at the time would not have recognised the sovereignty and treaty-making capacity of the Kings and Chiefs, and hence that the treaty was not 'governed by international law' and did not affect the capacity of Britain to subsequently dispose of the territory.[96] Proceeding, thus, on the basis that the treaty either did not really exist, or at least did not mean what it said,[97] the Court involved itself in a precarious exercise of revisionism. As Koskenniemi points out, 19th Century legal opinion was far from undivided on the question of the status of colonial treaties. Whilst there were those (such as Westlake and Rolin) who regarded such treaties as irrelevant to international law, there were also those (such as Bonfils and Fauchille) who assigned considerable significance to them.[98] Even if the Final Act of the Berlin Conference had apparently laid down the procedure for colonisation by way of effective occupation, this did not prevent King Leopold from seeking to establish a foothold in the Congo by means of reliance upon a series of treaties signed by envoys with local Kings and Chiefs in

---

[94] *Case Concerning the Land and Maritime Boundary Between Cameroon and Nigeria*, (Cameroon v. Nigeria, Equatorial Guinea intervening), *Merits*, ICJ Rep. 2002, 103, para. 207.

[95] For a discussion of this issue see Klabbers, 'Reluctant *Grundnormen*: Articles 31(3)(c) and 42 of the Vienna Convention on the Law of Treaties and the Fragmentation of International Law', in this volume, 148.

[96] There is some question as to how far this may be squared with the ICJ's position in the *Western Sahara* case, Advisory Opinion, ICJ Rep. 1975, 12, para. 80 in which it was held that State practice of the relevant period (1884) 'indicates that territories inhabited by tribes or peoples having a social and political organization were not regarded as *terra nullius*. It shows that in the case of such territories the acquisition of sovereignty was not generally considered as effected unilaterally through "occupation" of *terra nullius* by original title but through agreements concluded with local rulers.'

[97] See Dissenting Opinion of Judge Koroma in the *Case Concerning the Land and Maritime Boundary Between Cameroon and Nigeria, supra* note 94, 479, para 15.

[98] See generally M. Lindley, *Acquisition and Government of Backward Territory in International Law* (1926).

the region, nor did it prevent the European powers themselves subsequently relying upon such treaties as a basis for justifying their own claims to sovereignty.

This, of course, may be to expose the real sense of agreements of this kind. It is perfectly plausible to argue that, so far as the colonial powers were concerned, such treaties were not concluded with the local 'sovereigns' in mind at all, but functioned rather as a means of demonstrating a relationship of authority or control to other European powers. What would have mattered in other words, was not whether Britain assumed sovereignty over Old Calabar by means of the agreement, or indeed whether the Kings and Chiefs were regarded as sovereign themselves;[99] but whether other European understood that such territory was no longer open to annexation or other forms of informal influence.[100] The question of where sovereignty actually lay could thus largely be avoided so long as the preponderant interests of Britain in the region were given due recognition[101] and the obvious means by which such interest could be communicated was by the conclusion and publication of a public agreement to that effect.

If this is accurate then, and assuming the standpoint is that of the colonising powers, it would seem to be entirely beside the point to seek within the agreement or its surrounding circumstances an indication as to whether Britain or anyone else recognised the sovereignty of the Kings and Chiefs of Old Calabar. That would have been an 'academic point' of little serious consequence, and one that only few international lawyers would have committed themselves to on one side or another. That it has subsequently become important in virtue of Britain's purported cession of the territory to Germany in 1913, is no reason to read back into the history more than is palpably there, and is to obscure the obvious ambivalence that characterised discussions of treaty law and sovereignty at the time. One kind of response to the Court's problem would thus be to say that the issue was simply unanswerable because there was no sense that international lawyers within Europe in the 1880s thought it to be a question that needed to be answered. Whether or not the Kings and Chiefs might have had another view of the issue is, of course, another question and one suspects the answer to that is list to history.

For all the difficulties associated with reading the past, it is also evident that the past may actually be more accessible to the international lawyer – or at least provide international lawyers with a deeper understanding of their own discipline – than the

---

[99] Cf. Carty's observations about the Agreement of Sib, *supra* note 76.

[100] The general sense of the 1884 agreement as spelled out in articles 1 and 2 was that Britain undertook to extend to the Kings and Chiefs 'her gracious favour and protection' (art. 1). In return, the Kings and Chiefs agreed 'to refrain from entering into any correspondence, Agreement, or Treaty with any foreign nation of Power' (art. 2).

[101] Remnants of this kind of pragmatism in relation to claims of sovereignty are evident in the literature today. Thus Crawford observes, in commenting on the case, that the terms of the treaty itself did not really matter – what was important was the 'position which the parties themselves took and which were applied in practice'. He thus concludes that 'even if, after 1884, a party existed that might have espoused such a claim [to sovereignty], no claim contrary to Britain's own claim appears to have been made, and at the international level the Kings and Chiefs of Old Calabar . . . disappeared from view.' in J. Crawford, *The Creation of States in International Law* (2nd ed. 2005) 314.

present. In his contribution to this book, Carty points out that in the construction of customary rules, international lawyers necessarily seek both practice and *opinio iuris* and in the context of the latter, tend to rely upon the 'verbal positions' adopted by organs of the state in internal processes and external relations.[102] His point, however, is that the latter may be deeply misleading. On interrogation of archival evidence – in his case, the Foreign Office archives relating to the UK's intervention in Oman and Muscat in 1957 – a picture may emerge in which the formal pronouncements of the government appear to be largely at odds with the views or perceptions of the advisors and other key decision-makers as regards the questions of law with which they are dealing (views which, in fact, only emerge once the records concerned are made public). In the case in point, he observes that whilst the UK maintained the formal position that it was intervening in Muscat and Oman at the invitation of the local sovereign (and hence was not for Charter purposes unlawful), the underlying position of its advisors appeared to be that the Sultan could not plausibly be regarded as 'sovereign' given the lack of any historic effective control over the territory. Any insistence, thereby, that the Sultan was, indeed, sovereign could only be seen as 'window dressing' obscuring a continued policy of imperial ambition that continued beyond the time of formal decolonisation.

At one level Carty's argument may be taken to be a rather worrying critique of customary international law. He seems to insist, at the first stage, that if international lawyers are intent on taking customary international law seriously, they must necessarily seek to adduce from a variety of archival sources the outlook and normative preferences (the 'mentality') of key actors. This much is a reasonable demand and makes very clear the way in which historical research may be central to the development of any real understanding of international law (as opposed to an understanding built upon public utterances or formal statements). But what Carty then uncovers is a wholly unappealing world of imperial design, and mendaciousness posturing, which can barely be squared with the lofty ideals which international lawyers frequently associate with their discipline ('consent', 'non-intervention', the 'prohibition on the use of force' and so on). The history Carty unearths in this respect is both too bland and too radical to be effectively 'internalised' within the discipline. It is too radical in the sense that it leads to the obvious question as to whether anyone would possibly want to defend a rule permitting intervention by invitation if all the cases one relied upon were of this kind? Would anyone (even Walmsley's 'reasonable person') assume such practice to be a worthy precedent? What this might suggest, of course, is that only 'worthy' precedents should be sought – those not tainted by deception or malice, that demonstrate honesty, integrity and good faith – but it remains entirely open as to whether, once the history is revealed, any such examples exist.

It is also too bland in the sense that many will take it as read that States will have a multitude of reasons for behaving in the way they do, and that compliance with

---

[102] Carty, *supra* note 76, 234.

international law is likely to be only a minor consideration. Just because British officials may have had imperial designs in the pursuit of the war, it might be reasoned,
does not tell us a great deal about the validity or otherwise of the norm itself. Does
it really matter whether, for example, in advancing the idea that the war in Iraq was
legal, the British or US governments may have been motivated, like Holmes' 'bad
man', by sundry other less persuasive, or valid, concerns (oil, commercial opportu-
nity, or regional influence for example)? Is not the key, the question whether one
can plausibly justify the action under some legitimate head, or whether one can persuade others of the legitimacy of the position adopted? In this sense, it is the constraints placed upon actors in seeking the legitimation of their various projects
through the language of law and justice that are most important – albeit the case
that they are constraints that frequently operate only at the outer edges of everyday
activity. But here again, one may return to Carty's concern about the formulation
of the rules of legality that supposedly 'police' international actors, and the extent
to which they themselves are rooted in a practice of obnoxious imperialism: whose
violence is one legitimating when one posits a rule permitting intervention by invitation, and what history is one telling in the process?

International Law in History

The concerns that Carty appears to raise here, are not merely ones that relate to
international lawyers conversation with themselves, but also concern the place
international law is thought to assume in a broader social environment. As Carty
puts it, '[f]or the perplexed international lawyer, the question that is most pressing
is whether and how the Charter paradigm and language ... can retain not merely
formal validity but also a significant impact upon the forces at work in that society.'[103] The sense that international law has a place *within* history is thus just as
important for international lawyers as the sense that it has a history of its own.

In some respects, at least, the origination of this concern may be traced back to
the work of John Austin. As Lobban notes, in his contribution to this volume, since
the end of the 19th Century international lawyers in England, if not elsewhere,
have taken Austin's dismissal of international law as 'mere' positive morality to be a
central point of critique.[104] However much Austin's argument in this direction may
have been misconstrued (as Lobban suggests) it seemed to lay down two challenges:
one concerning the ability of international lawyers to justify to their legal colleagues (within or outside universities) the worth of their subject; the other, their
ability to represent to the wider world, the significance of international law for the

---

[103] *Ibid*, 243.
[104] Lobban, *supra* note 69.

everyday decision-making of governments. In as far as the significance of international law in its wider sense seemed to depend upon the prior question as to whether it was, indeed, law at all, the fixation of early scholars – Maine, Westlake, and Lawrence amongst them – was to interrogate the assumed connection between law, sovereignty, and the deployment of coercion. Their reaction to the Austinian critique, of course, was to assume different forms – the replacement of 'sovereignty' by 'society' in the definition of law; the insistence upon an plural conception of law; the emphasis upon ordering capacity of law rather than its coercive character; the re-definition of sovereignty as a product of, rather than a source of, law; and so on. But none of these forms of refutation involved a serious engagement with the second question – namely whether the demand for obeisance to international law exerted significant influence in international affairs, or whether to the contrary it was largely epiphenomenal. That, of course, was the direct challenge laid down in the inter-war years by the likes of Morgenthau and Carr, and a great deal of international law scholarship since that time has been centred around precisely that problematic.

Having reiterated this old question, Carty provides the 'perplexed' international lawyer no direct response. He rather confines himself to observing that 'the least one can say as an international lawyer is that *positions* taken up by the UK, or for that matter any other government, cannot be taken at face value, or even be treated with anything other than complete scepticism'.[105] He continues:

> 'Without consistent and comprehensive access to the governmental policy-making process in which government international lawyers may also have a significant input, it is impossible to assess the process of decision-making in such a way as to determine exactly how international law is being interpreted, applied, followed or ignored.'[106]

Taken as a critique of arguments sustaining the significance of international law merely by reference to external observation of 'practice' or to the verbalised positions of governmental organs adopted in public *fora.*, this is an important point. But Carty's argument also appears to go beyond this. In his example of British intervention in Muscat and Oman, he points out that the British were entirely duplicitous as regards their presentation of the legal position within the United Nations: although intervention was justified on the basis of consent of the sovereign, there was no real conviction that the Sultan could properly be regarded as sovereign. Even if strategic interests appear to have been important in this case, Carty is uncomfortable with the idea that one should thereby fall back upon a standard account of international relations which understands the world in terms of a competition of interests between 'a collection of primary, unknowable, self-defining subjects'. Rather, he argues, it is the model articulated by Robert Cooper (who suggests that

---

[105]　Carty, *supra* note 76, 243.
[106]　*Ibid,* 231.

international society is divided into three incommensurable regimes of order, and that relations between the 'modern' and 'pre-modern' worlds he identifies will inevitably assume an imperial form[107]) that has most descriptive purchase.

To the extent that Carty seems to re-affirm the subordinate, or dispensable, character of legal argument in this case – and the corresponding importance and centrality of imperial ideology – he might be thought to merely re-affirm the suspicion that international law is a largely insignificant phenomenon in international relations. He avoids any such direct conclusion, however, and one suspects that his account is not in fact susceptible to such kind of theorising: his concern being simply to employ a 'positivist' historiography for purposes of exploring the way in which British officials at the time understood the international legal issues and their relationship to a broader imperial culture. Had the account been of a different incident and concerned a different set of officials, the picture might have been quite different – what is surprising, after all, is how much time was clearly spent debating the legal issues.

Carty's apparent detached neutrality as regards the role played by international law in this incident is not one that is typically shared by mainstream international lawyers. For the most part, international lawyers are keen to insist upon the strength of international law – either in the form of bland semi-empirical assertions as to how nations behave, or by reference to constructivist accounts of regime formation or of the capacity for certain rules to exercise a pull to compliance. All such accounts, however, are written against a background image of the discipline's frailty – of the potential predominance of political discretion over rules, or power over law. Superficially, of course, this has been such as to encourage international lawyers to focus upon the problem of compliance or enforcement – to direct attention to the devising of mechanisms, strategies, or institutional initiatives to overcome what is thought to be an innate predisposition on the part of governments to ignore international commitments whenever they appear to be inconvenient. It has also been such as to foster the equation of law-breaking with a return to anarchy and violence and a sanctification or power politics.

But it is equally apparent that the constant reiteration of the discipline's potential marginality is an important rhetorical device insofar as it creates an innate predisposition in favour of whatever projects are given the soubriquet 'law' or 'legality'. The sense that international law represents the last bastion standing out against the collapse of international society into a lawless world of violence, conflict, deprivation or imperial dominance, is one that not only encourages the view that it is essentially benign (promoting peace, assuring security, engendering compliance with human rights obligations or a commitment to environmental protection), but is such as to render it immune to critique. One cannot be 'against' international law, or parts thereof, except in the name of some other legality. Far from being a threat, in other words, the image of a lawlessness world that is constantly present at the margins, is central to international lawyers' sense of their own discipline.

[107] R. Cooper, *The Breaking of Nations: Order and Chaos in the Twenty-First Century* (2003).

INTERNATIONAL LAW AND ITS HISTORY:
THE STORY OF AN UNREQUITED LOVE

Randall Lesaffer*

1. *International Law and Its History*

In a paper presented at the Royal Academy of Sciences of the Netherlands in 1953, the great Dutch historian of international law Johan Hendrik Willem Verzijl (Utrecht University) remarked that 'the historiography of the law of nations is still in a very unsatisfactory state'.[1] Verzijl did not feel this statement needed qualification when he published the same paper in the first volume of his monumental *International Law in Historical Perspective* fifteen years later.[2] The leading historian of international law from Germany of those days, Wolfgang Preiser, would certainly not have contradicted him. He too stated that the historical research into the law of nations was still underdeveloped. The history of the law of nations was, he said, the youngest branch of legal history.[3] Another German, Wilhelm Grewe, had it repeated as late as the year 2000 that 'this task [the history of the modern international law] has been severely neglected in the study of international law up to the present day'.[4]

These complaints by three leading international legal historians of the second half of the 20th century were not uttered without cause. The history of international law has been and still is a minor field in terms of academic interest. Until a decade ago, at no time since Robert Ward made the first attempt at writing a survey of the history of the law of nations in 1795[5] have there been more than a small number of scholars who regularly published on the subject and could make the claim of being specialists.

* Professor of Legal History at Tilburg University (The Netherlands) and Part-time Professor of Cultural History at the Law Faculty of the Catholic University of Leuven (Belgium). I would like to thank Amanda Perreau-Saussine (Cambridge) for her useful comments and the late Hildegard Penn (Tilburg) for her help in editing this text.
  [1] Published in the Academy's *Mededelingen, Letterkunde,* NS 16-2 (1953).
  [2] Verzijl, 'Research into the History of the Law of Nations', in J.H.W. Verzijl, *International Law in Historical Perspective*, vol. I (1968) 400.
  [3] W. Preiser, *Die Völkerrechtsgeschichte. Ihre Aufgaben und Methoden* (1964) 5.
  [4] W. Grewe, *The Epochs of International Law* (trans. Michael Byers, 2000) 1, translated from the German *Epochen der Völkerrechtsgeschichte* (1984) 19. The book was first published in 1944.
  [5] R. Ward, *An Enquiry into the Foundation and the History of the Law of Nations of Europe* (1795).

However, during the last decade, the interest in the history of international law has suddenly risen.[6] Never before have so many scholars been publishing or lecturing on the history of international law as today.[7] For the very first time, cautious attempts at a more coordinated and systematic study of the subject are made. The Max Planck Institute for European Legal History in Frankfurt initiated a project entitled 'The History of Academic Trends and Ideas in International Law from the *Kaiserreich* to National Socialism', in which some fifteen, mostly young, scholars participated.[8] At the Tilburg Law Faculty in the Netherlands, a group of scholars is working in the field.[9] In 1999, Professor R. St. J. Macdonald from Dalhousie University, Halifax (Canada) founded the *Journal of the History of International Law*, which is now continued by the Max Planck Institute for European Legal History and its counterpart for International Law at Heidelberg.[10] Apart from Nomos Verlag which publishes the books emerging from the Frankfurt project, other major academic publishers have regularly and increasingly printed books on the history of international law over the last years.[11] The first international conferences were also organised.[12]

---

[6] For a survey of recent developments: Hueck, 'The Discipline of the History of International Law', 3 *Journal of the History of International Law* (2001) 194.

[7] Today, courses in the History (and Theory) of International Law are taught, among others at the law faculties of New York University, Cambridge, Helsinki, Leyden, Rotterdam, Utrecht and Tilburg Universities. Most international legal historians are to be found in the United States, Canada, Britain, the Netherlands, Germany and Japan.

[8] The individual books resulting from this project are published by Nomos Verlag in the series 'Studien zur Geschichte des Völkerrechts'.

[9] By Autumn 2005 there were nine researchers working in this field. The research is done in the context of a subprogram of the Faculty's Centre for Transboundary Legal Developments, entitled 'The Westphalian Myth Revisited: State Sovereignty and the Process of International Law-Making and Law-Enforcement from the 16th Century to the Present'.

[10] First published by Kluwer Law International, and from 2003 (2nd issue) onwards by Brill/Martinus Nijhoff Publishers.

[11] E.g. Cambridge University Press: A. Anghie, *Imperialism, Sovereignty and the Making of International Law* (2005); D. Bederman, *International Law in Antiquity* (2001); R. Lesaffer (ed.), *Peace Treaties and International Law in European History: From the Late Middle Ages to World War One* (2004); M. Koskenniemi, *The Gentle Civilizer of Nations: The Rise and Fall of International Law 1870–1960* (2001); G. Simpson, *Great Powers and Outlaw States: Unequal Sovereigns in the International Law* (2004). Oxford University Press: H. Bull, B. Kingsbury & A. Roberts (eds.), *Hugo Grotius and International Relations* (1990); Y. Onuma (ed.), *A Normative Approach to War: Peace, War, and Justice in Hugo Grotius* (1993); R. Tuck, *The Rights of War and Peace: Political Thought and the International Order from Grotius to Kant* (1999). Martinus Nijhoff: S. Beaulac, *The Power of Language in the Making of International Law: The Word Sovereignty in Bodin and Vattel and the Myth of Westphalia* (2004).

[12] In addition to the conference 'Time, History and International Law' the papers of which are published in this volume, there were, e.g., the conference 'Peace Treaties and International Law in European History' at Tilburg University in March 2001 and the conference 'Sovereignty and the Law of Nations (16th–18th centuries) organised by the Royal Flemish Academy of Belgium for Science and the Arts in Brussels, April 2002. The *Deutsche Rechtshistoriker Tag* of 2004, organised by Mathias Schmoeckel in Bonn, included a session on 'Völkerrechtsgeschichte' convened by Karl-Heinz Ziegler, which was a first at such a national legal history conference. In September 2005 Heinhard Steiger hosted an important conference on the history of international law in Gießen.

This sudden boom in the historiography of international law is easily explained. Though the interest has never been so great, there have been periods in the past in which scholars, particularly international lawyers, suddenly showed an interest in the field. It is no coincidence that the first attempt at writing a history of international law dates from the Revolutionary Era (1795). In the years following both World Wars, there was a notable rise in activity as well. Now, some fifteen years after the Cold War and in these uncertain days of the 'War on Terror' international society is in turmoil and experiences major changes once again. It is this which causes scholars to turn from the more daily scholarly business of analysing and explaining existing international law and urges them to question the fundamentals of international law. The historical discourse is part of that 'enquiry into the foundations of the law of nations.'

One thing in all this is very striking, at least to a legal historian from continental Europe. The historiography of international law is an interdisciplinary subject with two natural constituencies: international lawyers and legal historians.[13] Today, as in the past, most specialists in the history of international law are primarily international lawyers, not legal historians. Whereas in most fields of the law, it is the legal historian who complains about the lack of interest of colleagues from current law, in the field of international law, the world is turned on its head.

There are two sides to this coin. First, international lawyers tend to have greater interest in the history of their field than municipal lawyers have – at least municipal lawyers from civil law countries. Second, legal historians have surprisingly little interest in the history of international law. The particular interest of international lawyers is easy to explain. Customary law plays a much larger part in international law than in most municipal law systems. The same goes for case law outside the world of the common law. This forces international lawyers to delve into the past. Furthermore, as was stated above, at a time of transition as we are in now, international lawyers tend to turn to history in order to get a grasp of current evolutions. On the whole, the interest displayed by international lawyers in their history is functional and is dictated by current needs. It is rarely born out of curiosity about the past itself.

The story of international law and its history can be read as a love story, albeit a sad one. Klio, the muse of history, desperately wants to marry into the house of Themis. Of all the sons of Themis, it is her youngest one who covets Klio the most. But in the eyes of Klio, he is the least eligible of all and she constantly pushes him away. Why is that, and what can be done to give this story a happy ending?

---

[13] Apart from these two categories, diplomatic historians and International Relations theorists have also made important contributions to the history of international law.

2. The Story of an Unrequited Love

Why is it that Klio turns down Themis's youngest son, International Law? There are three reasons.

A. An Unattractive Suitor

First, because he is not considered a good match. There is certainly a psychological and corporative dimension to the legal historian's reluctance to specialise in the history of international law. At least during the last fifty years, most legal historians have seen the relative position of their field – above all, of Roman law – decline within their law schools. It comes as no surprise, therefore, that legal historians sometimes – in their very worst moments, of course – exhibit the characteristics of an endangered species. In many European universities, recent ongoing reforms introducing Bachelors and Masters degrees have caused legal historians to dread another reduction in the credits devoted to legal history. And while, these fears have been realised in some cases, the international corps of professional legal historians tends – after years of continuous onslaught – to underscore and highlight the losses and forget about the, surprising, gains. In addition to being a self-defeating tactic, this betrays a defensive frame of mind.

Over the years, a considerable number of legal historians have tried to break out of the marginal position they felt they were in, by stressing that above all else, they are lawyers too. Regardless of the merits thereof, the concern with presenting credentials as 'real lawyers' helps to explain why legal historians do not easily turn their attention to what is still felt to be the least 'legal' of all branches of the legal profession and studies. Although the heyday of the sovereign state and of legal positivism that went along with it was in the 19th century and has now long since past, for many municipal lawyers international law still suffers from the stain the sceptics of international law of that century left it with. As most international lawyers have experienced, any breach of international law by a leading power tempts scholars from municipal law to do away with international law as 'political propaganda' or 'loose talk about ideals'. Choosing to study international law is hardly a clever option for the legal historian who wants to move from the margins to the centre of his law school. It comes thus as no surprise that international legal history has a strong place in law schools where international law is held in high regard. This is equally true for law schools where the field is worked by international lawyers – such as New York University and Cambridge – as where it is worked by legal historians – such as Utrecht and Tilburg.

In addition to this corporative reflex, there is another problem with international law that turns away legal historians. For a long time, historiography has suffered under the modern identification – again stemming from the 19th century – of the law of nations with the sovereign state. Thus, the scope of the field has been greatly reduced. The law of nations, so it is traditionally held, only emerged after the sovereign state came into being. Therefore, its history cannot go back beyond the beginnings of the sovereign state. Also, as the sovereign state and the international legal system based on it was a European invention, the relevant history of international law is – at least before the 19th century – a strictly European history.

Until the end of 19th century, it was held that the modern – or 'classical' as it, paradoxically, is also called – law of nations only emerged in the 17th century.[14] The Peace Treaties of Westphalia (1648) were commonly quoted as having laid down the foundations of the modern states system and its law.[15] The Dutch humanist Hugo Grotius (1583–1645), whose *De iure belli ac pacis libri tres* first appeared in Paris in 1625, was said to be the father of the modern doctrine and science of the law of nations.[16] In the decades before and after 1900, some scholars re-evaluated the role of the 16th-century writers on the law of nations such as the Spanish neo-scholastics Francisco de Vitoria (c. 1480–1546) and Francisco Suarez (1648–1617) or the Roman lawyer Albericus Gentilis (1552–1608).[17] Under the sway of the more general revaluation of the Late Middle Ages – the Renaissance of the Twelfth Century[18] – some students of international legal history moved further back the origins of the modern states system to that era. Wolfgang Preiser proposed 1300 as the starting point for the system of a modern law of nations in Europe.[19]

---

[14] By 'modern law of nations', I mean the law of nations that started to emerge in the 16th century, was elaborated in the decades after 1648 and endured until the end of the First World War. On this terminological confusion, see Grewe, 'Was ist klassisches, was ist modernes Völkerrecht?', in A. Böhm, K. Ludersen & K.-H. Ziegler (eds.), *Idee und Realität des Rechts in der Entwicklung der internationaler Beziehungen. Festschrift für Wolfgang Preiser* (1983) 111.

[15] See for examples: Lesaffer, 'The Grotian Tradition Revisited: Change and Continuity in the History of International Law', 73 *British Yearbook of International Law* (2002) 104, footnote 3.

[16] Bourquin, 'Grotius est-il le père du droit des gens', in *Grandes figures et grandes œuvres juridiques* (1948) 77–99, and more recently, Ziegler, 'Hugo Grotius als Vater des Völkerrechts', in P. Selmer and I. von Münch (eds.), *Gedächtniβschrift für Wolfgang Martens* (1987) 851; *idem*, 'Die Bedeutung von Hugo Grotius als Vater des Völkerrechts – Versuch einer Bilanz am Ende des 20. Jahrhunderts', 13 *Zeitschrift für historische Forschung* (1996) 354. Grotius' title as the father of international law has been disputed by e.g. Grewe, 'Hugo Grotius – Vater des Völkerrechts', 23 *Der Staat* (1984) 161 and P. Haggenmacher, *Grotius et la doctrine de la guerre juste* (1983) 622. See also *idem*, 'Grotius and Gentili: A Reassessment of Thomas E. Holland's Inaugural Lecture', in H. Bull, B. Kingsbury & A. Roberts (eds.), *Hugo Grotius and International Relations* (1992) 133.

[17] Kohler, 'Die spanische Naturrechtslehrer des 16. und 17. Jahrhunderts', 10 *Archiv für Rechts- und Wirschaftsphilosophie*, (1916/1917) 235; E. Nys, *Le droit de la guerre et les précurseurs de Grotius* (1882); J. Brown Scott, *The Spanish Origin of International Law: Francisco de Vitoria and his Law of Nations* (1934); C. von Kaltenborn, *Die Vorläufer des Hugo Grotius auf dem Gebiete des Jus Naturae et Gentium* (1848); T.A. Walker, *A History of the Law of Nations* vol. 1 (1899). On Scott's role in the 'rediscovery' of Vitoria and Suarez see C. R. Rossi, *Broken Chain of Being James Brown Scott and the Origins of Modern International Law* (1998).

[18] C.H. Haskins, *The Renaissance of the Twelfth Century* (1927).

[19] Preiser, 'Über die Ursprunge des modernen Völkerrechts', in E. Bruel (ed.), *Internationalrechtliche und staatsrechtliche Abhandlungen. Festschrift für Walter Schatzel zum 70. Geburtstag* (1960) 373. For more references, see Lesaffer, 'Grotian Tradition', *supra* note 15, footnote 105, note 6.

But however far back one places the origins of the modern, European law of nations, the association of the law of nations with the modern sovereign state still reduces the historiography of the law of nations in time and space. Wolfgang Preiser and his student Karl-Heinz Ziegler, both specialists in the Roman 'international law', escaped that reduction, but felt obliged to stress the continuities between international legal ideas and practices from Antiquity to European modernity.[20] Today, scholars who claim that 'international law' in Antiquity may be studied for its own sake without making the case of continuity remain a rarity.[21]

The debate about the origins of the modern, European law of nations (1500/1648–1919) is not the real debate about the history of international law and its outcome should not determine the scope of the field. The modern law of nations in its relation to the sovereign state should not define 'international law' in its historical setting. 'International law' as a historical concept should be defined as the law regulating the relations between political entities that do not recognise a higher authority. It is what Heinhard Steiger recently called the 'law between political powers'.[22] As such, international law is of all times and places and deserves to be the subject of historical enquiry, regardless of its relations to the modern law of nations and to current international law. It is only natural that current international lawyers who turn to history will primarily devote their time to those parts of the history that are most directly relevant to them. One cannot upbraid them for having neglected the other epochs. The fault lies with the legal historians who have systematically ignored the international legal systems of 'their' eras.

B. A Demanding Lover

Second, International Law is a demanding lover. As Verzijl already suggested in his 1953 paper, international legal historiography suffers from an abundance of sources.[23]

Traditionally, historians of international law have devoted a disproportionate amount of attention to doctrine to the detriment of international legal practice. The most obvious explanation for this is surely practical. The study of international legal practice is a huge undertaking. *Primo*, there is the abundance and the disparity of legal source material. Apart from the obvious 'international' sources such as treaties, declarations of war and decisions by international tribunals and arbitrators, there are many municipal law sources to be considered. This is even more important for those

---

[20] Preiser, *ibid*; K.-H. Zeigler, *Völkerrechtsgeschichte. Ein Studienbuch* (1994) 1–2.

[21] D. Bederman, *International Law in Antiquity* (2001) 6; A. Watson, *International Law in Archaic Rome: War and Religion* (1993).

[22] Steiger, 'From the International Law of Christianity to the International Law of the World Citizen – Reflections on the Formation of the Epochs of the History of International Law', 3 *Journal of the History of International Law* (2001) 181.

[23] Verzijl, *supra* note 2, 407–16.

eras where there was no strict distinction between the national and the international sphere, such as the Middle Ages or the 16th and 17th centuries. These municipal sources include legislation and the decisions of the most diverse courts of law. An example of what this may imply can be taken from peace treaty practice. Since the Late Middle Ages, peace treaties often contained stipulations about the restitution of private property. While these normally provided for special bodies to deal with the disputes arising out of these clauses, at times the regular courts judged these matters. To get a clear view of the execution of a peace treaty in any given border area, one should therefore browse through the archives of all the competent courts of the region, down to the lowest level. Such an exercise concerning one single treaty in one region might prove too onerous for one doctoral thesis. It should also be mentioned that for most eras in history the distinction between private and public law will not be helpful, because it either did not exist at the time or had little practical value. Statutes and cases from private law may therefore not be automatically disregarded because they address matters which in our view pertain to individual rights and obligations. Before the modern state became truly sovereign in the 18th century, the individual was not excluded from the international legal scenery to the same extent that he was afterwards. *Secundo,* studying historical international practice is a multi-disciplinary endeavour. In view of the underdevelopment of international legal history as a field, the scholar regularly needs to turn to International Relations Theory to get a grasp of his field. More importantly, if one wants to take the context of the legal practices one studies into account, one needs to take diplomatic history on board. The reasons behind a certain clause in a treaty or a certain justification for a war are almost always at least partly of a political or diplomatic nature. This in itself multiplies the sources international legal historians will have to deal with. Next to the strictly legal sources, diplomatic and political sources such as diplomatic instructions and correspondence, the reports of political debates in governmental councils and parliamentary assemblies as well as private letters will in many cases have to be perused by the international legal historian. These will not only provide contextual, political information but may also yield direct evidence concerning legal questions.

C. A Negligent Husband

Third, Klio fears that she will not be taken seriously. As was mentioned above, international lawyers show greater interest in historical discourse than municipal lawyers do, at least municipal lawyers from civil law countries. However, for most international lawyers their relation to history is a purely functional one. They look at history because they need it to better understand current issues and trends.

As a discipline, the history of international law has suffered from this pragmatic interest. This may not seem an honest statement to those scholars – international lawyers and legal historians alike – who devoted or devote much time and energy to the study of the subject. But these few dozens of historians of international law of past and present have not been able to sufficiently occupy the battleground as to mould the popular view of the history of international law to their liking. Today, as in the past, the popular view among international lawyers is still to a large extent based on broad and vague assumptions that rather bear witness to present-day concerns than to historical reality. If one wants to know what international lawyers in general know and think about the history of their field, it would serve more to browse through the historical introductions to general textbooks of international law or read the frequent historical reminiscences in international law books than to read the general surveys of its history like those of Nussbaum, Grewe or Ziegler.[24] For lack of an established methodology and theoretical frameworks for the study of the history of international law, International Relations Theory and its historical discourse traditionally take a place of honour in the 'popular' debate about the history of international law, sometimes for better, mostly for worse. International Relations theorists often treat historical facts in a most selective way, being on the outlook for those events and facts that corroborate their theses.[25] But one should not too easily upbraid International Relations theorists for the negative fall-out this has on international legal history, but reprove those who used their 'historical analysis' for what it was not meant to be: a comprehensive analysis and description of historical reality.

Much of what is generally accepted among international lawyers is the fruit of evolutional history. While there is no problem with evolutional history in itself, the problem is that it often concerns 'evolutional history of the worst kind'. It is history to which the famous dictum by T.S. Eliot 'the end is where we start from' would apply. With this kind of historiography, the researcher tries to find the historical origins of a present-day phenomenon by tracing back its genealogy. A prime illustration of this genealogical concern with history is what can be called the famous yet infamous 'first timers'. Thus, the trial of 1474 against Peter von Hagenbach has been cited as the very first conviction for a war crime before an international tribunal.[26] The aim is clearly not to understand what happened in 1474, but to give current ideas or practices roots in the distant past. This kind of historiography sins against the most basic rules of historical methodology, and the results are deplorable. This genealogic history from present to past leads to anachronistic interpretations of historical phenomena, clouds historical realities that bear no fruit in our own times and gives no information about the historical context of the phenomenon one claims to recognise. It describes history in terms of similarities

---

[24] W. Grewe, *Epochs of International Law*, supra note 4; A. Nussbaum, *A Concise History of the Law of Nations* (1954); K.-H. Ziegler, *Völkerrechtsgeschichte*, supra note 20.

[25] Osiander, 'Talking Peace: Social Science, Peace Negotiations and the Structure of Politics', in R Lesaffer (ed), *Peace Treaties and International Law in European History: From the Late Middle Ages to World War One* (2004) 290–300.

[26] G. Schwarzenberger, *International Law*, vol. 2, (1968).

with or differences from the present, and not in terms of what it was. It tries to understand the past for what it brought about and not for what it meant to the people living it. The cavalier way in which history is often dealt with is best of all illustrated by the fact that first-time claims are often rooted in no more than the researcher making the claim has not (or not yet) taken the trouble of considering a more remote period.[27]

However, students of the history of international law, and particularly professional legal historians, should not gloat over the 'amateurism' of international lawyers. If things are as they stand, it is primarily because the 'professional' legal historians have disdained to plough the field. Furthermore, many of the weakly founded generalisations of the history of international law have gone unchallenged by the specialists or have been adopted and confirmed without much serious, systematic and methodological research. Also, the evolutional streak has thrown its shadow over the discourse of specialists. The debate about the origins of the modern law of nations illustrates this point. The almost automatic and evident association of history and theory of international law, which is mostly an Anglo-American phenomenon, is another indication of the ancillary function of history to international lawyers. To many, history is not a self-standing concern. The past is only the mine where facts and figures are to be found to sustain and corroborate existing theories. While many scholars take history seriously when they try to prove their theories, others do not hesitate to force history by means of a Prokrustes-rotation into the box of their theory.

3. Brokering the Relation

The efforts of a few dozen true historians of international law of the past and the present notwithstanding, the history of international law remains underdeveloped. First, traditionally the stress is on the analysis of historical doctrine while state practice largely remains in the shadows. In this respect, little has changed since Preiser stated this complaint in 1964.[28] Second, leaving apart some exceptions, the historiography is largely limited in time and space to Europe and the West from the 16th or even 17th century onwards. Third, the history of this 'modern law of nations' is one-sidedly interpreted in terms of the emergence and rise of the sovereign state. In this sense, it is still dominated by the concerns of the early pioneers of the history

---

[27] Verzijl, *supra* note 2, 415. If one makes the claim about Von Hagenbach, one might as well refer to the role of heralds in upholding the code of chivalry in the Middle Ages. M.H. Keen, *The Laws of War in the Late Middle Ages* (1965) 23–44; T. Meron, *Henry's War and Shakespeare's Laws: Perspectives on the Law of War in the Later Middle Ages* (1993) 172–90.

[28] W. Preiser, *Völkerrechtsgeschichte*, *supra* note 3, 16–7. See also Steiger, 'Probleme der Völkerrechtsgeschichte', 26 *Der Staat* (1987) 103.

of international law from the heyday of the sovereign state, the 19th century. Everything that corroborated the 'Hobbesian' or 'Westphalian' interpretation of the law of nations since 1648 is placed in the spotlight and called fundamental to the system; everything that detracts from it is pushed into the shadows and rejected as exceptional. The 'revolution of international law' in the 20th century and the gradual decline of the sovereign state's dominance have done nothing to correct that view of the modern law of nations in the period between Westphalia and Versailles (1648–1919). On the contrary, underscoring the 'Westphalian' character of the period before 1919 enhances the significance of the changes afterwards.[29] It is only in the last decade or so that authors have started to nuance and fine-tune these views of the modern law of nations. The role played by natural law with the great 'positivists' of the 18th century, such as Cornelius van Bynkershoek (1673–1743) and Emer de Vattel (1714–1767) was rediscovered.[30] And outside the borders of a European international system where the Hobbesian order ruled supreme, a living Grotian system was resurrected in the relations between Europe and the outer-European world.[31] Also, the not so Hobbesian or Westphalian features of the 'Westphalian' system are currently being restated.[32] While I subscribe to these more nuanced views, I have to admit that they go remarkably well with the present-day discourse on the demise of the sovereign state, global governance and international protection of individual rights.

A. State Practice

What should be done to develop the field? First, in the historical research and discourse a balance should be struck between doctrine and legal practices. Often international legal historians consider doctrine to be convenient shorthand for what the law of nations of a certain period was. They act as if the writings of the 'classics of international law' offer a reliable or even authoritative statement of the then applicable law. They thus reduce the law of nations to what some influential authors said it was. Thereby, they tend to forget that these authors may have been more influential decades after their death and not so much during their lives. Furthermore, they all too readily overlook that many of the classics of international law – at least until

---

[29] Lesaffer, 'Grotian Tradition', *supra* note 15, 103–10.

[30] K. Akashi, *Cornelius van Bynkershoek: His Role in the History of International Law* (1998); E. Jouannet, *Emer de Vattel et l'émergence doctrine du droit internationale classique* (1998).

[31] In this system the 'state' was not the sole subject or author of the law of nations. Individuals or non-state entities held and created rights. Natural law and natural rights played a significant role. A. Anghie, *supra* note 11; E. Keene, *Beyond the Anarchical Society: Grotius, Colonialism and Order in World Politics* (2002); R. Tuck, *supra* note 11.

[32] S. Beaulac, *supra* note 11; R. Lesaffer, 'Grotian Tradition', *supra* note 15; B. Simpson, *supra* note 11.

deep in the eighteenth century – did not aspire at describing the law as it stood, but to outline an ideal, or at least a better system of the law of nations.[33]

In most eras of history, 'state' practices and customary law constituted a more important source for the law of nations than doctrine. In fact, it was only in the Late Middle Ages that something approaching an authoritative *communis opinio* in doctrine about some major issues of the law of nations came about. This doctrine of the *ius gentium* was part of the scholastic discourse of the later-medieval theologians, as well as Roman and canon lawyers of the *ius commune*. At the beginning of the 16th century, the Reformation shattered consensus on existing doctrinal rules and doctrine lost its authority.[34]

Therefore, international legal historians should delve deeper into state practice. There are two reasons why this has not been done. *Primo,* as was expounded above, this is a most tedious undertaking. *Secundo,* here too, the obsession with the sovereign state is at fault. After all, sovereignty is the ultimate shrinker of the law of nations. According to the most extreme Hobbesian interpretations of the Westphalian law of nations, there is little law of nations worth studying in the era of the modern law of nations. The thousands of treaties of the modern era should not be taken too seriously as sources of legal obligations, let alone as sources of law, because under the doctrine of *clausula rebus sic stantibus* sovereigns can always push them aside. The many hundreds of manifestos offering justifications of war are not worth a minute of the international legal historian's attention. What else can they be than mere propaganda at a time when the *ius ad bellum* was just that: an unlimited right of sovereigns to wage war whenever they saw fit? Therefore, their contents must have been as political as their purpose. Questions about the rights of individuals should not be addressed either, as the doctrine of dualism safely excludes the individual from the international legal sphere.

B. *Taking History Seriously*

Second, whatever the intentions and purposes of the scholar studying the history of international law, he should approach the past with proper respect. This means that he should make use of the basic rules of historical methodology. In itself, there is nothing wrong with the desire to learn something useful for the present from the past, nor with evolutional history. But before one can learn something from the past other than what one knows from the present, one first has to let the past be the past – at least as far as this is humanly possible. This means that one should work

---

[33] This claim has recently also been made to some extent for some of the great 'positivists' of the eighteenth century like Bynkershoek and Vattel, see *supra* note 30. In this context, see also A. Perreau-Saussine's chapter on Oppenheim in this volume.

[34] Lesaffer, 'Argument from Roman Law in Current International Law: Occupation and Acquisitive Prescription', 16 *European Journal of International Law* (2005) 34–8.

in two distinct phases. First, there is the analysis of history in its own right and on its own terms. Second, the historical data can be used in a wider framework, like a long-term evolution.

In this first phase, the rudiments of classical historical methodology should be respected. This comes down to nothing more or less to what historians have been doing since the days of humanistic scholarship: the textual and contextual analysis of their written sources. Historians should see to it that their sources are as authentic as possible. They should try to read them as the contemporaries of the authors would. And they should relate them to the contexts and the concerns of the authors.

This is easier said than done. Even today, there are hardly any trustworthy critical editions of even the main historical sources of international law, be it from doctrine or from practice.[35] Even the most frequently cited and used treaties have hardly been edited in a critical way.[36] Textual analysis often entails linguistic and philological skills. But it is in the contextual analysis that the greatest mistakes are made, although they are easiest to avoid. It is often, again, the concern with evolutional history that is at fault. Texts, and especially the writings of the great authors of international law are not read for what they said but for the significance they had for the further development of international law. They are read with knowledge of their future. One does not try to understand what the author wrote, but how he contributed to later developments. The enormous literature modern scholarship has produced on, for instance, Grotius's *De iure belli ac pacis* illustrates the point. As Grotius is considered the *fons originis* of the modern law of nations and its doctrine, his work is usually read with the concern of finding the roots of the later law. What one should do is try to understand why Grotius took a particular position[37] and consider what stand he took in relation to older authors and doctrines.[38] Grotius, like most other authors in history, entered into an ongoing debate. While he and other classical authors are often treated by current scholarship as if they dialogued with later authors, they dialogued with older authors. Here again, the history of international law bites its own tail. Traditional historiography has been so concerned with the debate about the origins of the modern law of nations and the modern states system that it has fallen into the trap of considering its father(s) – Grotius and his immediate predecessors – or its birth certificates – the Peace Treaties of Westphalia – as the original creators or creations.

---

[35] Steiger, 'Quellenkunde und Quellenedition für die Völkerrechtsgeschichte', 28 *Der Staat* (1989) 576–91; *idem*, 'Entwicklung des Völkerrechts von 1815 bis 1945 im Spiegel seiner Quellen', 34 *Der Staat* (1995) 130–9.

[36] One must do with either the uncritical publication of C. Parry (ed.), *The Consolidated Treaty Series* (1969–1981) as regards treaties since 1648 or with much older collections such as most famously Jean Du Mont, *Corps universel diplomatique du droit des gens* (Amsterdam, 1726). Currently, the Institute for European History, department of Universal History in Mainz is publishing early-modern peace treaties on the web. These editions are not critical: www.ieg-friedensvertraege.de.

[37] As one by Tuck, *supra* note 11, 78–108.

[38] As done by P. Haggenmacher, *Grotius et la doctrine de la guerre juste* (1983).

This may all seem evident, trivial and trite, but these are is not superfluous remarks to make. It never ceases to amaze how little this all is heeded in the historiography of the law of nations. One example will suffice to make this point. Probably the most widespread and repeated idea in the history of international law is the 'Westphalian myth'. Actually, it goes beyond the field and has become an idea shared with political and diplomatic historians, constitutional lawyers and international relations specialists.

The Westphalian myth holds that the Peace Treaties of Westphalia of 1648 laid the foundations for the sovereign states system and constitute the formative acts of the law of nations that went along with it. It has been claimed and repeated that the main features and principles of that system were introduced into the law of nations at Westphalia. These claims are made concerning sovereignty, religious equality, the constitution of Europe as an international legal society and the balance of power. They are so well spread that hardly anybody takes the trouble to check these claims or is likely to dispute them.[39]

However, in the context of the academic activities on the occasion of the 350th anniversary of the treaties in 1998 some scholars from very different backgrounds did just that. However surprising this will be to the reader who did not himself peruse the treaties, none of the above claims proved to have a foothold in the texts of the treaties themselves. There is no reference to either sovereignty, religious equality or the balance of power as principles of international law or relations, and the treaties do nothing to constitute a European legal order. And in as much as it contains concepts that may explain why historians have read into treaties what they did, these are anything but innovative, merely restatements of past principles, if not retrogressions into history.[40] Once again, the 'originality' of Westphalia seems to be

---

[39] See *supra* note 15.

[40] On the Westphalian myth and the challenge thereof: Beaulac, 'The Westphalian Legal Orthodoxy – Myth or Reality?', 2 *Journal of the History of International Law* (2000) 148; also *idem*, *supra* note 11, 71–97; Croxton, 'The Peace of Westphalia of 1648 and the Origins of Sovereignty', 21 *International History Review* (1999) 569; Eyffinger, 'Europe in the Balance: An Appraisal of the Westphalian System', 45 *Netherlands International Law Review* (1998) 161; Haggenmacher, 'La paix dans le pensée de Grotius', in L. Bély (ed.), *L'Europe des traités de Westphalie. Esprit de diplomatie et diplomatie de l'esprit* (2000) esp. 68–9; Lesaffer, 'The Westphalian Peace Treaties and the Development of the Tradition of Great European Peace Settlements prior to 1648', 18 *Grotiana* (1997) 71; Osiander, 'Sovereignty, International Relations and the Westphalian Myth', 55 *International Organization*, (2001) 251; Schröder, 'Der Westfälische Friede – eine Epochengrenze in der Völkerrechtsentwicklung?', in M. Schröder (ed.), *350 Jahre Westfälischer Friede. Verfassungsgeschichte Staatskirchenrecht,Völkerrechtsgeschichte*, Schriften zur europäischen Rechts-und Verfassungsgeschichte (1999) vol. 30, 119; Steiger, 'Der Westfälischen Frieden – Grundgesetz für Europa?', in H. Duchhardt (ed), *Der Westfälische Friede. Diplomatie, politische Zäsur, kulturelles Umfeld, Rezeptionsgeschichte* (1998) 33; K.-H. Ziegler, 'Die Bedeutung des Westfälischen Friedens von 1648 für das europäische Völkerrecht', 37 *Archiv des Völkerrechts* (1999) 129; *idem*, 'Der Westfälischen Frieden von 1648 in der Geschichte des Völkerrechts', in M. Schröder (ed.), *350 Jahre Westfälischer Friede*, 99.

vested in little more than that nobody ever took the trouble to compare the treaties with earlier treaties; everybody laid them besides more recent texts. And even now that the myth has been disproved, it is restated again and again.

All this does not imply that history can or may not be used in a wider discourse on current international law. However, as it was stated above, this can only be done in a second movement. Evolutional history is commendable, as long as the distinct phases of these evolutions are first studied in their own right and for their own sake. Only after having done that will it be possible to construct an evolutional theory that truly moves from past to present and to ensure that explanations are derived from the past and not dictated by the present. A similar, two-phased methodology has to be used for comparative history.

C. A Less Selective Approach

Third, international legal historians should extend their concerns with history beyond the spatial and temporal limits traditionally set to the sovereign state system and its law of nations. This is a double plea. *Primo,* it is a plea to study the international legal systems outside Europe and far beyond the 16th century. *Secundo,* it is also a plea for the historians of the modern, European law of nations to broaden their scope. This means that they should place that modern law of nations into its wider historical context and stop considering it as a highly exceptional *creatio ex nihilo* by the 'intellectual giants' of the early 17th or even 16th century. The precursors of Grotius and Westphalia need to be studied seriously if we are ever to understand the formation of this law of nations. It is impossible to comprehend Grotius without being aware of the intellectual tradition in which he stood. And whereas quite some attention has been devoted to his immediate inspirers such as the Spanish neo-scholastics or Balthasar de Ayala (1548–1584) and Albericus Gentilis (1552–1608), his main source of inspiration remains a blank spot on the historical map. I refer to the great tradition of medieval Roman and canon law, which has developed many important ideas on the law of nations.[41] And the concerns of the negotiators of Westphalia can never be correctly assessed if the upheaval brought about to the international legal system by the Reformation and the Discoveries is not correctly understood. Placing the modern law of nations into its wider context also presupposes more attention for the relations between Europe and the outer-European

---

[41] See, however, the chapters by K.-H. Ziegler, A. Wijffels, D. Bauer & L. Winkel in R. Lesaffer (ed.), *Peace Treaties and International Law in European History: From the Late Middle Ages to World War One* (2004). Also Muldoon, 'The Contribution of the Medieval Canon Lawyers to the Formation of International Law', 28 *Traditio* (1972) 483; *idem*, 'Medieval Canon Law and the Formation of International Law', 81 *Zeitschrift der Savigny-Stiftung für Rechtsgeschichte, kanonistische Abteilung* (1995) 64.

world. Over the last few years, several scholars have started on this road.[42] Apart from these temporal and spatial borders that need to be crossed, there is also a material one. International legal history is considered to be part of the history of public law. It is therefore of no interest to the vast majority of legal historians who work on private law. However, this too is a misconception. Historically, international law only became a distinct field of law, and thus of public law, far into the 17th century. And even then, as Sir Hersch Lauterpacht (1897–1960) brilliantly argued, it went on to take most of its inspiration from private law.[43]

D. International Legal History As a True Academic Discipline

Fourth, and probably most importantly, international legal history should be organised as a field and as a discipline. For the first time in history, today more than a handful of scholars regularly publish on the history of international law. However, their endeavours remain largely isolated and uncoordinated. This problem is enhanced by the fact that the field includes scholars from different constituencies, which in itself is a good thing. However, at times it is rather shocking to notice that scholars from one field, who propose certain ideas, are completely unaware of the fact that others from another field – even if they published in the same language and with major publishing houses – stated the same. Therefore, all kinds of initiatives that bring together scholars from these different backgrounds are laudable.

The need for coordination is great, not only because the field is wide but also because the field presupposes an interdisciplinary approach. Apart from international lawyers and legal historians, who are focused upon in this contribution, diplomatic historians and international relations specialists have a role to play. However, a first step would be for many international lawyers who work the field of history to lure more legal historians into working with them. After all, it is the legal historians who may be expected to do the groundwork, the work of the 'first phase'.

Legal historians often complain about their current law colleagues not having enough interest in or appreciation for historical discourse. It is ironic that the one field of current law in which the demand for historical research is the greatest is the most spurned by legal historians. They are wrong to do so, but will need to be convinced step by step. Therefore, legal history and international law need to break from their respective cocoons and reach out to and get acquainted with one another. To return to our metaphor of love: 'let them date'.

---

[42] Supra note 31.
[43] H. Lauterpacht, Private Sources and Analogies of International Law (1927).

FOREIGN OFFICE INTERNATIONAL LEGAL HISTORY

David J. Bederman*

Introduction

I take as a starting point of my discussion, Judge Rosalyn Higgins' seminal article, 'Time and the Law: International Perspectives on an Old Problem.'[1] International law as a discipline appears to be rooted in historical trends and realities to a far larger degree than other realms of law and jurisprudence, but the relationship between the domains of international law (as both an academic study and professional practice) and historiography remain cloudy and uncertain. The broad structure of Judge Higgins' argument is that time and history can be distinct elements in many international law doctrines and in forms of international law decision-making. In examining distinct temporal elements of particular rules – including jurisdictional consent and continuing acts under the international law of State Responsibility,[2] retrospective application of international law rules,[3] prescriptive limitations (including international statutes of limitations, laches, estoppel and acquiescence),[4] and the principle of intertemporal law[5] – history can play a crucial role.

The purpose of this contribution is to explore the contours of historiography in international law advocacy, decision-making and scholarship, while, at the same time, suggesting the need for standards and 'best practices' for international legal historians, especially those involved in aspects of international decision-making. In my view, international legal history can be a decidedly instrumental pursuit. Historical data is often 'mined' by advocates, desiring to win an important, disputed issue. Arbitrators and judges are increasingly called upon to consider historical evidence, and to render a forensic analysis of its putative weight and significance. International

---

* Professor of Law, Emory University. I am indebted to the organizers of the Time, History and International Law Conference, held on 1 October 2004, sponsored by Queen Mary University, the School of Oriental and African Studies and the British Institute for International and Comparative Law, and in particular Professor Malgosia Fitzmaurice and Dr. Matthew Craven. I am also grateful for comments received during an Emory University Law School conference on 'Alien Tort Claims after *Sosa v. Alvarez-Machain,*' held on October 22, 2004. This article is dedicated to my first instructor in international law, H.E. Judge Rosalyn Higgins, President of the ICJ.

[1] 46 *International and Comparative Law Quarterly* (1997) 501.
[2] *Ibid,* 501–07.
[3] *Ibid,* 507–11.
[4] *Ibid,* 511–15.
[5] *Ibid,* 515–19.

law scholars routinely have resort to historical materials to explain contemporary doctrines, chart the trajectory of customary international law or treaty compliance, or to elucidate general trends in the law.

It is thus vitally important to understand how international lawyers 'do' history. How do we create our own specialized genres of history? Is what we do as international legal historians a distinct sub-specialty, say, in comparison, with historians of international relations or diplomatic historians? Even more important, what kinds of history do we narrate? Are there any systemic or disciplinary blinders that we must be aware of? Does international law tend to ignore certain narratives, actors or participants in the international legal system? Are certain voices excluded from our counsels? Is all of this indicative of the much-discussed 'fragmentation' of international law?[6] Or, instead, does this manifest a new era of anxiety and uncertainty? Or is it, instead, a reflection of an old era of nostalgia?

I acknowledge that these portentous questions cannot all be fully addressed in this essay. I will try, instead, to focus on the key inquiry of what styles of international legal historiography are within the realm of acceptable scholarship, advocacy, and judicial decision. In this manner, I hope to open a discussion as to the best practices and methods of international legal history. To that end, this essay will unfold in three steps. First, I hope to chart the criticisms that have come to be levelled against many forms of legal history, as practiced by lawyers, judges, and (some) scholars. Derisively called 'law office history', the practices of some advocates and jurists in employing historical evidence and material have been attacked as overtly instrumental and misguided. I try to ascertain whether this critique can equally be applied to international legal history and to those who use historical materials in international advocacy and litigation contexts. Next, I offer up two case studies of relatively recent judicial decisions (one domestic and one international) in which international legal history figures prominently in the resolution of albeit very different kinds of disputes. I try to explore, through these case studies, the ways that advocates marshal historical evidence to make their points, and the ways that judges seek to resolve matters of historical uncertainty in reaching the decisions and conclusions they do. There is little point in discussing the uses (or abuses) of international legal history in the abstract, without recourse to specific litigation contexts and to the (sometimes) unique historical records that accompany these disputes.

---

[6] Simma, 'Fragmentation in a Positive Light', 25 *Michigan Journal of International Law* (2004) 845; Hafner, 'Pros and Cons Ensuing from Fragmentation of International Law', 25 *Michigan Journal of International Law* (2004) 849; Koskenniemi & Leino, 'Fragmentation of International Law? Postmodern Anxieties', 15 *Leiden Journal of International Law* (2002) 553. This issue has even received attention by the International Law Commission. See UN Doc. A/CN.4/L.663/Rev.1 (2004); Hafner, 'Risks Ensuing from Fragmentation of International Law' in *Report of the ILC on the Work of its Fifty-Second Session*, Doc. A/55/10, 321–339, available at: <http://untreaty.un.org/ilc/reports/2000/repfra.htm>.

1. The Question of International Legal History

In the United States, at least, because of the strong tradition of original intent in constitutional interpretation, recourse to historical sources and insights has become a consistent feature of both judicial decisions and academic commentary. The methodologically weak and (some might say) indiscriminate and instrumental uses of history in American legal discourse have resulted in a backlash, with such writing and decisions being derided as 'law office history',[7] or, even worse, 'History Lite'.[8] Part of this phenomenon can be attributed to the American jurisprudential love-affair with originalism, the goal of seeking legal truth from the intentions and desires of original law-makers (whether it be the drafters of a statute or the Framers of a Constitution). Professor Rebecca Brown has commented, in this regard, that

> originalists must be absolutely rigorous in their quest for accuracy and legitimacy in their historical investigations. The accusations of selective use of history, 'law office history', incomplete history, sloppy or strategic methodology, and lack of candor are all devastating critiques of the originalists, because their justifications for using history depend on a claim of truth and objectivity. The tenets of originalism, which justify the use of history in the first place, necessarily require that the history be objective, accurate, and 'true.' It is imperative, under the theoretical rationale, for the power of the past espoused by the originalist credo, that all aspects of the past be examined, that inquiry be complete and rigorous and honest, that conflicting evidence somehow be resolved, and that defensible answers be obtained. The difficulty of attaining that ideal has been, and continues to be, a serious problem for the originalists.[9]

But it would be a profound mistake to regard the historiographic pathologies of 'law office history' as being merely the moral failings of those who seek original intent, although certainly that is often how such has played-out in U.S. jurisprudential circles. Rather, the problem runs much deeper. It potentially affects all legal scholars, practitioners and jurists who occasionally or routinely use historical materials or methods in the pursuit of some forensic, scholarly, or juristic pursuit. As Martin Flaherty has observed:

> the legal community notoriously ignores the principle that the individual historical questions that its members commonly seek to answer cannot be understood except as 'part of a larger historical . . . whole.' Two methodological requirements follow. One is the necessity of thorough reading, or at least citation, of both primary and secondary source material generally recognized by historians as central to a given question. Too often, legal scholars make a fetish of one or two famous primary sources, and consider

---

[7] Richards, 'Clio and the Court: A Reassessment of the Supreme Court's Uses of History', 13 *Journal of Law and Politics* (1997) 809; Kleinhaus, 'Note, History as Precedent: The Post-Originalist Problem in Constitutional Law', 110 *Yale Law Journal* (2000) 121.

[8] Flaherty, 'History 'Lite' in Modern American Constitutionalism', 95 *Columbia Law Review* (1995) 523.

[9] Brown, 'History for the Non-Originalist', 26 *Harvard Journal of Law & Public Policy* (2003) 74.

their historical case made. Another procedural corollary requires viewing, or at least attempting to view, events, ideas, and controversies in a larger context. Here legal scholars, in what in its worst form is dubbed 'law office history', notoriously pick and choose facts and incidents ripped out of context that serve their purposes. In a phrase, persuasive historical procedure dictates genuine concern for facts, sources, and context. Abiding by just these standards is hard and time-consuming work, often too hard and time-consuming to meet the imperatives of legal scholarship.[10]

So it seems that the key attributes of 'law office history' are (1) a lack of analytic rigour in historical investigations, (2) selective use of historical materials, (3) sloppy or strategic methodologies in the review of historic sources, (4) overt or implicit instrumentalism in the selection of historic data and/or the conclusions drawn from such material, and (5) an unwillingness or inability to reconcile conflicting sources, or an inability to accept ambiguity or incompleteness in the historic record. Most devastating of all, the indiscriminate and instrumental use of history has been likened to a lawyer's brief where case-law citations are distorted or perverted, in order to make some point that has no basis in fact or reality.

In large measure, the growing concern for proper historiographic methodology in legal pursuits can be attributed to the growing influence of academic historians in legal scholarship, and in litigation. Professional historians, at least in the United States, have sought to bring to bear their formidable training and methods on legal questions, and to sometimes challenge the doctrinal views and opinions of academic lawyers. In short, there has been a growing turf war between history departments and law school faculties for the 'heart and soul' of legal history. Even more astonishingly, professional historians have come to wield increased influence in some forms of litigation by serving as expert witnesses or as amicus curiae brief-filers, in which they take strong stands as to the meaning and explication of the historic record as it affects some legal determination. To some degree, we are witnessing the growing 'professionalization' of history in legal circles.

How does all of this affect international law practice? Historical evidence can be much more significant in international disputes and the formation of rules of international law, than in domestic law and controversies. If anything, history matters more for international law than for domestic law. So, at least on the surface of things, there is a very real risk that international law advocacy and scholarship could be tainted by the same improper historiographic methods, just as 'law office historians' have done for domestic law. To put it another way, do we have – or could we have – the same problem with the international law decisions reached by both domestic and international tribunals? Are we seeing the emergence of a phenomenon of 'foreign office international legal history', as a counterpart to domestic 'law office history'?

---

[10] Flaherty, *supra* note 8, 553 (quoting Powell, 'Rules for Originalists', 73 *Virginia Law Review* (1987) 659).

By referring to 'foreign office international legal history,' I am by no means implying that it is the policy-makers or legal advisers of foreign ministries that are likely to be the chief culprits in the corruption of Clio in the pursuit of some instrumental objectives. If anything, such officials – because they are 'repeat players' in the process of international affairs and diplomacy – are more likely to respect historical fidelity and truth, and eschew attempts to subvert the integrity of historical evidence in the pursuit of some immediate policy or legal objective. Rather, it is more probable that advocates before domestic or international tribunals deciding international law issues, and the judges or arbitrators who decide these controversies, are likely to be affected by the Siren Song of historic instrumentalism or be afflicted by the pitfalls and challenges of historiographic method. It may also be that international law scholars and academics would be the ones that are most likely to succumb to the temptations of 'foreign office international legal history.'

That caveat aside, I also want it understood that there may be good and sufficient reasons why international law advocacy and scholarship may be *less* prone to historiographic instrumentalism, than are the participants in particular domestic legal systems (such as in the United States). The first is that while history *matters* in many international law controversies, originalism – and its hand-maiden of original intent for particular legal texts – does not. To take some obvious examples, the original intent of treaty drafters as to the meaning of particular provisions has only a subordinate role to play in the principles of treaty interpretation.[11] According to Article 32 of the 1969 Vienna Convention on the Law of Treaties, '[r]ecourse may be had to supplementary means of interpretation including the preparatory work of the treaty and the circumstances of its conclusion. . . .'[12] The 'supplemental means of interpretation' are only to be invoked when the text is 'ambiguous or obscure' or a plain reading of the treaty text leads to a 'manifestly absurd or unreasonable' result.[13] There are also well-understood reasons why the original intent of convention drafters should not necessarily be privileged as a matter of treaty interpretation. Not the least of these is that newcomers to any treaty system should not be bound by the original understandings (or side-deals) made by the original parties at the inception of a regime.[14] All of this applies as well to problems of constitutional

---

[11] I acknowledge that some international law doctrines, such as the *uti possidetis* rule for the recognition of former Colonial-period boundaries, may have a strongly originalist flavor. In actuality, though, this doctrine may be more of a Burkean conservative streak in international law rules. As the World Court observed, 'the maintenance of the territorial status quo . . . is often seen as the wisest course . . . to avoid a disruption [and promote] the essential requirement of stability.' *Frontier Dispute* case, (Burkina Faso/Republic of Mali), ICJ Rep 1986, 554.

[12] *Vienna Convention on the Law of Treaties*, 1155 UNTS 331. Signed on 23 May 1969, entered into force on 27 January 1980. Art. 32.

[13] *Id.*

[14] Separate Opinion of Judge Spender in *Certain Expenses of the United Nations*, Advisory Opinion, ICJ Rep 1962, 185.

interpretation in the international system, including the construction of such constitutive and organic documents as the United Nations Charter.[15]

A second reason that instrumental historiography may actually be less of a concern for international lawyers is that scholarship and advocacy for international law
has matured notably in the past decades. It has become less common for historical
evidence to be enlisted as part of some 'theological' approach to justify (or ration-
alize) particular international law doctrines. There is little perceived need today to
trace the lineage or pedigree of international law doctrines back to some clearly-
defined early-Modern, medieval, or possibly classical origins. More importantly, the
legitimacy or internal coherence of international law as a distinct legal system does
not necessarily depend on any historical role it has played in mediating disputes
between nations or as a guiding force for international relations under a rule of law.
To put it another way, 'boosterism' for international law – an indiscriminate and
(sometimes) counterproductive advocacy for compliance with international law at
all costs – can draw on many sources, but history is not usually one of them.

These cautions aside, there is still reason to be concerned that instrumental historiography – 'foreign office international legal history' – still poses a danger to professional international law advocacy, the proper disposition of international disputes,
and sophisticated international law scholarship. As has already been discussed, history and time do matter in the appreciation of international law sources, the understanding of international law doctrines, and the resolution of international
controversies. The historical contingencies of international law are probably more
notable than in domestic legal systems, even if (as already noted) the international
legal system does not necessarily privilege an original intent for international law
texts, nor the policy objectives and desires of 'first-movers' among international legal
actors. As I have intimated before, because history matters to international law, so
must responsible historiography.

2. Two Case Studies on the Importance of International Legal History

Having outlined the broad contours of the problem of instrumental historiography,
I now offer two case studies on the potential effects of 'foreign office international
legal history.' First, I must say that in narrating these two case studies, it is by no
means my intent to suggest that the historiographic errors or omissions that may
have been committed by lawyers in advocating certain cases, the judges who
decided them, or the scholars who commented on them, were intentional or even

---

[15] Sloan, 'The United Nations Charter as a Constitution', 1 *Pace Yearbook of International Law*
(1989) 61; Pair, 'Judicial Activism in the ICJ Charter Interpretation', 8 *ILSA Journal of International
and Comparative Law* (2001) 181.

the product of negligence. Actual international law disputes, like international incidents that might arise between countries,[16] are obviously contentious situations. It may be no surprise that history is enlisted to serve a legal argument in the same way as any evidence or material might be. In the heat of legal battle, norms and standards of good historiography can tend to be forgotten, or worse, deliberately ignored.

But one must recognize that one size does not fit all when it comes to international law disputes. The two case studies presented here are of strikingly different characters. I will briefly abstract them here, before launching into the details. The U.S. Supreme Court in June 2004 handed down a ruling in the *Sosa v. Alvarez-Machain* case,[17] concerning the status of the Alien Tort Statute, adopted by Congress in 1790, which gives a right of action to aliens seeking redress for 'violation[s] of the law of nations or a treaty of the United States.'[18] After extensive and hotly-contested briefing by the parties (including the United States government), the U.S. Supreme Court reached a ruling on the meaning of the 'law of nations' in eighteenth century English, American and international parlance and practice. But this was no academic exercise; the Court went on to rule that private rights of action were available under the Statute, and that the set of 'violations' so actionable could change and evolve with time. The Court sought to examine the intent of the drafters of the Alien Tort Statute and measure their understanding against the prevailing intellectual currents of international law at the time of creating the American constitution. The *Sosa* decision thus reflects international legal historiography sketched on a broad, compelling canvas. It is a narrative about 'history' on a macro-scale.

A somewhat more prosaic application of historiographic techniques to international decision-making is the International Court of Justice's 1999 decision in the *Kasikili/Sedudu Island* case (Botswana/Namibia).[19] This was a boundary dispute, the successful resolution of which has become a staple of the World Court's work. In boundary disputes, historical materials concerning the effective occupation of territory by the contesting nations are often implicated and often become decisive for the determination of the outcome of the case. *Kasikili/Sedudu* is not itself a significant decision, save for some disagreements registered by the parties and the members of the Court (particularly Judge Higgins) over the significance of

---

[16] Reisman, 'International Incidents: Introduction to a New Genre in the Study of International Law', 10 *Yale Journal of International Law* (1984) 1; Willard, 'Incidents: An Essay in Method', 10 *Yale Journal of International Law* (1984) 21; W. Michael & A.R. Willard (eds.), *International Incidents: The Law that Counts in World Politics* (1988).

[17] 124 S. Ct. (2004) 2739.

[18] 28 U.S.C. (2005) § 1350.

[19] *Kasikili/Sedudu Island* case, (Botswana/Namibia), *Merits,* ICJ Rep. 1999, 1045.

particular historical documents and evidence. Unlike the *Sosa* decision, *Kasikili/Sedudu* is international legal historiography writ small. This case is as much about 'time' (as distinct from 'history'), and the effects of time on internationally-cognizable claims. To put it another way, this is a case study about the 'micro-level' effects of arguments about custom, practice, and courses of dealing between parties. Nevertheless, the standards of quality history in international legal advocacy in such cases should be no less important.

A. The Sosa v. Alverez-Machain Case

The *Sosa v. Alvarez-Machain* case has had a long and convoluted trajectory in the United States court system. The underlying facts and procedural posture of the controversy certainly do not present the U.S. government's actions and conduct in the best light. The case arose from the 1985 kidnapping, torture and murder of U.S. Drug Enforcement agent, stationed in Mexico, by drug cartel operatives. A Mexican physician, Dr. Humberto Alvarez-Machain, was believed by U.S. law enforcement officials to have been involved in the torture and murder, and he was subsequently indicted by a U.S. court and a warrant for his arrest was issued. Having had no success with recourse to Mexican official procedures for extradition or rendition, U.S. officials contracted with private bounty-hunters to abduct Alaverez and bring him to the United States. Jose Francisco Sosa was one of these private contractors.[20]

Once in U.S. custody, Dr. Alvarez moved to dismiss the indictment on the ground that it violated the extradition treaty between the U.S. and Mexico. That issue reached the U.S. Supreme Court and, in a surprising and worrisome ruling,[21] the Court held that the plain meaning of the extradition treaty did not bar such unilateral exercises of abducting foreign suspects from the other side of the border. While this ruling was subject to a withering dissent by three members of the Court,[22] and hostile academic commentary,[23] it has no further bearing on subsequent proceedings in the case.

And what happened next was truly extraordinary – after trial, Dr. Alvarez was acquitted on all charges against him. He returned to Mexico in 1993, and proceeded to initiate a series of lawsuits in which Sosa was named a defendant, along with a number of government agents. The suits against the government agents were brought ostensibly in conformance with a federal statute known as the Federal Tort

---

[20] For the background facts, see *United States v. Alvarez-Machain*, 504 U.S. (1992) 657–58; *Sosa v. Alvarez-Machain*, 124 S. Ct. (2004) 2739, 2746 (hereinafter *Sosa*).

[21] *United States v. Alvarez-Machain, ibid* 663–70.

[22] *Ibid*, 670–88 (Stevens, J., dissenting).

[23] I certainly took this position in my academic commentary. See Bederman, 'Revivalist Canons and Treaty Interpretation', 41 *UCLA Law Review* (1994) 982, 1010–14, 1017–19.

Claims Act (FTCA), but the Supreme Court – in a ruling that need not detain our studies further – ruled that the FTCA's 'foreign country' exception applied and that the government agents could not be sued.[24]

That left the case against Sosa, which Dr. Alvarez brought, not under the FTCA, but a much older U.S. federal statute – the Alien Tort Claims Act (or Alien Tort Statute (ATS)) of 1789. That statute provides in its entirety: 'The district courts shall have original jurisdiction of any civil action by an alien for a tort only, committed in violation of the law of nations or a treaty of the United States.'[25] The fighting question for the U.S. Supreme Court – and the issue of international legal historiography that engages us here – is whether the First Congress of the United States intended this provision not only as a simple grant of jurisdiction to U.S. federal courts, but also 'authority for the creation of a new cause of action for torts in violation of international law.'[26] On this distinction – the ATS as a mere jurisdictional grant, as opposed to a robust and fulsome creation of new species of international causes of action under U.S. domestic law – much turned for the parties to the case. Dr. Alvarez, after all, had to show that U.S. courts had jurisdiction over his claims, and that (as a matter of substance) U.S. law had incorporated international standards of conduct regarding such 'tort[s] . . . committed in violation of the law of nations' like unlawful (but temporary) detentions. Sosa's counsel had merely to show that the ATS was solely a jurisdictional gateway, without providing any substantive law nor creating any international cause of action. Alternatively, he could show that temporary but unlawful detentions did not rise to the level of an 'offense against the law of nations or a treaty of the United States.' This is how the parties, and their counsel, drew the jurisprudential battle-lines in the case.

Ultimately, the crucial question that the parties (and their amici) briefed and that the Court decided was the historical question of whether the drafters of the Alien Tort Statute – essentially the same group that drafted the United States Constitution – contemplated that the Act would allow certain 'international law cum common law claims'[27] to be introduced directly into United States domestic law, and thus provide litigants with some substantive basis to bring tort claims

---

[24] See *Sosa supra* note 20, 2747–2754. The relevant statutory provisions for the FTCA can be found at 28 U.S.C. (2005) § 2680(k). See also *Smith v. United States*, 507 U.S. (1993) 197 ('foreign country' exception barred claims arising from Antarctica).

[25] 28 U.S.C. (2005) § 1350. The original language from 1789 was that the new federal district courts 'shall also have cognizance, concurrent with the courts of the several States, or the circuit courts, as the case may be, of all causes where an alien sues for a tort only in violation of the law of nations or a treaty of the United States.' First Judiciary Act, Act of Sept. 24, 1789, Chapter 20, § 9(b), 1 Stat. 79.

[26] *Sosa, supra* note 20, 2755.

[27] *Ibid*, 2754.

based on customary international law.[28] The key question for legal historians (both domestic and international) was the relationship between what was properly understood to be the 'law of nations' in 1789 and the contemporaneous common law of England and the United States. Superimposed upon these inquiries was a wider set of speculations as to the background political history of the formation of the American Republic, the weakness of the national government institutions during the Continental Congress (1775–1781) and Articles of Confederation (1781–1788) periods, the drafting of the Constitution in 1787, and its ratification and entry into force in the years following.

These inquiries implicate so much historical material that it could have kept a legion of legal historians busy. And, during the *Sosa* litigation in the Supreme Court, it did. Aside from the briefs of the main parties in the case (Alvarez, Sosa, and the United States Government),[29] some of the amicus briefs heavily engaged with historical materials and evidence.[30] The main party briefs in *Sosa* tended to be highly tendentious in their arguments and very selective in their use of historic evidence. Most of the citations were to Blackstone's *Commentaries* (assumed by all participants in the case as being the authoritative exposition of English common law at the time of the Founding),[31] the writings of the Framers, and early opinions of U.S. Attorneys General. Once again, an American penchant for originalism (this time in statutory interpretation, not constitutional construction) drove the parties into a mad-dash for contemporary statements that could lend any credence or support for their positions, and this evidence was presented in the briefs irrespective of historical context

---

[28] It should be noted that none of Alvarez-Machain's tort claims were premised on a provision in a 'treaty of the United States,' which would lead to a very different analysis of whether the subject provision was considered to be 'self-executing' and creating a private right of action under U.S. law. See *ibid*, 2763. 'Several times, indeed, the Senate has expressly declined to give the federal courts the task of interpreting and applying international human rights law, as when its ratification of the International Covenant on Civil and Political Rights declared that the substantive provisions of the document were not self-executing.' *Ibid*, 2767. This question of the interplay between treaty rights and claims under the ATS is quite significant, but is otherwise beyond the scope of this contribution.

[29] See Brief of the United States as Respondent Supporting Petitioner, *Sosa v. Alvarez-Machain*, U.S. S. Ct. 03-339, 2004 WL [Westlaw] 182581 (filed Jan. 23, 2004) (hereinafter 'U.S. Brief'); Brief of Petitioner, *Sosa v. Alvarez-Machain*, U.S. S. Ct. 03-339, 2004 WL [Westlaw] 162761 (filed Jan. 23, 2004) (hereinafter 'Sosa Brief'); Brief for the Respondent, *Sosa v. Alvarez-Machain*, U.S. S. Ct. 03-339, 2004 WL [Westlaw] 425376 (filed Feb. 27, 2004) (hereinafter 'Alvarez Brief').

[30] The most significant of these were the Brief of Amici Curiae National and Foreign Legal Scholars in Support of Respondents, *Sosa v. Alvarez-Machain* (U.S. S. Ct. 03-339), 2004 WL [Westlaw] 419427 (filed Feb. 26, 2004) (hereinafter 'Scholars' Amicus Brief'); and Briefs of Professors of Federal Jurisdiction and Legal History as Amicus Curaie in Support of Respondents, *Sosa v. Alvarez-Machain*, U.S. S. Ct. 03-339, 2004 WL 419425 (filed Feb. 27, 2004) (hereinafter 'Legal Historians' Amicus Brief').

[31] See, e.g., Berman & Reid, Jr., 'The Transformation of English Legal Science: From Hale to Blackstone', 45 *Emory Law Journal* (1996) 437; Bader, 'Some Thoughts on Blackstone, Precedent, and Originalism', 19 *Vermont Law Review* (1994) 5.

or historiographic methodology. The arguments advanced in the briefs tended to be highly focused on a handful of legal issues, and largely ignorant (or even dismissive) of wider concerns about the history of international relations or law at the time of the French and American Revolutions. Somewhat surprisingly, this observation even applies as to the *Sosa* parties briefing (or lack thereof) of the way in which U.S. political institutions (both state and national) dealt with foreign affairs issues – including the claims of foreigners – at the time of the Framing.

The one exception to the fairly mediocre employment of historical evidence by the *Sosa* briefs was that submitted by a self-styled group of 'Professors of Federal Jurisdiction and Legal History,' a collection of some of the leading academic international lawyers and scholars of legal history in the United States.[32] The mode of exposition adopted by the Legal Historians' Amicus Brief was straightforwardly simple: in arguing that the First Congress intended to provide a federal forum for cases where an alien sues for tort in violation of the law of nations, they submitted evidence that the adverse experiences under the Articles of Confederation led the Framers of the Constitution, and then the drafters of the First Judiciary Act, to conclude that adjudication of torts in violation of the law of nations should not be left exclusively to the states, and that there was an impelling need to provide uniformity in order to successfully discharge the nation's duty to provide redress for law of nations violations.[33] This section of the brief provided a coherent historic narrative as to conditions giving rise to the framing of the Constitution and the drafting of the Alien Tort Statute. Context is everything in the proper understanding of a statutory enactment, and this part of the Legal Historians' Amicus Brief marshals evidence from a diversity of sources, including minutes of debates in the Continental Congress, reactions to particular foreign affairs incidents (including the infamous 1784 Marbois Affair where the French consul general was assaulted on a Philadelphia street),[34] and contemporary writings of members of Congress.

The next step in the Legal Historians' Brief was to elucidate the First Congress's understanding that torts in violation of the law of nations were cognizable at common law, without the need for further action by Congress. In other words, the law of nations was believed by the Framers to be a legitimate part of the common law, and 'self-executing' in the sense that it was unnecessary for Congress to pass further legislation specifically designating certain torts as law of nations offences, cognizable in U.S. courts.[35] This was the argumentative core of the filing, essentially

---

[32] Included on the briefs were Professors Vikram Amar, William R. Casto, Sarah H. Cleveland, Drew S. Days, William S. Dodge, David M. Golove, Robert W. Gordon, Stewart Jay, John V. Orth, Judith Resnik, and Anne-Marie Slaughter. See Legal Historians' Amicus Brief, *supra* note 30, at cover.

[33] *Ibid*, 3–11.

[34] *Ibid*, 6–8. See also *Respublica v. De Longchamps*, 1 U.S. (1 Dall.) (1784) 111 (the criminal prosecution of the assailant, under the law of nations).

[35] See 'Legal Historians' Amicus Brief', *supra* note 30, 11–21.

engaging with the Petitioner's (Sosa's) and the U.S. Government's contention that the ATS was merely a jurisdictional 'gateway' without any substantive content. For this part of their brief, the legal historians relied not only on such canonical texts as Blackstone, but also on grand jury charges that incorporated law of nations terminology, Attorney General opinions, and case decisions handed-down immediately after the ATS was adopted.[36] In an important coda to the Amicus Brief, the legal historians also argued that the First Congress intended the ATS to include torts, committed in violation of the law of nations, that occurred abroad,[37] and even more importantly, that the First Congress expected that the law of nations – as a concept that would comprehend a growing set of violations – would necessarily evolve over time.[38] This was a significant line of argument because without a sense of such a continuing evolution of the 'law of nations,' there would be a real risk that a court might conclude that the only law of nations offences currently cognizable under the ATS were those that were actually recognized as such in 1789.[39]

Summing up the positions of the parties (and their amici), as well as framing the relevant issues for decision, the U.S. Supreme Court in *Sosa*, Justice Souter writing for the majority of the Court, observed:

> we think the statute [the Alien Tort Statute, or ATS] was intended as jurisdictional in the sense of addressing the power of the courts to entertain cases concerned with a certain subject. But holding the ATS jurisdictional raises a new question, this one about the interaction between the ATS at the time of its enactment and the ambient law of the era. Sosa would have it that the ATS was stillborn because there could be no claim for relief without a further statute expressly authorizing adoption of causes of action. Amici professors of federal jurisdiction and legal history take a different tack, that federal courts could entertain claims once the jurisdictional grant was on the books, because torts in violation of the law of nations would have been recognized within the common law of the time. . . . We think history and practice give the edge to this latter position.[40]

The Supreme Court then proceeded to analyze what it understood were the contours of the relationship between common law and the law of nations in the late eighteenth century. The Court appeared to accept the distinction, articulated by Emmerich de Vattel, James Kent and William Blackstone, that the law of nations

---

[36] See *ibid*, 11–13, 19–21 (citing Charge to the Grand Jury of Justice James Iredell for the District of South Carolina (May 12, 1794); (1792) 27; 1 Op. Att'y Gen. (1795) 57, 58–59; *Bolchos v. Darrel*, 3 F. Cas. 810 (D.S.C. 1795) (No. 1,607) and *Moxon v. The Fanny*, 17 F. Cas. 942 (D. Pa. 1793) (No. 9, 895)).

[37] *Ibid*, 22–25 (relying on English common law decisions regarding transitory torts, and Attorney General Bradford's 1795 opinion regarding a violation of the law of nations that occurred in Sierra Leone (1 Op. Att'y Gen. (1795) 58)).

[38] See *ibid*, 25–27 (relying on statements by Blackstone, record of the Continental Congress, correspondence from Secretary of State Thomas Jefferson, and later opinions in such cases as *United States v. La Jeune Eugenie*, 26 F. Cas. 832, 846 (C.C.D. Mass. 1822) (No. 15,551) (Story, J.)).

[39] See *TelOren v. Libyan Arab Republic*, 726 F.2d 774, 798 (D.C. Cir. 1984) (Bork, J., concurring).

[40] *Sosa, supra* note 20, 2755.

included three elements. The first was the customs and practices of nations in their relations with each other – the *ius inter gentes*.[41] This, the Court said, fell outside judicial cognizance at the time of the Framing.[42] The second, 'more pedestrian' element of the law of nations, one that 'did fall within a judicial sphere, as a body of judge made law regulating the conduct of individuals situated outside domestic boundaries and consequently carrying an international savour.'[43] Finally, there was a

> sphere in which these rules binding individuals for the benefit of other individuals overlapped with the norms of state relationships. Blackstone referred to it when he mentioned three specific offences against the law of nations addressed by the criminal law of England: violation of safe conducts, infringement of the rights of ambassadors, and piracy.[44] An assault against an ambassador, for example, impinged upon the sovereignty of the foreign nation and if not adequately redressed could rise to an issue of war.[45] It was this narrow set of violations of the law of nations, admitting of a judicial remedy and at the same time threatening serious consequences in international affairs, that was probably on minds of the men who drafted the ATS with its reference to tort.[46]

After reaching these conclusions, Justice Souter and the other members of the Court majority realized that they had to dig deeper into the historical record to acquire the forensic information they needed. As for the underlying purposes and objectives of the ATS, the Court looked to the constitutional history of the Confederation Period, the Marbois Incident, and the relative powerlessness of the pre-Constitution Congress in foreign affairs.[47] And, in a creditable act of historiographic candour, Justice Souter indicated that the historical evidence supported two propositions, which were in admitted tension with each other.[48] In addition,

---

[41] *Ibid*, 2756 (citing De Vattel, *The Law of Nations*, Preliminaries § 3 (J. Chitty et al. transl. and ed. 1883), and 1 James Kent, Commentaries 1)).

[42] *Id*.

[43] *Ibid*, (quoting W. Blackstone, *Commentaries on the Laws of England* vol. 4 (1765–1769) 67 for the proposition that this branch of the law of nations encompassed 'mercantile questions, such as bills of exchange and the like; in all marine causes, relating to freight, average, demurrage, insurances, bottomry . . . ; [and] in all disputes relating to prizes, to shipwrecks, to hostages, and ransom bills'.) I have elsewhere observed the strong connection between the early law of nations and admiralty law, see Bederman, 'Uniformity, Delegation and the Dormant Admiralty Clause', 28 *Journal of Maritime Law and Commerce* (1997) 1; *idem*, 'The Feigned Demise of Prize', 9 *Emory International Law Review* (1995) 31 (book review).

[44] W. Blackstone, *ibid*, 68.

[45] De Vattel, *supra* note 41, 463–464.

[46] *Sosa, supra* note 40.

[47] *Ibid*, 2756–57 (citing various debates from the Continental and Confederation Congress).

[48] *Ibid*, 2758–59 ('Still, the history does tend to support two propositions. First, there is every reason to suppose that the First Congress did not pass the ATS as a jurisdictional convenience to be placed on the shelf for use by a future Congress or state legislature that might, some day, authorize the creation of causes of action or itself decide to make some element of the law of nations actionable for the benefit of foreigners. The anxieties of the preconstitutional period cannot be ignored easily enough to think that the statute was not meant to have a practical effect. . . . The second inference to be drawn from the history is that Congress intended the ATS to furnish jurisdiction for a relatively modest set of actions alleging violations of the law of nations').

Justice Souter acknowledged that 'contemporaneous cases and legal materials referring to the ATS' were 'sparse', reflecting a thin historic record.[49] In the end, though,
the Court concluded that the ATS did countenance a narrow class of law of nations
offences as being incorporated into common law, and thus directly actionable.[50] 'In
sum,' the Court concluded,

> although the ATS is a jurisdictional statute creating no new causes of action, the rea-
> sonable inference from the historical materials is that the statute was intended to have
> practical effect the moment it became law. The jurisdictional grant is best read as hav-
> ing been enacted on the understanding that the common law would provide a cause of
> action for the modest number of international law violations with a potential for per-
> sonal liability at the time.[51]

The balance of the Court's opinion veered away from historical inquiries into more
contemporary concerns as to the creation of private causes of action, especially
under the Alien Tort Statue's 'law of nations'. The Court decided on a cautious
approach –

> there are good reasons for a restrained conception of the discretion a federal court should
> exercise in considering a new cause of action of this kind. Accordingly, we think courts
> should require any claim based on the present day law of nations to rest on a norm of
> international character accepted by the civilized world and defined with a specificity
> comparable to the features of the 18th century paradigms we have recognized.[52]

The Court thus sought to establish a 'high bar to new private causes of action for
violating international law, for the potential implications for the foreign relations of
the United States of recognizing such causes should make courts particularly wary
if impinging on the discretion of the Legislative and Executive Branches in managing foreign affairs.'[53] It was on this premise that the Court's majority diverged from
the position articulated in Justice Scalia's concurrence and dissent. Justice Scalia
would have had the Court defer to Congress in articulating particular torts as violating the law of nations;[54] the majority insisted this was in the province of the judiciary, although to be applied only sparingly.[55]

---

[49] *Ibid*, 2759 (discussing the *Bolchos v. Darrel* and *Moxon v. The Fanny* cases, as well as the 1795
opinion of Attorney General William Bradford).

[50] *Ibid*, 2759–61 (addressing, and then rejecting, Sosa's contrary historical arguments concerning
the availability of state law causes of action, and an ostensible distinction between 'public wrongs' and
'torts').

[51] *Ibid*, 2761. See also Stephens, 'Upsetting Checks and Balances: The Bush Administration's
Efforts to Limit Human Rights Litigation', 17 *Harvard Human Rights Journal* (2004) 187–88.

[52] *Sosa, supra* note 20, 2761–62.

[53] *Ibid*, 2763.

[54] *Ibid*, 2773–76 (Scalia, J., concurring and dissenting (joined by Chief Justice Rehnquist and
Justice Thomas)).

[55] *Ibid*, 2764–65.

And that is precisely what a unanimous Court proceeded to do. The *Sosa* Court held that the precise tort 'in violation of the law of nations' pled by the Dr. Alvarez as the plaintiff – a temporary, but arbitrary, arrest and detention – was not really supported by customary international law or by treaties as a real international law violation.[56] The Court concluded its judgment in these words:

> Whatever may be said for the broad principle Alvarez advances, in the present, imperfect world, it expresses an aspiration that exceeds any binding customary rule having the specificity we require. Creating a private cause of action to further that aspiration would go beyond any residual common law discretion we think it appropriate to exercise. It is enough to hold that a single illegal detention of less than a day, followed by the transfer of custody to lawful authorities and a prompt arraignment, violates no norm of customary international law so well defined as to support the creation of a federal remedy.[57]

With this statement, history and contemporaneity combined to produce the Court's opinion in the *Sosa* case.

Any historiographic evaluation of the *Sosa* case – its briefing, decision and scholarly commentary – must recognize the high stakes involved. It was not so much that the case's outcome determined the likely future of human rights and allied litigation under the Alien Tort Statute. The Court could have, after all, shut the door entirely on any contemporary uses of the Act. But it chose not to do so, relying on a nuanced, historical reading of the Statute in light of its original purposes.[58] But even more at issue in the *Sosa* litigation was a determination of whether matters of evolving customary international were even properly the province of a domestic judiciary. The real thrust of the arguments made by Sosa and by the U.S. Government was that the issues implicated in customary international law disputes (whether or not denominated as 'torts in violation on the law of nations') were simply beyond judicial purview, best left for the ad hoc and political judgments of the Executive Branch, or for particular legislation by Congress. The *Sosa* decision ultimately vindicated the continuing role of domestic courts in expounding the content of international law.

---

[56] *Ibid*, 2765–69 (reviewing substantive content of the *Universal Declaration of Human Rights* and the *International Covenant on Civil and Political Rights*, as well as the *Restatement (Third) of Foreign Relations Law of the United States*).

[57] *Ibid*, 2769. This particular aspect of the Court's ruling, as immensely significant as it is for future litigation involving particular torts under the ATS, is otherwise beyond the reach of this essay.

[58] For more on this, see Ku & Yoo, 'Beyond Formalism in Foreign Affairs: A Functional Approach to the Alien Tort Statute', *Supreme Court Review* (2004) 153 (also available at: <http://ssrn.com/abstract=652141>). See also Hufbauer, 'The Supreme Court Meets International Law: What's the Sequel to Sosa v. Alvarez Machain?', 12 *Tulsa Journal of Comparative and International Law* (2004) 77; Dodge, 'Bridging Erie: Customary International Law in the U.S. Legal System after Sosa v. Alvarez Machain', 12 *Tulsa Journal of Comparative and International Law* (2004) 87.

Also observed previously is that *Sosa v. Alvarez-Machain* was a case where history (and historians) were enlisted in the service of advocacy. Many of the litigants did, in fact, succumb to forms of instrumental historiography. This is not surprising, since there are few periods as well-documented as the founding of the American Republic and the beginnings of constitutionalism in the United States. Even so, the best briefs submitted in the case recognized the profound limitations of the historic record, as did a majority of the Court. Historiographic indeterminacy was accepted by these participants in the forensic process, and, even so, a creditable historic narrative evolved from the proceedings to illuminate this significant moment in legal history.

B. The Kasikili/Sedudu Island Case

I move now from the sublime to the prosaic; for my second case study involves a paradigmatic boundary dispute in the International Court of Justice. Unlike the *Sosa* controversy, no great intellectual battles were waged in the *Kasikili/Sedudu Island Case*,[59] disputed by Botswana and Namibia. Indeed, this case is exemplary of an important part of the World Court's current work: the resolution and adjustment of boundary disputes (both terrestrial and maritime). And while these cases are obviously significant to the nations involved, and the territorial conflicts can certainly raise the spectre of armed conflict, in most situations these disputes are resolved amicably and the Court's judgment respected and enforced. Such was the case here, where Botswana and Namibia submitted the dispute by Special Agreement of May 29, 1996,[60] and the Court ultimately ruled that Botswana had sovereignty overt the subject island.[61]

The fighting issue of the case was the proper construction of Article III of the Anglo-German Treaty of July 1, 1890,[62] which purported to establish the boundaries between Germany's colonial possessions of Southwest Africa, and Great Britain's colonial possessions of Bechuanaland, along the Caprivi Strip (where the modern-day land boundaries of Namibia, Botswana, Angola, Zambia and Zimbabwe nearly intersect).[63] The Chobe river was supposed to provide the land boundary between the two parties, but in the vicinity of Kasikili Island (as it was known to Botswanans) or Sedudu Island (as it was known to Namibians), the river splits into two channels; one running north and west of the island, the other running south and east. Obviously, if the North Channel was regarded as the

---

[59] *Kasikili/Sedudu Island* case, (Botswana/Namibia), *Merits*, ICJ Rep 1999, 1045.
[60] *Ibid,* 1047–51.
[61] *Ibid,* 1108–09.
[62] *Ibid,* 1060–61.
[63] *Ibid,* 1056 (detail map of region of the dispute).

boundary, Botswana would have sovereignty over the island; if the south channel was the boundary, Namibia would have title to the feature. As far as I can tell, the island has no intrinsic resources or strategic value. In short, this was a dispute about honour and history.

Article III of the 1890 Treaty marks the 'main channel' of the River Chobe as the international boundary. In German, the other language of the treaty, this phrase was rendered as '*Thalweg des Hauptlaufes*,' the centre of the main channel with the deepest soundings.[64] After discussing the relevant principles of treaty interpretation, as drawn from articles 31 and 32 of the 1969 Vienna Convention on the Law of Treaties,[65] the Court looked to the object and purpose of the 1890 Treaty, as well as any existing *travaux préparatoires* from its negotiation. The Court concluded that '[i]n referring to the main channel of the Chobe, the parties sought both to secure for themselves freedom of navigation on the river and to delimit as precisely as possible their respective spheres of influence.'[66] The *travaux* also 'support[ed] this reasoning,' insofar as the parties (in their earlier drafts and minutes of what would become the final agreement) essentially had reached an understanding to use the centre of the main channel.[67]

Any treaty interpreter's recourse to *travaux préparatoires* is essentially an historiographic investigation. The very process of analyzing contemporaneous documents surrounding a treaty negotiation is an exercise in parsing an historic record, often a very incomplete and fragmentary one. Of course, the vast majority of treaties have no negotiating history to speak of, and those that do are often strikingly incomplete or subjective. The process of drawing from treaty *travaux* is fraught with the same dangers as statutory interpretation in some common law countries – the evidence is limited and contradictory, and so one draws from the material favourable to one's position, and ignores or excludes the rest. The use of *travaux préparatoires* – just as with legislative history – can thus be described 'as the equivalent of entering a crowded cocktail party and looking over the heads of the guests for one's friends.'[68]

Perhaps it is for all of these reasons that the World Court did not place much emphasis on *travaux* in the *Kasikili/Sedudu Island Case*, preferring,[69] instead, to examine what the Vienna Convention calls the 'subsequent agreement between the

---

[64] *Ibid*, 1060–61. See also S.B. Jones, *Boundary Making: A Handbook for Statesmen, Treaty Editors and Boundary Commissioners* (2000) 118. The deepest point of the river principle has been applied in U.S. domestic litigation in *Arkansas v. Tennessee*, 246 U.S. 158 (1918); *New Jersey v. Delaware*, 291 U.S. 361 (1934); and *Louisiana v. Mississippi*, 282 U.S. 458 (1940).

[65] *Supra* note 12.

[66] *Kasikili/Sedudu Island* case, *supra* note 59, 1074.

[67] *Ibid*, 1075.

[68] *Conroy v. Aniskoff*, 507 U.S. (1993) 519 (Scalia, J., concurring in the judgment) (referencing anecdotally a description by Judge Harold Leventhal).

[69] *Kasikili/Sedudu Island* case, *supra* note 59, 1075–1076.

parties regarding the interpretation of the treaty or the application of its provisions,' or, better yet, 'any subsequent practice in the application of the treaty which establishes the agreement of the parties regarding its interpretation.'[70] This is the treaty counterpart in territorial disputes of looking at what has come to be called the 'effectivités' of actually exercising authority over the occupation of land.[71] The bulk of the Court's judgment was thus preoccupied with examining the historical evidence advanced by both Botswana and Namibia in support of their claims of either an agreed meaning to Article III of the 1890 Treaty or the effective occupation of the island.[72] The Court's analysis is careful and nuanced, especially in response to the parties' attempts to place undue weight on very slender pieces of evidence. Ultimately, the Court rejected Botswana's arguments that Namibia's former colonial powers (Germany, and later South Africa) were effectively placed on notice, through diplomatic correspondence, of Botswana's claim to the island.[73]

In examining these diplomatic exchanges, the Court exhaustively rendered the text of the notes, comments and documents. The point, however, was not the number of times that Bechuanaland authorities attempted to assert title to Kasikili Island, but, rather, the extent (if at all) opposing German or South African authorities favourably responded and acquiesced to those demands.[74] This was a far trickier move to capture in historic documentation. Indeed, in a February 14, 1949 document, the Union of South Africa authorities (which had taken over control of Southwest Africa from the Germans at the conclusion of World War One) sharply protested the Bechuanaland imputations of sovereignty.[75] Indeed, it appears that, at most, all the colonial authorities could agree to do was disagree, even while trying to conclude a 'gentleman's agreement,' resolving the sharpest elements of the dispute, without deciding the question of sovereignty.[76] For students of British colonial history in Africa, these documents make for interesting – if vaguely humorous – reading. But for the World Court, it was clearly frustrating that they yielded no

---

[70] *Vienna Convention*, Article.31(3)(a), (b).

[71] S.P. Sharma, *Territorial Acquisition, Disputes and International Law* (1997) 100–110; Rodriguez, 'L'uti possidetis et les effectivités dans les contentieux territoriaux et frontaliers', 263 *Recueil des Cours* (1997) 149; Lesaffer, 'Argument from Roman Law in current International Law: Occupation and Acquisitive Prescription', 16 *European Journal of International Law* (2005) 54–55; Donovan, 'Suriname-Guyana Maritime and Territorial Disputes: A Legal and Historical Analysis', 13 *Journal of Transnational Law & Policy* (2003) 41.

[72] *Kasikili/Sedudu Island* case, *supra* note 59, 1076 (summarizing Botswana's historical arguments), 1092 (doing the same for Namibia's).

[73] *Ibid* 1076–78 (regarding the Eason Report of 1910–11), 1078–87 (Ker correspondence of 1947–51) 1087–1092 (regarding correspondence between South Africa and Botswana after a shooting incident in 1984).

[74] *Ibid* 1077–78, 1087.

[75] *Ibid* 1080–81.

[76] *Ibid* 1084–85.

positive forensic value, at least rising to the standard of a 'subsequent practice' under the Vienna Convention.

From this mass of historical evidence, the Court reached the following conclusions:

79. The Court concludes from all of the foregoing that the subsequent practice of the parties to the 1890 Treaty did not result in any 'agreement between the parties regarding the interpretation of the treaty or the application of its provisions', within the meaning of Article 31, paragraph 3(a), of the 1969 Vienna Convention on the Law of Treaties, nor did it result in any 'practice in the application of the treaty which establishes the agreement of the parties regarding its interpretation', within the meaning of subparagraph (b) of that same provision.

80. However, the Court is bound to note that on at least three occasions, at different periods – in 1912, in 1948 and in 1985 – surveys carried out on the ground identified the channel of the Chobe to the north and west as the 'main channel' of the river around Kasikili/Sedudu Island. The factual findings that the parties concerned arrived at separately in 1948 were expressed in concurrent terms in a joint report. In addition, the survey made in 1985 was conducted jointly by the parties then concerned. The factual findings made on these occasions were not, as such, disputed at the time. The Court finds that these facts, while not constituting subsequent practice by the parties in the interpretation of the 1890 Treaty, nevertheless support the conclusions which it has reached by interpreting Article III, paragraph 2, of the 1890 Treaty in accordance with the ordinary meaning to be given to its terms. . . .[77]

In other words, while the historical evidence was insufficient to rise to the level of accepted mutual 'agreement' or 'subsequent practice' as between the contesting parties, within the meaning of the Vienna Convention, the data did disclose historic information as to the location of the main channel around the island. To put it another way, arguments as to historic title (*effectivités*) cannot trump the clear terms of title granted by treaty, a point made in other arbitral and World Court decisions.[78]

But it should be noted that there was a strong objection registered to the juristic methodology reflected in the above-quoted paragraphs of the Court's judgment. Judge Rosalyn Higgins observed that:

I add, to make my position clear, that I agree with all the Judgment has to say at paragraphs 47 to 63, regarding the legal significance of the diplomatic history of the matter. However – and unlike the Court – equally place no reliance at all in the facts said to be found by Eason, Trollope and Redman, whose methodology is not fully known to us and who were preoccupied with the question of depth; nor do I think it useful

---

[77] *Ibid*, 1096.

[78] *Eritrea-Yemen Arbitration (Territorial Sovereignty)*, 40 *International Legal Materials* (2001) 938, (PCA 9 October 1998): evidence of effectivités are 'voluminous in quantity but sparse in useful content' in para 239; *Case Concerning the Land and Maritime Boundary Between Cameroon and Nigeria*, (Cameroon v. Nigeria, Equatorial Guinea intervening), *Merits*, ICJ Rep. 2002, 303.

to accept as 'facts' findings of the Joint Team of Experts, such 'facts' not having been accepted by South Africa as determinative of the underlying legal issue.[79]

In other words, Judge Higgins would have neither recognized the subsequent course of dealing of the parties as a binding construction under Vienna Convention principles, nor assumed that the facts adduced from those prior dealings were necessarily dispositive. This caution, in the face of an ambiguous historical record, makes sense.

So returning to first principles of treaty interpretation, especially in the face of conflicting and contradictory historical evidence, seemed a logical choice for the Court to pursue in *Kasikili/Sedudu*. The Court's objective, after all, was simply to ascertain the location of the 'main channel' of the Chobe River, and thus determine title in the island. While map evidence would have been useful, leading to issues of cartographic history to resolve, ultimately this was inconclusive as well for the Court.[80] Indeed, in the face of such an indeterminate historical record, it may have been the only legitimate way to proceed.

3. Conclusions

The purpose of these two case studies was to illustrate possible uses and abuses of history in particular litigation or forensic contexts. They were not intended, as I have already indicated, to expound the full range of problems for instrumental historiography or 'foreign office international legal history.' Indeed, it does not require a fully-ripened international dispute or a litigation that has reached an ultimate decision-maker (such as a domestic supreme court or the International Court of Justice), in order for issues of instrumental historiography to arise. A law office (or foreign office) memorandum, an opinion letter to an international law client, a démarche to another country (or an opposing counsel), or a draft of a scholarly symposium submission can all implicate concerns as to the proper deployment and understanding of historical evidence in the pursuit of some lawyerly objective. As international lawyers, we are all called upon to 'do' international legal history. When we are so charged, what tools do we use to balance our duties of zealous representation, careful administration of justice, or dispassionate scholarship (as the case may be) with a larger (and higher duty) to the integrity and fidelity of history?

Clio demands that those who use historic materials in the pursuit of some legal objective have to recognize some enduring truths. The first of these is that legal history and legal truth are not always the same thing, and they certainly cannot be

---

[79] Declaration by Judge Higgins in the *Kasikili/Sedudu Island* case, *supra* note 59, 1115.
[80] *Ibid* 1096–1100.

ascertained by the same means and modalities. A lawyer's task is to assemble historical data that supports a client's position in a particular context, just as the judge's is to weigh the probative weight of that material, and reach a decision on the merits of the dispute. Legal historians just do not think in such result-driven ways, which gives rise to the concern of instrumental historiography.

The second truth that international lawyers have to understand is that, no matter how hard one tries, the historic record is often sparse and incomplete, at least on the issues that matter for the lawyers or judge. After all, the *Sosa* case featured an issue involving probably the best-documented period in all but contemporary history, and, even so, no definitive evidence on the construction of the Alien Tort Statute – no 'smoking-gun' as American lawyers like to say – was revealed. Ironically, the *Kasikili/Sedudu Island Case* involved a far more obscure period of history in a more far-flung place, and yet documentary evidence was plentiful. But, even so, a wealth of historical material does not necessarily yield a forensic result.

And that leads to a third enduring truth, and that is that even in cases of abundant historical materials, the historical record can still be ambiguous or contradictory. History does not always provide answers, or at least not in a form recognized by international lawyers. The most difficult task for the international historian *cum* international lawyer is to accept – and, indeed, embrace – the inherent indeterminacy of history, and historic materials, in these situations. Without such acceptance, international lawyers will often find themselves struggling against the tide of history and rowing upstream against the best methods of historiography.

Accepting these truths should also lead to the adoption of best practices for international legal historiography. Although I am mindful that there can be no central body for the imposition of these standards (nor should there be), I believe that, with time, the bench, bar and academy will see that some professional standards of international legal history may make sense. Obviously, to the extent that responsible judges and arbitrators understand the demands that historical analysis places on legal advocates, they may be in the best position to patrol the outer boundaries of acceptable historical arguments and to reject instrumental historiography. The scholarly academy also has a role to play in this process as well.

In recognizing the significance of historical inquiry in international legal pursuits, we need to be prepared to pass judgment on what are, and what are not, legitimate and proper techniques of historiography. Without such standards, the discourse of history and international law could well degenerate to the level of 'foreign office international legal history.'

ENGLISH APPROACHES TO INTERNATIONAL LAW IN THE NINETEENTH CENTURY

Michael Lobban*

Martti Koskenniemi has recently argued that there was a transformation in thinking about international law, which dated from the late 1860s and early 1870s, the era of the establishment of the *Revue de Droit International et de Législation Comparée* and the formation of the *Institut de Droit International*.[1] According to Koskenniemi, early nineteenth century continental jurists such as Georg Friedrich von Martens (1756–1822) and Johann Ludwig Klüber (1762–1837) took a highly rationalist view of international law, 'compress[ing] European reality into an *a priori* system of political ideas with little attention to the special nature and history of the relations between European sovereigns and even less to the political consciousness of European societies.'[2] By contrast, a new generation of jurists – Gustave Rolin-Jacquemyns (1835–1902), Tobias Asser (1838–1913) and Johann Caspar Bluntschli (1808–81) – having been raised in the era of Pandectism and the German historical school of Savigny, saw international law much more in terms of a common legal consciousness of a developing set of civilised nations, whose international *Volksgeist* was to be articulated by jurists. Law reflected the popular conscience of the people of Europe, but it was also a science. The norms derived from these sources were binding on states, for as Bluntschli put it, '[i]t is not up to the arbitrary will of the state to follow or reject international law.'[3]

Where did English jurists fit in this development?[4] Men such as Montague Bernard, John Westlake and T. E. Holland, certainly played prominent roles in the *Institut de Droit International*, which held its annual meeting in Oxford in 1880 and in Cambridge in 1895. Yet it was widely observed that the English approach to international law was distinctive from the continental one. Contrasts were often

---

* Professor of Legal History, Queen Mary College, University of London.
[1] M. Koskenniemi, *The Gentle Civilizer of Nations: the Rise and Fall of International Law 1870–1960* (2002), ch. 1.
[2] *Ibid*, 23.
[3] *Ibid*, 50.
[4] In what follows, I shall focus on English jurists exclusively, omitting discussion both of contemporary American and Scottish jurists. Though a jurist like James Lorimer (1818–1890) was a significant figure, I have omitted discussion of his work since my aim is to explore how common lawyers south of the border dealt with international law issues. English jurists like Holland and Pollock held that Lorimer's conception of international law '*pèche par la base*', (Holland, 'The Literature of International Law in 1884', 1 *Law Quarterly Review* (1885) 100).

drawn between continental approaches which were 'ethical and metaphysical', and *'L'école historico-pratique'* of the English which was 'distasteful' across the Channel.[5] John Westlake noted that while both English and continental scholars saw international law as rules, 'the former would think primarily of the rules, and then of the right as ordinarily measured by them, the latter primarily of the right, and then of the rules as ordinarily embodying it.'[6] In what follows, it will be suggested that English approaches to international law after 1850 were indeed distinct from continental ones, and were shaped by two strong influences. The first was practical: in the 1870s, in a number of high profile international disputes, English common lawyers stressed the nature of international law as a matter of practical politics and negotiation, rather than as a matter for jurists' speculation. The second was theoretical: any late nineteenth century writer on international law in England had to take into account the writings of John Austin, and meet the challenge of showing how international law could correctly be denominated law. While most international lawyers sought to distance themselves from Austin's definition of international law, their visions were often closer to Austin's than they admitted.

1. The Decline of Doctors Commons

Before turning to these questions, it is important to note a transformation in the profession, the result of which was that by the later nineteenth century, the mentality of international lawyers in England was far more dominated by a *common law* approach than had been the case before. In the early nineteenth century, international lawyers in England formed part of a closed professional elite: civilian lawyers, who were members of the College of Advocates and Doctors of Law, known as Doctors Commons.[7] Instead of practising in the courts of common law and equity, the civilians practised in a number of non-common law jurisdictions. The main body of their work was in the ecclesiastical courts, which until 1857 had an exclusive jurisdiction in testamentary suits and marriage litigation; but they also practised in the Court of Admiralty, which dealt with matters arising on the high seas, including prize

---

    [5] The quotations are taken from Lord Russell of Killowen, 'International Law', 12 *Law Quarterly Review* (1896) 322, and T.E. Holland's comment that W.E. Hall's work 'found success even among continental jurists, to whom as a rule Hall's adherence to what they called *L'école historico-pratique* was distasteful' (in T.E. Holland, rev. Pease-Watkin, 'William Edward Hall', 24 *Oxford Dictionary of National Biography* (2004) 670. For discussions of the 'rival' approaches, see also Lauterpacht, 'The so-called Anglo-American and Continental Schools of Thought in International Law', 12 *British Yearbook of International Law* (1931) 46.
    [6] L. Oppenheim (ed.), *The Collected Papers of John Westlake on Public International Law* (1914) xxvi.
    [7] See G. D. Squibb, *Doctors' Commons: A History of the College of Advocates and Doctors of Law* (1977).

disputes arising in wartime. The doctrine dealt with by civilians was not common law: the law of the ecclesiastical courts was the canon law of the Anglican Church (derived from the medieval canon law of Catholic Christendom), while the Admiralty dealt with the international law of the sea. As Sir William Scott (later Lord Stowell) pointed out in 1799, this 'law itself has no locality. It is the duty of the person who sits here to determine this question exactly as he would determine the same question if sitting at Stockholm.'[8] The body of lawyers who dealt with this law was extremely small. Whereas in the 139 years between 1681 and 1820, 6017 barristers were called to the bar (or 43 per annum), in the 344 years between 1512 and 1856, only 462 advocates were admitted (or a little over one a year).[9] In 1851, there were 25 practising advocates in Doctors Commons.

The civilians were trained at the Universities in Oxford and Cambridge, taking degrees in civil law. This education was not especially strong. While in the eighteenth century, both universities produced professors who lectured and published,[10] nineteenth century civilian education was weak.[11] In any event, the focus of attention for the civilian student was Roman law, rather than international law. As with common lawyers of this era, much of their learning was self-taught. Stowell (1745–1836) was educated at Oxford where he attended the lectures both of Blackstone and the Regius Professor of Civil Law, Thomas Bever. Stowell spent a number of years as Reader in Ancient History at Oxford, devoting much of his time to reading on Roman law and the law of nations.[12] While this kind of academic reading introduced a number of civilians to their subject, much more of their knowledge of international law came from practice in the Admiralty courts, and from the giving of diplomatic advice. Civilians had long been called on to give advice on international matters, including the making of treaties, for it was widely believed 'that the study of civil law helped to cultivate the art of statesmanship.'[13] At the very least, they spoke the same language as their continental legal counterparts.

---

[8] *The Maria* (1799), 1 *Christopher Robinson's Admiralty Reports* 350.

[9] See P. Searby, *A History of the University of Cambridge*, vol. 3. 1750–1870, (1997) 186–192. For the bar, see D. Lemmings, *Gentlemen and Barristers: the Inns of Court and the English Bar, 1680–1730* (1990) and *idem, Professors of the Law: Barristers and English legal culture in the eighteenth century* (2000). It should be recalled that many of those called as barristers did not practice.

[10] Cambridge's Samuel Hallifax published *An Analysis of the Roman Civil Law* (1774) while Thomas Bever published *A Discourse on the Study of Jurisprudence and the Civil Law* (1766).

[11] The Oxford Regius professor Joseph Phillimore told the Royal Commission on Oxford University in 1852 that his chair was underfunded and that both he and his predecessor (French Laurence) had a practice in London. He claimed only to have been chosen because none else was available. There were no lectures for they interfered with university exams. *Parliamentary Papers* 1852 (1482) XXII 1, Evidence 254–5.

[12] For Stowell, see H.J. Bourguignon, *Sir William Scott, Lord Stowell: Judge of the High Court of Admiralty, 1798–1828* (1987).

[13] B.P. Levack, *The Civil Lawyers in England 1603–1641. A Political Study* (1973) 26.

Thus, a jurist such as Stowell, though not a writer of treatises, drafted many opinions for the Foreign Office during the years when he was King's Advocate (1788–98). As Admiralty judge (after 1788), he also articulated his general views of law in a number of judgments.

While Stowell never wrote a treatise, a work entitled *Commentaries upon International Law* was written by Sir Robert Phillimore (1810–85), 'the last of the civilians.'[14] Phillimore set out a Grotian natural lawyer's view in this work. International law, he wrote, 'is not enacted by the will of any common Superior upon earth, but it is enacted by the will of God; and it is expressed by consent, tacit or declared, of Independent Nations.' He went on: 'Custom and usage, moreover, outwardly express the consent of nations to things which are *naturally*, that is by the law of God, binding upon them.' The aim of each state was to 'clothe with reality the abstract idea of justice.'[15] Phillimore dismissed any argument that a rule which lacked a sanction could not qualify as 'law' by saying that such arguments confused 'the physical sanction which Law derives from being enforced by superior power, and the moral sanction conferred on it by the fundamental principle of Right.'[16] For Phillimore, international law was rooted in justice and reason, but expressed via custom.

In taking this view, he followed the views of Lord Stowell, as expressed in his judgments. In *The Hurtige Hane*, in considering whether international law rules relating to blockades applied to the residents of Morocco, Stowell had conceded that many of the rules of international law which had been developed among European states were not applicable on the Barbary coast, for it 'is a law made up of a good deal of complex reasoning, though derived from very simple rules, and altogether composing a pretty artificial system, which is not familiar to their knowledge or observation.' But, the international rule on blockades had to be applied, for this was 'one of the most universal and simple operations of war, in all ages and countries, excepting such as were merely savage.' Stowell added that '[t]hey, in common with all other nations, must be subject to this first and elementary principle of blockade, that persons are not to carry into the blockaded port supplies of any kind: It is not a new operation of war; it is almost as old and as general as war itself.'[17]

This was to suggest that some principles were universally known, and could be known by reasoning alone, while others were more complex, and were the product of reason applied to a larger range of experiences. Echoing Sir Edward Coke's early seventeenth century view of the common law, he saw international law not as pure reason, but as reason manifested in usage. The law of nations, he said 'is introduced, indeed, by general principles; but it travels with those general principles only to

---

[14] *The Times*, 5 February 1885, col. 7a.
[15] R. Phillimore, *Commentaries upon International Law*, vol. 1 (1854) 1, 4.
[16] *Ibid*, 72.
[17] *The Hurtige Hane* (1801), 3 *Christopher Robinson's Admiralty Reports* 327–8.

a certain extent; and if it stops there, you are not at liberty to go farther, and to say, that mere speculations would bear you out in a farther progress.'[18] The judge could not invent rules by speculation, but had to root his decisions in the common practice of nations. In this system of reason and custom, the power of a national legislature was limited. For Stowell, a prize court was an international court, determining international law questions, and without jurisdiction to deal with municipal law matters. Though his court sat under the authority of the British King, it was open to all people, and 'what foreigners have a right to demand from it, is the administration of the *law of nations*, simply, and exclusively of the introduction of principles from our own municipal jurisprudence'.[19] British law could not affect the rights of foreigners in international law.[20] Given that the prime focus of Stowell's judgments concerned disputes arising in admiralty and prize courts, the view of law to be teased from them was one which downplayed the international relations aspects of international law. Moreover, Stowell saw the courts as agents of change. In *The Ringende Jacob*, concerning a question of contraband cargo, Stowell said that by 'the ancient law of Europe' the whole ship would have been condemned for carrying such cargo, a rule which would not have been unjust: '[b]ut in the modern practice of the Courts of Admiralty of this country, and I believe of other nations also, a milder rule has been adopted,' which he proceeded to apply.[21]

While lawyers such as Phillimore and Travers Twiss (1809–1897) were trained in the civilian school of Stowell, by mid-century, the closed world of the English civilians was under attack. From the 1830s, a number of parliamentary inquiries began to look into reforming the ecclesiastical courts, and the question was repeatedly raised whether the civilian lawyers should retain their monopoly on the probate jurisdiction. Phillimore had no doubts. In 1843 (with an ecclesiastical courts bill in parliament), he wrote a pamphlet, *The Study of the Civil and the Canon Law*, in which he defended the monopoly, claiming that without the ecclesiastical courts to support the civilians, there would be no civil law learning, without which there could be no Admiralty jurisdiction. 'What will it avail us,' he wrote, 'to have another Nelson to make prizes, unless we are likewise prepared with another Stowell to adjudicate on them?'[22] However, in 1857, the probate and matrimonial jurisdiction of the ecclesiastical courts was removed, and two new courts were opened up to common lawyers. The Court of Admiralty continued as a separate court until its

---

[18] *The Flad Oyen* (1799), 1 *Christopher Robinson's Admiralty Reports* 140. See also *The Henrick and Maria* (1799), 4 *Christopher Robinson's Admiralty Reports* 54: 'it is to be remembered that this is a matter not to be governed by abstract principles alone: The use and practice of nations have intervened, and shifted the matter from its foundations of that species.'

[19] *The Recovery* (1807), 6 *Christopher Robinson's Admiralty Reports* 349.

[20] See *Le Louis* (1817), 2 *Dodson's Admiralty Reports* 239.

[21] *The Ringende Jacob* (1798), 1 *Christopher Robinson's Admiralty Reports* 89.

[22] Quoted in 1 *Law Times* (1843) 276.

incorporation into the Supreme Court of Judicature in the reforms of 1873–5 (where Phillimore sat as a judge in the Probate, Divorce and Admiralty division until 1883). The reform spelled the end of a separate body of civilian lawyers, and Doctors Commons was wound up in 1865.

2. The New International Lawyers

By the second half of the nineteenth century, international law became less the preserve of a specialist branch of the profession, and more the preserve of a set of academic jurists, whose primary concerns focused less on the litigation of Admiralty courts and more on political issues. The teaching of international law in the universities was largely a development of later nineteenth century Oxford and Cambridge, although there had been some teaching of the subject earlier in the century in London. For instance, Austin's chair at London University (which he held between 1828 and 1835) was in jurisprudence and the law of nations, though he did not lecture on the latter topic. By contrast, his successor, J.T. Graves, who held the chair from 1838 and 1843, did lecture on international law, drawing largely on the texts of Vattel and Bynkershoek, and the decisions of Lord Stowell.[23] At King's College, Travers Twiss was appointed to a chair in International Law in 1848 which he held until 1854. With the revival of legal education at the Inns of Court after 1852, there was an attempt – encouraged by Henry Maine – to introduce law students to more philosophical and comparative approaches, by teaching Roman law and jurisprudence.[24] International law was taught at the Inns by the Readers in Jurisprudence, who made use of Wheaton's *Elements of International Law* as their textbook.[25]

The most significant developments however occurred later in Oxford and Cambridge. At Oxford, the Regius Chair in Civil Law was held from 1855 to 1870 by the civilian and international lawyer Travers Twiss, and from 1870 to 1893 by James Bryce. In addition, in 1859, in the wake of reforms brought forth as a result of the report of the 1854 university commissioners, All Souls College created the Chichele chair in international law, which was held first by Mountague Bernard (between 1859 and 1874), and subsequently by T.E. Holland (between 1874 and 1911).

---

[23] The lectures were published in 1843 in the *Law Times*.

[24] See in general: Brooks & Lobban, 'Apprenticeship or Academy? The idea of a law university, 1830–55' in J.A. Bush & A. Wijffels (eds.), *Learning the Law: Teaching and the Transmission of English Law, 1150–1900* (1999) 353–82.

[25] In the prospectus for 1864, the Reader in Jurisprudence and International Law announced that he would lecture on the history and present state of the law of blockade, and would give classes on the rights and obligations of neutrals 'using the work of Wheaton as the text-book, and referring to the works of the principal modern jurists, the decisions of the Admiralty and the Prize Courts of England and America, and Debates in Parliament, and State Papers relating to the cases under discussion'. This was of course a highly relevant topic at the time of the American civil war. (*The Jurist*, 19 March 1864.)

At Cambridge, William Whewell had suggested in 1847 that there should be more teaching of jurisprudence and international law,[26] and twenty years later a Whewell chair was set up in international law, which was held for twenty years by William Vernon Harcourt (with T.J. Lawrence as his deputy after 1883). He was succeeded for a brief period by Sir Henry Maine (who had in his early career been Regius Professor), who was in turn succeeded in the chair by John Westlake (1888–1908) and Lassa Oppenheim (1908–1919).

While legal education remained weak at Oxbridge throughout the late nineteenth century, in the age of Dicey, Holland and Anson, it began to develop its modern shape. While the new professoriate saw its role as that of university teachers of *law*, with the particular expertise of the legal scholar and common lawyer, it was an *academic* form of learning which would not amount to mere technical knowledge.[27] Moreover, if their classrooms were sparsely populated, they would speak to the world. For instance, Harcourt, made his name in this field from a series of letters to *The Times*, under the nom-de-plume *Historicus*, written on matters of current political concern (such as the position Britain should take vis-à-vis the parties in the American civil war). Westlake and Holland were equally regular correspondents on current matters, seeking to influence public opinion.[28]

Moreover, where many civilian lawyers entered their profession by following their fathers' footsteps, these new professors were men whose legal training was in the common law, but whose ambitions were aimed at a wider field. Many were drawn to the subject by a passion for politics and international relations. Vernon Harcourt (1827–1904) was a highly successful common lawyer who regarded international law as 'my passion, not my profession.' John Westlake (1828–1913) was another Cambridge educated barrister, whose interest in the subject was aroused both by his father (who had always encouraged him to take an interest in foreign affairs) and by the conveyancer whose pupil he was, who encouraged him to write a book on private international law.[29] Like Harcourt (who became a prominent liberal politician), Westlake was motivated by a broad political liberalism, rather than by any pettifogging concerns of practice: a member of the Social Science Association, he became its foreign secretary, and continued to preside over its jurisprudence department.[30]

---

[26] D.A. Winstanley, *Early Victorian Cambridge* (1940) 199.

[27] It may be noted that in 1851, jurisprudence was included in the Cambridge Moral and Natural Sciences Tripos (the Law Tripos only being set up in 1858), while in Oxford law and history was a joint degree until 1872.

[28] See Johnson, 'The English Tradition in International Law', 11 *International and Comparative Law Quarterly* (1962) 428; Pearce Higgins, 'Sir Thomas Erskine Holland', 42 *Law Quarterly Review* (1926) 471.

[29] See his obituary in *The Times,* 15 April 1913, col. 9g.

[30] Westlake's political career is well described by M. Koskenniemi, *supra* note 1, 59–60. See also L. Goldman, *Science, Reform and Politics in Victorian Britain: the Social Science Association 1857–1886* (2002) 103.

W. E. Hall (1835–94), who in 1856 took a first class degree in the recently established
school of Law and History in Cambridge, and who was called to the bar in 1861
never showed much interest in legal practice, but set about amassing materials for a
history of civilisation, and spent much of his life travelling in Asia, South America and
Africa.[31] T.J. Lawrence (1849–1919) was another graduate of the Cambridge Law
and History Tripos, and a Gladstonian liberal who was warden of the failed attempt
at Cavendish College to recruit lower middle class students to Cambridge.[32]

In the second half of the century, international lawyers often played a significant
role in public affairs, sitting on royal commissions which considered questions of
international law, and advising government on international questions. Thus, the
1867–8 Royal Commission on Neutrality laws included among its members older
civilians such as Phillimore and Twiss, and younger figures like Harcourt.
Mountague Bernard, who sat on the Fugitive Slave Commission in 1867, also negotiated with the United States on behalf of the British government in 1871 over the
Alabama affair; while Twiss advised the government at the Berlin West Africa
Conference in 1884. The world of the international lawyer after mid–century was
thus a more public and more political world than it had been half a century before;
and its practitioners were more likely to be interested in questions thrown up by
conflicts in international relations, than disputes between private parties.[33]

3. New Contexts and New Visions

If these new international lawyers sought to address a wider audience, international
law could itself no longer be regarded as the preserve of a specialist group developing
rules within their own courts. In the era after the outbreak of the American civil war,
new problems arose which raised questions both about how international law developed, and about how it related to domestic law. Given technological developments
and the expansion of commerce, new problems constantly arose which could not
simply be settled by the application of principles derived from eighteenth century

---

[31] Hall's taste for adventure never left him: four years after the publication of his treatise on international law (in 1880), he attempted to join the forces seeking to relieve General Gordon at
Khartoum. See the memoir in T.E. Holland, *Studies in International law* (1898).

[32] The domestic liberalism of many international lawyers should not mask their illiberal attitudes
to those they did not consider 'civilised': see especially Anghie, 'Finding the Peripheries: Sovereignty
and Colonialism in nineteenth century International law', 40 *Harvard Journal of International law*
(1999) 1, and Riles 'Aspiration and Control: International Legal Rhetoric and the Essentialisation of
Culture', 106 *Harvard Law Review* (1993) 723.

[33] See also Crawford, 'Public International Law in Twentieth-century England', in J. Beatson & R.
Zimmermann (eds.), *Jurists Uprooted: German-speaking Émigré Lawyers in Twentieth-century Britain*
(2004) 681–707, which stresses the practical and untheoretical nature of British approaches to international law in the nineteenth century.

natural law writings or the practice of prize courts. In an era of extensive commerce, international law was in a state of transition. As W.E. Hall put it, 'a certain number of doctrines appear to survive which can hardly in any true sense be said to live; and on the other hand, new applications of the old principles have constantly to be made to complex facts, in dealing with which there is no strict precedent, and sometimes a very doubtful analogy.'[34]

Developing the principles of international law was thus seen to be a more pragmatic and political exercise. For many jurists, it was no longer to be left to philosophers or civilian judges to develop the law: international law was to be found in state practice, and in the consent of nations as manifested in positive agreement or established usage. Moreover, the influential jurists were not necessarily specialists of international law. This can be seen from the impact of the ideas of the Chief Justice of the Queen's Bench, Sir Alexander Cockburn, in a number of celebrated disputes in the 1860s and 1870s. Cockburn was one of the commissioners in the Geneva arbitration in 1872, sat on the court which heard *R. v. Keyn* and sat on the 1876 Royal Commission on Fugitive Slaves. In these capacities, he read widely in the literature of international law, but brought a common law judge's mind to bear on many of the questions at hand.

The Geneva arbitration arose from the disputed American claim that the British government had violated its duties as a neutral during the civil war, by giving assistance to Confederate shipping. The loudest protests centred on the fact that the government had allowed a ship built at Liverpool for the Confederate government, the *Alabama*, to leave port, though the British authorities were aware that this unarmed vessel was to be armed at sea with weaponry also exported from a British port. The international law question at stake was moot. It was whether a neutral government had the duty to prevent the despatch from its ports of unarmed vessels *apparently* designed for war, and which it had *reason to believe* were constructed or intended for the service of a belligerent. The British position (against the proposition) was argued in a book by Mountague Bernard. He noted two relevant principles of international law. Firstly, merchants were free to trade in munitions to belligerents without compromising the neutrality of a state: for the belligerent could always seize contraband on the high seas. Secondly, no state was to allow its territory to be used as a base from which attacks could be launched. In Bernard's view, the latter duty would only be violated if an *armed* ship was allowed to depart.[35] The American position was that international law required more: that a state was to prevent the departure of unarmed ships if there was a reasonable suspicion they might be used for war; that if two apparently 'innocent' expeditions were

---

[34] W.E. Hall, *A Treatise on International Law* (1884) 552.

[35] M. Bernard, *A Historical Account of the Neutrality of Great Britain during the American Civil War* (1870) 391.

sent from the ports of the neutral country with the intention to unite them at sea, creating an armed force, then the neutral state had to take action to prevent it; and that neutral governments were bound to exert 'due' diligence when faced with this danger. By this was meant diligence proportioned to the danger; so that no government could claim to escape its obligations by allowing (as the British had) uncertain litigation to run its course in domestic courts. They had to act in proportion to the emergency, and amend domestic legislation if need be.

The Americans claimed damages from the British government for its breach of duty, and the matter was referred to arbitration at Geneva, under the terms of the 1871 treaty of Washington, in which the British government conceded the point that it was the duty of the neutral state to use diligence to prevent a ship leaving port which 'it has reasonable grounds to believe is intended to cruise or to carry on a war against a Power with which it is at peace.'[36] It was a political concession. The resolution of the dispute owed more to Britain's political need to bury the hatchet with the United States at a time of European diplomatic instability than to any agreement about the past principles of international law: for it was urged that the point conceded by negotiation had not been law at the time.[37] For our purposes, the _Alabama_ dispute and Geneva arbitration are important for showing the anti-speculative and pragmatic bent of English jurists at the time. In a review of Bernard's book in the _Revue de Droit International et de Législation Comparée_, Gustave Rolin-Jacquemyns regretted his concentration on positive law. He wrote

> Il eût dans tous les cas été digne d'un jurisconsulte de la valeur de M. Bernard de ne pas se borner à examiner cette grave question des devoirs de la neutralité au point de vue du droit positif existant. C'est par l'opinion hautement émise de savants comme lui, que les idées générales en matière de droit sont appelées à se rectifier et à se compléter.[38]

Addressing this point in his Geneva report, Cockburn raised a

> protest against the question being determined not according to 'existing positive law,' but to the opinion of 'savants' as to what law should have been, or should now be made. The Tribunal cannot, I apprehend, adopt such a principle in forming its judgment. Its functions are not to make the law, but to decide according to the rules of the Treaty.[39]

Cockburn took a similarly anti-speculative approach to international law on the Royal Commission on Fugitive Slaves. The question which they discussed – whether a fugitive slave who got on board a British ship could be given protection

---

[36] Article VI of the Treaty, quoted in Papers relating to the Geneva Arbitration, _Parliamentary Papers_ 1872 (61) LXIX 1, 23.

[37] Moreover, the two parties disagreed on the meaning of terms of the treaty, so that it was (as Hall saw it) unclear what impact it would have in future on the conduct of these two countries in respect of each other: Hall, _supra_ note 34, 570.

[38] Quoted in The Geneva Arbitration, _Parliamentary Papers_ 1873 (145) LXXIV 419, 23.

[39] _Ibid,_ 23.

or should be returned on request to the local authorities – was not determined by settled international opinion, and the practice of states differed. Cockburn attacked the theories of extraterritoriality according to which a fugitive slave could claim protection under the flag of the ship from local authorities. These theories derived from the 'doubtful authority of one or two publicists – a class of jurists to whose theories I am seldom disposed to ascribe very much weight, except when they are able to refer us to treaties or the settled practice of nations as an ascertained fact.'[40] In many respects, he felt, these jurists left crucial questions unanswered.[41] Cockburn also noted that in a number of circumstances, English law recognised property in slaves, so that care should be taken not to give instructions to commanders which might 'prove unable to stand the test of legal proceedings before our courts of justice.'[42] He also observed that

> no improvement in our own views on any principle of international law will justify us in forcing the law, as we view it, on another state, which does not take the same view that we do. It is not because we have come to look upon slavery with abhorrence, and have abolished it by our law, that we can take upon us to treat the law of a country which sanctions it as non-existent, or the rights which it gives as of no effect.[43]

Any attempt to impose a new view of international law on other states was likely to lead to conflicts.

Cockburn's fellow commissioners Maine, Phillimore and Bernard disagreed, noting that captains were not obliged to give up the slaves to the authorities on shore. Their view of international law was far less static. 'International law,' they observed,

> is not stationary; it admits of progressive improvement, though the improvement is more difficult and slower than that of municipal law, and though the agencies by which change is effected are different. It varies with the progress of opinion and the growth of usage; and there is no subject on which so great a change of opinion has taken place as slavery and the slave trade.[44]

Nonetheless, these three jurists (in common with the other commissioners) gave an ambiguous answer to the questions posed. While Cockburn felt that according to international law, fugitive slaves could be returned, 'I am very far from saying that there are not exceptional cases in which the strict rules of law and of abstract right should be made to yield to the more immediate and urgent considerations of humanity.'[45] Equally while the three jurists did not think captains were obliged by

---

[40] Royal Commission on Fugitive Slaves, *Parliamentary Papers* 1876 [C 1516–I] XXVIII 285 xxxi.

[41] Thus, on the issue of what to do when a criminal escaped onto a ship, Cockburn noted how 'completely does the professor [Bluntschli] leave us in the lurch just where we most need his assistance.' *Ibid*, xl.

[42] *Ibid*, xliv.

[43] *Ibid*, xxxvi.

[44] *Ibid*, xxv.

[45] *Ibid*, lv.

international law to return such slaves, they regarded it as a matter of policy whether the captain should allow slaves onto the ship in the first place, and did not feel that they should be encouraged to take slaves on board.

Cockburn's anti-speculative bent was also reflected in his judgment in *R. v. Keyn*, the case of the *Franconia*, where the Court of Crown Cases Reserved had to decide whether an English criminal court had jurisdiction to hear a case of manslaughter brought against the German captain of a German vessel, as a result of a collision which took place on the high seas, but within 3 miles of the British coast.[46] In this case, both Sir Robert Phillimore and Cockburn held that the Central Criminal Court had no jurisdiction, and rejected the crown's argument that according to international law, offshore waters within 3 miles of the coast were within the jurisdiction of the state. While Phillimore noted that '[t]he consensus of civilised independent states has recognised a maritime extension of frontier to the distance of three miles from low-water mark,' he rejected the proposition that this meant that a state exercised the *same* jurisdiction over this portion of the sea as was exercised over its land.[47] Cockburn (fortified by the readings made in preparation for Geneva) also noted that most writers agreed that the sea within three miles of the coast belonged to the littoral state:

> But it is equally clear that, in the practical application of the rule, in respect of the particular of distance, as also in the still more essential particular of the character and degree of sovereignty and dominion to be exercised, great difference of opinion and uncertainty have prevailed, and still continue to exist.[48]

Cockburn rejected the argument that the agreement of jurists that a state might treat the three mile zone as subject to its laws *ipso facto* conferred jurisdiction, since it was so unclear what the extent of the jurisdiction was. He proceeded:

> This unanimity of opinion that the littoral sea is, at all events for some purposes, subject to the dominion of the local state, may go far to shew that, by the concurrence of other nations, such a state may deal with these waters as subject to its legislation. But it wholly fails to shew that, in the absence of such legislation, the ordinary law of the local state will extend over the waters in question – which is the point which we have to determine.[49]

Cockburn's view was taken to mean that the assent of a state to a rule of international law had to be expressly given, either by legislation or though a court judgment, before it was incorporated into domestic law, a view which seemed at odds with the Blackstonian view that the law of nations was part of the common law.[50] But it should

---

[46] *R v. Keyn* (1876), 2 *Law Reports, Exchequer Division* 173.

[47] *Ibid*, 81.

[48] *Id.*

[49] *Ibid*, 191.

[50] See Sir H. Maine, *International law* (1888) 43. Crawford describes the Blackstonian claim (as articulated by Mansfield) as 'historically untenable.' (Crawford, *supra* note 33, 686.)

be borne in mind that the question addressed by Cockburn was whether international law could of itself confer on domestic courts a new jurisdiction they did not enjoy by the common law. In his view, while international agreement could *empower* parliament to legislate on matters over which it hitherto had no right to meddle according to international law, domestic courts could only obtain their authority to act from their parliament, and not from international opinion.[51]

The dissenting Lord Coleridge by contrast felt that the opinion of international jurists was indeed compelling, and held that international law was itself directly binding on English courts. 'Strictly speaking,' he ruled, 'international law is an inexact expression, and it is apt to mislead if its inexactness is not kept in mind. Law implies a law-giver, and a tribunal capable of enforcing it and coercing its transgressors. But there is no common law-giver to sovereign states; and no tribunal has the power to bind them by decrees or coerce them if they transgress.' However, where it was shown that there was a consensus of jurists (which he felt could be discerned here) and an international agreement, it was the practice of English courts to give effect to them as part of English law.[52] If the view of Coleridge (who was perhaps less familiar with the writers on international law than Cockburn) of the incorporation of international norms was one reflecting an eighteenth century conception, his language describing the law followed a nineteenth century positivist view.

In *R. v. Keyn*, in the Geneva arbitration and on the Royal Commission on Fugitive Slaves, Cockburn was worried about the unsettling effect of a *developing* international law, a law which was developed not in the decisions of courts on litigation brought before them, but by jurists discussing matters which directly concerned state policy. He was particularly worried about the impact of abstract jurists, and so constantly insisted that a changing international law could not rest on their opinions, but had to be rooted in agreed practice. Equally, while international law was a source of domestic law, which could be drawn on for the development of the common law in courts, it could not create new jurisdictions, any more than common law judges could extend their jurisdiction without legislation. He reflected a view which was sceptical about the function and role of international law.

Cockburn's views were taken up by J.F. Stephen in his comments on *R. v. Keyn*. In Stephen's view, the international 'law' which obtained between nations did not merit the name of law, as it was not enforced by a common superior. The obligation imposed by treaties, he said, was a moral and not a legal one. In Stephen's view international law remained an *a priori* subject, explored by writers whose theories 'all rest at last neither upon common usage, nor upon any positive institution, but upon some theory as to justice or general convenience, which is copied by one writer from another with such variations or adaptions as happen to strike his fancy'.

---

[51] 2 *Law Reports, Exchequer Division* 203.
[52] *Ibid*, 153–4.

For Stephen, any rules of international law applied by domestic courts were applied as *domestic* law.[53] This view reflected what might be called a 'vulgar Austinian' view of international law, hostile to it and uncomprehending of it. In fact as shall now be seen, Austin's position was more subtle.

4. The Challenge of Austin

Austin has long considered by many to be the great enemy of international law, for he defined international law to be part of the science of positive morality, rather than positive law, thereby apparently denying its status as law. Koskenniemi summarises by saying that Austin's view, while 'well-suited for a domestic system whose legitimacy was taken as self-evident . . . found no room for a law beyond sovereignty.'[54] Austin's position was assumed by many to be the following: since all law is the command of a superior sovereign backed by a sanction, any system of rules (such as international law) not backed by a political superior could not be defined as *law*, but could only be regarded as a non-binding set of moral norms.

In fact, Austin's position was less crude. It should be recalled that Austin's project was to define terms for jurists to use when analysing the law applied by the courts of a state, and that his terms were chosen to distinguish for practical reasons different kinds of norms. According to his definition, every law was a command issuing from a determinate superior which was backed by a sanction. His use of the word 'superior' was confessedly tautological: 'whoever can *oblige* another to comply with his wishes, is the *superior* of that other, so far as the ability reaches.'[55] Austin famously distinguished between three types of rules, each of which included law 'properly so called'. The first was divine law, set by God to his creatures, and backed by supernatural sanctions. The second he dubbed 'positive law', made up of laws 'which are set by men as political superiors, or by men, as private persons, in pursuance of legal rights.' The third type he called 'positive morality': but the rules of positive morality included both 'laws (properly so called) which are set by men to men, but not by men as political superiors' and 'laws which are closely analogous to laws proper, but are merely opinions or sentiments held by men in regard to human conduct.'[56]

Austin's aim was to make clear distinctions, though this task was sometimes frustrated by his use of terminology. Thus, he noted that every law 'properly so called' could be styled a 'positive law', since it was set 'by its individual or collective author.' For convenience of exposition, however, he used the term 'positive law' to apply to

---

[53] J.F. Stephen, *A History of the Criminal Law of England* 3 vols., (1883) 35, 38.
[54] M. Koskenniemi, *supra* note 1, 34.
[55] J. Austin, *The Province of Jurisprudence Determined*, (ed. by W.E. Rumble, 1995) 30.
[56] *Ibid*, 109.

law '*strictly* so-called', meaning the law set by political superiors to political inferiors, which he defined as the subject of jurisprudence.[57] Austin's occasional struggle to make his terminology clear can be seen from the following passage, where he argued that some rules of positive morality were properly speaking laws:

> Since no supreme government is in a state of subjection to another, an imperative law set by a sovereign to a sovereign is not set by its author in the character of political superior. Nor is it set by its author in pursuance of a legal right: for every legal right is conferred by a supreme government, and is conferred on a person or persons in a state of subjection to the granter. Consequently, an imperative law set by a sovereign to a sovereign is not a positive law strictly so called. But being *imperative* (and therefore proceeding from a *determinate* source), it amounts to a law in the proper signification of the term, although it is purely or simply a rule of positive morality.[58]

Austin's shorthand of 'divine law', 'positive law' and 'positive morality' was thus not designed to deny that each could be properly styled 'law'. However, he was keen to demarcate the distinct sources and ambit of the various kinds of norms.

A major part of Austin's project was the conceptual separation of law and morals, so that the existence of a human norm was not to be settled by reflection on its merits. It was therefore crucial for him to show the demarcation between divine laws – which for Austin could equally be dubbed 'natural law' or 'morality' – from human laws. Both positive law and positive morality were distinct from natural law, for they both flowed from human sources, and were capable of study without regard to their goodness or badness. Just as the validity of a norm of positive law did not depend on its conformity with natural law, so the existence and effectiveness of a norm of positive morality did not depend on its ethical content.[59] Austin's distinction between positive *law* and positive *morality* was drawn for the practical purpose of distinguishing those the rules dealt with within a political society, from those not enforced in its courts.[60]

For the most part, international law was not law properly so-called, but was 'analogous to laws proper', for it was comprised of 'rules set and enforced by *mere opinion*, that is, by the opinions or sentiments held or felt by an indeterminate body of men in regard to human conduct'.[61] Since there was no determinate body, the international community could not issue any commands, but could only express 'the *sentiment* which it feels'. Nor was the sanction determined: in consequence of the feeling, it was

---

[57] *Ibid,* 110.

[58] *Ibid,* 122.

[59] He thus criticized Grotius and Pufendorf for 'confound[ing] positive international morality, or the rules which actually obtain among civilized nations in their mutual intercourse, with their own vague conceptions of international morality as it *ought to be*.' *Ibid,* 160.

[60] He thus spoke of 'the human laws, which I style positive morality, as considered without regard to their goodness or badness.' *Ibid,* 111.

[61] *Ibid,* 20.

likely that the body or some member of it would be displeased and would visit the offender with 'some evil or another,' though it was not clear what that evil would be.[62] If this was to suggest that international law was less precise and less regularly enforced that domestic law, two features are worthy of note. Firstly, as a positive science, it was susceptible to study and elaboration (as had been done by international law writers).[63] Second, being analogous to laws proper, it generated similar effects: since some sanctions were likely to follow on breach, potential violators were in practice inclined to follow the rules dictated by opinion, and a uniformity of conduct developed which would otherwise not exist.[64] Thus, although Austin defined international law as 'positive morality', he did not deny that it generated rules which were observed, that the violation of international norms were often followed by sanctions, and that it was possible to study the rules of international law from the practice of nations. Most readers of Austin did not tease out these complexities, but attacked a straw man. Yet as shall be seen, in their defences of their subject, they often stated positions which would not have made Austin uncomfortable.

Austin's jurisprudence was well suited to the approach of common lawyers like Cockburn to international law. It opposed the idea that laws were binding insofar as they reflected a higher set of norms or any set of transcendent values. The sciences of positive law and of positive international morality were not speculative ones, but required the student to examine practice. In the international sphere, this required a close study of the rules which states regarded as binding on them, which required a close study of the behaviour of states. Such a view was not out of step with what many later nineteenth century English international jurists thought. But they had to combat the spectre of the 'vulgar' Austin who seemed to many to dismiss international law as so much private opinion.

5. The Responses to Austin

When faced with the Austinian attack, the 'old civilians' responded in traditional manner, looking back to Grotius and Vattel.[65] Twiss, for example, 'regretted at a time when much progress is being every where made in practice to establish the ascendancy of the Reason over the Will,' that Austin had 'adopted the primeval Notion of Law' as

---

[62] *Ibid*, 124. Austin went on to say that the law of nations was therefore only 'sentiments current among nations generally': but he noted that if any particular nation commanded another to forbear from conduct which the law of nations condemned, this would be 'law in the proper signification of the term' – though Austin immediately went on to qualify this, by saying that 'speaking precisely' for it to be a law, it would have to be issued as a political superior.

[63] *Ibid*, 112.

[64] *Ibid*, 126.

[65] See, *e.g.*, R. Phillimore, *supra* note 15, 72.

a command of a sovereign: 'a broader view of Law was taken by the Scholastic Jurists, who were the immediate predecessors of Grotius. Law according to them was an Ordinance of Reason promulgated for the Common Good.'[66] Following Vattel, Twiss argued that there was an involuntary and necessary natural law of nations, founded on the nature of independent states, which dictated such principles as non-interference, without which no state could subsist. There was also a positive law of nations derived from consent, and enforced by the isolation of the state which disregarded it.[67] But the view of the old civilians, as shall now be seen, was very untypical.

D.H.N. Johnson has noted that '[i]t is possible that to Maine more than anyone else we owe the fact that, despite the influence of Austin, the serious study of international law as a legal subject was able to survive in this country.'[68] Appointed to a chair of international law in the last year of his life, Maine gave lectures which were posthumously published. In his Cambridge lectures, Maine was respectful of Grotius and Vattel, and himself endorsed the idea that there was a natural and a positive law of nations. Moreover, while he saw international law as a mixture of general principles of justice, usages, customs and positive agreements, he claimed to regard it as improper to separate it from 'the same principles of right reason . . . and the same sanction of Divine revelation, as those from which the science of morality is deduced.'[69] But such comments masked the distinction between Maine's work and the Grotian tradition. In *Ancient Law*, Maine had attacked speculative approaches to the law of nature which, but for the pernicious influence of Rousseau, would in his view never have survived the historical method of Montesquieu.[70] In that pathbreaking work, Maine showed that there were no 'necessary' notions in law, but that concepts which in the modern age seemed essential categories of any legal system – such as contracts or wills – had developed in particular contexts out of institutions which fulfilled very different functions. Maine argued that much of the system of international law was 'made up of pure Roman law'; though it had descended by an 'an irregular filiation.'[71] By assuming that *jus gentium* and *jus naturale* were identical, he wrote, Grotius and his successors developed the idea 'that Natural Law is the code of states' and put in operation the process of 'engrafting on the international system rules which are supposed to have been evolved from the unassisted contemplation of the conception of Nature.'[72] But (Maine argued) no Roman lawyer would have

---

[66] T. Twiss, *The Law of Nations considered as Independent Political Communities, vol. 1 – On the Right and Duties of Nations in Time of Peace* (1861), v–vi.

[67] *Ibid,* 111.

[68] Johnson, *supra* note 28, 440.

[69] Sir H. Maine, *International Law, supra* note 50, 32.

[70] H. Maine, *Ancient Law: its connection with the early history of society and its relation to modern ideas* (1930) 97–8.

[71] *Ibid,* 106, 108.

[72] *Ibid,* 109.

imagined natural law to have obligatory force between independent common-wealths. The *jus gentium* was only a collection of rules and principles, derived from observing practices common to Rome and its neighbours,[73] which the Roman lawyer loved 'as little as he loved the foreigners from whose institutions it was derived and for whose benefit it was intended'. Only when Greek philosophy was added to it, was the theory transformed.[74] The historical specificity of modern notions of international law was confirmed for Maine by the fact that it was premised on the existence of territorial states – which only emerged with the decline of feudalism[75] – to which Roman concepts of property could be applied.[76]

If *Ancient Law* showed up the flaws of Austinian theory, it also revealed the histor-ical weakness of assuming that in the absence of a superior sovereign laying down pos-itive rules for states, an objective natural law binding on separate territorial units could be uncovered. Instead, as Maine showed, it was the theorists themselves, developing concepts by adapting them to modern needs, who had helped to create systems to maintain peace. Equally, his criticism of the idea of 'necessary notions' in law could be used against international lawyers, who defined rights of states which could be 'logically inferred from the mere fact that a state has existence'. As Maine showed, even the most basic premises of the state system had been fought over and contended.[77]

Maine's greatest contribution, as far as later international lawyers were con-cerned, however, lay in his critique of Austin's claims that all law derived from the commands of sovereigns: for this seemed to free them to speak the language of *law*. For Maine, Austin's theory was premised on a particular definition, which could not be applied in all contexts. There was nothing inherently wrong with that, for 'one sense of law is just as good and dignified as another, if it be only consistently used.' Austin's definition was perfectly useful for identifying and describing the rules applied by modern legal systems, and was entirely suitable for an age of legis-lation. But it was not helpful as a way to describe the evolution of customary sys-tems. For Maine, it was perfectly *logical* for Austin to say that no customary norm was 'positive law' until applied by a court, since by his definition 'positive law' only consisted of rules applied by courts. But his further implication, that in applying the norm for the first time judges were legislating, underestimated the extent to which judges were in practice limited by custom whose binding force could not be understood by calling it 'positive morality'. Commenting on Austin's argument that until courts applied a custom in a case, turning it into law, it remained only positive morality, Maine observed that '[t]he theory is perfectly defensible as a theory, but

---

[73] *Ibid*, 57.

[74] *Ibid*, 59.

[75] *Ibid*, 114.

[76] See Landauer, 'From Status to Treaty: Henry Sumner Maine's *International Law*', 15 *Canadian Journal of Law and Jurisprudence* (2002) 227–8.

[77] Sir H. Maine, *International Law, supra* note 50, 60–1.

its practical value and the degree in which it approximates to truth differ greatly in different ages and countries.'[78] Austin's concept of law as command could not help-fully be applied to societies such as India, where disputes were settled by customary norms, which did not depend on the coercive authority of the ruler (who himself never thought of altering them) but were followed by the community in the belief that they had always been law. To describe such norms as 'positive morality' was a 'mere artifice of speech.' Customs were applied by courts because they were regarded as binding already: they did not become binding merely because they were applied by a court. Turning to international law, he argued that the norms of inter-national law had spread in the same way that Roman law had spread throughout Europe, as the product of the learning of jurists and clerics. This process, he said, had little to do with legislation, but 'consisted in the reception of a body of doctrine in a mass by specially constituted or trained minds.'[79] Austin's definition, stressing the centrality of sanctions, overlooked the fact that most obedience to law came from habit, rather than fear. The founders of international law, he said, created not a sanction, but 'a law-abiding sentiment', which came from a general sense of approval of the laws.[80]

This attack hardly undermined the Austinian project, which had been tailored specifically to be applied to the law of modern states. Austin's theory (as has been seen) did not deny that there was a kind of 'law' beyond the courts: his point was to show that it was different in nature from the law he wished to study. He was no 'vulgar Austinian': for he did not rule out systematic study of customary norms. It is equally notable that therefore Maine conceded that international law was not law in Austin's sense of positive law:

> It is very convenient, when the main subject of thought is positive law, that we should remember that international law has but slender connection with it, and that it has less analogy to the laws which are the commands of sovereigns than to rules of conduct, which, whatever be their origin, are to a very great extent enforced by the disapproba-tion which attends their neglect.[81]

Moreover, Maine pointed to defects in international law which were traceable to the differences between that law and positive law: particularly that there was no authori-tative body to declare or enforce its rules.[82] Maine therefore took the edge out of Austin's language regarding international law, but without undermining his theory.

Writers following Maine took up his point, seeking to show that international law could properly be dubbed *law*, while admitting that it was distinct and less precise

---

[78] Sir H. Maine, *Lectures on the Early History of Institutions* (1875) 364.
[79] Maine, *International Law, supra* note 50, 26. For an analysis, see Landauer, *supra* note 71.
[80] Maine, *International Law, supra* note 50, 51.
[81] *Ibid,* 49.
[82] *Ibid,* 53.

than positive law.[83] Like many others, John Westlake admitted the utility of Austinian jurisprudence for analysing the law of a state, but contended that his methods were not suitable for a system lacking statutes and case law. The international lawyer sought rules 'existing in the international society and more or less enforced by it', by looking at 'the practice of states'. Austin's terminology of positive morality was not helpful, he felt, since it overlooked the fact that some international obligations were regarded as obligatory, while others were not.[84] Instead of looking at 'purely voluntary acts or abstentions', the student of international law had to ask whether 'the thing has been done or abstained from in obedience to a persuasion that such was the law.'[85]

For Westlake, domestic law and international law were different species of a genus of 'rules of conduct'.[86] Once four features of this genus – generality, precision, observance and recognition – had been identified, 'we have a positive rule'. Using these criteria, even Austin's positive international morality could be seen to be made up of such rules. Westlake noted that Austin singled out as 'law' rules which were set by a sovereign political authority: but he retorted that the key distinction 'lies not in how they come to be rules, but in their operation as rules, in the uniformity of their observance and of the expectation which attends it; in short, in their being or not being positive rules.'[87] Since it was composed of such rules, international law was law.

For Westlake, the jurist was to look not to the sovereign as the source of law, but to society itself. Wherever there was a society, he said, there had to be law, for no society could subsist as such without rules. He therefore distinguished law and morality in a different way from Austin. He defined 'law' as a body of rules expressing claims which were 'held to be enforceable and are more or less regularly observed'. A *legal* claim was one supported by a sentiment shared by the general mass of society 'that it would be justifiable to enforce it.' On the other hand, if the sentiment was not held so to be enforceable, it was only a moral claim.[88] As with Austin, the notion of a sanction or enforcement was thus essential to Westlake's definition of a law: but unlike Austin, he did not require the sanction to be imposed

---

[83] M. Bernard, *supra* note 35, 401 wrote, 'it is surely an error to treat rules of this kind as if they had all the sharpness and precision of municipal law, and created the same definite obligations, with the same perfect right to have every breach repaired by appropriate satisfaction. This is not their use or intention, nor are they capable of being so employed.'

[84] See J. Westlake, *International Law: Part I Peace* (1910) 13; see also F. Pollock, *Essays in Jurisprudence and Ethics* (1882) 35.

[85] J. Westlake, *Chapters on the Principles of International Law* (1894) x.

[86] J. Westlake, *Collected Papers, supra* note 6, 397. By observance, he meant that such rules were habitually followed in practice; and by recognition, the fact that it was recognised both by the person obliged and by others that he had no choice in the matter.

[87] *Ibid*, 399.

[88] J. Westlake, *Chapters, supra* note 85, 2–3. Westlake noted Austin's use of the adjective 'positive' to show that the international 'rules so described are sufficiently enforced and observed to have an objective existence'; but objected to the noun 'morality' as confusing socially obligatory rules with private ethics, *ibid*, 8.

by a determinate source to qualify as 'law'. For Westlake, international lawyers had to trace the rules which would be regarded as enforceable by states. This involved not merely examining state practice, but the opinion which motivated it, since 'through a change of opinion, an old practice [may have] ceased to be accompanied by the general persuasion of enforceable right without which it cannot be law.'[89]

In practice, Westlake admitted that the rules of international law were less determinate and its enforcement less certain than in the case of domestic law. On the one hand, he argued that international rules were for the most part obeyed without any need to resort to force. Indeed, if statesmen frequently complained of violations, 'it is more correct to say that international law is an imperfect body of rules than that, so far as it is perfect, it is not obeyed.' But on the other, he noted that when a state was justly offended, it was often left to fight its own battles. In this process, it received 'a moral support from the general recognition that its resort to arms was the exercise of a right', while the offending party was sooner or later 'made to feel the loss of sympathy which his conduct has occasioned.'[90]

This was to rename Austin's terms but without undermining the theory. International law remained a less perfect system than state law.[91] Moreover, Westlake's view was one of a 'positive' system of norms which applied to a certain society: it was not a rationalist, universal system. The peoples of Europe, European descent and Japan were 'the peoples by whose consent it exists, and for the settlement of whose differences it is applied.' Outside that pale, there were 'facts of the same nature as some of those which international law deals with', such as independent governments, and there were 'the same principles of natural justice to which international law ought to conform'; but those facts alone gave it no more force in those areas than the law of England had beyond its own territory.[92] Though changing Austin's terms, Westlake did not reject his project. Indeed, while noting Mainite objections to Austin, he commented that the analytical school was right 'in maintaining that, if we give the name of law to anything which we so discover in a remote state of society before we have fixed in our minds what we mean by that name, we beg the question, and have no security that our language has any consistent, or therefore useful, sense.'[93]

---

[89] *Ibid*, x.

[90] *Ibid*, 8, 7.

[91] This can be seen in the following definitions he gave: 'A rule set by a sovereign political authority is contained in a statute-book, or in writings or traditions which are authoritative in the eyes of a judge, whose decisions will in their turn be carried into effect by the executive department. A rule which forms part of International Law is contained in writings, traditions or sentiments which are authoritative in the eyes of civilized men, whose judgment on its breach will receive a pretty effective execution by the force, or at least by the disapprobation, of the states concerned.' J. Westlake, *Collected Papers, supra* note 6, 398.

[92] J. Westlake, *Collected Papers, supra* note 6, 622–3. See also the discussion in Anghie, *supra* note 32.

[93] J. Westlake, *Chapters, supra* note 85, viii. Anghie, *supra* note 32, 31–2 notes the irony of international lawyers like Westlake claiming that Austin used the word 'law; in a special and limited sense, only to do the same themselves in order to exclude the 'uncivilized' from its ambit.

Like Westlake, T.J. Lawrence also argued that Austin's definition only looked to one particular aspect of law. Lawrence argued that Austin had erred by focusing on the issue of force, rather than on order. While (he argued) it might have been the case that under medieval monarchs, the power of law rested on the royal ability to enforce it, in modern societies, particularly in democracies, '[l]aw no longer emanates from the mere will of the rulers, but from the wisdom of the community. Its chief support is not the force controlled by government, but the general sense of its goodness and utility.'[94] For Lawrence, it was the concept of order which was crucial in his definition of law as a 'rule of conduct actually observed among men.'[95] The notion of sanctions was important for distinguishing the different species of law, rather than identifying law itself. Thus, municipal law was ultimately backed by the coercive power of the state; moral law was backed by disapproval; and international law was 'provided with [clearly defined] sanctions as regards some of its rules, while others depend for their coercive force on nothing but the general opinion of rulers and peoples, and the probability that nations which disobey them will suffer some undefined evil from some state of states not capable of being pointed out beforehand.'[96] Like Westlake, Lawrence had in effect recast Austin's terminology, but without essentially challenging his distinctions.

A third jurist who took a similar view was Lord Russell of Killowen. Rejecting Austin's focus on force, he noted that international law comprised 'the sum of the rules or usages which civilized states have agreed shall be binding upon them in their dealings with one another.'[97] But (like Westlake and Lawrence) he was clear to show that international law was not made up of higher norms, derived from speculative ethics: just as it was of the essence of municipal law that its rules were enacted or recognized as binding by the sovereign, international law contained only rules 'recognized as binding by the nations constituting the community of civilized mankind.'[98] It was also clear that Russell saw international law as being different in kind from municipal law, and that it had certain defects: notably that a state might repudiate any agreement, for instance to submit to arbitration. '[U]nless and until the great powers of the world, in league, bind themselves to coerce a recalcitrant member of the family of nations,' he noted, 'we have still to face the more than possible disregard by powerful states of the obligations of good faith and of justice.' Nonetheless, a form of sanction existed in the power of public opinion.[99]

---

[94] T.J. Lawrence, 'Is there a true International law?' in T.J. Lawrence, *Essays on some disputed questions in modern International law* (1885) 16.

[95] *Ibid*, 26.

[96] *Ibid*, 23.

[97] Russell, *supra* note 5, 313.

[98] *Ibid*, 317.

[99] *Ibid*, 331–2.

These approaches, which downplayed the role of sanctions in any definition of law, raised some objections from more analytical jurists, such as T.E. Holland. Holland's definition of law took account of Maine's objections. For him, law was 'a general rule of external human action *enforced* by a sovereign political authority'.[100] He observed that '[i]f you define 'Law' with Professor Westlake as 'positive rule' or with Dr. T.J. Lawrence as 'any kind of rule or canon whereby actions are framed' (so following Hooker), you are evidently sacrificing the distinction between Law and Morality'.[101] The word 'law' he argued had to be applied to the rules which the state applied: any rules which were observed voluntarily, if habitually, by states could only be given the name 'law' as a matter of courtesy. Holland noted that 'international Law is, in fact, a beneficent application of legal ideas to questions which, from the nature of the case, are incapable of a legal solution'.[102] Like his mentor Austin, Holland admitted that there were agreed conventional rules which governed the conduct of states, and whose violation both shocked the conscience and was held to justify a resort to war; but they could only be dubbed 'law' by analogy.[103]

Frederick Pollock, who often derided the work of Austin, also echoed Holland's scepticism about the approach of Westlake and Lawrence. In review of works by Holland, Hall and James Lorimer, Pollock rejected the *Naturrecht* approach of the Scot as dealing with philosophical matters outside the province of jurisprudence. He accepted the proposition that positive law assumed the existence of society and morality. But – in an exposition owing much to Austin – Pollock went on to say that a further precondition for the existence of law, as distinct from morality, was the existence of 'a general understanding that some rules of conduct are fit to be enforced by definite means of compulsion, and in the last resort by the whole power of society, and others are not'.[104] Beyond that, it was necessary for the commonwealth to assume a power to issue binding rules on morally indifferent matters. In his review, Pollock endorsed W.E. Hall's empirical approach to international law, regretting that Hall had not devoted more attention to the nature of sanctions in international law.

Hall, who in common with the other international lawyers doubted Austin's definition since it omitted a body of rules regarded as having the force of law by those it addressed,[105] had defined international law as 'certain rules of conduct which modern civilised states regard as being binding on them in their relations with one another with a force comparable in nature and degree to that binding the conscientious

---

[100] T.E. Holland, *The Elements of Jurisprudence* (1882) 34. Emphasis added.
[101] T.E. Holland, *Lectures on International Law*, (ed. by T.A. Walker & W.L. Walker 1933) 26.
[102] *Ibid*, 6.
[103] *Ibid*, 9: 'We have here the central fact which makes possible a Science of International Law, *viz.*, an Opinion, widely enough spread to produce important historical results, to the effect that States may have Rights and Duties similar or, at least, analogous to the legal Rights and Duties of individuals.'
[104] F. Pollock, *supra* note 84, 23.
[105] W.E. Hall, *supra* note 34, 15–16.

person to obey the laws of his country, and which they also regard as being enforceable by appropriate means in case of infringement.' But what were the appropriate means? Since there was no international judicial or administrative machinery, individual states were left to vindicate their own rights, ultimately by the sanction of war. In theory, he noted, international law should set out precisely the causes of a just war, marking 'out as plainly as municipal law what constitutes a wrong for which a remedy may be sought at law'. But this was scarcely possible, and in practice, self-interest often intervened. The obedience paid to the law therefore had to be a 'willing obedience, and when a state has taken up arms unjustly it is useless to expect it to acquiesce in the imposition of penalties for its act.[106]

This did not satisfy Pollock. Noting the trite observation 'that international law differs from law proper in that the parties are judges in their own cause', and the fact that war was the ultimate sanction, he asked, '[h]ow can we speak of a war as legally unjust when there is no penalty save the risks of the war itself, which may turn out, for anything that can be pronounced beforehand, to the unjust combatant's advantage?'[107] Pollock observed that the greater the offence, the less capable it was of being punished in kind, by way of reprisals. Ultimately, the sanction which made belligerents follow humane conduct in war was 'the general opinion of civilized people.' Pollock concluded by effectively accepting Westlake and Lawrence's understanding of the operation of international law, while rejecting their definition of is as properly 'law'.

> Should we not, then, regard public opinion as the final sanction of international law in every case, – a sanction with physical force behind it, no doubt, in one or another shape, but a force latent and undefined, and to be called into action only in an extreme case? This would bring out more clearly than the common view does the analogy between international law as governing the relations of States, and the rules of morality as governing those of individuals.[108]

6. Conclusion

Faced with the new international order of the second half of the nineteenth century, and the increasing intervention of common lawyers in international law, there was a general rejection of the earlier civilian approach to the subject, which cast its rules in abstract terms derived from natural law thinking. International law was to be rooted in facts, not speculation. It has been argued that an Austinian approach was suitable for this new approach, although his language – particularly when set out in the vulgarised version of Stephen – offended by its implication that international law was simply

---

[106] *Ibid* 59–60.
[107] F. Pollock, *supra* note 84, 34.
[108] F. Pollock, *supra* note 84, 37.

morality. As has been seen, the criticism of the 'vulgar Austinian' position attacked a straw man, for Austin's own views were more subtle. For Austin, international law was distinct both from abstract ethics, and from the law of a political society. He dubbed it *positive international morality* to distinguish it both from abstract morality (hence it consisted of 'posited' rules) and from positive law (which issued from a determinate superior with powers to enforce). Those who attacked Austin equally sought to distinguish obligatory international rules from mere rules of conscience, and conceded that it was different in nature from domestic law. But seeing it as a system capable of scientific study, they were unhappy at Austin's reluctance to call it 'law'.

According to Austin's 'strict' definition, positive law was identified by the nature of its source. It was a command which came from a definite source which had the power to impose a definite sanction. Since it had neither definite source nor sanction, international law was not properly called law, though it did have rules which could be identified by focusing on conduct, and which were to be studied regardless of their merits. 'Positive international morality' was also to be identified by its sources, although they were different and less precise than those of proper law. The more these sources could be identified, the more precise the science could be, and the more like 'law' their subject. A number of international jurists took up this 'Austinian' challenge of identifying the sources. Thus, for writers such as Hall,[109] the obligations of international law could only change through the positive agreement of states to it, or through developing usages as manifested in state actions. It was therefore up to each state to participate in the development of these rules, agreeing or disagreeing according to its own ideas. For the jurist, the advantage of such an approach was that it reflected the *Realpolitik* of late nineteenth century international relations, under which rival states often took positions regarding key questions of international law (notably those affecting commerce) reflecting their self-interest. A second advantage was that this made it easier to identify what the agreed rules were, more precisely, thereby participating in the Austinian project of identification and clarification.

A number of writers, including Westlake and Lawrence, looked to broader sources, including a general informed opinion. In doing so, Lawrence insisted that he was not confusing 'ought' and 'is', for he argued for an approach to his subject based on 'historical' rather than 'ethical' methods, since those who administered the rules of international law 'determine[d] them mainly by a reference to precedent and usage'.[110] But he proceeded to point out that it was nevertheless the duty of writers to make ethical

---

[109] Johnson, *supra* note 28, 439 noted that Hall was regarded by many as the best writer on this subject produced by Britain.

[110] T.J. Lawrence, *The Principles of International Law*, (2nd ed., 1897) 22. He went on, 'The principles and the rules based upon them may be morally good or morally bad; but they determine the conduct of governments in relation to one another, they define the rights of states and set forth their obligations, and therefore they, and they alone, are International Law', *ibid*, 23.

judgments on the rules they were describing. Lawrence's view seemed to suggest that the separation of law and morals was less effective when it came to international law. In contrast to disputes over municipal law, which were settled by legislation, disputed questions of international law could only be settled by reasoning or violence. 'He who in such a case bases his reasoning on high considerations of morality may succeed in resolving the doubt in accordance with justice and morality,' Lawrence advised. While nations would never forget their own self-interest, 'the publicist should rise above national prejudice, and endeavour so to use his influence as to make the system he expounds at the same time more scientific and more just.'[111] Moreover, if the foundations of international law were found in public opinion, or the feelings of the community as informed by enlightened jurists, then its content would change as general feelings of humanity became more refined. International law, by this token, would reflect the morals of the international community. But by the same token, it would become more difficult to identify what the rules of international law actually were.

---

[111] *Ibid*, 24.

A CASE STUDY ON JURISPRUDENCE AS A SOURCE OF INTERNATIONAL LAW: OPPENHEIM'S INFLUENCE

Amanda Perreau-Saussine*

Introduction

Lassa Oppenheim's two volume *Treatise on international law* was first published by Longmans and Green in London and New York, the first volume *Peace* (on international law in peace time) in 1905 and the second *War and neutrality* (on international law in time of war) in 1906. Through nine editions, the *Treatise* has remained the leading British reference book on general public international law, frequently relied upon by English advocates and judges and often cited before and by international and domestic tribunals. Arthur Nussbaum, writing in 1947 (at the time of the sixth edition), concluded that Oppenheim's *Treatise* remained 'by common consent the outstanding and most frequently employed systematic treatise on the subject in the English-speaking countries'.[1] Michael Reisman, reviewing the ninth edition, concludes that Oppenheim's *Treatise* has been and remains 'the premier modern international law treatise in English . . . quoted and relied upon by governments and domestic and international tribunals, often as the final authoritative statement of international law on a particular point'.[2] There 'is no doubt', concludes James Crawford, surveying English-language treatises on international law produced between 1836 and 1960, 'that Oppenheim's *International Law* won the battle of the international law textbooks. It did so not only because of the eminence

---

* University Lecturer, Faculty of Law, University of Cambridge; Assistant Director, Centre for Public Law; Fellow of Newnham College.

** This paper draws on lectures presented as a seminar at the Cambridge Lauterpacht Research Centre for International Law in April 2004, at a public lecture at the Institute for Advanced Legal Studies delivered under the 'Legal History Series' in May 2004, and at the conference on whose proceedings this volume is based. I am indebted to the audiences at those lectures for their comments and suggestions. I develop the broader themes of this paper in two other essays: 'Foreign views on eating aliens: The roots and implications of recent English decisions on customary international law as a source of common law limits on executive power' in C. Warbrick & S. Tierney (eds.), *Towards an international legal community? The sovereignty of states and the sovereignty of international law* (2006) and 'Three ways of writing a treatise on public international law: textbooks and teachers as a contemporary source of public international law' in A. Perreau-Saussine & J.B. Murphy (eds.), *The nature of customary law: philosophical, historical and legal perspectives* (Cambridge University Press, forthcoming 2006).
    1   A. Nussbaum, *A Concise History of the Law of Nations* (1947) 277.
    2   Reisman, 'Lassa Oppenheim's Nine Lives', 19 *Yale Journal of International Law* (1994) 256.

of his inter-war editors, McNair and then Lauterpacht, but initially through its own merits.'[3] This essay considers how and why Oppenheim and his *Treatise* came to be so widely regarded as authoritative.

Oppenheim (1858–1919) initially lectured at the University of Freiburg im Breisgau and then at Basle, becoming well-known for his work on criminal law, but also teaching the philosophy of law, constitutional law, and international law. At the age of thirty-seven, he moved to England and 'since he could not hope to continue his criminal-law studies in a common-law system, he instead turned his attentions to the universal topic of international law, which transcended all common law or civil law boundaries'.[4] He arrived to live at the Albany in Piccadilly in 1895, the year in which the new London School of Economics and Political Science (LSE) was founded and at which, in 1898, he was appointed to a lectureship in international law. According to one of his friends, Edward Whittuck:

> No man ever pursued the object of mastering a subject with more method or with greater determination. He at once began to form what became a unique library of international law, spending a considerable portion of a not very large income upon it. The fact that the Foreign Office has had not infrequently to borrow books from this collection is some testimony to its usefulness.[5]

Oppenheim remained at the LSE for ten years, taking British citizenship in 1900 and marrying an Englishwoman, Elizabeth Cowan, in 1902. In 1908, he was

---

[3] J. Crawford, 'Public international law in Twentieth-century England' in J. Beatson & R. Zimmerman (eds.), *Jurists uprooted: German-speaking Émigré lawyers in Twentieth-century Britain* (2004) 697.

[4] Brierly, 'Oppenheim, Lassa Francis Lawrence (1858–1919)', rev. by Nathan Wells, 41 *Oxford Dictionary of National Biography* (2004) 899–900. How far if at all anti-Semitism influenced the move is unknown. Brierly writes that 'His was not a strong constitution, and he felt that the English climate and mode of life would suit him. It was also convenient in that his brother had been living in London for some time.' On Oppenheim, see also Whittuck, 'Professor Oppenheim', 1 *British Yearbook of International Law* (1920–1921) 1. Oppenheim's obituary was the first article in the first edition of the British Yearbook, a journal he had been involved in founding and first edited by one of his favourite students, Picciotto, on whom see text below. A rich and thought-provoking study of Oppenheim's work can be found in Kingsbury, 'Legal Positivism as Normative Politics: International Society, Balance of Power and Lassa Oppenheim's Positive International Law', 13 *European Journal of International Law* (2002) 401. For a detailed series of essays on Oppenheim see: Schmoekel, 'The Internationalist as a Scientist and Herald', 11 *European Journal of International Law* (2000) 699–700; *idem*, 'The Story of a Success: Lassa Oppenheim and his 'International Law'' in M. Stolleis & M. Yanagihara (eds.), *East Asian and European Perspectives on International Law* (2004) 57; *idem*, 'Lassa Oppenheim' in J. Beaston and R. Zimmermann (eds.), *supra* note 3, 583; *idem*, 'Consent and Caution: Lassa Oppenheim and his reaction to World War I' in R. Lesaffer (ed.), *Peace treaties and International Law in European History* (2004) 270.

[5] Whittuck, *supra* note 4, 5. Oppenheim dedicates the first edition of his *Treatise* to Whittuck 'whose sympathy and encouragement have accompanied the progress of this work from its inception to its close'. The London School of Economics and Political Science was founded in 1895 with a bequest of the Fabian Society; Whittuck is the seventh on the list of signatories and guarantors (Sidney Webb being the first) on LSE's documents of incorporation in 1901.

(apparently with reluctance on his part) elected to the Whewell Chair of International Law at Cambridge on the strength of the impression made by the first edition of his *Treatise* on the retiring Whewell Professor, John Westlake.[6]

On the most sceptical account, the influence of Oppenheim's *Treatise* would be explained by tracing a chain of relations of filial piety – helped by a bequest in Oppenheim's will to finance subsequent editions of the *Treatise* – which sustained a small chain of scholarly editors, scholars trained and teaching subsequent generations at the LSE and Cambridge and adjudicating at English and international tribunals. After the first two editions of Oppenheim's treatise (1905–1906; 1912) edited by Oppenheim himself, the third edition (1921) was edited (working on revisions Oppenheim had made before his death in October 1919) by 'one of Oppenheim's favourite pupils', Ronald Roxburgh, 'at great self-sacrifice'.[7] Roxburgh had written a Whewell scholarship dissertation[8] under Oppenheim's supervision in 1913–1914, published in 1917 as part of a series of monographs edited by Oppenheim. Roxburgh would later move into practice at the English bar and ultimately became a High Court judge.

The fourth edition (1928) was edited by Arnold Duncan McNair, again a Cambridge-trained lawyer and a protégé of the Roman lawyer William Buckland.[9] McNair seems to have become interested in international law only after the First World War,[10] possibly sitting in on lectures by Alexander Pearce Higgins (who had replaced Oppenheim at LSE in 1908 and succeeded Oppenheim to the Whewell chair in 1920). McNair replaced Pearce Higgins[11] at the LSE, and in turn succeeded Pearce Higgins in the Whewell Chair at Cambridge in 1935; he was elected (in 1945) the first British Judge of the International Court of Justice (ICJ), and subsequently acted as President both of the ICJ and of the European Court of Human Rights.

---

[6] *Ibid*, 6: 'Oppenheim was not originally a candidate for the post, but on Westlake's insisting on his standing he finally consented to do so and was elected.'

[7] *Id.*

[8] R. Roxburgh, *International Conventions and Third States: A Monograph* (1917). Written in 1913–14, and published by Longmans in 1917. This was edited by Oppenheim and published in a series called 'Contributions to International Law and Diplomacy'. Roxburgh also published a monograph entitled *The Prisoners of War Information Bureau in London* (1915), again published by Longmans and with a preface by Oppenheim.

[9] McNair had applied to study law at Gonville and Caius College in Cambridge because, on enquiring 'as to the best teacher of law in Cambridge, the answer was that 'if you are prepared to gamble on Buckland's precarious state of health you can't do better than go to Caius' ': McNair's obituary of Buckland, co-authored with P.W. Duff: 33 *Proceedings of the British Academy* (1946) 284. McNair was later to co-author with Buckland, *Roman law and the Common law* (1936), a book based on a series of lectures Buckland had given to small group of fellow academics in 1931.

[10] In his obituary of McNair, Gerald Fitzmaurice writes: 'It was really during, and in consequence of, the war of 1914–1918 that his attention was first attracted to international law as a subject' in Fitzmaurice, 'Arnold Duncan Lord McNair of Gleniffer', 47 *British Yearbook of International Law* (1974–1975) xiii.

[11] McNair's obituary of Pearce Higgins in 22 *Proceedings of British Academy* (1935) 5: 'Pearce Higgins was from the student's point of view a good lecturer, as I can testify.'

McNair befriended and encouraged Hersch Lauterpacht and his wife Rachel after their arrival in England in 1923 as immigrants from Lwów via Vienna.[12] McNair supervised Lauterpacht's research at the LSE and handed over to his 'former pupil and friend'[13] full editorial control of the fifth edition (1935–1937) of Oppenheim's *Treatise*. Lauterpacht continued as editor of the sixth (1940–1947), seventh (1948–1952) and eighth (1955, volume I only) editions of the *Treatise*, succeeding McNair first at LSE and then as Whewell Professor of International Law at Cambridge in 1937, and in 1955 as the British judge at the ICJ.

The much later ninth edition of volume I (1992) was edited by Robert Jennings and Arthur Watts. Jennings attended McNair's lectures as an undergraduate at Cambridge, replaced Lauterpacht at the LSE (in a more junior post) when the latter took up the Whewell Chair in Cambridge, and was nurtured by Lauterpacht when he moved to teach at Cambridge; he succeeded Lauterpacht in the Whewell chair in 1955 and was in turn (in 1985) elected the British judge and later President of the ICJ. Watts too was an undergraduate (studying economics and law) and then LLM student at Cambridge, graduating as the Whewell scholar of 1955 in Lauterpacht's last year at Cambridge; he joined the British diplomatic service as a legal adviser, remaining there until 1991 (becoming Deputy Legal Adviser and then Legal Adviser in the Foreign and Commonwealth Office) when he moved to practice at the Bar. He advises on international law issues and acts as an internationally appointed mediator and a member of various international arbitration tribunals, while continuing work on the new edition of Volume II of the *Treatise*.

The enduring influence of these 'elder statesmen of public international law',[14] this LSE, Cambridge and ICJ tradition,[15] itself raises questions about the sufficiency of an account of customary law as simply an articulation of the customs of a small, privileged elite. *Why* did the first editions of Oppenheim's *Treatise* have the impact they did? And why has this tradition endured: why has Oppenheim's *Treatise* continued to be accepted as authoritative?

For many commentators, Oppenheim's *Treatise* has had enduring appeal for international lawyers because of its 'combination of the German passion for organization

---

[12] See Jennings, 'Hersch Lauterpacht: A Personal Recollection', 8 *European Journal of International Law* (1997) 301; Lauterpacht, 'Biographical note: Sir Hersch Lauterpacht 1897–1960', 8 *European Journal of International Law* (1997) 313.

[13] L. Oppenheim, *International Law, A Treatise*, vol. I (1928), Preface.

[14] A phrase from another elder statesman of public international law, Gerald Fitzmaurice, in his obituary of McNair, *supra* note 10, xi.

[15] Holders of the Whewell Chair of International Law in Cambridge (established in 1868 'to lay down such rules and to suggest such measures as may tend to diminish the evils of war and finally to extinguish war between nations'): 1869 Harcourt; 1887 Maine; 1888 Westlake; 1908 Oppenheim; 1920 Pearce-Higgins; 1935 McNair; 1938 Lauterpacht; 1955 Jennings; 1981 Bowett; 1992 Crawford. British judges of the ICJ: McNair 1946–1955; Lauterpacht 1955–1960; Fitzmaurice 1960–1973; Waldock 1973–1981; Jennings 1982–1995; Higgins 1995–.

and the English love of detail'.[16] Brierly heralded it, writing in 1927, as 'the most complete and systematic account of contemporary public international law yet published.'[17] And a similar theme unites a recent series of essays on Oppenheim's work and influence by Matthias Schmoeckel: the success of Oppenheim's work, Schmoekel argues, is due 'to a clear systematic approach underlying Oppenheim's legal theory'.[18] Crawford also links the success of Oppenheim's *Treatise* with the fact that it was 'clear, accessible and well-organized.'[19] And although Martti Koskenniemi attributes the influence of Oppenheim's *Treatise* to Lauterpacht rather than Oppenheim, he too argues (of the Lauterpacht editions) that 'there are no contestants to a more methodologically complete vision of the whole field of public international law.'[20]

So around what principles was the *Treatise* organised? What renders it clear, systematic and 'methodologically complete' in a way in which, these commentators imply, rival textbooks on international law were not? After all, the previous two generations of English speaking international lawyers before Oppenheim had produced a significant series of treatises on public international law by highly regarded scholars.[21] Each of these rival texts – with the qualified exception of Moore's *Digest*[22] – was systematic: to systematise an area of law is, after all, the aspiration of any textbook writer. What, then, was different about the principles around which Oppenheim organised his textbook? And why have later editions of Oppenheim endured? These two questions frame this essay.

---

[16] Janis, 'The New *Oppenheim*', 16 *Oxford Journal of Legal Studies* (1996) 330–331, referring to Westlake, reviewing the first volume of the first edition (21 *Law Quarterly Review* (1905) 432), on the 'special character' of the book which 'consists of the German mould in which the thought is cast, while the details coincide largely with those to which we are accustomed in English writings'.

[17] Brierly, 'Oppenheim', *supra* note 4.

[18] Schmoekel, 'The Internationalist as a Scientist and Herald', *supra* note 4, 701.

[19] J. Crawford, 'Public International Law in Twentieth Century England', *supra* note 3, 697; for the other reasons Crawford gives for its success, see below, section III.

[20] M. Kosekenniemi, 'Hersch Lauterpacht (1897–1960)' in J. Beatson and R. Zimmerman, (eds.), *supra* note 3, 602.

[21] For a full list of international law treatises published in the UK between 1800 and 1970, see the appendix to James Crawford's 'Public international law in Twentieth-century England', *supra* note 3, 702–706. For a discussion of Phillimore, Hall, Holland and Brierly see my 'Three Ways of Writing a Treatise on Public International Law: Textbooks and Teachers as a Contemporary Source of Public International Law' in A. Perreau-Saussine and J.B. Murphy (eds.), *The Nature of Customary Law: Philosophical, Historical and Legal Perspectives*, (Cambridge University Press, forthcoming 2006)

[22] *Cf.* Reisman, *supra* note 2, 259: 'As a title, the word 'digest' is really a misnomer. Digests of international law do almost no 'digesting'. Like the American casebook, they select and reproduce chunks of documents and cases relevant to particular problem areas that the decision maker is likely to encounter. In this sense, the digest is a useful counterweight to rule-oriented treatises. The documents and particularly the diplomatic correspondence show human beings applying policies and adapting institutional arrangements to every-changing situations. So despite its nominal jurisprudence, the digest is much more representative of the actual process of international decision making. On the other hand, the materials that are selected for inclusion and exclusion reflect policy choices. Documents and incidents that could be extremely relevant to subsequent practice may be suppressed or reproduced so selectively that they give the reader quite a different impression of what transpired.'

1. Oppenheim As a Noble Liar

In the Preface to the first edition of his *Treatise*, Oppenheim explains confidently:

> I have everywhere tried to establish either the opinion I approve or my own opinion as firmly as possible, but I have nearly always taken pains to put other opinions, if any, before my readers. The whole work, I venture to hope, contains those suggestive and convincing qualities which are required in a book for students. Yet I have, on the other hand, been careful to avoid pronouncing rules as established which are not yet settled. My book is intended to present International Law as it is, not as it ought to be.[23]

As Oppenheim acknowledges, international law is a system of customary law.[24] But writers of textbooks on customary law find themselves in a curious position: it is philosophically impossible to treat customary law – as Oppenheim explains he will do – as a system of clear, settled rules: there is no way of settling authoritatively the correct text or formulation of those rules. As Brian Simpson writes in a celebrated essay on English common law,

> we all know that no two legal treatises state the law in the same terms, there being a law of torts according to Street, and Heuston, and Jolowicz and James and the contributors to Clerk and Lindsell, and we buy them all *because* they are different. And what is true of the academics is true perhaps even more dramatically of the judges, who are forever disagreeing, often at inordinate length. . . . As a system of legal thought the common law then is inherently vague; it is a feature of the system that uniquely authoritative statements of the rules which, so the positivists tell us, comprise the common law, cannot be made.[25]

What is true of English law, to echo Simpson, is at least as true of public international law, on which not only academics and individual judges but also tribunals and courts disagree, similarly often at inordinate length.

There 'comes a time in the development of every civilised State', argues Oppenheim, when codification 'can no longer be avoided'; and with codification, the 'science of Law receives a fresh stimulus', a 'great deal of fresh and healthy blood is brought into the arteries of the body of the law in its totality' and a 'more uniform spirit enters into the law'.[26] For Oppenheim it 'was not before 1861 that a real attempt was made to show the possibility of codification' of international law. Central to this, in Oppenheim's account, was the 'draft code' published by his former teacher, Bluntschli, in 1868 and 'translated into the French, Greek, Spanish and Russian languages, and the Chinese Government produced an official Chinese translation as a

---

[23] Preface to Oppenheim, *supra* note 13, vol. I (1905) ix.

[24] E.g., *ibid*, 22.

[25] Simpson, 'The Common Law and Legal Theory', in A.W.B. Simpson (ed.) *Oxford Essays in Jurisprudence* vol. II (1973) 89–90.

[26] L. Oppenheim, *supra* note 13, vol. I (1905) 40.

guide for Chinese officials.'[27]. Wholesale codification was of course the end sought by late eighteenth and early nineteenth century law reformers.[28] In 1792 the French Convention resolved to create a Declaration of the Rights of Nations.[29] In England, Bentham had ambitious codification plans for both English and international law, each code to be structured around his master principle of utility.[30]

But any project aiming at total codification is doomed to fail.[31] To argue that a particular formulation is the correct view of a rule of customary law, as do teachers, text-book-writers, judges and counsel, is, as Simpson argues, 'to participate in the system, not simply to study it scientifically.'[32] No written law *can* give exhaustive directions on its own interpretation, so customary rules and practices will be needed not just to resolve 'a fault that codification has made'[33] but to guide judicial interpretation – and these guiding customary rules and practices will themselves be subject to change and development through interpretation.[34] Codify it, repeal it, abolish it; some form of customary law will inevitably reappear. The only question for a treatise writer is that of what view to take, what account to assume of the nature of this customary law.

Four rival accounts of the nature of customary law underpin rival treatises on international law, and it is the last of these four accounts which I will argue Oppenheim assumes.[35] For a sceptic, customary law is but a disguise for the further-ance of writers' or judges' motives, motives which are usually self-interested and 'sinister'. For a mid-wife, rules of customary law become manifest or emerge thanks to a spirit sustaining that customary system and those (the mid-wives) who stand by to deliver its rules using only formal rules of reason. For a natural lawyer, rules of customary law are ultimately anchored in principles of justice or natural law

---

[27] *Ibid*, 36.

[28] For an international law context see: M. Koskenniemi, *The Gentle Civilizer of Nations: the Rise and Fall of International Law 1870–1960* (2002), ch.1 and 2.

[29] Having charged Abbé Grégoire to draft the declaration, in 1795 the Convention rejected the principles he laid out as a twenty-one article code.

[30] On the Benthamite legislator see: R. Harrison, *Bentham* (1983) 106–166; D. Lieberman, *The Province of Legislation* (1989) 257–290; Schofield, 'Jeremy Bentham: Legislator of the World' in M.D.A. Freeman (ed.), 51 *Current Legal Problems* (1998) 115 (reprinted in G. Postema (ed.), *Bentham: Moral, Political and Legal Philosophy*, vol. II (2002), 126–129); Perreau-Saussine 'Bentham and the boot-strappers of Jurisprudence', 63 *Cambridge Law Journal* (2004) 346.

[31] *Cf.* G. Postema, explicitly developing Simpson's argument in his study of Bentham: 'what the courts *do* has an important (though not necessarily decisive) impact on what the law *is* and what it requires' in G. Postema, *Bentham and the Common Law Tradition* (1986) 456–457.

[32] Simpson, *supra* note 25, 97.

[33] L. Oppenheim, *supra* note 13, vol. I (1905) 41.

[34] *Cf.* N. Simmonds, *The Decline of Juridical Reason* (1984) esp. 117–8; R. Dworkin, *Law's Empire* (1986). *N.B.* this point has no necessary link with the doctrine of precedent. On this last point see in particular Goodhart, 'Precedent in English and Continental Law', 50 *Law Quarterly Review* (1934) 53–54.

[35] On the other three accounts, see my 'Three Ways of Writing a Treatise', *supra* note 21.

(including a principle recognising the moral value of a stable system of rules). And for a noble liar, arguments in terms of rules of customary law veil law making by benign (*not* self-interested) writers or judges.

Oppenheim's approach, I will argue, is that of a noble liar. For a noble liar, lawyers must discriminate between two kinds of customary rules, rejecting on their demerits those customary rules which are inimical to moral or political reasoning. This discrimination between valuable and dangerous customs will be made in terms of principles which the noble liar claims are manifest within and learnt from engagement with the set of customary rules with which she is working. Her account of customary law will be structured around these principles, conferring a higher status on customary rules in which the principles are manifest (so that these higher status rules prevail over lower-order inconsistent rules). She will also offer an account of how she would aim to adjudicate between or reconcile apparently conflicting customary rules (including those with the special higher status).

A natural lawyer believes that these crucial principles are principles of justice or natural laws. But a noble liar believes that there is no (or at least not yet sufficient) *philosophical* justification for the principles on which she nonetheless relies: no rationally justifiable natural laws or moral principles have yet been found, and so at present discrimination between customary legal principles requires *political* rather than rational judgment.[36] For a noble liar, particularly in the realm of the regulation of state power, such judgments are generally more safely made by an aristocracy of judges rather than by the very politicians who exercise that power, although for political reasons, *this* belief is generally best kept quiet and their position better presented as that of a natural lawyer or of a mid-wife delivering principles that are conceived within (rather than simply evidenced and developed within) customary practice. For noble liars, analysis of customary practices is unlikely to offer a set of rational constitutional principles, but in so far as (and only in so far as) some set of principles is needed to sustain legal and political stability, it should be imposed as if some kind of 'higher' or 'better' law did actually underpin international law. The noble liar – or in contemporary terms 'spin doctor' – deliberately weaves a misleading story in defence of what she believes to be a politically noble position.

A. *The Principles Underpinning Oppenheim's First Edition*

What, then, distinguished the early editions of Oppenheim's *Treatise* from those of its rivals? Oppenheim claims in the first edition that there is 'no English treatise

---

[36] *Cf.* J. Waldron, 'Legal and Political Philosophy', in J. Coleman & S. Shapiro (eds.), *The Oxford handbook of Jurisprudence and Philosophy of Law* (2002) 377: 'In the contested issues of politics, objective truth never manifests itself *in propria persona*; it presents itself always as someone's opinion, usually someone's contested opinion; and it cannot be made politically effective, nor the condition for any political action unless someone's determination is taken for practical purposes as the truth of the matter.'

which provides such a bibliography' as those he gives at the start of each of section of his discussion (listing relevant treatises and monographs). But while this format (giving bibliographical lists) and the structure of his book *were* different from those found in Phillimore or Hall, it follows closely standard German treatments of the time.[37] And Oppenheim's range of references is far narrower and thinner than that found in Phillimore – Oppenheim himself acknowledges later in his *Treatise* that 'Generations to come will consult Phillimore's volumes on account of the vast material they contain and the sound judgment they exhibit.'[38] Particularly strikingly, Oppenheim's table of cases in the first volume of his *Treatise* is only one side long, citing fifty-four cases – as against, for example, nine sides of cases cited in only the first of Phillimore's four volumes.

Oppenheim, unlike either Phillimore or Hall[39], offered a confidently and explicitly positivist account of international law as a matter of empirical fact: 'We know nowadays that a Law of Nature does not exist. Just as the so-called Natural Philosophy had to give way to real natural science, so the Law of Nature had to give way to jurisprudence, or the philosophy of the positive law. Only a positive Law of Nations can be a branch of the science of law.'[40]

International law, for Oppenheim, must be treated as inherently separable from moral principles, natural law and national legal systems:

> If we exclude the law of nature and what is called 'natural' international law altogether, and if we consider international law real law, the method to be applied by the science of international law can be no other than the positive method.... The positive method is that applied by the science of law in general, and it demands that whatever the aims and ends of a worker and researcher may be, he must start from the existing recognized rules of international law as they are to be found in the customary practice of the states or in law-making conventions.[41]

---

[37] Reisman, *supra* note 2, 263 notes that Oppenheim 'largely follows the table of contents of Johann Bluntschli's work on international law'.

[38] L. Oppenheim, *supra* note 13, vol. I (1905) 91.

[39] Thomas Holland (1835–1926) had produced a short volume of explicitly positivist essays on international law, entitled *Studies in International Law* (1898), three years after Oppenheim's arrival in England – and the year in which Oppenheim was appointed as a lecturer at the LSE. Although Oppenheim lists Holland's *Studies in International Law* (1898) and his much more famous *Elements of Jurisprudence* (1882) as books 'very often referred to' in his own *Treatise*, and as such ones for which he uses abbreviations, he does not discuss Holland in his summary of British Treatises or of the early twentieth century development of international law, (*ibid*, 87, 90–93). Holland is mentioned *only* twice in the short bibliographical references, in both cases referring to theoretical (and positivist) discussions in the *Studies* on the 'Relations between international and municipal law' (*ibid*, 25, citing *Studies* at 176–200) and on 'The Science of the Law of Nations' (*ibid*, 76, citing *Studies* 1–58, 168–175).

[40] Oppenheim, *supra* note 13, vol. I (1905) 92.

[41] Oppenheim, 'The Science of International Law: Its Task and Method', 3 *American Journal of International Law* (1908) 333.

Such customary practice, asserts Oppenheim, just *is* a matter of rules: 'Just as we see streams of water running over the earth, so we see, as it were, streams of rules running over the area of law.' The existence of such rules is a matter of fact, a matter for empirical observation: rules of law 'rise from facts in the historical development of a community.' As an example, Oppenheim offers Great Britain where 'a good many rules of law rise every year from Acts of Parliament. "Source of law" is therefore the name for a historical fact out of which rules of conduct rise into existence and legal force.'[42] Historical 'facts' however must act in tandem with something extra: elsewhere Oppenheim recognises that they generate rules thanks to pre-existing customs, so that 'all statute or written law is based on unwritten law in so far as the power of Parliament to make statute law is given to Parliament by unwritten law'.[43] Such a custom exists 'when a clear and continuous habit of doing certain actions has grown up under the aegis of the conviction that these actions are, according to International Law, obligatory or right' – as distinct from 'usage' which is a habit without this conviction.[44]

What then is this crucial 'conviction' which transforms general usage into an obligatory rule? At this point, Oppenheim would distinguish between moral and legal rules. A rule is a moral rule, he states, 'if by common consent of the community it applies to conscience and to *conscience only*; whereas, on the other hand, a rule is a rule of law, if by *common consent* of the community it shall eventually be *enforced by external power*.'[45] By enforcement, Oppenheim explains that given 'the absence of a central authority for the enforcement of the rules of the Law of Nations, the States have to take the law into their own hands. Self-help, and intervention on the part of other States which sympathise with the wronged one, are the means by which the rules of the Law of Nations can be and actually are enforced.'[46]

So a practice or usage of states is at best a moral rule if 'common consent' recognises it as a rule but not an enforceable one: common consent that a state may use force in defence of the rule transforms that usage into a rule of law. How then is this crucial 'common consent' to be discerned in the case of rules of international law? For Oppenheim, it is not found in the scholarly Anglican and civilian consensus of Phillimore, nor in the pragmatic English consensus of Hall: common consent is found in

> the express or tacit consent of such an overwhelming majority of the members that those who dissent are of no importance whatever, and disappear totally from the view of one who looks for the will of the community as an entity in contradistinction to the wills of its members. The question whether there be such a common consent in a special case, is *not a question of theory, but of fact only*. It is a matter of observation and

---

[42] Oppenheim, *supra* note 13, vol. I (1905) 15.
[43] *Ibid*, 4.
[44] *Ibid*, 17.
[45] *Ibid*, 4 (emphasis added).
[46] *Ibid*, 9.

appreciation, and not of logical and mathematical decision, just as is the well-known question, How many grains make a heap?[47]

Here then Oppenheim presents his role as one of delivering from out of state practice a set of rules recognised and accepted by those states themselves. But unlike the mid-wife, Oppenheim insists that what he is doing remains throughout a matter of observing empirical, scientific facts. The contents and existence of rules of international law can be determined without moral evaluation, although discerning those rules will require reference to states' views which themselves *will* often be manifest within particular moral or political or domestic legal arguments.

Oppenheim presents social reality as a matter of fact from start to end – although those facts include the meanings or subjective intentions with which particular governments, diplomats, legislators or courts act. For Oppenheim, although Phillimore was 'a powerful author . . . who may on the whole be called a Positivist of the same kind as Martens and Klüber', he 'applies the natural Law of Nations to full up the gaps of the positive'. As such, these writers' works were inadequate, based ultimately on 'no real Positivism since these authors recognised a natural Law of Nations, although they did not make much use of it.'[48] Even Bluntschli's book 'must, in spite of the world-wide fame of its author, be consulted with caution, because it contains many rules which are not yet recognised rules of the Law of Nations.'[49]

Oppenheim fears that basing international law on natural law arguments can offer 'a breach through which the deniers of the law of nations can easily come in and attack the very existence of international law': they are 'not only without any value whatever, but directly detrimental' because they distract a writer from what should be a focus on real practice, real facts, and so real law. 'There is', writes Oppenheim, 'no better and quicker way to the realization of international ideals than to present the facts of international life and the rules of international law as they really are. For the knowledge of the realities enables the construction of realizable truths, in contradistinction to hopeless dreams.'[50] A theory of natural law 'weakens the eyes of those who profess it', it 'prevents the criticism of the existing positive law' and 'constantly mixes up the past, the present and the future': its place 'is no longer in our textbooks, law schools, and universities, but in the museums where the scientific tools are preserved with which future generations did their best to lay the foundation of our present scientific knowledge.'[51] Not only are natural law theories untenable (a claim which Oppenheim backs up by arguing both that 'the innumerable systems' of natural lawyers conflict, and that 'it is impossible

---

[47] *Ibid*, 11.
[48] *Ibid*, 91–92, continuing: 'Real positivism must entirely avoid a natural law of Nations.'
[49] *Ibid*, 92–93.
[50] L. Oppenheim 'The Science of International Law', *supra* note 41, 355.
[51] *Ibid*, 329.

to find a law which has its roots in human reason only and is above legislation and
customary law'), but they obscure the real foundations of international law in customary practices and 'law-making conventions': 'It requires much more scientific
skill to expose the real existing rules of international law, to lay bare their history
and real meaning, and to criticize them in the light of reason, justice, and the
requirements of the age, than to teach the rules of the law of nature in the clouds.'[52]

Yet in focussing on the understandings and judgments of state officials,
Oppenheim is not concerned with the non-arbitrary verification of an empiricist:
he is acting as an interpreter, aiming to tease out shared meanings, understandings
and judgments. He aims to attain a greater clarity of understanding than the officials involved – an understanding that enables him to show not only 'how things
have grown in the past, but also to extract a moral for the future out of the events
of the past'. Five morals, Oppenheim argues, 'can be said to be deduced from the
history of the development of the Law of Nations':

(i)   first, and principally, that international law can exist 'only if there is an equi-
      librium, a balance of power, between the members of the Family of Nations.'
(ii) That international politics, and in particular the use of force, should be con-
      ducted 'on the basis of real State interests' *rather than* to preserve dynasties or
      to act 'in favour of legitimacy'.
(iii) 'that the principle of nationality is of such force that it is fruitless to stop its
      victory', so international politics should 'enforce the rule that minorities of
      individuals of another race shall not be outside the law, but shall be treated on
      equal terms with the majority'.
(iv) That 'every progress in the development of International Law wants due time
      to ripen' although the establishment of the permanent Court of Arbitration
      in the Hague and the codification of parts of the Law of Nations (which 'will
      in due time arrive' following the Geneva Conventions on land warfare) will
      'make the legal basis of international intercourse firmer, broader, and more
      prominent than before'.
(v)   'that the progressive development of International Law depends chiefly upon
      the standard of public morality on the one hand, and, on the other, upon eco-
      nomic interests' and that it may 'fearlessly be maintained that an immeasura-
      ble progress is guaranteed to International Law, since there are eternal moral
      and economic factors working in its favour.'[53]

Oppenheim later added two more morals, both defending a notion of an international rule of law: one new moral connects the progress of international law with the
'victory everywhere of constitutional government over autocratic government, or,

---

[52] *Ibid*, 330.
[53] L. Oppenheim, *supra* note 13, vol. I (1905) 51.

what is the same thing, of democracy over autocracy'; the other links the progress of international law with the 'prevailing' of 'the legal school of international jurists' (who aim at 'codification of firm, decisive, and unequivocal rules of International Law' and 'work for the establishment of international courts') over the 'diplomatic school' (which 'considers International Law to be, and prefers it to remain, rather a body of elastic principles than of firm and precise rules').[54]

These morals show how Oppenheim's work was consciously intended to *alter* state officials' actions (often radically) in so far as his 'morals' would be internalised as their own self-interpretations:[55] no more striving at hegemony nor use of force to preserve dynasties or to restore a legitimate successor; minorities to be treated on equal terms with the majority; the Court of Arbitration and general codification projects to be supported as part of a fearless confidence that international law (and, with the later morals, the rule of international law more generally) will 'progress'.

What then is the point of Oppenheim's repeated insistence that he is acting as a scientific observer, delivering rules of international law which do *not* rely on – and are quite separable from – any moral or political principles? One way of understanding Oppenheim's claim is as an insistence on the separation of correct, objective principles which *are* a source of scientific law from the conventionally accepted but unfounded principles of natural lawyers. In Oppenheim's case, these scientific principles build on a belief in there being a society of states, in the importance of a balance of power, and his 'faith in the progress of nations towards peace and civilization'. The science of international law can be conducted 'only by those workers who are imbued with the idealistic outlook on life and matters':

> He who believes that the essential characteristic of law is the policeman who protects it is not properly fit to work at the science of international law, nor is he who has not a deep-rooted faith in the progress of nations towards peace and civilization. International law is at present an unfinished and uncrowned system and building. He who has no faith in the possibility of accomplishing it is not wanted among us. We require men possessed of that idealism which sits down to historical research because it sees the present and the future in the past, and the past in the present and future, although it does not confound them; which criticises the existing law for the purpose, not of pulling it to pieces, but of preparing its improvement and its codification; which believes in the good instincts of the masses and therefore helps to popularize

---

[54] For a thought-provoking (and generally sympathetic) discussion of Oppenheim's morals, see Kingsbury 'Legal Positivism', *supra* note 4 and Schmoekel's series of essays, *supra* note 4.

[55] *Cf.* Taylor, 'Interpretation and the Sciences of Man', 97 *Review of Metaphysics* (1971) 3, reprinted in C. Taylor, *Philosophy & the Human Sciences: Philosophical Papers*, vol. 2 (1985) 27. How then is the superiority of one position, one interpretation, one set of common meanings to be shown? Taylor relies on the classical argument that 'from the more adequate position one can understand one's own stand and that of one's opponent, but not the other way around' but he acknowledges that this argument can only have weight for those in the superior position (at 53–4). Those in the less adequate position will be told that it is not simply that they do not understand, but that they will need to change themselves *in order* to understand: 'Our capacity to understand is rooted in our own self-definitions hence in what we are.'

international law in the hope of thereby improving international relations and working for the cause of peace.[56]

This equates scientific principles with truly moral principles or 'ideals', and so returns
us to the core of natural law theories – making Oppenheim into a defender of a liberal natural law theory, one more progressive or less conservative than (for example)
Phillimore's.[57] Oppenheim's 'science' is then but a rival natural law theory.[58]

But I suggest that Oppenheim's insistence on the separability of his legal account
from moral claims is best understood as a noble lie, a *political* claim which he knows
is untrue. His account *does* depend upon and is structured around specific moral and
political principles, ones which Oppenheim invokes to encourage commitment to
international law in states whose illiberal practices he hopes international law will
transform. Opinions of 'famous writers' on international law, he explains, 'may influence the growth of International Law' by 'creating usages which gradually turn into
custom'.[59] But Oppenheim believes his principles need to be disguised or hidden as
the science of international law will succeed only if 'all authors endeavour to write in
a truly international and independent spirit, and [...] to *keep in the background* their
individual ideas concerning *politics, morality, humanity, and justice*.'[60]

A classic noble liar would see her noble lie, her purportedly scientific principles,
as a temporary substitute for her enlightened ideas, ones which it is hoped philosophers will one day find a convincing way of justifying. In the meantime, the separability claim encourages commitment to her account of international law and so to
enlightened principles, while reassuring governments of the separability of law
from ('positive', 'subjective') morality. Law would then encourage a gradual conversion from conventional practices into enlightened ones respecting Oppenheim's
'background' ideals (for which no sufficient justification has yet been found): the

---

[56] L. Oppenheim, 'The Science of International Law', *supra* note 41, 355–356.
[57] This seems to be the category into which Lauterpacht would place Oppenheim. H.
Lauterpacht, *Private Law Sources and Analogies of International Law* (1927) 33: 'Being unable to
afford the consistency of totally ignoring both private and natural law, [modern positivist writers who
reject both as sources of international law] put in their place 'the reason of the thing', 'the demands of
logic', and 'the principles of general jurisprudence. . . . There remains, however, the danger that this
general jurisprudence might become a purely abstract philosophy of law – the very natural law from
which they wish to purify the science of international law'.
[58] *Cf.* J. Brierly, *The Law of Nations* (1928) 9: 'Modern legal writers, especially in England, have
sometimes ridiculed the conception of a law of nature, or they have recognized its great historical
influence but treated it as a superstition which the modern world has rightly discarded. Such an attitude, however, proceeds from a misunderstanding of the medieval idea; for under a terminology
which has ceased to be familiar to us the phrase stands for something which no progressive system of
law either does or can discard'. For Brierly, the range of cases and rival positions which natural law
arguments have been used to support is not an argument against the conception of natural law itself,
ibid: 'there was nothing arbitrary about the conception itself, any more than a text of Scripture is arbitrary, because the Devil may quote it.'
[59] L. Oppenheim, *supra* note 13, vol. I (1905) 24
[60] L. Oppenheim, 'The Science of International Law', *supra* note 41, 354 (emphasis added).

grounds of political or moral and legal judgment (*mores* and enlightened principles) will eventually coincide as law transforms discordant conventional practices and beliefs into harmonious enlightened ones.

This in effect is the picture of Oppenheim presented by Schmoekel, who argues that Oppenheim 'had to discuss the principles so that the new law became intelligible.' For Schmoekel, it 'is of little importance whether science is regarded as an independent source of law or – as Oppenheim did – as a means to perceive the law so that it gradually becomes accepted through consent or custom.'[61] The summary of Oppenheim's position is apposite, but the comment seems less so: as we have seen, Oppenheim argues that common consent or acceptance that violations of a particular practice can be punished is the only marker that distinguishes a rule of international law from other customary rules and practices. If the principles 'perceived' by Oppenheim are not yet accepted, let alone accepted as enforceable principles, then on Oppenheim's own definition they are at best political or moral rather than legal principles.

A more radically positivist noble liar would believe she has no grounds for expecting a satisfactory justification *ever* to be found for her enlightened liberal principles: both the separability claim and her enlightened principles themselves are noble lies, but those who are sufficiently noble to choose to pursue those enlightened principles regardless will seek to impose them through textbook writing and dissembling judgments, and to persuade those less noble than themselves that whatever 'moral' principles those others hold, enlightened principles are a necessary source of *law*.

There are grounds for fitting Oppenheim into this last category. For Oppenheim, moral rules result from a concordance of free, conscientious opinions: a rule 'is a moral rule, if by common consent of the community it applies to conscience and to conscience only'[62]. But, as Kingsbury highlights, Oppenheim's view of the role of public opinion in international law matters 'was at the cautious end of the spectrum prevalent in late-Victorian and early Edwardian England: a liberal disposition to regard it as part of achieving progress in law and public policy, epitomized by Dicey's *Law and public opinion in England*, but a lack of conviction that a truly international public opinion was really possible.'[63] On Oppenheim's own account of the common consent or opinion needed to justify a moral rule, he seems to have thought that a satisfactory justification for his liberal principles would be found when, and only when, those principles came to be widely accepted – something which would happen when, and only in so far as, public opinion came to be transformed in line with his fifth moral. And for Oppenheim, the best hope for this transformation was through the teachings of his textbook.

---

[61]   Schmoekel, 'Consent and Caution', *supra* note 4, 288 and footnote 27.
[62]   *E.g.*, L. Oppenheim, *supra* note 13, vol. I (1905) 8.
[63]   Kingsbury, 'Legal Positivism', *supra* note 4, 411, quoting A. Carty, *The Decay of International Law* (1986) 90.

B. A Case Study: Oppenheim's Account of the Relation Between English Law and Public International Law

I referred above to four different accounts of customary law, each one of which might be assumed by a treatise-writer on international law. For a sceptic, the grounding of rules in their continued reception is but a disguise for the furtherance of an elite's self-interested, 'sinister' motives. For a mid-wife (like Hall), the continued acceptance of a rule of customary law manifests the benign spirit sustaining that legal system. For a natural lawyer (like Phillimore or Brierly), the continued acceptance of a rule of customary law is evidence of its links with anchoring principles of justice or natural law (including a principle recognising the moral value of a stable system of rules). And for a noble liar like Holland or Oppenheim, arguments in terms of the continued acceptance of a rule of customary law veil law-making by benign (*not* self-interested) judges. One area where these different understandings of the nature of customary law come to the fore is in treatment of the relation between English law and public international law.

The difficulty *and* interest in this area is that any treatment of this question must suppose an account both of the nature of customary international law and of the nature of the Common law. Both a natural lawyer and a mid-wife would expect to be able to show a direct link between international law and the common law. For the mid-wife this would be so in so far as the benign spirit which she believes sustains the development of customary international law is a spirit shared by English Common law or vice-versa; for a writer like Hall the benign spirit sustaining the development of English (and to a lesser extent American) Common law spilling over into nurturing the emergence of a system of customary international law. A natural lawyer would expect to find the same natural laws interlinking domestic and international law, although only in the rare cases where there is but one way of deriving a legal principle directly from a rule of natural law *and* where that legal principle is one that plays a role in both domestic and international law would she expect to show a direct connection.[64] (Developments or concretizations of natural laws at the international level she would also treat as sources for the common law and vice versa.)

A noble liar is likely to adopt either a noble liar's or a sceptic's approach to the Common law, depending on how far decisions of domestic courts can be invoked to further her political ends. For a writer like Oppenheim, treating the sovereignty of states as an underpinning principle of international law, a government *must* be treated as constrained only by its voluntarily assumed international obligations and unfettered by its own courts let alone by purportedly objective principles of justice

---

[64] Since those very principles will be central principles of procedural fairness or equity or of the law of murder, theft, marriage or contract, she is unlikely to need to establish that the principle is just in order to establish that it *is* part of the law – even though, a natural lawyer would argue, it is the justice of the principle that makes it so central to a particular branch of law.

or natural law. Sure enough, Oppenheim decrees that 'the Law of Nations can neither as a body nor in parts be *per se* a part of Municipal Law' because it 'lacks absolutely the power of altering or creating rules of Municipal Law': 'adoption' by municipal custom or statute is required, he argues, to transform a rule of international law into a rule of English law.[65] For Oppenheim this is not a matter of accepted practice but of principle, reflecting the fact that international law and municipal law are 'essentially different': the former is based on 'custom grown up within the Family of Nations and law-making treaties concluded by the members of that family' and the latter on 'custom grown up within the boundaries of the respective State and statutes enacted by the law-giving authority'; the former regulates relations between states, the latter relations between 'individuals under the sway of the respective State and the relations between this State and the respective individuals'; and while the latter is 'a law of a Sovereign over individuals subjected to his sway', the former 'is a law not above, but between Sovereign States, and therefore a weaker law.'[66] Decisions of municipal courts *cannot* 'directly concern international law' because it is the recognition or otherwise by 'the government of the land' rather than its courts 'which is decisive'.[67] For Oppenheim, a truly sovereign government must by definition be able to override decisions of its own courts: the will of a government must prevail over arguments of its courts, while in the spirit of internationalism, the will of no one government can prevail over a majority consensus.[68]

Yet having insisted on this principle, Oppenheim also argues that 'practices' of municipal courts are 'of the greatest importance for the science of international law'. A 'universal practice' means 'it may be taken for granted that a universally recognized rule of international law is at its background', while if decisions of municipal courts diverge greatly, 'the science of international law can examine the different decisions; can point out the relative value of the different groups; can single one out as the most adequate, reasonable and just; can thereby foster the growth of future unanimity'.[69] In addressing conflicts of these kinds, writers on international law dealing with decisions of municipal courts are prone to commit one of two 'grave sins of method'. Either, like Hall, they 'fall on their knees and worship the decisions of the courts of their own country, while they abuse the differing decisions of foreign courts.'[70] Hall's focus on the practice of English courts and the interests of the UK was incompatible with the perspective needed for a compelling account of international law, one which must be motivated by 'the conviction that all the

---

[65] Oppenheim, *supra* note 13, vol. I (1905) 26.
[66] *Ibid*, 25–6.
[67] Oppenheim, 'The Science of International Law', *supra* note 41, 340.
[68] On Oppenheim's notion of civilised States and on the role assumed for power politics in his account of international law, see generally Kingsbury, 'Legal Positivism', *supra* note 4.
[69] Oppenheim, 'The Science of International Law', *supra* note 41, 339.
[70] *Ibid*, 340–341.

civilised States form one Community throughout the world in spite of the various factors which separate the nations from one another; the conviction that the interests of all the nations and States are indissolubly interknitted, and that, therefore, the Family of Nations must establish international institutions for the purpose of guaranteeing a more general and a more lasting peace than existed in former times.'[71] Or, continues Oppenheim, writers tend to 'pile case upon case ... without sifting them and without abstracting the rules they are supposed to bring into view', a practice that is 'without any value for the science of international law, unless it is done only for the purpose of collecting material.'[72]

Oppenheim himself cites not one case or example of state practice to defend his own position on the relation between international and domestic law,[73] nor to defend his insistence that municipal courts 'cannot by themselves alter the Municipal Law to meet the requirements of the Law of Nations.'[74]

Yet although this view was not taken by Oppenheim's predecessor, John Westlake,[75] in terms of twentieth century English writers on the question, Oppenheim might appear to be in good company. The correct view, writes Brierly in 1935, is that 'international law is not a part, but is one of the sources, of English law.'[76] The 'modern view', echoes Holdsworth in 1938, 'is that international law is not a part, but a source, of English law'.[77] 'Rather than saying that international law is part of the law of England, a kind of subdivision thereof', reiterates John Collier, 'it is more accurate to regard it as a *source* of English law. . . . This was all pointed out

---

[71]　L. Oppenheim, *The League of Nations and its Problems* (1919) 12.

[72]　Oppenheim, 'The Science of International Law', *supra* note 41, 340–341.

[73]　He offers a few to US domestic practice and law as an example of a state which he argues has 'adopted' the law of Nations.

[74]　L. Oppenheim, *supra* note 13, vol. I (1905) 28. The British case of *The Franconia (R v Keyn)* often cited by 'transformationists' as the leading case on this question Oppenheim treats as wrongly decided, arguing that where a state has not renounced its rights under international law – as here, concerning maritime jurisdiction – 'its courts ought to presume that, since by the Law of Nations the jurisdiction of a State does extend over its maritime belt, their Sovereign has tacitly consented to that wider range of its jurisdiction.' (*Ibid*, 29).

[75]　'The English courts must enforce rights given by international law as well as those given by the law of the land in its narrower sense, so far as they fall within their jurisdiction in respect of parties or places, subject to the rules that the king cannot divest or modify private rights by treaty (with the possible exception of treaties of peace or treaties equivalent to those of peace), and that the courts cannot question acts of state (or, in the present state of the authorities, draw consequences from them against the Crown). The international law meant is that which at the time exists between states, without prejudice to the right and duty of the courts to assist in developing its acknowledged principles in the same manner in which they assist in developing the principles of the common law.' Westlake, 'Is International Law Part of the Law of England?', 22 *Law Quarterly Review* (1906) 14, reprinted in L. Oppenheim (ed.), *Collected Papers* (1914) 518.

[76]　Brierly, 'International Law in England', 51 *Law Quarterly Review* (1935) 31.

[77]　W.S. Holdsworth, *A History of English Law*, vol. X (1938) 372–3.

by the late J.L. Brierly many years ago. There is really no mystery about it at all and there is no need for doctrinal squabbles to enter into the matter.'[78]

But each of the arguments defending Oppenheim's position in the previous paragraph can be traced back to the direct influence of Oppenheim himself. Both Collier and Holdsworth rely on Brierley – and, in Holdsworth's case, the historian Adair, whom I discuss below. Brierley in turn invokes an article by Edwin Dickinson and a book by Piccioto. And, as I will show below, the arguments of Dickinson, Piccioto and Adair can all be traced directly back to one source: Oppenheim.

Dickinson, in his 1930 article 'Changing concepts and the doctrine of incorporation', writes, directly echoing Oppenheim's 'history' of the law of nations, that:

> In the 18th century, judicial concepts of the law of nations were dominated by concepts of the law of nature. In the 19th century the law of nations was founded increasingly upon usage sanctioned by consent. . . . The law of nations was necessarily and literally a part of national law in the 18th century, since the two systems were assumed to rest in their respective spheres upon the same immutable principles of natural justice. In the 19th century, with changing concepts of law and of the limitations of judicial method, the doctrine of incorporation assumed more modest proportions. The law of nations became a source, rather than an integral part, of the national system.[79]

The only citation Dickinson gives for this last claim is a reference to Piccioto's book.

And Cyril Moses Picciotto's short book, *The relation of international law to the law of England and of the United States: a study*, turns out to be an elaboration of his rather crude Whewell Scholarship dissertation, writing at and under the encouragement of and with an introduction by Oppenheim.[80] Picciotto quotes frequently from Oppenheim's second edition, insisting (with the triumph of positivism pushed back by a century) that:

> The Positive writers had not much influence in the seventeenth century, during which the Naturalists and Grotians carried the day, but their time came in the eighteenth century. . . . It is not too much to say that the modern view (dating, roughly, from the middle of the last century) is now predominantly supreme, and that the basis of

---

[78] Collier, 'Is International Law really part of the Law of England?', 38 *International and Comparative Law Quarterly* (1989) 935. Main cases invoked by 'transformationists': *R. v Keyn (The Franconia)* (1876) 2 Ex D. 63; *West Rand Gold Mining Co. v R.* [1905] 2 KB 391; *Mortensen v Peters* (1906) 8 F. (JC) 93 (Scottish High Court of Judiciary); *Commercial and Estates Co. of Egypt v Board of Trade* [1925] 1 KB 271; *Chung Chi Cheung v The King* [1939] AC 160. Main cases (up to *Trendtex*) relied on by incorporationists: *Barbuit's case* (1737) Cas. temp. Talbot 281; *Triquet v Bath* (1764) 3 Burr. 1478; *Heathfield v Chilton* (1767) 4 Burr. 2015; *Dolder v Lord Huntingfield* (1805) 11 Ves. 283; *Viveash v Becker* (1814) 3 M.& S. 284, 292, 298; *Wolff v Oxholm* (1817) 6 M.& S. 92, 100–6; *Novello v Toogood* (1823) 1 B.& C. 554; *De Wütz v Hendricks* (1824) 2 Bing. 314, 315; *Emperor of Austria v Day* (1861) 30 LJ Ch. 690, 702 (reversed on appeal on different point); *West Rand Gold Mining Co. v R.* [1905] 2 KB 391; *In re Ferdinand, Ex-Tsar of Bulgaria* [1921] 1 Ch. 107; *Trendtex Trading Corporation v Central Bank of Nigeria* [1977] 1 QB 529.

[79] Dickinson, 'Changing Concepts and the Doctrine of Incorporation', 26 *American Journal of International Law* (1932) 239.

[80] Picciotto was to be the first general editor of the British Yearbook of International Law.

International Law is now entirely Positivist; it rests upon fact and practice, and no longer upon speculation.[81]

In English law, he asserts – wrongly and so unsurprisingly without citation of any case law – that international law is 'a question of fact, like foreign law, for example; the Court takes no judicial cognisance of it. . . . It would follow from this that nothing which requires proof in a Court can be in itself law to be applied unless and until such proof has been satisfactorily adduced.'[82] Wrong in terms of English precedent though this position is, Picciotto's book was published and praised by Oppenheim, who inserted a marginal reference to it in the section on English law and international law in the typed lecture notes that served as the manuscript for the third edition of his *Treatise*.[83]

Adair's book, a history of ambassadorial and diplomatic immunity in the sixteenth and seventeenth centuries, is far richer than Picciotto's but remains a curious account, offering a detailed but partial survey of juristic or diplomatic reliance on established custom as 'another way of saying that the Positivist point of view is growing in importance'[84]. Where judges held that the law of nations is part of English law, Adair dismisses the precedents as factually unsound:

> Judicial rulings are merely evidences of the opinion current at the moment when they were made; many of them are entirely valueless because they were founded upon an ignorance of the facts or upon a wrong historical interpretation of them, yet the majority of lawyers still go on accepting and quoting them as though the wisdom of the judge was above that of other men, as though Midas-like his word turned dross to gold. It is too often forgotten that judges may make law, but they cannot make facts; their interpretation may be accepted for a time as legal history, but that does not make it true history.[85]

---

[81] C.M. Picciotto, *The Relation of International Law to the law of England and of the United States: A Study* (1915) 15–16.

[82] *Ibid*, 104–5.

[83] Trinity College, Cambridge: Add. ms. a338. The references appear in footnotes to section 21a, referring readers (on English law and international law) to Blackstone, Westlake, 'but chiefly Picciotto' – references that are then published in A. McNair, *Oppenheim's International Law, A Treatise*, vol. I (1928) 31 footnote 1.

[84] E.R. Adair, *The Exterritoriality of Ambassadors in the Sixteenth and Seventeenth Centuries* (1929) 38–39.

[85] *Ibid*, 2. On Mansfield's argument in *Triquet v Bath* that the act of 7 Anne, cap. 12, was not occasioned by any doubt 'whether the law of nations, particularly the part relating to public ministers, was not part of the law of England, and the infraction criminal', Adair writes that 'both parts of this opinion are entirely unsound':

   – 'before 1709 violation of an ambassador's special immunities was not criminal, punishment for such violation was a matter for prerogative action, and this part, at any rate, of the law of nations was not part of the common law.' (*Ibid*, 241).

   – 'executive action was, and to some degree still is, the only protection an ambassador can invoke, and reprimand of the over-zealous official may often be the beggarly cloak under which the government hedges its own connivance in the breach of international customs or its impotence to override the laws of the land.' (*Ibid*, 243).

Yet while dismissing as historically unsound cases that would otherwise under-mine Adair's thesis, he claims to show how in the mass of minor European cases in the 16th and early 17th centuries on exterritoriality of ambassadors in foreign countries, 'a body of precedent was built up that told in the ambassador's favour', that precedents, however historically ungrounded, *did* gradually make law and as such, 'Midas-like', *did* make history:[86]

> it is case law that is triumphant in this matter of the ambassador's exterritoriality; this branch, at least, of international law by the end of the seventeenth century can throw away the two crutches that had aided it in its earlier infirmities – Roman law and the law of Nature – and relying on case law alone can go forward with confidence to estab-lish the ambassador in the liberties that he enjoys today.[87]

Given the thesis driving Adair's account of the superseded 'crutches' of Civil law and natural law no longer needed by international law,[88] it is unsurprising to discover that the book is dedicated to 'the late Professor L. Oppenheim whose genial scholarship remains a fragrant memory in the hearts of his pupils'. Adair begins his Preface by explaining that 'To some considerable degree this book owes its inception to the late Professor Oppenheim of Cambridge, for it was he who first directed my attention to the need for a more detailed examination of the early history of International Law.'

Writing on Dicey on Parliamentary sovereignty, Simpson notes:

> it is very generally agreed today that there are no legal limitations upon the legislative competence of Parliament. The explanation for this is very largely connected with the fact that the basic book and the best written book, is Dicey, and it is around Dicey that nearly all lawyers study constitutional law. This has been so for a long time now. Dicey announced that it was the law that Parliament was omnicompetent, explained what this meant, and never devoted so much as a line to fulfilling the promise he made to demonstrate that this was so. The oracle spoke, and came to be accepted.[89]

Oppenheim's views on the relation between law and public opinion were very close to Dicey's. And just as Dicey oriented English public law around a principle of Parliamentary sovereignty, so Oppenheim offered an account of international law oriented around sovereign states, announcing that international law could neither

---

Cf. W.S. Holdsworth, *supra* note 77, 373, footnote. 3 & 4: Blackstone's view (agreeing, if less sweepingly, with Mansfield) 'is historically incorrect; but if Mansfield is right in his report of Holt's, Talbot's and Hardwicke's dicta, it was in accordance with the prevailing trend of legal opinion.'

[86] 'It is probably perfectly just to say that ambassadors established their immunities more as a result of political pressure than of any very strong respect for international law; but what of that? The fact that they were established is enough, for precedents make law.' (E.R. Adair, *supra* note 84, 251).

[87] *Ibid*, 253.

[88] *Cf.* L. Oppenheim, *supra* note 13, vol. I (1905) 53, 59: 'The Law of Nations supplied the crutches with whose help history has taught mankind to walk out of the institutions of the Middle Ages into those of modern times.... We know nowadays that a Law of Nature does not exist.... Only a positive Law of Nations can be a branch of the science of Law.'

[89] B. Simpson, *supra* note 32, 96.

as a body nor in parts be *per se* a part of Municipal Law without citing even one case to help demonstrate that this was so.

But in spite of the work of students writing under Oppenheim's direction, attempting to provide the necessary demonstration, English international lawyers – and English common law – have never quite come to accept Oppenheim's view on this particular issue. It is not endorsed by either McNair or Lauterpacht as will be seen below. Nor is it endorsed by some of the most eminent contemporary British writers on international law.[90] The final section of this essay considers briefly why Oppenheim, unlike Dicey, failed to make his position on this question into law.

2. Conclusion: Oppenheim's Influence

For one who adopts a noble liar's account of the nature of international law, Oppenheim's limited success in influencing debates on the relation between English and international law reflects his limited success as a noble liar. And this, it might be argued, was due in large part to the undermining of principles central to Oppenheim's noble lie by his own subsequent editors – who selected and defended principles in places contrary to Oppenheim's own ones.

On the specific question of the relation between English law and international law, McNair qualified Oppenheim's position, emphasising that 'it would be more correct to say that, when treaties require for their enforcement a modification of the law (common law or statutory) administered in English courts, the necessary statutes must first be passed'[91] and explaining in a later paper that 'We deny to international law any external authority which can override our own domestic law, but we recognize and apply it as part of our own law.'[92] Lauterpacht had earlier

---

[90] (Crawford, 'Case No. 9', 48 *British Yearbook of International and Comparative Law* (1976–1977) 353: 'Probably the *dicta* which have been regarded as embodying the 'doctrine of transformation' have been attempting to convey two distinct propositions, both qualifying rather than displacing the basic principle that international law is part of the law of England. First, attention is drawn to the need for clear and satisfactory evidence that the customary rule is as contended for, and that it has according to its terms legal effects as part of the municipal law. (The real point in *Thakrar* [*Regina v. Secretary of State ex parte Thakrar* [1974] QB 684 CAJ]). Secondly, emphasis is placed on the status of any such rule, once incorporated, as a distinct and independent rule of English law, subject to the normal rules of *stare decisis*'; I. Brownlie, *Principles of Public International Law* (2003) 41, 44: 'The dominant principle, normally characterized as the doctrine of incorporation, is that customary rules are to be considered part of the land and enforced as such, with the qualification that they are incorporated only so far as is not inconsistent with Acts of Parliament or prior judicial decisions of final authority. . . . The authorities, taken as a whole, support the doctrine of incorporation, and the less favourable dicta are equivocal to say the least. . . . Where it is appropriate to apply international law [. . .] the courts will take judicial notice of the applicable rules, whereas formal evidence is required of foreign (municipal) law.'

[91] L. Oppenheim, *supra* note 13, vol. I (1928) 31, footnote 3, referring readers on 'the whole subject' to his article in 9 *British Yearbook of International and Comparative Law* (1928) 59.

[92] A. McNair, 'The Method whereby International Law is made to prevail in Municipal Courts on an Issue of International Law', XXIX *Grotius Soc.* (1944) 21.

emphasised more directly, although with qualifications relating to statute, that 'the universal law of the *civitas maxima* is part and parcel of the law administered by the courts'.[93] And as editor of the *Treatise,* he reaffirms the 'classical' doctrine that 'all such rules of customary International Law as are either universally recognized or have at any rate received the assent of this country are *per se* part of the law of the land'.[94] Lauterpacht explicitly presents Oppenheim's position as stemming from a dualist view 'shared emphatically' with Triepel,[95] concluding that given rival monist views and so the 'wide divergence of doctrine it is necessary to inquire into the actual legal position in the principal countries' on the question. Citing the standard English cases, distinguishing 'dicta of some judges in *The Franconia* case', and speeding through a two side survey of US law with brief reference to France, Belgium, Switzerland and Germany, Lauterpacht concludes:

> The doctrine that International Law is part of the law of the land is a rule of positive law. For that reason alone, it ought not to be lightly abandoned. From a more general point of view it must be regarded as a beneficent doctrine inasmuch as it brings into prominence the fact that the obligations of International Law are, in the last resort, addressed to individual human beings. To that extent it serves as yet another explanation of the reason why the general principles of law and morality must also lie at the basis of rules of International Law.[96]

On the more general question of Oppenheim's positivist approach to the sources of international law, in the fourth edition (acknowledging in the preface his deep debt to 'my friend and former pupil, Dr H. Lauterpacht'), McNair appends a note to Oppenheim's insistence on the death of natural law:

> the rather uncompromising opinion expressed by the author on this point is no longer in keeping with recent developments in the science of International Law. It is now urged by many writers that:
>
> (a) International Law may, without losing its character as a legal science, be fittingly reinforced and fertilised by recourse to rules of justice, equity, and general principles of law, it being immaterial whether those rules are defined as a Law of Nature in the sense used by Grotius, or a modern Law of Nature with variable contents;

---

[93] H. Lauterpacht, 'Is International Law part of the Law of England?', XXV *Grotius Soc.* (1939) 51, reprinted in E. Lauterpacht (ed.), *Collected Papers of Hersh Lauterpacht*, vol. II (1975) 459, 555: 'The doctrine of incorporation ... does not imply the supremacy of international law. For it is through the will of the State that the general act of incorporation has taken place. The State may, with an effect binding upon municipal courts, set aside the Law of Nations thus generally incorporated. [...] But so long as that overriding will has not been clearly manifested, the universal law of the *civitas maxima* is part and parcel of the law administered by the courts.... The doctrine of adoption is not concerned with the question of the supremacy or otherwise of international law. Its essence is expressed in the fact of the direct operation of the Law of Nations. Statutes may override the common law. It has not been asserted on this account that the common law is not part of the law of the land.'

[94] L. Oppenheim, *supra* note 13, vol. I (1948) at s. 21a.

[95] *Ibid,* 20, footnote 1.

[96] *Ibid,* 41–42.

(b) that recourse to such rules is a frequent feature of the practice of States . . .;

(c) and that the rigid elimination of the Law of Nature from International Law has not been conducive to the development of the latter.[97]

Oppenheim's passage treating as characteristic of rules of law that 'they shall, if necessary, be enforced by external power' (as against rules of morality which apply to 'conscience only') McNair qualifies with a note emphasising that the distinction is 'by no means generally recognised, for there are many writers who deny to the rules of law the essential characteristic that they shall, if necessary, be enforced by external power.'[98] And although McNair leaves intact Oppenheim's list of 'morals' for international lawyers, a footnote qualifies Oppenheim's leading moral by drawing attention 'to the fact that, although the necessity of a balance of power is generally recognised, there are some writers of great authority who vigorously oppose this principle.'[99]

In Lauterpacht's editions, the body of Oppenheim's text is transformed at two of these three points. Oppenheim's passage on the distinction between legal and moral rules is retained (along with McNair's qualifying note). But Oppenheim's account of the victory of positivism becomes an account of a late nineteenth century blip:

> In denying the validity of sources of International Law other than the will of States [positivism] constituted yet another manifestation of the extreme doctrine of State sovereignty which, at that time, was typical of the science of law and of politics. So uncompromising was the positivist attitude that it denied the character of science to any other than the purely positive Law of Nations.[100]

In Lauterpacht's editions, three of Oppenheim's seven morals disappear. Lauterpacht retains only the two later 'rule of international law' morals and two of Oppenheim's original five morals, those on the equal treatment of minorities and on the link between the progressive development of international law and the 'rising of the standard of public morality and growth in importance of international economic interests'. Gone is Oppenheim's defence of the balance of power as crucial to the development of international law; gone too is the prohibition on striving at hegemony and on the use of force to preserve dynasties or to restore a legitimate successor; and gone is Oppenheim's emphasis on the 'due time to ripen' needed by International Law.

For a noble liar, this simply reflects a deep disagreement between Lauterpacht and Oppenheim on which principles *are* fundamental to a liberal internationalist vision of international law: Lauterpacht's noble lie is different but he makes no more attempt than does Oppenheim to justify his preferred principles. One of the

---

[97] L. Oppenheim, *supra* note 13, vol. I (1928) 121.

[98] *Ibid,* 7–8 (citing Vinogradoff).

[99] *Ibid,* 100 (citations omitted).

[100] L. Oppenheim, *supra* note 13, vol. I (1948) 102, footnote 2 explaining that this 'was also the view of the author of this book.'

richest and most thoughtful contemporary studies of Oppenheim concludes with an argument for a return to 'Oppenheim's fundamentals':

> there may be a case for brushing off and updating some of Oppenheim's fundamentals, rather than consigning them to dusty shelves. . . . If Oppenheim's positivism entrenches the *status quo* and disempowers visionaries, a formal international law based on consent has an increasing hold on the democratic imagination and on the growing number for whom anti-formalism is a specific or systematic threat.[101]

But the position Kingsbury seeks to reinstate seems *not* to be one founded on Oppenheim's seven morals. Kingsbury accepts Anthony Carty's objection to the triumph of Oppenheim's advocacy of the balance of power over his recognition that nationalism (the principle of nationality) 'is of such force that it is fruitless to try to stop its victory'; he concedes that 'The suspicion of some unevenness in Oppenheim's balance of power doctrine is reinforced by his position on the Monroe Doctrine – he not only accepted it as lawful, but seemed quite supportive of it, confining himself to observing that a balance of power will emerge in the Americas only if another great power grows up there.'[102] And most importantly of all, Kingsbury acknowledges that 'the balance of power has no fixed meaning; its usual justification by reference to history involves very subjective assessments; it entails self-judging that is largely a cloak for the interests of the powerful; it operates on the premise of a war of all against all; and it has caused at least as many wars as it was supposed to prevent.'[103]

In one sense, Kingsbury's conclusion is close to the one I have suggested. Oppenheim's very appeal to subsequent generations of readers, he argues, lies in 'the implicit sense' of 'the ethical view that legal positivism provides the best means for international lawyers to promote realization of fundamental political and moral values.'[104] Acknowledging that 'the positivist separation of law from moral argument and from politics is itself a moral and political position,'[105] Kingsbury presents his essay as a defence of normative positivism, a defence – invoking the work of Joseph Raz – of the political and moral worth of insisting on the separability of legal from political and moral argument. While this is not the place to challenge the coherence of Raz's normative positivism,[106] it is striking that Kingsbury argues:

> Oppenheim shared the widely held view that an international law expressive of general morality could help to *construct that morality* and shore up its generality. But he did *not* think that international law was strong enough to play this role *very boldly*, nor

---

[101] Kingsbury, 'Legal Positivism', *supra* note 4, 436.
[102] *Ibid*, 418 referring to A. Carty, *supra* note 63.
[103] *Ibid*, 419.
[104] *Ibid*, 401–2.
[105] *Ibid*, 103.
[106] On which see my chapters on J. Raz and G. Radbruch in my *Old Questions for New Natural Lawyers*, (Princeton, forthcoming 2007).

that the corpus of general morality was extensive or deep enough to propel rapid development of new legal rules.[107]

Here Kingsbury argues – again in accord with my earlier suggestions – not just that Oppenheim's account of international law was *of* political and moral worth, but that there are moral principles 'expressed' *within* Oppenheim's account of international law, principles which Oppenheim hoped would become part of a general public morality. It is one thing to say (with 'normative positivists') that there are moral and political reasons to separate law from morality; it is another to say (with my noble liars) that law is not (in spite of the previous claim) actually separated from moral and political argument. And given Kingsbury's dismissal of Oppenheim's morals, one is left suspecting that the real 'fundamental' that Kingsbury seeks to revive is the approach of a noble liar.[108]

One who offers a mid-wife's account of the nature of international law might offer a very different account of Oppenheim's influence. Just as a mid-wife hopes to stand by at the birth of a baby, intervening as little as possible and ideally not at all, so a mid-wife of international law believes that customary rules emerge from legal practices and customs and that the emergent rules will point their own way out of any apparent internal conflict. The reasoning of a text-book writer plays at most a formal role, drawing on literary traditions and formal structures or schemes to assist at and embellish the delivery of principles from within a spontaneously developed system of practice. On this account, knowledge of legal principles is unattainable without understanding their variable manifestations or actualisations in a wide range of sources: international lawyers' reasoning can only be guided by customary understandings, and the relevant principles will necessarily be manifest in or emerge from a careful study of customary practices.

For a mid-wife, to suggest that particular treatise writers could have an attributable influence on the development of international law is akin to suggesting that assisting at the delivery of a child makes one a biological parent. Thus James Crawford writes that 'there is a fundamental problem with assigning and measuring influence in international law, which is the ultimately collective character of so much of the work.' The collective work of international lawyers is rooted in a reflective professional tradition with a long history. Central to this tradition is a style and culture traceable to Grotius and other creators of modern international

---

[107] Kingsbury, 'Legal Positivism', *supra* note 4, 427 (emphasis added).

[108] See similarly, but with less philosophical sophistication, Schmoekel, 'The Internationalist as a Scientist and Herald', *supra* note 4, 703: 'Mankind's only chance is in the constant struggle for perfection. In this goal he is justified by the belief in the constant progress of mankind for the better. The primary sources of law and the subsidiary means have accordingly to be seen together: the analysis of the present is necessary for criticism; criticism is necessary for the evolution of law; [*Theorie der Rechtsqueelen* (1929, reprinted 1989)] calls this overt politics. I find this evaluation to be exaggerated and evolution is necessary for the acceptance of the present law.'

law and one 'still-existing, and no longer merely European'. It is a tradition that individuals 'may influence but hardly decisively', not least since 'its outcomes at any time, though expressed definitively in terms of current international law, are at the same time part of a process, and are to that extent provisional': 'Rise and fall, rise and fall, that is its enduring significance'. On this account, the history of Oppenheim's influence would be best treated as a history of the work of the different editors of the *Treatise*, themselves articulating a history of the work of a professional tradition, of advocates' and judges' 'shared attempt at addressing and resolving the problematic of order in a diverse world'.[109]

For a natural lawyer, the most fundamental role of a text-book writer is that of discriminating between valuable and dangerous customary practices, rejecting on their demerits those customary rules which are inimical to moral and political reasoning. This discrimination between valuable and dangerous customs she makes in terms of natural laws or principles of justice, and those natural laws, she argues, will themselves be manifest within and learnt from engagement with the set of customary rules with which she is working. For her, then, the emphasis on case law in later editions of the *Treatise* reflects this crucial process of learning, through which some of Oppenheim's morals were proved wanting or dangerous while others could be retained as wisely chosen and well grounded principles of natural law. She would argue that the *Treatise* has endured because Lauterpacht perceived that international law relies not (as Oppenheim had thought) on the growth of new, positivist fruits but on the 'revival of authority of natural law', a revival which he argues has 'tended to undermine the rigid positivism of the nineteenth century' and is 'likely to receive an accession of strength as the result of the experience preceding the Second World War.'[110]

Any conclusion, then, on the real nature of Oppenheim's influence hinges on a deeper account of the nature and history of customary international law. For a midwife, the treatise-writer's influence reflects and can be but a product of influences at play within a professional tradition focussed on resolving practical problems. For both the natural lawyer and the noble liar, the very resolution of those practical problems will have required systematised argument drawing on the principles and arguments offered in contemporary textbooks;[111] for them, the deepest question concerning the influence of a writer is of whether and if so how those principles were justified.

---

[109] J. Crawford, 'Public International law in Twentieth-Century England', *supra* note 3, 692, 699, 700–701.

[110] L. Oppenheim, *supra* note 13, vol. I (1948) 103.

[111] *Cf.* A. Carty, *supra* note 63, 95–96: 'One cannot simply study the practice of States as evidence of law because it is logically inconceivable to examine any evidence without *a priori* criteria of relevance and significance.'

TIME, HISTORY, AND SOURCES OF LAW PEREMPTORY NORMS: IS THERE A NEED FOR NEW SOURCES OF INTERNATIONAL LAW?

Hazel Fox*

Introduction

The boundaries of international law have recently come under review by historians of international law. They have challenged the assumption which has largely prevailed over the past three hundred and fifty years that the emergence of international law is to be dated from the recognition and establishment of the territorial sovereign State. The Peace of Westphalia in 1648 has been traditionally accepted as the turning point when the rule of both the Pope and the Holy Roman Emperor was broken and replaced by the law of nations, later known as international law, which provided principles and rules to regulate the relations between States

But international law, particularly since the Second World War, has undergone change: change as to content, as to the persons to whom it is addressed and its method and point of application. Instead of law made by and derived wholly from the consent of the State members of the international community, the content of international law has expanded to include standards enjoying 'the recognition of contemporary society' which reflect 'the social conditions of the time',[1] and which operate to prohibit conduct 'inconsistent with justice', which 'outrages human decency' or which 'offends against the worth and dignity of human beings that are common to all peoples'.[2] The former constraints by which one State could not intervene in the domestic jurisdiction of another State nor question the latter's treatment of its nationals within its own territory have been swept aside by the obligations in human rights conventions to secure their observance within the territories of the States parties and wherever such States exercise jurisdiction or control. National courts entrusted with the judicial power of a State increasingly construe national laws so as to apply them in conformity with international standards.

---

* Q.C., Barrister; Vice President, British Institute of International and Comparative Law; Honorary Fellow of Somerville College, Oxford University.
[1] Application No. 20190/92, *C.R. v. UK* (1994), DR 31, at paras. 60 & 62; *C.R. v. U.K.*, ECHR (1995) Series A, No. 335-C, 58.

[2] *Streletz and Kessler*, German Federal Constitutional Court, Judgment of 24 October 1996, cited by A. Cassese *International Criminal Law* (2003) 140, footnote 9.

Nowhere is the shift from a State-orientated law to one embracing a 'community of mankind' (a term used in the Joint Opinion of Judges Higgins, Kooijmans and Buergenthal in the *Arrest Warrant* case[3]) so clearly identified as in the decisions of the International Criminal Tribunal for former Yugoslavia applying the customary rules of war to armed conflict taking place within the boundaries of one State. The classic justification for the regulation by international law of the conduct of belligerent States in time of war was precisely because the territory where war raged was in dispute. There was doubt as to which State's internal system of laws applied. There was a hiatus in regulation which was filled by international rules relating to the conduct of war. The new approach is very different; it treats the standards set to regulate inter-State war as superior to any regulation of civil disorder in a State's internal law and, because the commission of atrocities are no longer confined to the conduct of inter-State war, imports and applies these international standards within a single legal national system.

> A State-sovereignty-orientated approach has been gradually supplanted by a human-being-orientated approach. Gradually the maxim of Roman law *hominum causa omne jus constitum est* (all law is created for the benefit of human beings) has gained a firm foothold in the international community as well. It follows that in the area of armed conflict the distinction between interstate wars and civil wars is losing its value as far as human beings are concerned. Why protect civilians from belligerent violence, or ban rape, torture or the wanton destruction of hospitals, churches, museums or private property, as well as proscribe weapons causing unnecessary suffering when two sovereign States are engaged in war, and yet refrain from enacting the same bans or providing the same protection when armed violence has erupted 'only' within the territory of a sovereign State? If international law, while of course safeguarding the legitimate interests of States, must gradually turn to the protection of human beings, it is only natural that the aforementioned dichotomy should gradually lose its weight.[4]

Given then, that the content, application and methods of enforcement have changed, it would seem that the sources on which this law is based must also change. This is the issue which I want to address in this paper – whether the new international law requires a new approach to its sources. The old law was based on a horizontal system where laws of equal validity were made and enforced by the member States of the community. The new law introduces relativity of norms: some laws are given superior rank, are described as peremptory permitting no derogation; based on jus cogens, they are considered as universally obligatory without express consent.

---

[3] Joint Separate Opinion of Judges Higgins, Kooijmans and Buerghental in the *Arrest Warrant of 11 April 2000* (Democratic Republic of the Congo v. Belgium), ICJ Rep (2002), 3. para. 75.

[4] *Prosecutor v. Tadic*, Case No. IT-94-1, Appeals Chamber, Interlocutory Appeal on Jurisdiction, 2 October 1995, para 97.

My enquiry as to the need for new sources will be particularly directed as to their relevance for the establishment, continuance and replacement of peremptory norms based on jus cogens. It is an enquiry that really goes to the immutability and duration of a jus cogens norm.

1. Definition of a Peremptory Norm

What is the point of time at which a jus cogens norm comes into force? Is this a contradiction of its nature? Does it not operate, like divine law dependent on the will of God or natural law dependent on reason, out of time? or for all time? Does the lex lata/lex ferenda distinction apply to jus cogens? These are profound questions more suited to philosophers than lawyers, but as I hope to show, aspects of these questions raise legal issues for which lawyers require some solution.

In part, as some may argue, the problem may be one of definition; thus Fitzmaurice defines natural law as follows: 'when a rule of law is found which could not be other than it is, could not *not* exist and does not require to be accounted for or justified in terms of any other rule,-it is a rule of natural law'.[5] In effect, the qualities of the rule itself provide a self-evident proof of its normative character. But in providing illustrations of such natural law – pacta sunt servanda, municipal law is no defence in international law – Fitzmaurice treats his rules of natural law as embracing the rules which are logically inherent in any legal system,[6] rather than rules applicable to an international community enjoying superior legal effect by reason of their moral force.

More relevant, because it was employed when considering the applicable rules for annulment and invalidity of treaties is the definition supplied by the International Law Commission, 'A rule of *jus cogens* is an over-riding rule depriving any act or situation which is in conflict with it of legality'.[7] Accordingly the Commission identified, as a ground of invalidity of treaty, its conflict with such a rule of jus cogens, and in doing so it widened the sources to which reference might be made in the recognition of such a jus cogens rule, and perhaps even more significantly accepted that such peremptory norms might not be immutable. Article 53

---

[5] Fitzmaurice, 'Some Problems regarding Formal Sources of International Law', in F.M. van Asbeck (ed.), *Symbolae Verzijl* (1954) 164, reproduced in M. Koskentiemi (ed.), *Sources of International Law* (2000) 62.

[6] The third element in the list of sources in Article 38(1)(c) of the Statute of the ICJ 'general principles of law recognised by civilised nations' would seem to include these rules. Whether they also may be drawn upon in identifying 'the constitutional foundations of the international community' identified by Tomuschat and Cassese is questionable, see below note 35, and also Degan, *Sources of International Law* (1997) 88–9.

[7] *Report of the ILC on the Work of its Eighteenth Session*, Doc. A/CN.4/191, *YBILC* (1966), vol. II, 261 (Commentary on draft Article 64(61)).

of the 1969 Vienna Convention on Treaties provides: 'A treaty is void if, at the time of its conclusion, it conflicts with a peremptory norm of general international law. For the purposes of this present Convention, a peremptory norm of general international law is a norm accepted and recognized by the international community of States as a whole as a norm from which no derogation is permitted'.

The Vienna Convention here dates the effect of a peremptory norm on a treaty by reference to 'the time of its conclusion' and it specifically contemplates such a norm as being of limited duration by adding 'and which can be modified only by a subsequent norm of general international law having the same character'. According to this text a peremptory norm may have a commencement date and be of limited duration. Similarly in Article 64: 'If a new peremptory norm of general international law emerges, any treaty which is in conflict with that norm becomes void and terminates'. But note such effect is not so as to have 'retroactive effect on the validity of the treaty. The invalidity is to attach only as from the time of the establishment of the new rule of *jus cogens*.'[8] The International Law Commission and the States who negotiated and ratified the Vienna Convention on Treaties would seem to have accepted that a peremptory norm, though of higher obligatory effect than other rules of law, was itself relative and capable of change over time. With regard to the ILC, it made this plain when, in providing for modification of a peremptory norm in VCT 53, it stated in the commentary: 'it would clearly be wrong to regard even rules of *jus cogens* as immutable and incapable of modification in the light of future developments'[9].

2. Passage of Time and Progressive Enforceability of a Peremptory Norm

Acceptance of such lack of total permanence surely supports a view that the process of articulation of the standards to be found in peremptory norms takes place over time. One is well aware that positions formerly taken on moral issues become no longer tenable with change over time of economic interests and social habits.[10] For instance, the acceptance of the slave trade as a legitimate business endeavour and the promotion of tobacco sales regardless of their effect on health are two public positions which no 'civilised' country now supports. Increasingly, in part due to the more rapid flow of information, attitudes of tolerance to harmful practices harden into denunciation and crystallize into legal regulation.

---

[8] *Ibid*, 248 (Commentary on draft Article 50); see also *ibid*, 268 (Commentary on draft Article 71).

[9] For the challenge to the universality of a peremptory norm by the 1969 Vienna Convention on Treaties' provisions limiting its enforcement to parties to the treaty, see G. Gaja, 'Jus cogens beyond the Vienna Convention', 172 (III) *Recueil de Cours* (1981) 283.

[10] E.g. as to the absolute prohibition against torture, M.D. Evans & R. Morgan, *Preventing Torture* (1998) Chapter 1.

This process whereby moral positions are converted into propositions with legal effect must be of concern to the lawyer. He or she needs, in gauging the applicability of the rule and its sanctions, to understand and date the processes of conversion of a moral exhortation to a fully enforceable legal rule; processes by which a politically correct statement, for example that aid is given to developing States, or that foreign investment in another State's territory should not cause environmental pollution, are converted first into a legal rule, secondly elevated to a peremptory norm and then moved forward to a definition of an international crime.

An example of the later stages in that process is given by Byers in a recent note on policing the high seas where he provides an interesting historical summary of the outlawing of the transatlantic slave trade. The entry into bilateral treaties providing a right of visitation of State parties' ships eventually led to a multilateral visitation treaty but never matured into a customary international right of visitation in respect of a non-consenting State, suspected of slave trading.[11]

Or take the use of child soldiers in war: once a recognised practice of civilised States, from exhortation as morally abhorrent, it was strengthened first into a legal prohibition, and then into an international crime. Unusually, the conversion into a legal prohibition of the use of child soldiers in war was first effected at the international level by its recognition as an international obligation upon States, rather than imposed by national legislation. Ultimately, it led to the identification of recruitment, forced or not, of children under the age of fifteen into the armed forces as an international crime. The Special Court at Sierra Leone recently had to grapple with this problem of evolution over time and the dating of a rule of international law. Whilst the majority judgment antedated the existence of an international crime of child recruitment prior to 1996 when the Court acquired its jurisdiction and the acts of the accused Norman were alleged to have taken place, Judge Geoffrey Robertson QC in a strong dissent concluded that the articulation of the rule had proceeded in stages, and that its recognition as an international crime post-dated 1996. After noting that the use of children in warfare in respect of activities unconnected with hostilities was long tolerated in the practice of States, he formulated the issue as follows:

> The enlistment of children of fourteen years and below to kill and risk being killed in conflicts not of their making was abhorrent to all reasonable persons in 1996 and is abhorrent to them today. But abhorrence alone does not make that conduct a crime in international law . . . So when did child enlistment-as distinct from forcible recruitment of children or subsequently using them in combat – become a war crime? That depends, as we shall see, on first identifying a stage-or at least a process – by which prohibition of child enlistment became a rule of law binding only on States (i.e. on their governments) and with which they were meant to comply (although nothing could be

---

[11] Byers, 'Policing the High Seas: The Proliferation Security Initiative', 98 *American Journal of International Law* (2004) 535.

done if they declined). Then, at the second stage, on further identifying a subsequent turning point at which that rule- a so-called "norm" of international law-metamorphosed into a *criminal law* for the breach of which individuals might be punished, if convicted by international courts.[12]

The principle of legality and retroactivity, in Judge Robertson's view, made essential the precise identification and dating of the second stage process. Otherwise a man might be convicted in respect of acts that were not recognised as criminal at the time of commission. I shall return to this aspect later.

I would suggest that this process of articulation, of progression of a legal proposition through stages of increasing legal effect and sanction requires new sources of law. The classic sources of treaty, custom and general principles are not located in the right time or place or have the right antennae to receive and record the emergence and changes of such new standards. Paul Ginsborg in writing the recent history of Italy in his book states that it entails 'the almost complete abandonment of the traditional tools of the historian's craft, – the patient work in the archives, the attention to primary documentation … I have been at work on virgin territory, heavily dependent on sociological surveys, on the anthropologist's eye, on newspaper reports, oral history, economists' texts, judicial transcripts, parliamentary inquiries'.[13]

I would suggest that similar types of evidence may be required to capture and date the new international law and that such evidence may not readily be categorised under the traditional heads of treaty, custom or general principles of law. Reisman, in his 1981 Harold D Lasswell Memorial lecture focusing on the theory of communications, confirms the need for a wider catchment area of sources:

> The traditional diplomatic conduits, by which territorial-based elites have communicated and clarified their common interests, continue to be important, but many other international conference and parliamentary arenas have come into operation. In some of these non-official actors may participate in direct or indirect fashion. In all of them, the ever-present media of the non-communist, industrial world monitor and diffuse what they believe is occurring as rapidly as possible.[14]

---

[12] Dissenting Opinion of Judge Geoffrey Robertson QC in *Prosecutor v. Norman*, Case No. SCSL-03-I, Trial Chamber, Decision on preliminary motion based on lack of jurisdiction, 31 May 2004. A further example is provided by the debate over the prohibition of human cloning. In place of the treaty which the US sought to have approved in November 2004 the UN General Assembly adopted, by a divided vote of 84, 34 against and 37 abstaining, a resolution calling on all UN member states 'to prohibit all forms of human cloning inasmuch as they are incompatible with human dignity and the protection of human life'. GA Resolution 591/280.annex, para. (b), (8 March 2005) reported in 90 *American Journal of International Law* (2005) 718–9.

[13] P. Ginsborg, *Italy and its Discontents 1980–2001: Family, Civil Society, State* (2003) xiv.

[14] W.M. Reisman, 'International Law-making: A Process of Communication', *ASIL Proceedings* (1981) 106.

Whilst the first type of international law historically is closely linked with the emergence of the territorial State after the Peace of Westphalia in 1648, the second is derived from a much longer diverse culling of human experience and culture. My approach thus aligns itself with the modern trend to extend and widen the historical sources from which international law is drawn and to shun forcing such teeming sources of experience, ideas, political, economic and social theories into the Procrustean narrow bed of legal concepts derived from a relatively short European-oriented period of time.

I propose to address this question by first briefly looking at the traditional sources and identifying some of their defects. Second, by reviewing approaches to the new law which deny the relevance or applicability of sources of law to their recognition. Such approaches can be at the level of general theory or of legal method in regulating problems of time. And third, by elaborating on the nature of the problems that arise in dating new law, particularly where claimed to be of a jus cogens character, as to the degree of legality to be accorded to a particular rule.

3. Inadequacy of the Classic Sources of International Law

Classic international law was based largely on the diplomatic history of the day recording the working out in detail of the relations of the new States in their external relations with each other. Article 38(1) of the Statute of the International Court of Justice is widely accepted as setting out the sources of this international law and those sources – the international conventions, international custom and general principles of law recognised by civilised nations – were based on first, the external communications between States and their diplomats by exchange of notes, initialled minutes, protocols and second, the documentation internal to each single State formulating and putting into effect its foreign relations policy by means of communications preserved in national archives between ministers, their chancelleries, and consultation with interested parties.[15] Basically the documentation, providing the evidence to support the recognition of sovereign States, their exercise of jurisdiction, definition of boundaries, entry into treaties and dispute settlement, was bureaucratic in nature. The relevance of the three sources is stated to be formal, that is, the basis on which legal validity and enforceability is given to a proposition.[16] The material substance of the rule, its moral or social content is irrelevant, and put on one side as a matter of extra-legal import.

---

[15] M. Toscano, *History of Treaties and International Politics* (1966) 7–9.

[16] G. Fitzmaurice, *supra* note 5, 154: 'The formal legal and direct sources consist of the acts or facts whereby their content, whatever it may be and from whatever source it may be drawn, is clothed with legal validity and obligatory force'.

A useful summary prior to 1800 is provided by Peter Macalister-Smith and Joachim Schwietzke in a study prepared for the Max Planck Institute at Heidelberg and they identify four main sources of international law: general works on the history of international law, general documentary material with an emphasis on treaties, studies by learned and influential authors, and commentaries.[17] They and others criticise this material as literary in character, derived from secondary rather than original sources and with legal questions subordinated to the exposition of foreign policies and their consequences.[18]

A. Inadequacy As To Actors

Certainly, as recent international proceedings and arbitrations have demonstrated, these sources need to be supplemented by non-governmental documents. Such documents may be generated by the interactions of non-governmental actors and are capable of creating practices giving rise to a set of entitlements.[19] Reisman writes concerning the formation of a norm of international law of 'the existence and content of the expectations of politically relevant individuals and groups. These expectations will be sustained and changed by the continuation or abatement of streams of communication about authority and the credible control intentions of those whose support is needed for the norm's efficacy.'[20] In more concrete terms, Kritsiotis envisages the international community of States as expanding to embrace the legislators, addressees and adjudicators of the system of international law.[21] This expansion to non-State actors is particularly necessary in respect of the formation and enforcement of a peremptory norm because 'States rarely take to heart the fulfilment of international obligations where none of their direct interests is involved.'[22]

Source material from such 'non-governmental elites' may be derived from oil companies as to concessions, airlines as to overflight and flight routes, fishing communities as to maritime limits. Thus, in the *Tunisia/Libya case*, the International Court relied upon the terms of oil concessions agreed by companies in the area: 'This line of adjoining concessions, which was tacitly respected for a number of years and which approximately corresponds furthermore to the line perpendicular

---

[17] Macalister-Smith & Schwietzke, 'Literature and Documentary Sources relating to History of Public International Law: An Annotated Bibliography', 1 *Journal of History of International Law* (1999) 136. See also 'Bibliography of Textbooks and Comprehensive Treaties on Positive International Law of the 19th Century', 3 *Journal of History of International Law* (2001) 75.

[18] Preiser, 'History of the Law of Nations: Basic Questions and Principles', 2 *Encyclopaedia of Public International Law* (1992) 716.

[19] A. D'Amato, *International Law: Prospect and Process* (1995) 123–47.

[20] W.M. Reisman, *supra* note 14, 113.

[21] Kritsiotis, 'Imagining the international Community', 12 *European Journal of International Law* (2002) 973–7.

[22] G. Gaja, *supra* note 9, 289.

to the coast at the frontier point which had in the past been observed as a de facto maritime limit, does appear to the Court to constitute a circumstance of great relevance to the delimitation.'[23]

An arbitral tribunal held under the auspices of the Permanent Court of Arbitration embraced a wider concept of relevant sources in the *Eritrea/Yemen Maritime Delimitation Award* 1998. The tribunal there referred to the *Qur'an* and the *sunna* as embodying 'fundamental moralistic general principles' and stated Islam 'is not merely a religion but also a political community (*Umma*) endowed with a system of law' and the sovereignty awarded to Yemen had to be seen as a sovereignty 'that respects and embraces and is subject to the Islamic concepts of the region'.[24] The Arbitral Tribunal also relied on evidence from local fishing communities: the remote location of the named offshore islands 'meant they were put to a special use by fishermen as way stations and as places of shelter, and not just, or perhaps, even mainly as fishing grounds. These special factors constituted a local tradition entitled to the respect and the protection of the law.'[25] Similarly in the *Rann of Kutch Arbitration*[26] the reminiscences of nomadic herdsmen or fishermen were relied on in the delimitation of territorial sovereignty and in the *Kasikili/Sedudu Island* case before the International Court of Justice, evidence was produced designed to support the Namibian title from tribes of the E Caprivi Strip, in particular the elderly members' accounts of cultivation of crops on the disputed island.[27]

---

[23] *Application for Revision and Interpretation of the Judgment of 24 February 1982 in the case concerning the Continental Shelf* (Tunisia v. Libyan Arab Jamahiriya), *Merits,* ICJ Rep 1985, 192.

[24] *Eritrea/Yemen Maritime Delimitation Award,* Permanent Court of Arbitration (1998), para.95. This approach of international law may be compared to that of municipal law. Financing agreements entered into by a bank incorporated under the laws of Bahrain contained a governing law clause which provided 'subject to the principles of the Glorious Sharia'a, the agreements should be governed and construed in accordance with English law.' The English Court of Appeal held the financing agreements were governed by English law alone, 'a law commonly adopted internationally as the governing law for banking and commercial contracts, having a well-known and well-developed jurisprudence in that respect whch is not open to doubt or disputation on the basis of religious or philosophical principle'. The intention of the parties at the outset had been for the agreements to be binding, and the court should lean against a construction which would or might defeat that commercial purpose. The reference to the principles of Sharia'a was simply intended to reflect the Islamic banking principles according to which the bank held itself out to do business, rather than incorporating a system of law intended to 'trump' the application of English law as the law to be applied in ascertaining the liability of the parties under the terms of the agreement (*Shamil Bank of Bahrain v. Beximco Pharmaceuticals Ltd* [2004] EWCA Civ 19, [2004] 4 All ER 1072, per Potter LJ, at paras 47 & 54.)

[25] *Eritrea/Yemen Maritime Delimitation Award, ibid,* para 527; Eritrea/Yemen Maritime Delimitation Award, Permanent Court of Arbitration (1999), paras. 94 & 95; Antunes, 'Casenote', 50 *International and Comparative Law Quarterly* (1999) 302–3.

[26] *Rann of Kutch Arbitration (Indo-Pakistan West Boundary) Case,* 50 *International Law Reports* (1976) 2.

[27] *Kasikili/Sedudu Island* case (Botswana/Namibia), *Merits,* ICJ Rep 1999, 1045.

B. *Inadequacy As To Period of Time*

A further defect of the traditional sources arises from its restriction to events post 1648 and thereby excluding prior periods when rules of substantive law developed. An example has already been given in the reliance in the *Tadic* case of the Appeals Chamber of the International Criminal Tribunal for former Yugoslavia on a general dictum of Roman law that 'all law is created for the benefit of human beings'. The date of 1648 arbitrarily excludes the whole of jus gentium as applied during the Roman Empire, in existence for some five hundred years, from the second century BC to the end of the third century AD,[28] and the jus commune of the Holy Roman Empire dating from the coronation of Charlemagne in Rome in 800 AD until the acknowledgment in the Treaty of Westphalia of the independence of territories ruled by protestant princes. Arguably, international elements of law are better found in periods of empire where unification of the source of authority results in the harmonisation of rules of conduct regardless of tribal or feudal boundaries. From the Roman ius gentium derive fundamental rules relating to obligations, acquisition of title, prescription, and natural justice; while precepts of natural law including the concept of just war are derived from Papal canon law and feudal jus commune.

C. *Inadequacy As To Content*

A final defect of the traditional sources is the absence of substantive content relating to standards of conduct of States and individuals.[29] As already stated, since 1945 and the end of World War II and more particularly the year 1989 with the collapse of the Soviet Empire, the content of international law has undergone change – new values have been asserted, if not enforced, for the international community as a whole; new actors with degree of locus standi; new rules, not solely of an external nature, applicable between States, but also of an internal nature, setting standards for a State's conduct with regard to its own territory and people. Structurally the shape of rules has changed with the recognition of hierarchy and ranking. Although the matters coming within the new categories of peremptory norms and erga omnes obligations remain controversial, there can be little doubt that the recognition of such categories gives rise to new enquiries for which new sources would seem required. Surely new sources are required to date the point in time when a hierarchy of norms emerged? or

---

[28] 168 BC, the date of the Battle of Pydna when the Seleucid ruler, Antiochus IV was driven back by Roman legate may be taken as marking the end of a system of independent States of equal rank; such a system only emerges again in 389 AD when the Roman Emperor Theodosius I concluded an agreement over Armenia with Bahram IV of the New Persian Empire (Preiser, *supra* note 18, 721).

[29] For Oppenheim's view that a law of nature does not exist, and its influence on international lawyers, see the chapter of Perreau-Saussine included in this volume.

at least the point in time when a particular rule changed from a dispositive to a mandatory requirement? Evidence would seem required to determine the commencement, duration and termination of higher norms.

4. Alternative Solutions To Providing Superior Enforceability of a Peremptory Norm

One response is to treat the problem, not as a question of sources, but of theory, of method, or of legal technique. Even though it may be acknowledged that classical sources require supplementing, many jurists do not see the emergence of new international norms as requiring new sources.

A. Theory

First, at the level of theory and constitutional structure, if the existence of rules enjoying primacy over other rules is denied, it follows that traditional sources will remain sufficient. As Prosper Weil so convincingly argued[30], international law should be seen as a horizontal system based on consent; to introduce norms of a peremptory character undermines its coherence, blurs the normative threshold as well as the distinction between unratified and ratified treaties, and elevates soft law without imposing upon it the constraints of enacted law. Thereby it both erodes the obligatory force of law by applying it to States who have not consented, and by denying the right of objection denies the independence and status of the persistent objector.

It would, however, seem too late to return to a purely consensual horizontal system. The international community at large, not solely composed of its original members, territorial States, has embraced the system of international law as a guarantee of the rule of law over and above State politics. In consequence, a system of relative normativity would seem now to be widely accepted.[31] The 1969 Vienna Convention on Treaties has been widely ratified[32] and much of its provisions treated as the statement of customary international law; Articles 53 and 64 to which reference has been made, clearly constitute a recognition of the relative

---

[30] Weil, 'Towards Relative Normativity in International Law?', 77 *American Journal of International Law* (1983) 43.

[31] It is certainly at the present time politically correct to do so, though I note indications that even the most progressive thinkers see some advantages in the classical system, e.g. see in the Separate opinion of Judge Higgins in *Legal Consequences of construction of Wall in occupied Palestinian Territory*, Advisory Opinion, ICJ Rep 2004, 217.

[32] Even France, long opposed to these provisions in Part V has now ratified the 1969 Vienna Convention.

quality of jus cogens. The latest draft ILC Articles on State Responsibility, of which the General Assembly took note commending them to governments,[33] though modifying Ago's original concept of international crimes of a State (article 19), recognise in Articles 26, 40, and 42, the category of peremptory norms and in Article 48, the obligations owed to the international community as a whole. In its advisory opinion on the *Legality of the Threat or Use of Nuclear Weapons* the International Court of Justice, although refraining from discussing the legal character of a jus cogens norm, recognized the existence of superior ranking norms:

> It is undoubtedly because a great many rules of humanitarian law applicable in armed conflict are so fundamental to the respect of the human person and "elementary considerations of humanity" as the Court put it in its Judgment of 9 April 1949 in the *Corfu Channel* case (*I.C.J. Reports 1949*, p. 22), that the Hague and Geneva Conventions have enjoyed a broad accession. Further these fundamental rules are to be observed by all States whether or not they have ratified the conventions that contain them, because they constitute intransgressible principles of international customary law.[34]

Even though a system of relative normativity is accepted, some thinkers treat the topic as purely a question of theory, of a comparison of positivism to natural law, of deductive or inductive methods of determining rules of international law. Van Hoof compares the formal and material sources of international law to those of a national constitution containing 'two types of provisions: the procedural constitutional provisions on the one hand which outline the legal/organisational structure of the society concerned; the material constitutional provisions on the other hand, that lay down the fundamental (political) orientation in the form of basic values or ideas which society wants to uphold or attain.' He concludes that: 'International *jus* cogens, of course, belongs to the 'material constitutional provisions' of international law'.[35]

Similarly, jurists such as Tomuschat and Cassese adopt a deductive approach and rank these new norms of a different nature to dispositive rules of international law. These peremptory norms in their view form part of the fundamental structure of international law and require no evidence of State practice in their support. Thus, Tomuschat in his Hague lectures of 1993 identifies certain principles as the 'constitutional foundations of the new international community', which can be 'derive[d] directly from the core philosophy of humanity as it is enshrined in the-unwritten-constitution of the international community, as well as in the Charter of United Nations.' He includes sovereign equality, non-use of force and common values of mankind under which he lists equality of human beings, protection of human life,

---

[33] GA Res. 58/83, 12 December 2001.
[34] *Legality of the Threat or Use of Nuclear Weapons,* Advisory Opinion, ICJ Rep 1996, 257.
[35] G.J.H. van Hoof, *Rethinking the Sources of International Law* (1983) 151.

and physical integrity, freedom from torture and slavery. He accepts, referring specifically to the Nuremberg Tribunal's prosecution of crimes against peace, that 'it would be difficult to show that indeed in accordance with classical criteria of formation of customary rules the punishable character of breaches of elementary norms of international law has evolved through a constant practice supported by *opinio juris.*'[36]

It flows from the logic of this approach that the breach of peremptory norms by States does not disprove their legal nature. As the ICJ stated in the *Nicaragua* Case:

> The Court does not consider for a rule to be established as customary, the corresponding practice must be in absolute rigorous conformity with the rule. In order to deduce the existence of customary rules, the Court deems it sufficient that the conduct of States should in general be consistent with such rules and that instances of State conduct inconsistent with a given rule should generally have been treated as breaches of that rule, not as indications of the recognition of a new rule.[37]

The dangers of such an inductive approach are obvious if it is applied to anything more than the basic *Grundnorm*, or seeks to go beyond the broad concepts of pacta sunt servanda or equality of States. Once the inductive approach is extended to asserting precepts of human rights or humanitarian law without requiring evidence of State practice or opinio juris, these precepts become vulnerable to formulation based on subjective values.

Koskenniemi, as a publicist of the Rhetorical school of thought, equally rejects the need for sources to support peremptory norms. He dismisses the search for support for such fundamental principles as self referential: 'Genocide – or better the unthinkability of genocide – brings to the surface the limits of rational argument and the character of normative knowledge. Chains of argument and proof can always be traced to a point at which something can no longer be proved but must be axiomatic, as something that we know because we could not think otherwise.'[38]

B. Legal Method and Techniques

Just as theory acknowledges limits in its search for the source of fundamental principles, legal techniques may also preclude challenges to the establishment of such principles and provide an alternative route by which any need for new sources is avoided. Principles of certainty, constitutional process, and non-retroactivity have

---

[36] C. Tomuschat, 'Obligations arising for States without or against their Will', 241 *Recueil des Cours* (1993) 302. See also A. Cassese, *International Law* (2004) 46–8, 64–7.

[37] *Military and Paramilitary Activities in and Against Nicaragua* (Nicaragua v. United States of America), *Merits,* ICJ Rep 1986, 98.

[38] Koskenniemi, 'Faith, Identity, and the Killing of the Innocent: International Lawyers and Nuclear Weapons', 10 *Leiden Journal of International Law* (1997) 157.

been developed to avoid direct investigation into whether the law itself has changed in terms of its effectiveness. Intertemporal law ensures an issue is determined by reference to the applicable law in force at the relevant time. For questions of treaty interpretation the applicable law will be the law in force at the time the treaty came into force – that being the law to which the State parties gave their consent. Where the parties can be shown as coordinating their policies in new areas, the use of the legal concept of a 'situation' to bring the facts within a new legal regime may resolve any dispute as to the meaning of original terms. Lawyers here manage time as divided into segments according to the relevant law prevailing and fit the facts either to the time period when the treaty came into force or to the present period to which continuing facts belong. Similarly, questions relating to the application of law prior to the date a treaty came into force or jurisdiction was conferred on an international tribunal, are resolved by strict rules as to cut-off or counter presumptions based on implied consent, or knowledge.[39] The solution adopted, rather than addressing the question whether the applicable law itself has changed, is to apply legal devices to identify artificially the period in time into which the issue falls for determination. Thus, the question of whether the law itself has undergone change over time – or is undergoing such change, either by a strengthening of its legal validity or a progressive weakening is avoided.

A recent decision of the US Supreme Court relating to the retrospective character of the Foreign Sovereign Immunities Act 1976 (FSIA) provides an illustration of how legal technique can avoid awkward questions as to the effect of a change in the law on parties' expectations. The court directed its focus to the claim as presented today rather than to the past facts on which it was based. The Austrian Government sought to plead immunity to a claim relating to the wrongful expropriation of property (paintings by Klimt) which the Austrian National Gallery had obtained in 1948 and argued that at that time, foreign States enjoyed absolute immunity under US law. By focussing on the present claim and proceedings, the Supreme Court was able to apply the present law in force, that is the FSIA, even though the claim related to facts occurring at a time before the Tate letter was sent in 1952 when US Courts applied a doctrine of absolute immunity. Any disregard of expectations as to immunity based on that absolute doctrine which the defendant State might have held in 1948, could be met by political decision, the Court said, by the filing of a statement of interest by the State Department, following which the court would probably apply immunity.[40]

In calling attention to the inadequacies of the classic sources of international law, it is not intended to deny the utility of the basic method which they deployed,

---

[39] See Higgins, 'Time and the Law: International Perspectives on an Old Problem', 46 *International and Comparative Law Quarterly* (1997) 501.

[40] *Altmann v Austria*, 124 *Supreme Court Reporter*, 2240, (2004).

namely, the citing of examples of previous behaviour, organised according to the principal problems arising for states in their relations one to another from which rules can be extracted. As Bobbitt explains, in discussing classic sources, Grotius' method 'is no more than the way things are done; not the substance of the law, not the things being done themselves . . . and not the divine law, but the ordinary, every-day methods of arguing and putting forward interpretations.'[41] This paper does not seek to impugn the basic method, but to argue that the changing relative nature of international law requires that 'the ordinary everyday methods' be enlarged to include those employed by nonstate actors, over a longer period of time and with regard to different subject-matter involving social rather than political choices.

The classic sources were of use at a time when Prosper Weil's conception of international law as a horizontal consensual system was generally accepted. But it is suggested that the emergence of a hierarchy of norms presents a much wider range of choices as to the degree of legality to be accorded to a particular rule, choices which actors other than states, drawing on areas of expertise and conduct other than political, can perhaps better assess as producing a fair and just outcome. Peremptory norms cannot adequately be compartmentalised into periods of total validity or complete nullity. Such a hierarchy requires legal techniques to evaluate the content of a rule and to fix by reference to a specific date the various stages of enforceability and the widening circle of legal consequences that flow from norms of higher rank. Sources are required to provide recognition of those higher norms and legitimation of those stages.

It is suggested that acts and expressions of consent between States are insufficient to provide that recognition and legitimation. Hence new sources are required. The case of *Bouzari v. Islamic Republic of* Iran in the Canadian courts illustrates the need for such new sources. The Ontario Superior Court held there to be evidence that the prohibition on torture was a rule of *jus cogens* but sought in vain from the traditional sources for evidence of 'the scope of the norm, as to whether 'the prohibition of torture includes an obligation to provide a civil remedy against a foreign state for acts that occurred within the state.'[42] A similar search was conducted by the English Court of Appeal in the claim brought by British nationals against individual officials in the Saudi police and prison service for torture allegedly carried out in a Saudi state prison; to obtain an answer Mance LJ resorted to applying to an international convention the techniques used to construe an English statute.[43]

The legal consequences which result from the recognition of the peremptory status of a rule of law are an independent and too extensive topic to be included in the

---

[41] P. Bobbitt, *The Shield of Achilles: War, Peace and the Course of History* (2002) 515–6.

[42] *Bouzari v. Islamic Republic of Iran*, Ont. S.C., 125 *International Law Reports* (2002) 428 paras. 61–2; *Bouzari*, [2004] 243 D.L.R. (4th) 406 (Ont. C.A.), paras. 77–8.

[43] *Jones v. Ministry of Interior Saudi Arabia and Lt Col Abdul Aziz (Minister)*, [2004] EWCA Civil 1394.

present paper.[44] All that is attempted in this final section is to indicate some of the possible stages of that process and refer to one or two instances where the need for new sources is apparent.

5. Stages in Enforceability of a Peremptory Norm

Sources may be required: first, to find as contrary to international law conduct which is not incorporated as a rule in any ratified convention or international custom; second, when a rule has emerged, the conferment on it of the status of a peremptory norm; and third, to establish the consequences which may, but do not necessarily flow from such status. Such consequences may take effect at the international or national level. On the international inter-state level they may include the recognition of a general prohibition, its articulation as an international crime, its application to a dispute governed by *lex specialis,* the undertaking by States of an obligation to include such a crime in their national penal codes, or the undertaking to exercise universal jurisdiction over persons accused of its commission of whatever nationality and wherever such a crime is committed. At the national level, in order to bring a State's national law in line with the international norm, such consequences may take the form of the conferment of primacy on the norm over the national constitution, legislation to give it both substantive and procedural effect and clear words to overrule countervailing principles based on international law, such as State and diplomatic immunity.

A. First Stage: The Transition of a Moral Principle to a Rule of Law

An example of the first stage – the transition from moral principle to legal rule – is to be found in the resort to sources other than treaty or custom when, in the prosecution of prominent Nazi leaders for war crimes and crimes against humanity, the Nuremberg Tribunal was confronted with the principle of legality, 'there can be no punishment of crime without pre-existing law – *nullum crime sine lege, nulla poena sine lege*'. To avoid the charge of retroactivity with regard to its indictment for crimes committed by a State against its own people, when such crimes had not been enacted into German national law nor by international treaty, the Nuremberg Tribunal declared that the absence of a crime at a time when the crime was committed does

---

[44] For a useful discussion of some of the legal consequences of the peremptory norm prohibiting torture, see De Wet, 'The prohibition of torture as an international norm of jus cogens and its implications for national and customary law', 15 *European Journal of International Law* (2004) 97. See also Roucounas 'Time limitations for claims and actions under international law', in E. Yakpo & T. Boumedra (eds.), *Liber Amicorum Mohammed Bedjaoui* (1999) 236.

not absolve one from criminal responsibility provided 'the act or omission which, at the time when it was committed, was criminal according to the general principles of law recognised by civilised nations.' It found evidence of those principles in various unratified international declarations and agreements which declared aggressive war to be an international crime and which warned that persons engaged in waging such a war might be prosecuted.

This same exception to the principle of legality in respect of criminal liability appears in Article 7.2 of the European Convention of Human Rights and was relied upon by the European Court of Human Rights in *Streletz, Kessler, and Krenz v. Germany* to resolve a question arising from 'the transition between two States governed by different legal systems' where, after reunification, the German courts convicted three former senior East German officials for causing the death of persons trying to cross the intra-German border. The applicants contended that to uphold the convictions would be contrary to the principle of legality since at the time of the offences no one had been prosecuted for them in the GDR. The court rejected the application holding that at the time when the acts were committed they constituted offences defined with sufficient accessibility and foreseeability by the law of the GDR or international law:

> The Court considers that a State practice such as the GDR's border-policing policy, which flagrantly infringes human rights and above all the right to life, the supreme value in the international hierarchy of human rights, cannot be covered by the protection of Article 7.1. That practice, which emptied of its substance the legislation on which it was supposed to be based, and which was imposed on all organs of the GDR, including its judicial bodies, cannot be described as "law" within the meaning of Article 7.[45]

Judge Levits in his concurring opinion was more explicit:

> ... interpretation and application of national or international legal norms according to socialist or non-democratic methodology (with intolerable results for a democratic system) should from the standpoint of a democratic system be regarded as wrong. That applies both to *ex post facto* assessment of the legal practice of previous non-democratic regimes (as in the instant case, although the same situation may obviously arise in other new democracies) and to assessment of the actual legal practice (for example regarding the International Covenant on Civil and Political Rights) of today's non-democratic regimes.[46]

As this quotation makes plain, resort to the exception to the principle of legality introduces considerable judicial freedom of interpretation.

Not all courts have shown themselves ready to exercise such a freedom. In a strictly legalistic approach the Dutch Supreme Court applied the principle of

---

[45] *Streletz, Kessle and Krenz v. Germany, ECHR Reports of Judgments and Decisions* (2001-II) 422.

[46] Concurring Opinion of Judge Levits, *Streletz, Kessle and Krenz v. Germany, ibid,* 460.

legality to deny jurisdiction. The Dutch Court refused to treat the prohibition of torture as jus cogens norm which overrode any national or international law to the contrary. Consequently, prosecution of the accused Bouterse for ordering the torture of fifteen persons, later executed, by a group of military personnel under his control in Surinam on 8 or 9 December 1982 was denied because at the time of the alleged offence his conduct was not defined as criminal by Dutch law. The offence with which Bouterse was charged, of torture committed outside the Netherlands by an alien was only made a crime by a Dutch law which came into force in 1989.[47]

In this context, it is reassuring to find that the exception introduced by the Nuremberg Tribunal does not appear in the Rome Statute of the International Criminal Court's formulation of the principle of legality, (Articles 22–24). Article 22.1 restricts criminal responsibility to crimes within the jurisdiction of the Court and paragraph 3 merely declares that this provision shall not affect the characterization of any conduct as criminal under international law independently of this Statute.[48]

B. Second Stage: Conferment of the Status of a Peremptory Norm

Moving to the second stage, the conferment of the status of a peremptory norm upon a rule, the distinguishing feature of a peremptory norm, according to the Vienna Convention on Treaties, article 53 and the ILC Articles 26 and 48 on State Responsibility, is its recognition by and applicability to the international community as a whole (the 1969 Convention speaks of that community as one of States but arguably the express endorsement of States is no longer required).[49] Accordingly, in addition to evidence establishing the transposition of a moral imperative into a rule, its transformation into a peremptory norm requires recognition of its fundamental, universal and non derogable nature. Van Hoof speaks of the 'double consent requirement' consisting of _opinio juris cogentis_ in addition to _opinio juris_ as 'necessary to avoid uncertainty concerning the exact character of

---

[47] _Bouterse_ Netherlands, Supreme Crt., Judgment of 18 Sept 2001, reprinted in 32 _Netherlands Yearbook of International Law_ (2001) 282; see Zegveld, 'The Bouterse Case', 32 _Netherlands Yearbook of International Law_ (2001) 97. See also _Habré_, Senegal, Crt. of Cassation, Judgment of 20 March 2001, 125 _International Law Reports_ (2004) 569, where the presence of the former head of State of Chad was held insufficient to found jurisdiction, in the absence of procedural legislation conferring on the Senegalese courts universal jurisdiction in respect of acts of torture committed abroad.

[48] According to the 1969 Vienna Convention on the Law of Treaties, peremptory norms never have retroactive effect. On this point see also G. Gaja, _supra_ note 9, 292, footnote 48 and authorities there cited.

[49] Kritsiotis, 'Imagining the international community', 12 _European Journal of International Law_ (2002) 961, discussing Thomas Franck's view of the 'international community' in T. Franck, _Fairness in International Law and Institutions_ (1995).

international peremptory norms. If no additional evidence was required, it would be impossible to tell peremptory norms apart from ordinary rules of international law'. Later he envisages change or extinction of jus cogens requiring the same higher standard of proof.[50]

It is suggested that rather than one act of recognition of the 'cogent' force of a particular norm, such recognition may be fragmented into a number of stages. The issue in the *Norman* case in the Special Court for Sierra Leone illustrates one later stage when, after the prohibition of child enlistment had become a peremptory norm binding upon States it, in the words of the dissenting judge, Geoffrey Robertson QC, 'metamorphosed' into an international crime for the breach of which an individual might be punished. Sources other than States' commitment to the prohibition were required to support the attainment of that stage including statements of the Secretary General and the President of the UN Security Council.[51]

C. Third Stage: Conferment of Legal Consequences at the International and National Level

There are a number of decisions of national courts demonstrating the need for independent source material if a norm at the international level is to have legal consequences at the national level. The rapid development of the new international law is placing strains on the established framework of national legal systems. As Lord Browne-Wilkinson commented in *Pinochet No.3* 'though a norm may be effective at international law, its enforcement in a municipal court may require it to be 'a fully constituted crime'.[52] For example, the acts with which an individual is charged in a national court, though categorised as international terrorism may not fall within any international obligation of the forum State so as to take primacy over a customary international law that grants immunity to a serving head of State. Thus the French Court of Cassation dismissed a prosecution brought against Colonel Gaddafi, the serving head of State of Libya, for complicity in bombing a French registered civilian aircraft with loss of life on the ground that France was under no international obligation relating to terrorism which required the disregard of the immunity which international law accorded to a serving head of State.[53]

Similarly the prohibition against aggression though generally recognised to be of a peremptory nature may lack, even in international law, complete clarity as to its consequences, so as to make it impossible for a national court to give it full effect. The English Court of Criminal Appeal had recently to decide whether the crime of

---

[50] G.J.H. van Hoof, *supra* note 35, 157, 167.

[51] See *supra* note 12.

[52] *Pinochet No. 3*, 2 All ER [1999] 114.

[53] *In re Ghadafi, SOS Attentat and Castelnau d' Esnault v Khadafi*, France, Crt. of Cassation, Crim Chamber, March 2001, JDI (2002) 129, 803; 125 *International Law Reports* (2004) 272.

aggression in international law was capable of having an effect in English law, and if so, what effect. The accused, charged with malicious damage, declared that he intended to set fire to an aircraft on a RAF base in order to prevent the bombers from taking part in the crime of an illegal war in Iraq. He relied on the defence in English law under section 3 of the Criminal Law Act 1967 that he was using such force as was reasonable in the circumstances for the prevention of a crime. The Criminal Court of Appeal dismissed the defence on the ground that aggression could not be treated as a crime for the purposes of a defence to a charge of malicious damage. 'The mere fact that an act can clearly be proscribed by international law, and is described as 'a crime' does not necessarily of itself determine its character in domestic law unless its characteristics are such that it can be translated into domestic law in a way which would entitle domestic courts to impose punishment'.[54]

Once established, subsequent change in the peremptory nature of a rule is not to be overlooked. The passage of time may bring about a loss to a rule of its compelling quality and a return to a status where in certain conditions it may be set aside by consent. Such a situation is described by Reisman in his account of how the ratification of the Treaty banning Nuclear Weapons Test in the atmosphere in Outer Space and Under Water of 1963 established a peremptory norm contradicting the previous perception as lawful of US/USSR atmospheric testing over oceans in the 1950s. He maintains that the International Court of Justice confirmed in its order for provisional measures of 22 June 1973 the peremptory nature of the ban given to France to 'avoid nuclear testing causing the deposit of radioactive fallout on Australian territory' but later, by failing to repeat such an order at the final merits stage implicitly recognised that the rule lacked such a peremptory status.[55]

6. Conclusion

To sum up, international law has moved from a horizontal consensual model to a hierarchy of relative normativity and in doing so has given effect to standards of a wider community than that of States. In consequence, the traditional sources of international law, treaty, custom and general principles of law, based solely on the practice of States, are inadequate to provide support for this new law and its progressive enforceability. The classic sources are too narrow in scope as to actors, period of time and content. Merely to attribute the existence of peremptory norms to the constitutional set-up of the international community or to avoid the issue by application of legal techniques such as intertemporal law, does not address the need

---

[54] *Jones and Milling, Olditch, Pritchard and Richards v. Gloucestershire Crown Prosecution Service,* 2004 EWCA Crim 1981, per Latham LJ, para. 24.
[55] W.M. Reisman, *supra* note 14, 115–117.

for new sources for this new international law of relative normativity. Failures in enforcement in international tribunals and national courts are inevitable if the new law is not properly articulated on the basis of such sources.

Thus, this paper has endeavoured to show, by reference to the greater specificity now occurring in the implementation of international law, a need to elaborate and expand the sources supporting peremptory norms. Without the acceptance of such novel sources and their elaboration, peremptory norms as law must fail. The status of peremptory norms continues to generate criticism and its lack of certainty generally weakens international law as a credible system of law. Christenson writes of jus cogens as 'a normative myth masking power arrangements that would avoid substantive meaning until later decision, thereby postponing and inviting political and ideological conflict.'[56] The enlargement of sources as to the period of time, by reference to content and inclusion of conduct of new categories of actors are indeed necessary if the 'emptiness of jus cogens'[57] is to be proved false.

---

[56] Christenson, 'Jus cogens guarding interests fundamental to International law', 28 *Virginia Journal of International Law* (1988) 590.

[57] Weisburd, 'The Emptiness of the concept of jus cogens: as illustrated by the war in Bosnia-Herzegovina', 17 *Michigan Journal of International Law* (1995) 1.

RELUCTANT *GRUNDNORMEN*: ARTICLES 31(3)(C) AND 42 OF THE VIENNA CONVENTION ON THE LAW OF TREATIES AND THE FRAGMENTATION OF INTERNATIONAL LAW

Jan Klabbers*

Introduction

The law of treaties, as laid down in the 1969 Vienna Convention on the Law of Treaties, has a somewhat ambivalent relationship with externalities, including history and time. The most obvious example of this ambivalence is, as far as its relation to history goes, the discrepancy between the rules on interpretation (consigning a treaty's drafting history to the proverbial dustbin, not even including it as part of the context of a treaty), and the circumstance that international lawyers typically, when confronted with interpretative difficulties, have recourse to the drafting history of the provision in question; and where they do not have recourse to the *travaux préparatoires*, it will usually only be because of an awareness as to how a phrase was intended or has been applied in the past.[1]

If the use of *travaux préparatoires* provides a convenient example of the Vienna Convention's ambivalent attitude to time and history, it is not the only one.[2] A more fundamental battle took place when drafting the Convention on precisely this issue: what to do with the factor of time and, therewith, what to do with both yesterday and tomorrow? On the one hand, in Waldock's 1964 report (and Waldock was the first of the special rapporteurs to address issues of interpretation) a proposal was included that the Vienna Convention comprise a rule on intertemporal law. Draft article 56 provided that a treaty be interpreted in light of the law in force at the time of its drafting, whereas its application be governed by the rules of international law in force when the treaty was to be applied.

---

* Professor of International Organizations Law, University of Helsinki and Director of the Academy of Finland Centre of Excellence on Global Governance Research.

[1] For further exploration, see Klabbers, 'International Legal Histories: The Declining Importance of Travaux Préparatoires in Treaty Interpretation?', 50 *Netherlands International Law Review* (2003) 267.

[2] For an analysis of the factor of time with respect to the Convention itself, see Rosenne, 'The Temporal Application of the Vienna Convention on the Law of Treaties', 4 *Cornell International Law Journal* (1970–71) 1. The moment a treaty is deemed to have been concluded is discussed in Vierdag, 'The Time of the Conclusion of a Multilateral Treaty: Article 30 of the Vienna Convention on the Law of Treaties and Related Provisions', 59 *British Yearbook of International Law* (1988) 92. For a general overview see Nascimento e Silva, 'Le facteur temps et les traités', 154 *Recueil des Cours* (1977) 215.

Be that as it may, there is yet a different story to be told. Waldock's draft article 56 eventually became article 31, paragraph 3(c) of the Vienna Convention, the single most relied on provision to quell anxieties about the fragmentation of international law. Curiously enough, and underlining the Convention's ambivalence on externalities, the Convention contains another article, article 42, which had the potential to do much the same.

Article 42 aims, on its face at least, to place the Convention's regime in a vacuum, isolating it from the influences of external and extraneous factors including the workings of time. Article 42 places the Vienna Convention as the sole possible source of arguments to contest the validity of a treaty and arguments to terminate a treaty or suspend its operation, and therewith aims to create a vacuum around the Vienna Convention or, in yet other (and sometimes over-used) words: it aims to create a self-contained regime. And since the law of treaties touches all of international law, this would amount to turning international law into a unified system, governed by the Vienna Convention. Article 42 reads:

Validity and continuance in force of treaties

1. The validity of a treaty or of the consent of a State to be bound by a treaty may be impeached only through the application of the present Convention.

2. The termination of a treaty, its denunciation or the withdrawal of a party, may take place only as a result of the application of the provisions of the treaty or of the present Convention. The same rule applies to suspension of the operation of a treaty.

Partly, the idea is obvious and, really, not all that remarkable: it gives flesh to the notion that treaties can be invalidated, terminated, or suspended by the operation of law.[3] What is remarkable, however, is the Convention's attempt to carve the concept of 'the operation of law' in stone.

This paper then aims to contrast the stories of article 42 and draft article 56 with each other, in light of the ongoing discussion amongst international lawyers about the fragmentation of international law: one is an attempt to close off international law from anything (including the factor of time), whereas the other aimed to regulate how exactly the factor of time could be incorporated. Both, therewith, were potential basic norms (*Grundnormen*),[4] keeping the international legal order together. The irony, or tragedy, is that neither story could be played out to the full. As a result, nothing is regulated or, if you will, everything is: article 31, paragraph 3(c) of the Vienna Convention admonishes interpreters to take into account any possible

---

[3] This obviously applied also prior to the Vienna Convention. See generally, e.g., Parry, 'The Law of Treaties', in M. Sörensen (ed.), *Manual of Public International Law* (1968) 175.

[4] The notion was famously developed by Hans Kelsen. See in particular his *Introduction to the Problems of Legal Theory* (1992), esp. 55–64. An excellent discussion of Kelsen's work can be found in J. von Bernstorff, *Der Glaube an das universale Recht: Zur Völkerrechtstheorie Hans Kelsens und seiner Schüler* (2001).

rules of international law applicable between the parties when interpreting a treaty. In an additional irony, or tragedy, this attempt at regulation without being regulatory (as the rule is about as open-ended as it could possibly be) merely places the burden of decision-making back into the hands of the interpreter: the very thing that both articles 31 and 42 were designed to prevent. Interpretation thus becomes yet another instrument for the exercise of power.[5]

1. Tomorrow is a Long Time

While two of the ILC's four special rapporteurs on the law of treaties devoted much of their non-ILC work to issues of treaty interpretation (Lauterpacht as rapporteur for the Institut de Droit International, Fitzmaurice as chronicler of the decisions and opinions of the International Court of Justice), it was only with Sir Humphrey Waldock, late in the drafting process, that issues of interpretation first manifested themselves.[6] And generally, that first appearance was a rather unenthusiastic appearance: Sir Humphrey himself, and quite a few of the ILC members, seemed less than convinced about the utility of trying to capture what Sir Humphrey referred to as the 'art' of interpretation in a set of rules.[7]

Nonetheless, in his third report, in 1964, he formulated a number of draft articles, one of which, draft article 56, made provision for intertemporality.[8] The main idea was twofold. First, the will of the parties ought to be decisive as to the meaning of a treaty. Hence, draft article 56 included a provision that treaties be interpreted in light of the law in force at the time of drawing up the treaty. The reference to the time of drawing up suggests that drafters can, logically, only 'intend' or 'will' things which are acceptable or recognizable possibilities to begin with. One cannot interpret a 19th century treaty on fighting crime as covering also computer crime, since the very concepts of computers and computer crime were not yet known at the time. Thus, in order to pay respect to the drafters' intentions, interpretation should take place in light of the law as it was then.

---

[5] This should not come as a surprise. On the connections between law and power, see M. Foucault, *Society Must Be Defended: Lectures at the Collège de France 1975–1976* (2004).

[6] The first special rapporteur on the law of treaties, J.L. Brierly, never got around to discussing rules of interpretation, and never managed to work up much enthusiasm for drafting a Convention to begin with.

[7] For a general discussion, see Klabbers, 'On Rationalism in Politics: Interpretation of Treaties and the World Trade Organization', 74 *Nordic Journal of International Law* (2005) 405.

[8] The text ran: '1. A treaty is to be interpreted in the light of the law in force at the time when the treaty was drawn up. 2. Subject to paragraph 1, the application of a treaty shall be governed by the rules of international law in force at the time when the treaty is applied.' See Waldock, 'Third Report on the Law of Treaties', Doc.A/CN.4/167 and Adds.1–3, *YBILC* (1964) vol. II, 8–9. For a brief discussion, see Nascimento e Silva, *supra* note 2, 265–270.

However, things would be different with respect to the application of treaties. Surely, so Sir Humphrey suggested,[9] states should not be allowed to violate present-day international law under reference to an older agreement. To uphold a 19th century treaty condoning an activity that would later be rendered illegal under general international law would be problematic.

The underlying distinction between interpretation and application, while not uncommon,[10] itself already indicates deeply felt ambivalence on all things temporal. It presupposes (and proposes), on the one hand, that an interpretation, once established, remains settled: the interpretation of the term 'aggression' (for example) in the United Nations Charter, on this view, would have been carved in stone in 1945, and would thus be incapable of further development, no matter how hard the General Assembly might work at a further definition.[11] What might change is not the meaning of the provision, but the surrounding legal instruments; this then ought to be taken into account when applying that interpretation arrived at earlier. In practice, however, there is a good chance that the two (interpretation and application) might lapse into each other – such would seem well-nigh inevitable, if only because it would be difficult to apply something without at the same time interpreting it, and to interpret a term without a context in which to apply it.[12]

The initial discussion within the ILC proved a bit inconsequential. While many of the ILC members agreed that there ought to be some role for some version of the notion of intertemporality, others objected, echoing the thoughts of Judge Jessup, that it might create instability to have treaties adapting to changing international law.[13] Jiménez de Aréchaga, for one, worried that article 56 might result 'in longstanding treaties concerning frontiers being called in question on the ground that they had been secured by coercion. . . .'[14]

---

[9] Actually, he did nothing of the sort: his brief commentary on draft article 56 traced the development of the intertemporal rule through the cases, but hardly addressed any reasons as to why such a rule would be useful or desirable. See Waldock, *ibid*, 8–10.

[10] It finds its roots in Max Huber's classic dictum in the 1928 *Island of Palmas* arbitration, 2 *RIIA* (1928) 829.

[11] See GA Resolution 3314 (XXIX), 14 December 1974. For an informed discussion, see Stone, 'Hopes and Loopholes in the 1974 Definition of Aggression', 71 *American Journal of International Law* (1977) 224.

[12] Many sensible things about interpretation have been written by Stanley Fish. See for a more systematic explication of this position, the essays collected in S. Fish, *Doing What Comes Naturally: Change, Rhetoric, and the Practice of Theory in Literary and Legal Studies* (1989).

[13] See Jessup's famous commentary on Judge Huber's award in the *Island of Palmas* arbitration: Jessup, 'The Palmas Island Arbitration', 22 *American Journal of International Law* (1928) 740. Following Jessup, W.J.B. Versfelt too finds Huber's dictum 'highly disturbing. Every state would continually have to be considering: does international law still recognize my sovereignty over such or such part of my territory or has it developed new requirements, which I do not now fulfil?' See: W.J.B. Versfelt, *The Miangas Arbitration* (1933) 15.

[14] ILC, 728th meeting, *YBILC* (1964) vol I, 34.

What most of the members of the ILC seemed worried about were two things. First, many seemed to suggest that the principles laid down in article 56 were really, or at least seemingly, contradictory. Castrén for instance made that point, as did Tabibi, suggesting that the two notions nullified each other.[15] Rosenne, suggesting that neither of the two principles 'was subordinate to the other', was plagued by similar worries.[16]

The point was most forcefully (if perhaps somewhat inadvertently) expressed by Bartos. Distinguishing between two conceptions of treaties (treaties as legal acts between parties, and treaties as sources of law) he held that 'it was not only logical, but essential to distinguish between the two points of time mentioned in the article.'[17] And he proceeded: 'It was necessary to understand what the parties had wished to do and to determine what legal relationships they had wished to establish . . . , but it was also necessary to consider the effects of treaties as legal norms.'[18]

This, however, gave rise to thoughts about the proper place of the two principles of intertemporality. If one was about interpretation, and the other about application, then why not separate the two and place them in different articles, perhaps even in different parts of the Convention? This, at least, would have had the benefit of preventing the appearance of contradictions in one and the same provision.[19]

The second thing on the minds of the ILC members was the question of whether the distinction made between a treaty's interpretation and its application, while analytically plausible, could be maintained in any meaningful way in practice. Verdross suggested, in wonderfully optimist language, that 'once a treaty has been correctly interpreted, in [sic] had to be applied according to that interpretation.' In light of this, he did 'not think it was possible to draw a distinction between the interpretation of a treaty and its application.'[20] Paredes, in a similar vein, suggested that 'interpretations were made in order to perform the treaty.'[21] De Luna, likewise, insisted that 'a treaty was interpreted so that it could be applied',[22] while Yasseen suggested much the same when claiming that 'in speaking of application it was necessary to speak of interpretation.'[23]

---

[15] ILC, 729th meeting, *ibid,* 35.
[16] *Ibid,* 36.
[17] *Ibid.*
[18] *Ibid.*
[19] Several members, accordingly, advocated such a split, most explicitly perhaps Tabibi (729th meeting, *supra* note 15, 35) and De Luna, *ibid,* 37.
[20] ILC, 728th meeting, *supra* note 14, 33.
[21] *Ibid,* 34.
[22] ILC, 729th meeting, *supra* note 15, 37.
[23] *Ibid.*

Indeed, Sir Humphrey himself, forced to defend the positioning of the two principles in one and the same article, pointed out that they were really inseparable:
interpretation is 'often a necessary preliminary to application.'[24] But thus put, of
course, the one problem ends up undermining the other: by positing that interpretation and application are not all that different, Sir Humphrey ended up shooting
himself in the foot; there now was no longer a solid reason to have two distinct
principles, and it became possible to discuss the notion of intertemporality in connection with the rules on interpretation. This result was not immediately visible;
the meeting's chairman, Roberto Ago, merely proposed that further consideration
of article 56 be postponed and that Sir Humphrey would reconsider the matter.[25]

Sir Humphrey would get around to drafting rules on interpretation in his sixth
report. He presented a general rule of interpretation which included the injunction
that a treaty shall be interpreted in light of 'the rules of general international law in
force at the time of conclusion.'[26] Hence, this covered the first principle of
intertemporality, but not the second; the earlier distinction between interpretation
and application had been abandoned.

Some governments responded on this point, but none was very enthusiastic. The
Dutch government suggested that the element of intertemporality would best be
considered subsumed under the general notion of good faith,[27] whereas Greece
remarked that the reference to international law 'in force at the time of conclusion'
would result in stasis: excluding any development.[28]

While Sir Humphrey was less than fully convinced by the Dutch position,[29] he
did nonetheless present a different version for discussion in the Commission.
Under this new draft, introduced at the ILC's 869th meeting, any hint at anything
temporal or intertemporal had vanished. The redraft merely provided (amongst
other things) that a treaty be interpreted in light of 'the rules of international law.'[30]

This struck a chord with the Commission members, who seemed above all relieved
by the fact that the thorny problem of intertemporal law had been disposed of.[31] As a
result, the discussion revolved around the question as to whether the reference to

---

[24] ILC, 729th meeting, *supra* note 15, 39; a few sentences earlier, he had made essentially the same
point: 'many other articles of the draft ... also involved interpretation as a preliminary to application
of a treaty.'

[25] *Ibid*, 40.

[26] Draft article 69, as reproduced in *YBILC* (1966) vol. I, 183.

[27] Waldock, 'Sixth Report on the Law of Treaties', Doc.A/CN.4/186 and Adds.1-7, *YBILC*
(1966) vol. II, 92.

[28] *Ibid*, 93.

[29] *Ibid*, 96.

[30] ILC, 869th meeting, *YBILC* (1966) vol. I, part II, 184.

[31] If the intertemporal problem were to have been taken into account, then, as Herbert Briggs suggested, the most adequate formula would be somewhat convoluted: 'The rules of international law in
force at the time of its conclusion as well as those rules in force at the time of its interpretation.' See
ILC, 870th meeting, *YBILC* (1966) vol. I, part II, 187. Note, incidentally, that in Briggs' formulation
any distinction between interpretation and application has disappeared.

international law was meant as a reference to general or customary international law, or whether it should also cover locally or regionally applicable rules. Either way, following the Dutch suggestion, the ILC seemed to have come around to the position that 'the temporal element should be regarded as implicitly covered by the concept of good faith.'[32] As Sir Humphrey concluded, with a fine sense of understatement, he had the 'impression that the Commission was generally disinclined to deal with the problem of intertemporal law in the draft articles.'[33]

In the end, the Commission proposed, in draft article 27, paragraph 3(c), that when interpreting, there shall be taken into account '[a]ny relevant rules of international law applicable in the relations between the parties,'[34] and explained indeed 'that correct application of the temporal element would normally be indicated by interpretation of the term in good faith.'[35]

The Vienna Conference[36] by and large could live with this. Some delegations[37] thought it sounder to have all rules relating to interpretation included in a single article (this would arguably have turned the rule-based approach of the ILC into something like a list of maxims to pick and choose from, more or less along the lines of what Fitzmaurice suggested in his academic writings), and Germany thought that the paragraph on international law should also make reference to obligations of one or more of the parties to a treaty, but in the end, the text remained as proposed.

The entire discussion suggests that it would be difficult to consider treaties in a vacuum.[38] This holds true at least (on this point, the ILC seemed to be unanimous) when interpretation is concerned. Perhaps Yasseen best summed up the general position at a session he was chairing: 'The reference to the rules of international law was indispensable, for just as a term could only be understood in a sentence, a sentence only in an article, and an article only in the treaty as a whole, it was impossible to understand the treaty except within the whole international legal order of which it formed a part, which it influenced and by which it was influenced.'[39]

---

[32] So, e.g., Jiménez de Aréchaga, *ibid*, 190.

[33] ILC, 872nd meeting, *ibid,* 199.

[34] The reference to the law as applicable in the relations to the parties seems to have been included by the Drafting Committee without any particular urging on the part of, or discussion within, the ILC. See ILC, 883rd meeting, *YBILC* (1966) vol I, 267.

[35] *Report of the ILC on the Work of its Eighteenth Session,* Doc. A/CN.4/191, *YBILC* (1966) vol. II, 222.

[36] *Official Records of the United Nations Conference on the Law of Treaties,* Vienna, (hereinafter Vienna Conference), (1968–69) 149–151.

[37] Most notably the USA and the Philippines, *ibid.*

[38] And there seems something quite natural about this. Recall, e.g., that already in its first ever contentious case, the PCIJ was asked to interpret the provisions of the Versailles Treaty concerning the Kiel Canal in light of other instruments on international waterways, and in light of the law of neutrality. See *Case of the SS Wimbledon*, PCIJ Series A, (1923), No. 1, 231. On Wimbledon, see Klabbers, 'Clinching the Concept of Sovereignty: Wimbledon Redux', 3 *Austrian Review of International and European Law* (1998) 345; for a useful discussion of the work of the PCIJ, see O. Spiermann, *International Legal Argument in the Permanent Court of International Justice: The Rise of the International Judiciary* (2005).

[39] ILC, 871st meeting, *YBILC* (1966) vol. I, part II, 197.

Yasseen's position seems indisputable, at least as far as interpretation goes.[40] Yet, while opening up the interpretation of treaties to the influence of international law, the ILC simultaneously aspired to close off from international law other aspects of the law of treaties, in particular the rules on invalidity and termination.

3. Time in a Bottle

While the intertemporal provision of draft article 56 had a respectable (if controversial) pedigree in the form of the classic *Island of Palmas* arbitration,[41] article 42 is typically a legislative provision, and could not possibly have had its origins in customary international law. It is not, so to speak, a substantive rule of the law of treaties, but rather a rule on how to use some of the substantive rules of the Vienna Convention; a methodological device, if you will. In the standard textbooks or overviews, article 42 is either not mentioned at all,[42] or only mentioned in passing,[43] but never discussed at length or in depth.[44] Nor am I aware of any scholarly article or book chapter on article 42 specifically.

It is sometimes claimed that the main function of article 42 is to make sure that the Vienna Convention's mechanisms on establishing invalidity and termination (articles 65 and 66 in particular) might actually be useful.[45] While there is little in the drafting history of article 42 itself to corroborate this particular thesis, there is a recognized connection between article 42, the dispute settlement machinery,[46] and the provisions on the consequences of a finding of invalidity.[47] This focus on settlement may help explain why the potential of article 42 has long remained unrecognized.[48]

Article 42 first made a sustained appearance in the drafting of the Vienna Convention in 1963, in Sir Humphrey Waldock's second report. Under the heading 'The presumption in favour of the validity of a treaty', Sir Humphrey posited

---

[40] The ICJ made grateful use of article 31, paragraph 3 (c) in its decision in the *Case Concerning Oil Platforms* (Islamic Republic of Iran v. United States of America), ICJ Rep 2003, 182.

[41] For a balanced discussion, see Elias, 'The Doctrine of Intertemporal Law', 74 *American Journal of International Law* (1980) 285.

[42] See Fitzmaurice, 'The Practical Workings of the Law of Treaties', in M. Evans (ed.), *International Law* (2003) 173.

[43] See, e.g. A. Aust, *Modern Treaty Law and Practice* (2000) 224.

[44] A relative exception is the attention afforded in I. Sinclair, *The Vienna Convention on the Law of Treaties* (1984) 162–165.

[45] See, e.g. Capotorti, 'L'extinction et la suspension des traités', 134 *Recueil des Cours* (1971) 455.

[46] A. Aust, *supra* note 43, 245, pithily observes that article 65 is a 'key provision, its procedural safeguards being designed to deter states from arbitrary action, though it is often not followed.'

[47] In particular article 69 of the Vienna Convention.

[48] An example highlighting the connection between article 42 and articles 65 and 69 is H. Mosler, *The International Society as a Legal Community* (1980) 102.

the rule that treaties ought to be presumed valid and in force upon the parties unless they lack 'essential validity' under the draft articles, or unless they had 'ceased to be in force' under the draft articles.[49] A brief commentary (a single paragraph) explained that the point of the provision was to highlight the presumption of validity (and, one may add, of being in force). As Waldock explained:

> ... the onus is upon a party which asserts that a regularly concluded treaty is not binding upon it. Unilateral assertions of a right to avoid or denounce treaties on one or other of the grounds covered in this part [of the draft – JK], simply as a pretext to escape from inconvenient obligations, have always been a source of insecurity to treaties; and one of the most difficult problems in this part is to formulate the grounds of invalidity in terms which do not open the door too wide to unilateral avoidance or denunciation of treaties.[50]

It is one thing, in other words, to insist that treaties are binding upon the parties and should be kept by them in good faith; it is quite another, however, to actually rely on good faith. As Waldock's words suggest, good faith may not always be present, and may need a helping hand in the form of a provision which explicitly recognizes that on occasion, bad faith may manifest itself.

Perhaps precisely because it hinted at the possibility of bad faith, the proposal met with an initially somewhat antagonistic response within the ILC. At the 702nd meeting of the Commission, on 18 June 1963, many of the ILC members voiced their doubts as to the wisdom or necessity of including such a provision in the Convention.[51] Castrén, Jiménez de Aréchaga, Yasseen and Tunkin all held that the proposal would be unnecessary, as did Amado. Some of the other members were rather more in favour of its inclusion, but still only moderately so. De Luna explicitly referred to the possibility of states acting in bad faith, and Gros thought it 'natural' to include a rule which would hold a treaty to be binding 'subject to the special provisions on the essential validity and termination of treaties . . .'[52]

Waldock himself made clear that the association of article 42 with bad faith was perhaps a mite overblown: his article was not concerned with the notion that *pacta sunt servanda*, as some of the ILC members apparently thought (most explicitly Amado) – there could be good reasons for not executing a valid treaty in force.[53] But if not related to the *pacta sunt servanda* maxim, then what was it related to? Waldock himself left this unanswered, but perhaps a clue can be found *a contrario* in one of Cadieux' remarks. Cadieux proposed 'as an intermediate solution', that the

---

[49] Waldock, 'Second Report on the Law of Treaties', Doc.A/CN.4/156 and Adds.1-3, *YBILC* (1963) vol. II, 39.

[50] *Ibid*, 39.

[51] See the discussion during the 702nd meeting, in *YBILC* (1963) vol. I, 194–196.

[52] *Ibid*, 195.

[53] Presumably, he was thinking here about limits to territorial or temporal application. He referred to his next report, which deals with such issues.

article should retain the presumption of validity while omitting the reference to contesting the validity of treaties.[54] That seems to suggest that, within the ILC, there was an understanding that Waldock's draft covered two distinct topics: first, the creation of a presumption of validity and bindingness, and second, listing (and thus limiting) the possibilities to rebut that presumption.

Despite Cadieux's plea, many ILC members were against the very idea of a presumption of validity and bindingness. Jiménez de Aréchaga recalled that presumptions usually, in civil law, relate to rules of evidence; thus, there was no place for a presumption in an instrument on the law of treaties. Tunkin, for his part, felt that presumptions were matters of logic, not law, and others simply held that they did not think Waldock had been laying down a presumption (something Waldock himself remained silent about). In the end, the 702nd meeting was concluded, on Jiménez de Aréchaga's proposal, with a decision to submit the matter to the Drafting Committee for redrafting.

The Drafting Committee presented a reformulated version which, however, still contained a strong element of presumption. The title to the article was to start with the term 'Presumption'; the provision itself would specify that a rebuttal could only result 'from the provisions of the present articles.'[55] The Commission adopted it with 16 votes to none, with one abstention.

Sir Humphrey's Fourth report, submitted in 1965, contained the comments of some governments to what had now become draft article 30. Those were by and large positive, save for proposing some drafting changes in the French and Spanish translations.[56] One remarkable thing happened though, and is included in the statement by the Venezuelan delegation. Venezuela opined that it was necessary to determine the result of the application of the rules of the Vienna Convention relating to validity 'before the question whether a particular treaty is void can be settled.'[57] This, if taken literally, would amount to reversing the presumption: on the Venezuelan proposal, a treaty would be presumed to be void unless the opposite could be demonstrated.

Perhaps in a variation on the same theme, the United States delegation raised the issue of the completeness of the law.[58] Sir Humphrey picked up on the suggestion, and invited the Commission to consider 'whether the draft articles cover all the possible grounds of invalidity, termination and suspension.'[59] Much of the answer could depend, so he hinted, at whether phenomena such as obsolescence or desuetude could be subsumed under other headings and thus safely be left unaddressed.

---

[54] ILC, 702nd meeting, *supra* note 51, 195.

[55] ILC, 717th meeting, *YBILC* (1963) vol. I, 296.

[56] Waldock, 'Fourth Report on the Law of Treaties', Doc.A/CN.4/177 and Adds.1-2, *YBILC* (1965) vol. II, 65–67.

[57] *Ibid*, 65.

[58] *Ibid*, 65.

[59] *Ibid*, 66.

The ILC did not get around to discussing the topic in its 1965 session, but did include a draft article in its final set of draft articles. Draft article 39 no longer carried the word 'presumption' in its heading, and differs on important technical points (but not on points of principle) from what would later become article 42.[60]

In its commentary, the ILC once again underlined that the basic idea behind article 42 was to safeguard the stability of treaties, and therefore formulate a rule holding that 'the validity and continuance in force of a treaty is the normal state of things which maybe set aside only on the grounds and under the conditions provided for in the present articles.'[61]

During the later stages of drafting, one central question slowly but irresistibly came to the fore: to what extent could the provision meet its aspiration of relating to a complete set of grounds for invalidity, termination and suspension? During a meeting in early 1966, several ILC members began to voice concerns on this topic.

For instance, Rosenne, subtle as always, held that the article could not begin to cover cases whose *sedes materiae* would rest outside the law of treaties; the law of state succession came to mind as an example.[62] Yasseen, by contrast (supported by Bedjaoui) turned the issue into a more overtly political issue, claiming that under positive international law (but not under the proposed Vienna Convention), treaties concluded under economic or political coercion would be void.[63] Hence, to their mind, to include a provision which would find the grounds of invalidity mentioned in the Vienna Convention to be exhaustive would pre-empt any discussion on economic or political duress. Verdross, likewise, pointed out that as long as the ILC could not reach agreement on what to do in case of corruption of a state representative, the list of causes of invalidity was incomplete.[64]

Half a year later, this turned out to be the central theme in the drafting of the commentary. By now, it was clear that the Vienna Convention would not address issues of state succession, nor issues of state responsibility. As a consequence, Manfred Lachs advocated the inclusion of 'the exceptions relating to the effects of State succession and responsibility on treaties'. Interestingly, where earlier attempts had aspired to create a closed system, the Commission by now had come around to the idea that such a closed system would be well-nigh impossible; Lachs' routine use of the term 'exceptions' is telling. Eventually, it was decided that article 42 would

---

[60] There are two technical differences in paragraph 1. One is that article 42 distinguishes between the validity of a treaty and the validity of an expression of consent; draft article 39 made no such distinction. The second is that draft article 39 spelled out that an invalid treaty would be void; this is left out of article 42, and found a place in article 69 on a French initiative: see *Vienna Conference, supra* note 36, 159.

[61] *Report of the ILC on the Work of its Eighteenth Session,* Doc. A/CN.4/191, *YBILC* (1966) vol. II, 236–237 esp. 236.

[62] ILC, 841st meeting, *YBILC* (1966) vol. I, part I, 123.

[63] *Id.*

[64] *Ibid,* 124.

not be preceded by a savings clause, but that a general savings clause be added to the Convention: this became article 73.

At the Vienna Conference, nothing much of import happened as regards article 42. Various technical amendments were proposed, but nothing of eye-catching substance. Probably the most relevant decision was that the earlier reference to 'the present articles' was replaced, upon a Vietnamese proposal, by reference to 'the present Convention.'[65]

4. Time Waits for No One

It has become commonplace to explain the role of article 42 within the Vienna Convention's scheme as a defensive move, so as to safeguard the binding and valid nature of treaties. As Nahlik notes, some 40 per cent of the Convention's articles deal with termination and invalidity, and '[t]his fact alone caused some anxiety: so many articles to restrict the binding force of treaties by making it possible either to impeach their validity, or to terminate them, or, at the very least, to suspend their operation?'[66] Sinclair likewise invokes the psychological make-up of international lawyers when he explains: 'The spelling out in conventional form of a long series of separate and unrelated grounds for the avoidance of treaties is a disturbing phenomenon for the majority of international lawyers . . .'[67]

As noted, however, article 42 aims not merely to pacify lawyerly anxieties about the sanctity of treaty commitments: this would be too rosy a picture in a world where many do their best to escape from that sanctity by concluding non-binding agreements, making far-reaching reservations, or engaging in heated debates about the proper methods of interpretation.[68]

Instead (or additionally), article 42 aspires to create a vacuum around the Vienna Convention by positing that only the application of the Convention may result in invalidity of treaties, and only the application of the Convention or a treaty itself

---

[65] See *Vienna Conference, supra* note 36, para. 16 (a) of the introduction to the report. This change was made throughout the Convention.

[66] Nahlik, 'The Grounds of Invalidity and Termination of Treaties', 65 *American Journal of International Law* (1971) 737.

[67] I. Sinclair, *supra* note 44, 162. Note however that some turn the causality around, holding that the idea to safeguard the sanctity of treaties 'required the Commission to produce a series of articles to deal with all the grounds on which a claim could legitimately be made that a treaty was invalid or subject to termination, denunciation, withdrawal or suspension.' See Kearney & Dalton, 'The Treaty on Treaties', 64 *American Journal of International Law* (1970) 526.

[68] Best summed up in the title of R.B. Bilder, *Managing the Risks of International Agreement* (1981).

may result in termination of a treaty or suspension of its operation. The reason for doing so remains a bit obscure, and probably taps as much into psychological considerations as Sinclair's explanation: the wish to keep things under control by creating a regime that is both part of and separate from general international law.

In fact, perhaps contrary to what the drafters self-consciously realized, the potential of article 42 is enormous. Article 42 would not just have posited the Vienna Convention as a self-contained system; that alone would have been remarkable enough. Its main import, however, would have been to place this self-contained system at the apex of international law: if a treaty can only be invalidated or terminated on the basis of the Vienna Convention, or anything allowed by it, then it follows that the Convention must be seen as superior to anything else. Supervening custom, e.g., would not be a solid reason for terminating a treaty anymore, unless it could be cast in terms acceptable to the Vienna Convention. In short, while its drafters may not have realized the full extent of the aspirations behind article 42 at the time, article 42, if successful, would have turned international law into a veritable hierarchical legal order.

The obvious question arising then is whether it works this way. And the answer – already anticipated by the ILC and fleshed out by the general exception with respect to state succession, state responsibility and the outbreak of hostilities – is in the negative. Precisely by excluding state succession, hostilities and the law of responsibility from the scope of the Vienna Convention, the drafters have opened the door for considerations other than those listed in the Convention itself to impeach the validity of a treaty or to bring it to an end.

Various commentators have added further examples of their choice to illustrate how unrealistic the wording of article 42 is. Thus, Nahlik recalls that the Convention does not include anything specific on the extinction or disappearance of a state as a ground for termination, nor on the outbreak of hostilities,[69] whereas Crawford and Olleson underline that while the Convention is silent on issues of state responsibility, breaches (non-material breaches, at any rate) may well result in a treaty's termination or a suspension of its operation.[70] Jennings & Watts, in their edition of *Oppenheim's International Law*, list as a possible additional ground for invalidity the possibility of uncertainty[71] and Hersch Lauterpacht, it is perhaps worth recalling, had discussed conflicting treaties initially in terms of validity: a

---

[69] See Nahlik, *supra* note 66, 752–753.

[70] See Crawford & Olleson, 'The Exception of Non-performance: Links Between the Law of Treaties and the Law of State Responsibility', 21 *Australian Yearbook of International Law* (2000) 55.

[71] See R.Y. Jennings & A. Watts, *Oppenheim's International Law* (1992) 1285, footnote 1. They suggest, furthermore, that a strict reading of article 42 would be difficult to reconcile with the last recital of the Vienna Convention's preamble, which keeps the door open for customary international law.

treaty conflicting with a prior commitment would be invalid.[72] Article 42, however, would render such a conclusion unlikely.[73]

The International Law Commission itself had already discussed whether such things as obsolescence or desuetude would not constitute separate grounds for termination; it came to the conclusion that in such cases, the termination would be traceable to the consent of the parties (however implied perhaps), and would thus come within the ambit of article 54 of the Convention. Some have been critical of this position, claiming that desuetude or obsolescence do not rest upon implied consent to terminate, but rather on supervening custom.[74] And supervening custom is, again, not referred to as a ground for termination.[75]

To make a long story short, it seems abundantly clear that article 42, as laid down in the Vienna Convention, does not meet its aspiration of creating a vacuum around the Vienna Convention. The Convention simply is not exhaustive as far as grounds for invalidity and termination are concerned and, what is more, could never have been expected to be exhaustive: as with other things in life, invalidity and termination are intensely political matters, the meaning of which is not carved in stone but is fluid.

The attraction of article 42 as a norm holding the international legal system together must have been all the greater in light of the dawning realization, shared by some of the more influential members of the Commission at least, that the law of treaties could not, and should not, be based on contractual notions alone. Rosenne, whose academic work thoughtfully advocates coming to terms with the community interest in the law of treaties,[76] was the first to embrace the idea of article 42 among the members of the ILC.[77]

But in much the same way in which attempts to protect the community interest have been shipwrecked before, so too article 42 does not seem to work: international law simply cannot afford to ignore the interests of states, their positivist and selfish

---

[72] See Lauterpacht, 'First Report on the Law of Treaties', Doc. A/CN.4/63, *YBILC* (1953) vol. II, 156–159. McNair too treats this under the heading of validity; see A. McNair, *The Law of Treaties* (1961) 213–236.

[73] As conflicting obligations are, eventually, not listed among the grounds of invalidity in the Vienna Convention, it would be difficult to argue that nonetheless invalidity should ensue.

[74] Capotorti, *supra* note 45, 44 and 446–447. Capotorti is approvingly referred to by Sinclair, *supra* note 44, 64.

[75] Writing well before the Vienna Convention, E. Vitta mentioned lack of registration as a ground for invalidity. See E. Vitta, *La Validité des Traités Internationaux* (1940) 245.

[76] See already Rosenne, 'Bilateralism and Community Interest in the Codified Law of Treaties', in W. Friedmann, L. Henkin & O. Lissitzyn (eds.), *Transnational Law in a Changing Society: Essays in Honor of Philip C. Jessup* (1972) 202. In it, he subtly suggests (esp. at 208–211) that the community interest underlying rules on validity (almost by definition) is canceled out by the bilateralism of the procedure to be followed under the Vienna Convention's regime.

[77] At least, he was the first to publicly endorse the idea, after some of his colleagues had deemed it 'unnecessary'. See ICL, 702nd meeting, *supra* note 51, 195.

desires, without running the risk of falling into oblivion. It is one thing for a rule to proclaim that it, and it alone, can be applied to certain circumstances; it is quite another to stop states from doing (ever so reasonable) things outside that rule. If two states were to decide, amongst themselves, to, say, consider a treaty between themselves as being terminated upon the outbreak of hostilities, then there is fairly little international law can do about it while remaining faithful to the basic ideas of sovereignty and state consent. The only alternative is to draft a rule so broad as to encompass all possible manifestations of state consent; but doing so will immediately take the sting out of the very rule. If it is broad enough to accommodate all cases where states would wish to declare treaties invalid or terminated, it loses its utility.

By the same token, excluding in advance such things as state succession, state responsibility and the outbreak of hostilities signified that the rule would be of little use; it is no coincidence, furthermore, that both courts and academics have seen fit to somehow reconcile the terms of article 42 with the desires of states. Some authors have argued, with force, that cases of state succession generally are (and probably ought to be) treated as ever so many examples of fundamental changes of circumstances.[78] In diplomatic practice too, this would not seem to be unusual.[79] Moreover, famously (or notoriously, as some might have it), the European Court of Justice has subsumed the outbreak of hostilities under the *rebus sic stantibus* rule.[80] Therewith, instances of state succession or the outbreak of hostilities come within the scope of the Vienna Convention and thus within the reach of article 42, notwithstanding the formal exclusion by means of article 73. The (inevitable)[81] blurring of the distinction between the material breach of a treaty, triggering the application of the law of treaties, and a 'regular' breach, possibly triggering the application of law of state responsibility, has had much the same result: any breach of some magnitude can come within the ambit of the Vienna Convention as reworked in judicial practice and in the practice of states.[82]

---

[78] See briefly, e.g., Oeter, 'State Succession and the Struggle over Equity: Some Observations on the Laws of State Succession with Respect to State Property and Debts in Cases of Separation and Dissolution of States', 38 *German Yearbook of International Law* (1995) 73.

[79] For an example, see Lehto, 'Succession of States in the Former Soviet Union: Arrangements Concerning the Bilateral Treaties of Finland and the USSR', 4 *Finnish Yearbook of International Law* (1993) 222–225.

[80] Most notably in the decision of the European Court of Justice in case C-162/96, *A. Racke GmbH & Co. v. Hauptzollamt Mainz*, [1998] ECR I-3655. For further discussion, see Klabbers, 'Reinventing the Law of Treaties: The Contribution of the EC Courts', 30 *Netherlands Yearbook of International Law* (1999) 57–59.

[81] Given the wording of article 60 (stressing the relevance of the norm breached rather than the gravity of the breach), it was well-nigh inevitable that courts would take article 60 not quite literally. See generally Simma, 'Reflections on Article 60 of the Vienna Convention on the Law of Treaties and its Background in General International Law', 20 *Österreichische Zeitschrift für Öffentliches Recht und Völkerrecht* (1970) 5.

[82] See generally Klabbers, 'Side-stepping Article 60: Material Breach of Treaty and Responses Thereto', in M. Tupamäki (ed.), *Finnish Branch of International Law Association 1946–1996* (1998) 20.

And as far as the internal consistency of the Vienna Convention goes, on this point too it was unlikely that article 42 would live up to its ambitions. For one thing, the idea of such a fundamental norm closing off a system is difficult to reconcile with the more liberal attitude of the Convention on the whole: many of its rules are generally recognized to be residual in nature.

More specifically, where article 42 would create a veritable *Grundnorm*,[83] article 5 strips it of possible effects to a considerable extent by carving out a separate niche for the treaty practice of international organizations. And most interestingly, as discussed above, the thought of including a provision advocating the use of intertemporal law would have undermined article 42 even further.[84] The intertemporal provision never materialized, but became, in a watered down version, what is now article 31, paragraph 3(c) of the Vienna Convention, instructing interpreters to take into account 'any relevant rules of international law applicable in the relations between the parties.' Interestingly, it is this provision which is presently often regarded as the possible remedy to the ailment of the fragmentation.

5. Unity in Fragmentation

The main attraction, to be sure, of laying down article 42 (and no doubt the reason why the ILC, initial misgivings notwithstanding, swiftly came around to the idea) is that it taps into the sentiment that international law can be a real legal system, just like domestic law. To have a closed, self-contained system relating to invalidity and termination is to close things off for the possibly diverging will of the parties; it is to introduce a public law element in a system largely made up of private-law type relations, and serves thereby to underpin that very system. Koskenniemi refers to article 42 as a 'Münchausen-provision', which precludes other regimes from being self-contained. After all, at least the first paragraph of article 42 (on invalidity) creates 'the 'minimum-level' at which the Vienna Convention regulates everything that happens in the world of regime-building and regime-administration.'[85]

Potentially then, article 42 could have been the answer to anyone's worries and anxieties about the fragmentation of international law: if taken seriously, it would have had the potential to keep a fragmenting system together. Its open-ended nature, however, ensures that its potential was lost before the ink on the Vienna

---

[83] It has been noted that it is somewhat awkward to speak of a *Grundnorm* situated at the apex of a legal order; this usage might suggest a tension inherent in the notion. See D. Dyzenhaus, *Legality and Legitimacy: Carl Schmitt, Hans Kelsen and Hermann Heller in Weimar* (1997) 103, footnote 4.

[84] I am indebted to Anja Lindroos for intelligent discussion on this point.

[85] See Koskenniemi, 'Preliminary Report on Function and Scope of the *Lex Specialis* Rule and the Question of 'Self-contained Regimes', UN Doc. ILC(LVI)/SG/FIL/CRD.1/add.1, 40, paras. 187–188.

Convention was dry. Hence, the quest continues for a norm that can somehow keep the system together.

The latest candidate to have been proposed is article 31, paragraph 3(c) of the Vienna Convention, the residue of what was once planned to become a rule on intertemporal law in the law of treaties. But instead of using the closing tactics of article 42, article 31, paragraph 3(c) uses the opposite tactic: it aims to keep the system hanging together by making sure that everything relates to everything else.

The fragmentation of international law manifests itself in at least two fundamental ways. The first is that the various sub-regimes of international law are thought to become self-determining, more or less self-contained, units.[86] The most discussed example at present is no doubt the World Trade Organization, around which a wild debate rages concerning its relationship to general international law, involving such questions as whether WTO law should give way to environmental standards or labour standards.[87]

Much of that debate takes place in terms of general international law doctrine. Thus, the leading study of conflicting norms and the WTO is set up as a study on conflicting treaty provisions, studying articles 30 and 41 of the Vienna Convention in some detail, advocating a more widespread use of the *lex specialis* maxim, *et cetera*.[88] The thought underlying it, in other words, is that fragmentation means, really, a separation of one state-controlled system (the WTO) from a more general state-controlled system (public international law), to be analyzed within the discourse of the general system. Technically, the room for doing so is created by WTO law itself: article 3, paragraph 2 of its Dispute Settlement Understanding, after all, allows (perhaps even orders) public international law to enter into WTO law. The only alternative way of looking at it would be to reverse the relationship and place the WTO in the driving seat.[89] Technically this too would be possible by invoking the same provision and pointing to its limits: it does, after all, merely refer to the customary rules of treaty interpretation. Anything else can thus, *a contrario*, be excluded; and if the WTO drafters had wished the WTO to take labour or environmental concerns into account, they would have, could have, and should have indicated as much.

---

[86] The *locus classicus* is Simma, 'Self-contained Regimes', 16 *Netherlands Yearbook of International Law* (1985) 111.

[87] On the fundamentals of the relationship, see, e.g., Kennedy, 'The International Style in Postwar Law and Policy', *Utah Law Review* (1994) 7. See also MacMillan, 'International Economic Law and Public International Law: Strangers in the Night', 10 *International Trade Law & Regulation* (2004) 115.

[88] See J. Pauwelyn, *Conflict of Norms in Public International Law: How WTO Law Relates to Other Rules of International Law* (2003).

[89] Such a vision is endorsed (albeit not in very open terms) by the so-called 'Sutherland report'. See Consultative Board to the Director-General Supachai Panitchpakdi, *The Future of the WTO: Addressing Institutional Challenges in the New Millennium* (2004). For commentary on this issue, see Klabbers, 'New Logo: The Sutherland Report and the Re-branding of the WTO', 2 *International Organizations Law Review* (2005) 177.

While quite obviously this debate on fragmentation raises and discusses serious issues, what the debate misses is that there is a second threat to the unity (which may always have been more postulated than real at any rate) of international law: the fragmentation involved in non-state centered regulation.[90] As Gunther Teubner in particular, writing alone or with others, has made clear, standards for behaviour are not only set in public bodies anymore:

> Law-making also takes place outside the classical sources of international law, in agreements between global players, in private market regulation by multinational concerns, internal regulations of international organisations, interorganisational negotiating systems, world-wide standardisation processes that come about partly in markets, partly in processes of negotiation among organisations.[91]

Here the problem becomes more difficult to handle. Any attempt to insist on discussing a situation such as the AIDS/HIV crisis in terms of the TRIPS agreement may be countered not just by referring to different standards set up under auspices of the World Health Organization or some set of social justice norms promulgated by the United Nations, but also under reference to standards set by pharmaceutical companies inter se, or by codes of conduct developed by health workers.[92] Where the classic interplay of fragmentation of various public regimes could still invoke general rules, this becomes a lot harder when it is not just public authority but also private authority that demands precedence, or at least offers itself as an alternative.[93] There is no convincing legal reason[94] why rules emanating from public authority should be preferred over the other, in particular given the circumstance that rules emanating from non-public sources may be far better equipped to deal with the relevant aspects, and may boast a far more impressive degree of legitimacy precisely because they result from bottom-up procedures.[95] At the very least, the authority of public norms has lost some of its lustre as public decision-making

---

[90] Sometimes referred to as 'deformalization'. See, e.g., Koskenniemi, 'Global Governance and Public International Law', 37 *Kritische Justiz* (2004) 241.

[91] See Teubner, 'Societal Constitutionalism: Alternatives to State-centred Constitutional Theory' in C. Joerges, I.-J. Sand & G. Teubner (eds.), *Transnational Governance and Constitutionalism* (2004) 16.

[92] The example is adapted from A. Fischer-Lescano & G. Teubner, *Regime-Kollissionen: Kompatibilität durch Vernetzung statt Rechtseinheit* (unpublished paper, 2004, on file with the author).

[93] An interesting discussion is Fischer-Lescano, 'Die Emergenz der Globalverfassung', 63 *Zeitschrift für ausländisches öffentliches Recht und Völkerrecht* (2003) 717, (holding that law is self-reflexive with the final decisions on validity being taken by courts, but that fundamental norms take communication between legal orders to a higher level).

[94] For a normative critique, suggesting that there might be solid non-legal reasons for favouring public elements, see Cohen, 'Whose Sovereignty? Empire versus International Law', 18 *Ethics & International Affairs* (2004) 1.

[95] Some pertinent themes are explored in K.-H. Ladeur (ed.), *Public Governance in the Age of Globalization* (2004).

has not always been as accountable as one would have hoped for.[96] In such a setting, it is perhaps the case that article 42 could not do its work at any rate. Formalism, as Roberto Unger observed many years ago, inevitably brought forth deformalization, and vice versa.[97] The attempt to create a *Grundnorm* in article 42 automatically called for attempts to undermine that very *Grundnorm* (or at least to defuse its foundational potential), and it should come as no surprise that fragmentation is now being fought not by closing off the system, but rather by radically opening it up. For that is what article 31, paragraph 3(c) of the Vienna Convention entails: it does not close off international law from the workings of time, politics, or anything else, but rather embraces externalities wholeheartedly. Through the backdoor of interpretation, international law, whatever its form or manifestations, is invited to join the party; and not just some international law, but 'any relevant rules'. While it is an open question whether the drafters of the Vienna Convention would have had things like the *lex mercatoria*, or ISO standards, or such phenomena as the Global Compact[98] in mind, there is no good reason, in law, to exclude those as not really being international law, at least not without adopting an unfashionably strict attitude as to how international law is made.[99]

Fragmentation then is being fought by embracing it and clutching it (to continue an awkward metaphor) to death. For if fragmentation is total, then everything hangs together again: fragmentation becomes the unifying trait. It is this that reliance on article 31, paragraph 3(c) may help to accomplish: unity in fragmentation.

Even so, success is not guaranteed. Obviously, for the purposes of fighting fragmentation, the use of article 31, paragraph 3 (c) should not be limited to what might be called 'hard cases';[100] if so limited, separate treaty regimes would still be allowed to develop as long as their own terms were clear enough, no matter how much those clear terms would depart from other (general) legal instruments or norms. In other words: all cases should be construed as 'hard cases' to make fullest use of the unifying potential of article 31, paragraph 3 (c).

Yet doing so would change the very basis of treaty interpretation in international law, and therewith stumble upon formidable theoretical objections (and those have a habit of manifesting themselves in practice as well).[101] Treaty interpretation

---

[96] For some reflections focusing on how international organizations are affected, see Klabbers, 'Constitutionalism Lite', 1 *International Organizations Law Review* (2004) 31.

[97] See generally R.M. Unger, *Law in Modern Society: Towards a Criticism of Social Theory* (1976).

[98] On the latter, see V. Engström, *Realizing the Global Compact* (2001).

[99] For a treatment of all sorts of norms as part of an 'autonomous global legal order', see Brunkhorst, 'Globalising Democracy without a State: Weak Public, Strong Public, Global Constitutionalism', 31 *Millennium* (2002) 675.

[100] This seems to be where William Mansfield is heading in his report to the ILC. See UN Document ILC (LVI)/SG/FIL/CRD.3/Rev.1, para. 63.

[101] On the theoretical twists involved in turning from a consent-based system into something more 'public', see also the discussion in Craven, 'Legal Differentiation and the Concept of the Human Rights Treaty in International Law', 11 *European Journal of International Law* (2000) 489.

would cease to be a search for the intentions of the parties; it would, instead, become a quasi-legislative exercise, a search for the best way to keep the system intact, and would thus be vulnerable to the criticism that it does away with what the parties may have had in mind.[102]

6. Time to Conclude

The attempt to create a vacuum, temporal and otherwise, around the Vienna Convention and to posit article 42, however unwittingly perhaps, as the *Grundnorm* of the post-Vienna Convention international legal order, failed. By the same token, the simultaneous (and contradictory) attempt to specifically introduce an intertemporal provision failed. What is left is something much less ambitious: an injunction that when interpreting treaties, any relevant rules of international law applicable between the parties are to be taken into account. And perhaps nothing more could have been expected, as historically, the existence of international law as a legal system (let alone a coherent one) has often enough been put in doubt among both statesmen[103] and legal theorists.[104]

In an important sense, ordering interpreters to take any relevant rules into account is tantamount to stating the obvious: it would have been implausible to think of interpretation as an act taking place *in vacuo*,[105] in complete disregard of existing substantive rules. While the law might strive to conjure up a self-contained world without conflicts or politics, there is always the nagging suspicion that in real life (whatever that may be) outside factors cannot so easily be excluded.

The drawback will be obvious: if everything is law and if everything can be taken into account when interpreting treaties, then there is no end to what the law could possibly signify. It is no surprise that simultaneously to the observed fragmentation and deformalization of international law, one can hear increasingly vocal affirmations of the general rules on interpretation as embodied in the Vienna Convention, and increasingly urgent admonitions that departures from those rules are not to be recommended.[106] This suggests a deep paradox though: a quest for certainty in limits by

---

[102] See, e.g., Separate Opinion of Judge Higgins in the *Oil Platforms* case, *supra* note 40, 237. Incidentally, she may be mistaken in suggesting that article 31, paragraph 3 (c) would refer, under the Vienna Convention, to international law as part of the context; a literal reading would suggest that international law comes in 'together with' the context of a treaty.

[103] See the discussion in A. Carty, *The Decay of International Law* (1986), esp. Chapter 5.

[104] Famously, H.L.A. Hart, *The Concept of Law* (1961), esp. Chapter 10. The fine biography by N. Lacey, *A Life of H.L.A. Hart: The Nightmare and the Noble Dream* (2004), provides little additional insight on Hart's thoughts on international law.

[105] Which adds a new dimension to the old adage about the *horror vacui* of law.

[106] See, e.g., D. Verwey, *The European Community, the European Union and the International Law of Treaties* (2004) 257.

invoking the very rules which allow for an unlimited variety of factors to be taken into account. Quite apart from the point that attempts to lay down the process of interpretation in rules betray a rationalist conception of legal reasoning and are bound to remain forever frustrated,[107] article 31 of the Vienna Convention bites itself in the tail by making the rule as open-ended as it is.

As a result, reliance on seemingly technical devices such as rules of interpretation ends up a fig-leaf for the exercise of power;[108] indeed, it is no accident that the politically explosive notion of intertemporal law came to be reinvented as a technical device aiding interpretation. Under reference to article 31 of the Vienna Convention and its third paragraph, the interpreter can literally include anything – or, as the case may be, exclude things.[109] This very open-endedness and ambivalence also offers hope, though, for as Koskenniemi puts it, '[l]egal structure does not realize a prepolitical justice but acts as the surface on which the search for justice is conducted.'[110] It is precisely by being so open-ended that interpretation can indeed contribute to justice; it is precisely because article 31, paragraph 3(c) is a manifestation (however sanitized) of the doctrine of intertemporal law that it has, like so much international law, an emancipatory potential.[111] But this is also yet another reminder that institutional (or legal) design is subservient to individual characteristics: with so much power resting in the hands of the interpreter, the crucial question is not so much how interpretation should proceed, but who gets to undertake the interpretation.

---

[107] For an explanation, see Klabbers, *supra* note 7.

[108] See generally also Kennedy, 'The Turn to Interpretation', 58 *Southern California Law Review* (1985) 275 (noting that the turn to interpretation implies a turn to elite management, which 'reconfirms the structured distinction between truth and power which in turn sustains the position of the manager.')

[109] Although there might be, in case of interpretation by judicial bodies, considerations relating to jurisdiction to take into account. See Separate Opinion of Judge Buergenthal, *Oil Platforms* case, *supra* note 40, 278–9.

[110] See Koskenniemi, 'Legal Universalism between Morality and Power in a World of States', in S. Cheng (ed.), *Law, Justice, and Power: Between Reason and Will* (2004) 62.

[111] For a fine illustration of the emancipatory potential of international law, K. Knop, *Diversity and Self-determination in International Law* (2002).

THE TIME OF CONCLUSION AND THE TIME OF APPLICATION OF TREATIES AS POINTS OF REFERENCE IN THE INTERPRETATIVE PROCESS

Don Greig*

Introduction

It is not the purpose of this paper to examine in detail the various meanings that can be attributed to references to the conclusion of a treaty. For present purposes, we shall take the moment of a treaty's conclusion as the time when the parties agree to the text of a treaty, which in the case of a treaty with a limited number of parties will often also be the time of consent to the treaty itself. In the context of the present discussion, it will not be necessary to distinguish between the steps by which a treaty is finalised and brought into force.

From the point of view of how a treaty is to be applied, the circumstances surrounding the treaty's conclusion will be a relevant factor, though it will also be necessary to consider the extent to which the treaty's application is affected by the circumstances existing at the time of application. This raises the issue of whether the interpretation of a treaty is separate from the matter of its application, or whether they constitute a single process in which the two factors are brought together.

At the outset, it should be said that the 1969 Vienna Convention on the Law of Treaties[1] and its development in the work of the International Law Commission (the ILC) give decidedly mixed messages on the question of whether the interpretation of a treaty and its application constitute part of the same process. This issue is connected to the problem of how changes during the period a treaty is in force can affect the way in which it is interpreted and applied. Linked to these matters is the approach that is adopted in relation to the interpretation of treaties and it is with this question that the paper commences.

1. Interpretative Approaches

We are all familiar with Fitzmaurice's helpful discussion of what he termed the 'three main schools of thought' on how to approach the interpretation of a treaty.[2]

---

* Visiting Fellow, College of Law, Australian National University and Honorary Fellow, British Institute of International and Comparative Law.
[1] 1155 UNTS 331. Signed on 23 May 1969, entered into force on 27 January 1980.
[2] Fitzmaurice, 'The Law and Procedure of the International Court of Justice: Treaty Interpretation and Certain Other Treaty Points', 28 *British Yearbook of International Law* (1951) 1.

These he described as the textual or ordinary meaning of the words view, the intentions of the parties or founding fathers approach, and the aims and objects basis
with its potentially teleological operation.

No one would deny that the text of an instrument provides the starting point of
the act of interpretation so that the differences between the various approaches are
very much a contest over what additional material might be consulted and for what
purpose. A textualist would not gainsay the significance of the parties' intentions
but would emphasise the text as the best source of what those intentions might be.[3]
Indeed the subordinate role of supplementary means of interpretation in Article 32
of the Vienna Convention is a classic example of textualist rhetoric.[4]

In contrast, a supporter of an intentions' approach would seek to ascertain the parties' intentions in order to ensure that the text of the treaty did give proper effect to
those intentions. A proponent of this view of treaty interpretation was Lauterpacht
who, as the Rapporteur of the Institut de Droit International's project on the topic,
put forward the following as the first sentence of his proposed resolution:[5]

> La recherche de l'intention des parties étant le but principal de l'interprétation, il est
> légitime et désirable, dans l'intérêt de la bonne foi et de la stabilité des transactions
> internationales, de prendre le sens naturel des textes comme point de départ du proces-
> sus d'interprétation.[6]

As Lauterpacht explained of the interpretative process:

> The very choice of any single rule [of interpretation] or of a combination or cumulation
> of them is the result of a judgment arrived at, independently of any rules of construction,
> by reference to considerations of good faith, of justice, and of public policy within the
> orbit of the express or implied intention of the parties or of the legislature.[7]

However, in his view 'the main task of interpretation' remained 'the discovery of
the intention of the parties.'[8]

---

[3] As Fitzmaurice said in criticism of the intentions' approach: 'It ignores the fact that the treaty was,
after all, drafted precisely in order to give expression to the intentions of the parties, and must be presumed
to do so. Accordingly, this intention is, prima facie, to be found in the text itself, and therefore the primary
question is not what the parties intended by the text, but what the text itself means: whatever it clearly
means on an ordinary and natural construction of its terms, such will be deemed to be what the parties
intended', Fitzmaurice, 'The Law and Procedure of the International Court of Justice 1951–4: Treaty
Interpretation and Certain Other Treaty Points', 33 *British Yearbook of International Law* (1957) 205.

[4] See further below under Section 3(a).

[5] The Report of Lauterpacht appears in 43 – I *Annuaire d l'Institut de Droit International* (1950)
366, as translated by J-F Lalive.

[6] *Ibid,* 433.

[7] This appears in a different version of Lauterpacht's Report, published under the title of
'Restrictive Interpretation and the Principle of Effectiveness in the Interpretation of Treaties', 26
British Yearbook of International Law (1949) 53.

[8] *Ibid,* 55.

Lauterpacht acknowledged that, of course, the intention might have to be an imputed one because of the absence of any common intention. Of this occurrence, he provided three examples:

> In the first instance, there may be no common intention for the reason that the parties, although using identical language, did not intend the same result ... Secondly, it is possible that the different meanings attached to the same expression by the parties to the dispute is due not to an accident but to the deliberate design of one or more of the parties bent upon benefiting from an ambiguity surrounding the expression or provision which it succeeded in having inserted – or which it allowed to be inserted – in the treaty without the other party being aware of the pitfall thus prepared for it ... Thirdly, and this is one of the most typical aspects of the subject here discussed, the absence of an effective common intention may be due to the circumstance that, being unable to reach an agreed solution, the parties are content to use an ambiguous or non-committal expression and to leave the divergence of views to be solved in the future by agreement or in some other way.[9]

In its more conservative form the aims and objects approach is not so very different from that of the intentions' school. After all, the intentions of the parties provide the framework for the aims and objects of their treaty. Nevertheless, though those intentions may be of some relevance, a teleological approach requires an identification of the aims and objects of a treaty against which its interpretation must be measured. However, in the case of multilateral treaties creating organizations or other forms of international regulatory regimes, the aims and objects of the original treaty may change with time. To a teleologist these changes should also be reflected in the interpretation of such an instrument.

Obviously enough, in the early life of a treaty's history, the intentions of the parties and the aims and objects they had in mind are likely to be essentially similar whatever might be the theoretical differences between them. In time, those differences might suggest that one would give a greater emphasis to a particular point of departure than another. For example, a teleologist is likely to be more influenced than an adherent of the other two schools by what he or she perceives to be the changing nature of the aims and objects of the treaty in question. As far as supporters of these other approaches are concerned, though the question is how the treaty is to be applied today, the text, the objects and purposes of the treaty and the intentions of the parties are essentially those that existed at or with the treaty's creation.

2. The Codification of the Law

Lauterpacht's intentions approach to treaty interpretation was not acceptable to the Institut, some of the most trenchant criticism coming from his British colleagues. According to McNair:

> La première fonction d'un tribunal est celle de constater le sens naturel et ordinaire des termes d'une phrase, prise dans son contexte. Cela fait, le tribunal doit chercher à donner

---

[9] *Ibid,* 76–77.

effet à la phrase. Si les mots, pris dans leur sens naturel et ordinaire et à lumière du con-
texte, ont une certaine signification . . . , il incombe au tribunal de constater cette signification, même s'il peut estimer qu'une autre signification serait meilleure ou plus utile. Le
tribunal n'a pas le droit de substituer ses propres idées aux intentions des parties.[10]

Beckett was even more scathing:

> It seems to the present writer . . . that these statements of ascertaining the intention are
> rather clichés tending to obscure rather than illuminate the real task of the Tribunal.
> In fact the task of the Tribunal is that of interpreting a written document, a statute, a
> will, a contract in writing, or a treaty, and it has to proceed on the assumption that it
> finds the intention expressed in the words of the document which it has to interpret.
> There is a complete unreality in the references to the supposed intention of the legis-
> lature in the interpretation of the statute when in fact it is almost certain that the point
> which has arisen is one which the legislature never thought of at all. This is even more
> so in the case of the interpretation of treaties.[11]

This view resulted in the Institut's final version of its suggested approach in the resolution it adopted in 1956, Article 1(1) of which was in terms very similar to the
text of Article 31(1) of the Vienna Convention. In the Institut's resolution:

> The agreement of the parties having been embodied in the text of the treaty, it is nec-
> essary to take the natural and ordinary meaning of the terms of this text as the basis of
> interpretation. The terms of the provisions of the treaty should be interpreted in their
> context as a whole, in accordance with good faith and in the light of the principles of
> international law.[12]

There are certainly differences in emphasis between the Institut's formulation and
the one adopted in the Vienna Convention. For example, while 'the object and purpose' of a treaty is included as part of the general rule of interpretation in Article
31(1) of the Convention, according to the Institut, in 'a case brought before an
international tribunal, it will be for the tribunal . . . to consider whether and to what
extent there are grounds for making use of other means of interpretation', including
a 'consideration of the objects of the treaty'.[13] Where this approach creates a significant difference is in the treatment of *travaux préparatoires*. Article 32 of the
Convention firmly places them in a position of subordination to the general rule of
interpretation in Article 31, Article 32 providing:

> Recourse may be had to supplementary means of interpretation, including the
> preparatory work of the treaty and the circumstances of its conclusion in order to

---

[10] Lauterpacht, *supra* note 4, 449.

[11] *Ibid,* 438.

[12] For the adoption of this text in French, see 46 *Annuaire de L'Institut de Droit International*
(1956) 349; this translation appears in the Appendix to Jacobs, 'Varieties of Approach to Treaty
Interpretation: With Special Reference to the Draft Convention on the Law of Treaties before the
Vienna Diplomatic Conference', 18 *International and Comparative Law Quarterly* (1969) 344.

[13] Article 2, *ibid.*

confirm the meaning resulting from the application of Article 31, or to determine the meaning when the interpretation according to Article 31:

(a) leaves the meaning ambiguous or obscure; or
(b) leads to a result which is manifestly absurd or unreasonable.

In contrast, Article 2 of the Institut's resolution of 1956 equates the *travaux* with the objects of a treaty by including, amongst 'the legitimate means of interpretation' not only the objects of the treaty, but also recourse to preparatory work.[14]

This was a subtle means of allowing access to the *travaux* in a manner regarded as appropriate and helpful to the tribunal charged with interpreting a treaty, or with settling a dispute linked to the interpretation of a treaty. It was also a way of saving Lauterpacht's view from being totally discarded. In his proposed resolution the first sentence of Article 2 read as follows:

> Le recours aux travaux préparatoires, lorsqu'ils sont accessibles, est notamment un moyen légitime et désirable aux fins d'établir l'intention des parties dans tous les cas où, malgré sa clarté apparente, le sens d'un traité prête à controverse.[15]

To an extent the objections to this proposal stemmed from the opposition to the idea that treaty interpretation had anything to do with (finding) the intentions of the parties. As already pointed out, for a textualist it is the text which is the repository of the parties' intentions. Not that this can be entirely true because, if the treaty has to be interpreted in light of its objects, or object and purpose, how is this to be differentiated from the parties' intentions in making the treaty? Beckett was highly critical of the use of the *travaux* because they were 'uncertain and unequal and confusing'.[16] If this were so in a particular case then the *travaux* would be excluded on the basis that they are valueless.[17] On the other hand, if they do throw light on the meaning of provisions of a treaty, they should be admissible as an aid to interpretation. This is, of course, what the Institut's proposal would have

---

[14] *Ibid.*
[15] Lauterpacht, *supra* note 4.
[16] *Ibid*, 442.
[17] Beckett provided as an example of the inadequacies of the *travaux* the gaps that will exist when there has been what he termed a 'compromise behind the scenes', which he described as follows:
'Something appears to have happened but there is no record of it at all. At a certain stage the records seem to be inconsistent with what went before ... What, of course, has happened is that as the conference was making heavy weather, some private meeting was called. There is either no record of it at all or the only records of it ... will not appear in the minutes of the conference. Delegations may have their private records but they will not be quotable against anybody else. That private meeting probably results in the adoption of a text, and the text is a compromise, but what people said about it at the time they agreed to it is not on record anywhere' (*ibid*, 443). Beckett's elimination of 'private records' hardly seems sustainable in light of the use made of the Politis letter in the *Aegean Sea Continental Shelf* case, (hereinafter the *Aegean Sea* case), (Greece v Turkey), ICJ Rep 1978, 26–8.

achieved, though, in this respect, Article 32 of the Vienna Convention is unduly restrictive.

More in keeping with the reality of interpretation was the attempt of the United States at the Vienna Conference to replace Articles 31 and 32 with the following version of the factors to be taken into account in the interpretative process:

A treaty shall be interpreted in good faith in order to determine the meaning to be given to the terms in the light of all relevant factors, including in particular:

(a) the content of the treaty;
(b) its objects and purposes;
(c) any agreement between the parties regarding the interpretation of the treaty;
(d) any instrument made by one or more parties in connection with the conclusion of the treaty and accepted by the other parties as a instrument related to the treaty;
(e) any subsequent practice in the application of the treaty which establishes the common understanding of the meaning of the terms as between the parties generally;
(f) the preparatory work of the treaty;
(g) the circumstances of its conclusion.
(h) any relevant rule of international law applicable in the relations between the parties;
(i) the special meaning to be given to a term if the parties intended such term to have a special meaning.[18]

The proposal was rejected by a substantial majority.[19] However, it is difficult to contest the substance of the American view that a government legal officer asked to advise on the meaning to be attributed to a treaty provision, or to argue its meaning before an international tribunal, could hardly carry out the task properly without taking account of the various factors listed in the American proposal. As Myers McDougal argued on behalf of the United States at the Conference:

The text of a treaty and the common public meanings of words would be made the point of departure of interpretation, but not the end of the inquiry. The text would be treated as one important index among many of the common intent of the parties. No fixed hierarchy would be established among the elements of interpretation; the amendment sought to make accessible to interpreters whatever element might be significant in a particular set of circumstances, including ordinary meaning, subsequent practice and preparatory work, but not excluding others that might be also relevant.[20]

---

[18] *Official Records of the United Nations Conference on the Law of Treaties,* Vienna, (hereinafter *Vienna Conference*), (1968–69) 149, para 269 (i) (a).

[19] By 66 votes to 8 with 10 abstentions, *ibid,* 150, para 271 (a).

[20] *Vienna Conference, supra* note 18, 1st Session, 168, 31st Meeting of the Committee of the Whole, para 49. See also the observation of the Greek representative, Krispis, *ibid,* 172, 32nd Meeting of the Committee of Whole, para 7: 'it seemed impossible to draw up guidelines on interpretation in the form of rules of law. One had to be content with a description of the various factors which would facilitate the task of interpretation. Jurists should be given the means of discovering the ideas conveyed by the words used by the authors of a treaty to express their intention.'

Despite the considerable majority by which the ILC's version was adopted as the basis of Articles 31 and 32 of the Convention, the arguments favouring this conclusion were scarcely convincing. Not surprisingly, being a member of the ILC, the representative of Uruguay was one of the strongest supporters of the ILC's text. To demonstrate its acceptability, he relied principally upon the criticisms voiced of Lauterpacht's views by members of the Institut. The contentions he employed were, however, as destructive of the ILC's version as they were supposed to be inconsistent with the proposed American amendment. For example, it may be true, as Beckett had claimed, that a supposed intention is a fiction because 'it often occurred that the difference between the parties to the treaties arose out of something which the parties had never thought of when the treaty was concluded and that, therefore, they had absolutely no common intention with regard to it.' The same criticism could be made of any specific object and purpose which the parties could be claimed to have had at the particular level of a disputed provision of a treaty. The Vienna Convention attempted to avoid this issue by referring, in Article 31(1), to the 'meaning to be given to the terms of the treaty in *their* context and in the light of *its* object and purpose.'[21]

However, it is hardly realistic to suggest that the general object and purpose of a treaty is of greater importance to the interpretation of a specific provision than the object and purpose which the parties appeared to have had in mind in drafting that provision. To reconcile this factor with Article 31(1), the object and purpose that emerges from the apparent meaning of a specific provision would have to be taken into account in assessing the object and purpose of the treaty as a whole. In any case, the implication in Article 31(1) that a treaty has only one object and purpose makes little sense in dealing with a multifaceted instrument. The UN Charter has a variety of different objects and purposes, only one or some of which might be relevant to the interpretation of particular provisions. Nevertheless, the content of such a provision, or group of provisions, may also be of relevance in determining the scope and significance of those objects and purposes. The text of a provision may itself be suggestive of the object and purpose the parties had in mind in drafting it in this way.

Viewed from this perspective, it is difficult to understand why the Institut was so dismissive of Lauterpacht's adoption of the intention of the parties as a basis for treaty interpretation. Admittedly, the intention may well be a fiction as no shared intention may have existed. However, the same could also be true of the object and purpose of a treaty as a guide to what the parties must have 'meant' by a particular provision. To be of any value in such a specific context, it is likely that the process of identifying the intention of the parties or the object and purpose they had in mind when drafting the provision in question is likely to be as much speculative as analytical.

---

[21] Emphasis added.

Despite the efforts of the Institut de Droit International and of the International Law Commission to exclude the intentions of the parties from consideration in the interpretative process, their intention has a crucial role to play in assessing the nature of a treaty as well as its object and purpose. It would be difficult to accept that the nature of a treaty and its object and purpose can exist without any consideration of the parties' intentions.

The classic example of the significance of those intentions was provided by the International Court of Justice in its examination of mandate agreements in the *Namibia* case.[22] South African forces had seized the German colony of South West Africa in the course of the First World War. A segment of recalcitrant Boers from South Africa had gone over to the German side, but what united the rest of the Boers with the British community in South Africa was support for the annexation of the colony. To them, the mandate agreement accepted by Britain on South Africa's behalf was no more than a stepping stone to eventual annexation. It was this attitude, which persisted after 1946 and the winding up of the League of Nations, that brought South Africa into confrontation with the United Nations over the powers to supervise the due performance of the mandate which the United Nations claimed to have inherited from the League.

After twenty years of this confrontation, the General Assembly, in 1966, by Resolution 2145 (XXI), purported to terminate the mandate, and the Security Council, by Resolution 276 (1970), declared South Africa's continued presence there to be illegal and spelt out the consequences of this illegality for other States.[23] The basis of the act of termination was said to be South Africa's failure to carry out its obligations under the mandate agreement so that it had been in material breach of that agreement in contravention of Article 60 of the Vienna Convention. By paragraph (3) of that Article, a material breach is defined as:

(a) a repudiation of the treaty not sanctioned by the present Convention; or
(b) the violation of a provision essential to the accomplishment of the object or purpose of the treaty

The view of the General Assembly in adopting Resolution 2145 was that the material breaches in this case had taken both forms.[24] For this to have occurred out of the mandate, the instrument of 1920 must have developed in such a way as to have rendered South Africa's administration of the Territory unacceptable, not by the standards of its inception, but by reference to the existing view of what was necessary in order to satisfy the standards of the sacred trust as envisaged by the developments that had taken place post 1945. The Court justified the evolutionary nature

---

[22] *Legal Consequences for States of the Continued Presence of South Africa in Namibia (South West Africa) notwithstanding Security Council Resolution 276 (1970)*, Advisory Opinion (hereinafter *Namibia* case), ICJ Rep 1971, 16.
[23] *Ibid*, 45.
[24] *Ibid*, 47.

of the mandate by reference to the original intention of the parties with regard to such agreements:

> Mindful as it is of the primary necessity of interpreting an instrument in accordance with the intentions of the parties at the time of its conclusion, the Court is bound to take into account the fact that the concepts embodied in Article 22 of the Covenant – "the strenuous conditions of the modern world" and "the well-being and development" of the peoples concerned – were not static, but were by definition evolutionary, as also, therefore, was the concept of the "sacred trust". The parties to the Covenant must consequently be deemed to have accepted them as such. That is why, viewing the institutions of 1919, the Court must take into consideration the changes which have occurred in the supervening half-century, and its interpretation cannot remain unaffected by the subsequent development of law, through the Charter of the United Nations and by way of customary law. Moreover, an international instrument has to be interpreted and applied within the framework of the entire legal system prevailing at the time of interpretation. In the domain to which the present proceedings relate, the last fifty years, as indicated above, have brought important developments. These developments leave little doubt that the ultimate objective of the sacred trust was the self-determination and independence of the peoples concerned.[25]

This outcome could be regarded as giving some reason for jubilation amongst supporters of a teleological view of treaty interpretation. The object and purpose of the mandate system, even with regard to the least advanced of territories, those in Category C, was now seen as their independence in performance on the part of the Mandatory State of the 'sacred trust of civilization' principle, contained in Article 22 of the League Covenant. This was clearly a development of the notion of 'sacred trust' because States administering Class C territories regarded the assumption of this role as a precursor to annexation, and this continued to be South Africa's policy towards South West Africa.

There would also have been delight amongst the advocates of an intentions approach to treaty interpretation. The Court was able to attribute taking into account changes in attitude towards the sacred trust of civilization in Article 22 of the Covenant to the evolutionary nature of that provision. That evolutionary nature was ascribable entirely, in the Court's opinion, to the original intentions of the parties to the Covenant. The only comfort for supporters of a textualist approach to treaty interpretation is to regard these institutions as explicit in or necessarily to be implied from the text of Article 22.

3. Interpretation and Application in the Jurisprudence of the World Court: Two Stages or Just One?

These ways of ascribing the substance of the Court's advisory opinion in the *Namibia* case to the different schools of interpretation should not conceal the great significance

---

[25] *Ibid,* 31.

of the time of application to the interpretation of Article 22 of the League Covenant and of the mandate agreement made thereunder with respect to South West Africa. But it does not follow from this factor that the interpretative process involves two distinct stages, of interpretation followed by the application of that interpretation as best one can to the circumstances of the case. While a teleological approach is concerned with a contemporary appreciation of a treaty's aim and objective, it is the interpretation made in that light which is applied to solve the disputed issue. As for adherents of the other two schools, it was their support for the intention of the makers of the Covenant and of the mandate agreement which enabled them to apply Article 22 in light of modern conditions. From whichever standpoint one views the interpretative process, it seems to speak as a single whole in which the way it is to be applied constitutes the appreciation of the treaty and its meaning which we call interpretation.

Despite this appearance of the singularity of the process, it has to be admitted that the existence of a distinction between the act of interpretation and its subsequent application to the circumstances of a case finds support in a number of international instruments.

(a) Understanding Articles 31 and 32 of the Vienna Convention

A two stage process is clearly envisaged by the interpretative rules prescribed by the Vienna Convention on the Law of Treaties. According to Article 31(1), that contains the general rule:

> A treaty shall be interpreted in good faith in accordance with the ordinary meaning to be given to the terms of the treaty in their context and in the light of its object and purpose.

It seems to be necessary for the interpreter to establish a provisional meaning for a disputed text before the interpreter can consider whether the supplementary means can be taken into account under Article 32:

> Recourse may be had to supplementary means of interpretation, including the preparatory work of the treaty and the circumstances of its conclusion, in order to confirm the meaning resulting from the application of Article 31, or to determine the meaning when the interpretation according to Article 31:
>
> (a) leaves the meaning ambiguous or obscure; or
> (b) leads to a result which is manifestly absurd or unreasonable.

A meaning has to be deduced by virtue of Article 31 before it is possible to confirm that meaning by reference to the supplementary means available under Article 32. *A fortiori*, a meaning has to be found by the application of Article 31 before it is possible to decide whether its application is hindered or even excluded by the circumstances covered by Article 32(a) or (b).

The alternative view of the balance between Articles 31 and 32 is to regard it as based upon a fiction. The idea that no reference can be made to the supplementary means until the first stage is completed and a meaning established in accordance with Article 31, and then only if the prerequisites for their consideration under Article 32 are satisfied, is totally unrealistic.[26] The interpreter, whether the government lawyer advising on how a treaty should be interpreted, or a judge or arbitrator called upon to give a meaning to a treaty, would be conversant with the supplementary means as part of the process. That knowledge may or may not influence the outcome of the process, but it is certainly not made available only once an initial interpretation has been placed on the text.[27] Yet, as we have seen, this fiction was deliberately adopted by the Vienna Conference in rejecting the United States' proposal that the interpretative process would be better represented by the combination of the factors in Articles 31 and 32 in a single provision.[28]

As a consequence of the Conference's decision, whatever use is made of supplementary material will normally be justified in terms of those provisions. Thus, for example, even if such material appears to have been disregarded on the basis that the requirements of Article 32 for its reception have not been satisfied, this determination will only have been made after an examination of the material in question.

There is a further avenue by which access might be permissible to the *travaux* in determining the intentions and objectives of the parties in making their treaty. Article 31 refers to the need to place the provisions of a treaty in their context. In a later section of this paper there will be a fuller examination of what is meant by 'context' in relation to a treaty. However, it is worth making the point at this juncture that it is a term of uncertain provenance with regard to the interpretation of treaties. The reason for the doubts is because Article 31 provides a much narrower definition of what is meant by 'context' than one would normally associate with the word. Thus, according to paragraph (2) of that provision, 'context' for the purpose of interpreting a treaty, that is, as it is to be employed in applying paragraph (1), is primarily 'the text' of the treaty itself, 'including its preamble and annexes'.

As it is only a treaty's provisions which have to be viewed in 'their context', this would seem to be incompatible with a broader notion of 'context' as requiring the treaty to be examined in or against the historical circumstances in which it was made. The historical record would inevitably involve a reference to the events surrounding the drawing up of the treaty. It would be difficult to imagine that the context of a

---

[26] This point was trenchantly made by Rosenne as a member of the ILC, in its 766th meeting, *YBILC* (1964) vol I, 283.

[27] As Waldock observed: 'it was unrealistic to imagine that the preparatory work was not really consulted by States, organisations and tribunals whenever they saw fit, before or at any stage of the proceedings even though they might afterwards pretend that they had not given it much attention', *ibid,* 314.

[28] *Supra* note 17.

treaty in this broader sense could exist independently of the history, including the *travaux*, of how it came to be made.

As will be discussed in more detail later,[29] the International Court of Justice has on occasion adopted the broader view without making it at all clear why it was departing from the essentially textual definition of context in Article 31(2). In the *Aegean Sea* case,[30] for example, the Court had to consider whether the following communiqué issued at the end of a meeting between the Prime Ministers of Greece and Turkey at Brussels on 31 May 1975 constituted an agreement bestowing jurisdiction on the Court:

> They decided that those problems [which had arisen between the two States] should be resolved peacefully by negotiations and as regards the continental shelf of the Aegean Sea by the International Court at the Hague.[31]

In reaching its decision to reject Greece's attempt to rely on the Communiqué, the Court explained that it had to 'have regard' not only to the 'actual terms' of the instrument, but also to 'the particular circumstances in which it was drawn up'.[32] This involved the Court in placing the Communiqué in the context of Turkey's previously stated position that the parties should agree on the terms of a joint submission on the matter to the Court, and of the continuation of the negotiations between the parties to this end, even after the Brussels Communiqué was issued.[33]

The Court did not deny that the Brussels Communiqué was capable of constituting an international agreement. All the Court decided was that the Communiqué did not bestow jurisdiction on the Court with regard to the continental shelf dispute. It avoided considering the legal effects of the Communiqué, contenting itself with the observation that it was 'for the Governments themselves to consider . . . what effect, if any, is to be given to the Joint Communiqué in their further efforts to arrive at an amicable settlement of their dispute.'[34]

We shall return to consider the significance of the *Aegean Sea* case with regard to the 'context' of a treaty at a later stage. However, the issue was raised of how the decision could be fitted within the confines of Articles 31 and 32 of the Vienna Convention. It is possible to read the *Aegean Sea* case as providing support for the provisional interpretation view of the process envisaged by Articles 31 and 32 of the Vienna Convention. After all, it could be said that the Brussels Communiqué did appear to bestow jurisdiction on the International Court, though it did so in a manner that was hardly free from ambiguity. Accordingly it was permissible under Article 32 to consult additional means of interpretation including the *travaux* and

---

[29] See below Section 4.
[30] *Id.*
[31] *Aegean Sea* case, *supra* note 17, 3.
[32] *Ibid*, 39.
[33] *Ibid*, 43.
[34] *Ibid*, 44.

the subsequent conduct of the parties. However, this would be to adopt an artificial view of how the Court disposed of the issue. The Court regarded the additional material as relevant, not because it was supplementary under Article 32, but because it formed part of the context in which the Communiqué was issued.[35]

No one pretends that the *travaux* are not invariably placed before the Court or other tribunal engaged to settle a dispute involving matters of treaty interpretation. If a broader meaning of 'context' is permissible, the overlap between what constitutes the context in which a treaty is set, and the *travaux* which can be employed only if one or other of the requirements prescribed by Article 32 has been satisfied, is sufficient to justify the Court or tribunal making whatever use it wishes of the material placed before it. It is for this reason that the question posed by Judge Schwebel in the *Qatar and Bahrein* case, when he asked 'what happens when the *travaux préparatoires* turn out not to confirm but contradict the meaning arrived at by application of the general rule of interpretation?'[36] is not of critical significance. If, despite the contradiction in the context, the tribunal decides upon a particular interpretation of the treaty, the contradiction is inadmissible, in legal terms, because it does not satisfy the requirements of Article 32, and, in practical terms, because it has already been assessed as part of the context by the tribunal in reaching the conclusion it did as to the treaty's contrary meaning.

(b) The Contentious Jurisdiction of the International Court

In a case involving the interpretation of a treaty, the ICJ Statute and the Rules of Court would seem to require that the interpretation can only take place with respect to an actual dispute between the parties and in relation to the treaty's application to those parties.

The State making an application to the Court commencing proceedings must, under Article 38(2) of the Rules of Court, specify not just the 'legal grounds upon which the jurisdiction of the Court is said to be based', but also 'the precise nature of the claim, together with a succinct statement of the facts and the grounds on which the claim is based'. Although the position where the basis of jurisdiction is a special agreement between the parties is less clear,[37] whether the application is

---

[35] *Ibid*, 41: 'The divergence of views as to the interpretation of the Brussels Communiqué makes it necessary for the Court to consider what light is thrown on its meaning by the context in which the meeting of the 31 May 1975 took place and the Communiqué was drawn up.'

[36] Dissenting Opinion of Judge Schwebel in *Maritime Delimitation and Territorial Questions between Qatar and Bahrain Case,* (Qatar v. Bahrain), (hereinafter *Qatar and Bahrain* case), *Jurisdiction and Admissibility*, ICJ Rep 1995, 31.

[37] In such a case, the proceedings are commenced by notification of the special agreement (Rules of Court, Article 39(1)), which must accompany the notification, and the 'notification shall also, in so far as this is not already apparent from the agreement, indicate the precise subject of the dispute and identify the parties to it' (Rules of Court, Article 39(2)).

made under Article 38 or 39 of the Rules, the initial Memorial 'shall contain a statement of the relevant facts, a statement of the law, and the submissions'.[38] The response is by way of Counter-Memorial which 'shall contain: an admission or denial of the facts stated in the Memorial; any additional facts, if necessary; observations concerning the statement of law in the Memorial; a statement of law in answer thereto; and the submissions'.[39] Hence the interpretation of a treaty could arise only with regard to its application to a matter in issue in the case.

The only limitation to this feature of the Court's contentious jurisdiction is the power which it has to decline to deal with matters which do not, or are no longer, an issue between the parties. There have been occasional recourses to this power by the Court of which two may be mentioned.

The *Northern Cameroons* case[40] concerned allegations by Cameroon that the United Kingdom had, 'in the application of the Trusteeship Agreement of 13 December 1946, failed to respect certain obligations directly or indirectly flowing therefrom'. After the First World War, the League of Nations had created two mandated territories out of the German protectorate of Kamerun, one to be administered by France, the other by the United Kingdom. With the winding up of the League in 1946, the Mandate Agreements were replaced by Trusteeship Agreements, each administered by the same State. The French Territory became the Republic of Cameroon on 1 January 1960 and was admitted as a Member to the United Nations on 20 September 1960. The United Kingdom had administered its Territory of the Cameroons separately as northern and southern parts attached to two different regions of Nigeria. With independence in prospect the General Assembly arranged with Britain that plebiscites should be held in the two parts of the territory. The southern part opted to join the independent Cameroon, but the northern part eventually voted for incorporation as part of Nigeria. The application to the Court by Cameroon was made on 30 May 1961; the Trusteeship Agreement had been terminated by the General Assembly to take effect from 1 June 1961.

The objective of Cameroon in starting these proceedings was to publicise its complaint that the outcome of the referendum in the northern Cameroons was the inevitable consequence of the failure by the United Kingdom to administer the whole of its Territory of the Cameroons separately from Nigeria.[41] The difficulty was that the case as presented by Cameroon could serve no useful purpose. Cameroon was not seeking damages for the alleged past breaches of the Trusteeship Agreement. Moreover, as the date of termination of the Agreement two days after the application to the Court was made had already been set by the General

---

[38] Rules of Court, Article 49(1).

[39] *Ibid*, Article 49(2).

[40] *Case Concerning the Northern Cameroon,* (hereinafter *Northern Cameroons* case), (Cameroon v UK), *Preliminary Objections,* ICJ Rep 1963, 15.

[41] *Ibid,* 31.

Assembly, a declaration that there had been past breaches of the Agreement by the United Kingdom would have been without legal effect.[42] As the Court said:

> The function of the Court is to state the law, but it may pronounce judgment only in connection with concrete cases where there exists at the time of adjudication an actual controversy involving a conflict of legal interests between the parties. The Court's judgment must have some practical consequence in the sense that it can affect existing legal rights or obligations of the parties, thus removing uncertainty from their legal relations. No judgment on the merits in this case could satisfy these essentials of the judicial function.[43]

The Court adopted a similar approach in the *Nuclear Test* cases,[44] in which Australia and New Zealand sought orders that France should not carry out any further nuclear weapons tests in the atmosphere in the South Pacific.[45] The Court held that a number of public statements by members of the French Government[46] amounted to unilateral declarations binding on the French Government to cease such tests once the current round of tests was completed.[47] After citing the *Northern Cameroons* case, the Court went on to say:

> The Court therefore sees no reason to allow the continuance of the proceedings which it knows are pointless ... It does not enter into the adjudicatory functions of the Court to deal with issues *in abstracto*, once it has reached the conclusion that the merits of the case no longer fall to be determined. The object of the claim having clearly disappeared, there is nothing on which to give judgment.[48]

The lesson from these two cases appears to be that, as far as its compulsory jurisdiction is concerned, the Court could only apply a treaty in the context of a subsisting and defined dispute between the parties. The 'abstract' nature of a dispute as a

---

[42] See the separate opinions of Judge Fitzmaurice, *ibid* 97–99, and Judge Wellington Koo, *ibid*, 50–61, who took the view that, as Cameroon had raised the issues before the General Assembly, the Assembly's determinations adverse to the arguments advanced by Cameroon were conclusive of those issues. This was totally different from the circumstances of *Certain Phosphate Lands in Nauru*, (hereinafter *Phosphate Lands* case), (Nauru v Australia), *Preliminary Objections*, ICJ Rep 1992, 250–253, in which the Assembly resolutions granting independence to Nauru did not definitively determine the issue of compensation for the alleged failure of the administering powers, Australia, New Zealand and the United Kingdom, to rehabilitate the large parts of the island from which the phosphate had been removed.

[43] *Northern Cameroons* case, *supra* note 40, 33–34. In the *Phosphate Lands* case, however, Nauru was seeking 'appropriate reparation in respect of the loss caused to the Republic of Nauru as a result of breaches of Australia's legal obligations' as set out *inter alia* in Article 76 of the UN Charter and Articles 3 and 5 of the Trusteeship Agreement, 243–244.

[44] *Nuclear Tests* (Australia *v.* France), *Merits*, Judgment of 20 December 1974, ICJ Rep 1974, 253; *Nuclear Tests* (New Zealand *v.* France), *Merits*, Judgment of 20 December 1974, ICJ Rep 1974, 457.

[45] *Ibid*, 256; the New Zealand application was somewhat broader in scope, *ibid*, 460.

[46] *Ibid*, 265–267, 469–471.

[47] *Ibid*, 269–270, 474–475.

[48] *Ibid*, 271, 477.

reason for declining to decide the matter relates solely to its current justiciability. A dispute is not justiciable in this sense if determination of the issue would no longer have practical consequences for the contesting States. This may be because the matter has already been decided by a competent body,[49] or as a consequence of one of the parties agreeing to comply with the demands of the other side.[50]

(c) The Court's Advisory Jurisdiction

As will be explained in a moment, the term 'abstract' is employed by the Court in the context of its advisory jurisdiction, though its use is significantly different from the way it has been employed in a contentious setting. It does not follow, however, that the Court would be prepared to employ its advisory competence in such a way as to give an opinion on a matter that was abstract in that sense.

In the *Western Sahara* case,[51] the General Assembly asked two questions of the Court concerning an event and its surrounding circumstances in the relatively distant past:

> I. Was Western Sahara . . . at the time of colonization by Spain a territory belonging to no one (terra nullius)?
> If the answer to the first question is in the negative,
> II. What were the legal ties between this territory and the Kingdom of Morocco and the Mauritanian entity?

There is little doubt that if such questions had been the central issues of a contentious case between Spain and Morocco and/or Mauritania, the Court would have declined to decide them along the lines of its judgment in the *Northern Cameroons* case. That outcome was not determinative in the present case because an 'advisory opinion of the Court on the legal status of the territory at the time of Spanish Colonization and on the nature of any ties then existing with Morocco and with the Mauritanian entity may assist the General Assembly in the future decisions which it is called upon to take.'[52] As the Court went on to explain:

> In any event, to what extent or degree its opinion will have an impact on the action of the General Assembly is not for the Court to decide. The function of the Court is to give an opinion based on law, once it has come to the conclusion that the questions put

---

[49] *Northern Cameroons* case, *supra* note 40; but not the *Phosphate Lands* case, *supra* note 41.

[50] This is an adequate explanation of the *Nuclear Test* cases, *supra* note 44, with regard to Australia, though it is less convincing with respect to New Zealand. Whereas Australia had sought an order that France should not carry out any more tests (ICJ Rep 1974, 256), New Zealand's claim included that 'the conduct by the French Government of nuclear test in the South Pacific region that give rise to radio-active fall-out constitutes a violation of New Zealand's rights under international law, and that these rights will be violated by any further such tests' (*ibid*, 460).

[51] *Western Sahara, Advisory Opinion*, ICJ Rep. 1975, 12.

[52] *Ibid*, 36.

to it are relevant and have a practical and contemporary effect, and, consequently, are not devoid of object or purpose.[53]

The use of the term 'abstract' with regard to the Court's advisory jurisdiction has a totally different meaning. It refers to the tendency of the Court to avoid relating the question or questions which it has been requested to address by an international organization, to the political circumstances giving rise to the request. In the *Admission* case,[54] the Court was asked:

> Is a Member of the United Nations which is called upon, in virtue of Article 4 of the Charter, to pronounce itself by its vote, either in the Security Council or in the General Assembly, on the admission of a State to membership in the United Nations, juridically entitled to make its consent to the admission dependent on conditions not expressly provided by paragraph 1 of the said Article? In particular, can such a Member, while it recognizes the conditions set forth in that provision to be fulfilled by the State concerned, subject its affirmative vote to the additional condition that other States will be admitted to membership in the United Nations together with that State? [55]

With respect to the nature of the questions, the first question was patently more abstract than the second. Nevertheless, the Court was certainly apprised of the various factors which States had employed to justify the votes they had cast on applications for admission.[56] Even so, the Court regarded itself as precluded by the abstract nature of the Assembly's request for the Opinion from considering the validity or otherwise of such factors, though it can hardly be claimed that the Court provided a very clear explanation of why this was so.[57]

In the view of the Court, Article 4(1) did prescribe the necessary and only conditions of membership, that an applicant 'must (1) be a State; (2) be peace–loving;

---

[53] *Ibid*, 37.

[54] *Conditions of Admission of a State to Membership in the United Nations (Art 4 of the Charter)*, (hereinafter *Admission* case), Advisory Opinion, ICJ Rep 1948, 57.

[55] *Ibid*, 58.

[56] Details of the various applications and the reaction to them were provided by Kerno, representing the UN Secretary-General, in his Statement to the Court, in the *Admission* case, ICJ Pleadings, 48–52.

[57] In the Court's words (ICJ Rep 1948, 60–61): 'the General Assembly can hardly be supposed to have intended to ask the Court's opinion as to the reasons which, in the mind of a Member, may prompt its vote. Such reasons, which enter into a mental process, are obviously subject to no control. Nor does the request concern a Member's freedom of expressing its opinion. Since it concerns a condition or conditions on which a Member "makes its consent dependent", the question can only relate to the statements made by a Member concerning the vote it proposes to give. It is clear from the General Assembly's Resolution ... that the Court is not called upon either to define the meaning and scope of the conditions on which admission is made dependent, or to specify the elements which may serve in a concrete case to verify the existence of the requisite conditions. The clause of the General Assembly's Resolution, referring to "the exchange of views which has taken place . . .", is not understood as an invitation to the Court to say whether the views thus referred to are well founded or otherwise. The abstract form in which the question is stated precludes such an interpretation'.

(3) accept the obligations of the Charter; (4) be able to carry out these obligations; and (5) be willing to do so.'[58] In assessing whether an applicant did satisfy these criteria, a member of the United Nations, voting on the application, could take into account:

> any factor which it is possible reasonably and in good faith to connect with the conditions laid down in that Article. The taking into account of such factors is implied in the very wide and very elastic nature of the prescribed conditions; no relevant political factor – that is to say, none connected with the conditions of admission – is excluded.[59]

As to the second question asked of the Court, which concerned 'a demand on the part of a Member making its consent to the admission of an applicant dependent on the admission of other applicants',[60] such a requirement was unacceptable:

> Judged on the basis of the rule which the Court adopts in its interpretation of Article 4, such a demand clearly constitutes a new condition, since it is entirely unconnected with those prescribed in Article 4. It is also in an entirely different category from those conditions, since it makes admission dependent, not on the conditions required of applicants, qualifications which are supposed to be fulfilled, but on extraneous considerations concerning States other than the applicant State.[61]

It is possible to explain the Court's approach in terms of a division between the act of interpretation, that, irrespective of what factors a State might take into account in deciding how to vote on an application for admission, Article 4(1) described the only relevant criteria, while the act of applying that interpretation was sufficient to exclude the conduct referred to in the second question of making the admission of an applicant dependant upon the admission of other applicants at the same time. In other words, once the interpretation was established in the first stage, the act of application followed automatically, and was insulated from an evaluation of the circumstances to which it was to be applied.

Though the second part of the question was more specific than the first, it was still expressed with a degree of generality. It was true to say, therefore, that neither question really addressed the actual dispute giving rise to the question(s) submitted to the Court. Judge Zoričić was clearly correct in his criticism of the Court for isolating the interpretative issue from how the ultimate question of the application of the text to the matter to be addressed should be answered. As the Judge pointed out:

> The work of the Court of Justice involves primarily the application of rules of law to concrete cases. It follows that the first task of the Court is to consider what are the concrete cases from which the application for an opinion arises. That this should be the

---

[58] *Ibid,* 62.
[59] *Ibid,* 63.
[60] *Ibid,* 64.
[61] *Ibid,* 65.

Court's procedure is the more evident from the fact that concrete examples have been drawn to its attention in the documents supplied by the Secretariat of the United Nations.[62]

Once one does examine the 'concrete' circumstances, a different complexion is given to the Court's task. Five former enemy States, Finland and Italy, favoured by western countries, and Bulgaria, Hungary and Romania, supported by the Soviet Union, were the relevant candidates. The western case against the last three States was that they were not peace-loving in view of the conduct of their governments in restricting the human rights of their citizens, in breach of the terms of the respective peace treaties.[63] The Soviet counter-argument was based on the fact that both the Potsdam Declaration of 1945, and the Peace Treaties with the five States involved, contained an obligation on the part of the signatory powers to support the individual applications for admission of those five States.[64]

The inadequacy of the Court's abstract question approach thus becomes all too clear. According to the majority Opinion, the conditions contained in Article 4(1) were exhaustive, setting the parameters on the right of a State voting on admission to support or oppose a candidate. While relevant political factors could be brought into a voting State's assessment of a candidate, in so far as they related to the requirements set out in Article 4, they could not be turned into an additional requirement, and certainly not in the manner contemplated by the second question.

There was a joint dissenting opinion which took the view that Article 4(1) was not exhaustive of the requirements for admission. In particular:

> The resolutions which embody either a recommendation or a decision in regard to admission are decisions of a political character; they emanate from political organs; by general consent they involve the examination of political factors . . . It follows that the Members of such an organ who are responsible for forming its decisions must consider questions from every aspect, and, in consequence, are legally entitled to base their arguments and their vote upon political considerations.[65]

However, the four Judges held that, once it was admitted that a political consideration might be employed to justify voting in a particular manner, the issue of whether such a motive as the admission of other States at the same time as a particular applicant was permissible was a 'political consideration' which could be

---

[62] *Ibid*, 103.

[63] The defects in the dispute settlement clauses in these treaties were subsequently considered by the Court in *Interpretation of Peace Treaties,* Advisory Opinion, ICJ Rep 1950, 65; and *Interpretation of Peace Treaties*, Advisory Opinion (second phase), ICJ Rep 1950, 221.

[64] See Dissenting Opinion of Judge Zoričić in Admission case, *supra* note 54, 105–106 and Dissenting Opinion of Judge Krylov, *ibid*, 114.

[65] See Joint Dissenting Opinion of Judges Basdevant, Winiarski, McNair and Read, *ibid,* 85.

assessed only 'from a political point of view'. Such an issue was not a legal question and could not therefore be answered by the Court.[66]

It cannot be said that the adoption of this 'abstract' approach by the Court has much to commend it. It may have been thought necessary at one time to preserve the appearance that the Court was not dealing with the actual dispute between States without their consent so that there could be no justification for the Court declining to exercise its advisory jurisdiction.[67] Nevertheless, as Judge Zoričić observed:

> Although the second question is an abstract one, it must evidently relate to the only concrete case of this nature that has arisen, namely to the discussion on the admission of ex-enemy States. This discussion took place in the Security Council during the meetings referred to in the recitals of the General Assembly's Resolution of 17 November 1947 [requesting the Court's Opinion]. Consequently, however abstract the Court's reply may be, it will necessarily be understood as an indirect judgment on the action of certain members of the Council. Moreover, this interpretation will be given in complete ignorance of the exceptional circumstances of the case and of the arguments then put forward.[68]

The final sentence in the above passage needs clarification. Of course, a state of complete ignorance did not exist because the issues were raised in written submissions to the Court[69] and in oral presentations before the Court.[70] Nevertheless, treating a question as 'abstract' inevitably gives an air of unreality to the answer provided. After all, if the Soviet claim had been correct and Western powers were in breach of their undertakings in the Potsdam agreement and in the Peace Treaties to support the candidature of the various applicants, what was an appropriate response? For the Soviet Union to have voted in favour of candidates supported by the West and to have allowed the applications of candidates of which it approved to be thwarted would have been politically unacceptable. The compromise which it proposed was no different from a suggestion made earlier by the United States,[71] and was the arrangement which eventually resolved the difficulty with the admission of 16 States by a 'package deal' in 1955.[72]

It is not the purpose of this paper to examine the history of the Court's use of the abstract nature of a question to enable it to provide answers to issues which were in fact in dispute between States.[73] The significance of the Court's approach is to

---

[66] *Ibid,* 93.

[67] As had happened in *Eastern Carelia Advisory Opinion,* PCIJ Series B, (1923), No 5, 27.

[68] *Admission* case, *supra* note 54, 104–105.

[69] Observations submitted by Governments, Letter from Australian Minister at the Hague to the Registrar of the Court, *Admission* case, ICJ Pleadings, 30–32.

[70] Oral Statement by Mr. Kerno on behalf of the UN Secretary-General, *ibid,* 55–57; Oral Statement by Dr. Lachs (Poland), *ibid,* 101–107.

[71] Though then rejected by the Soviet Union, see Oral Statement by Mr. Kerno on behalf of the UN Secretary-General, *ibid,* 55–56.

[72] See Gross, 'Progress towards Universality of Membership in the United Nations', 50 American Journal of International Law (1956) 791.

create an artificial divide between the interpretation of a provision and its application. Application remains part of the process, but the provision is applied not to,
but in, an artificial situation.

The *Admission* case offers a striking illustration of that artificiality. To the majority,
the interpretation it placed on Article 4(1) of the Charter led to the inescapable conclusion that the proposed solution to the political disagreements alluded to in the second question was impermissible. However, once it was admitted that political factors
could be taken into account in assessing whether an applicant for membership satisfied
the criteria contained in that provision, it is difficult to understand how the political
difficulties involved in the process could not be resolved by political compromise.

Seen from this perspective, the view of the Joint Dissenting Opinion has some
merit:

> If the request for an opinion involved the Court in approving or disapproving the
> desire thus expressed by a Member of the United Nations to procure the admission of
> other States at the same time as the applicant State, it would only be possible to assess
> this political consideration from a political point of view. But such an assessment is not
> within the province of the Court. An opinion on this subject would not be an opin-
> ion on a legal question within the meaning of Article 96 of the Charter and Article 65
> of the Statute. It is one thing to ask the Court whether a Member is legally entitled to
> rely on political considerations in voting on the admission of new Members; that is a
> legal question and we have answered it. It is quite another thing to ask the Court to
> assess the validity of any particular political consideration upon which a Member
> relies; that is a political question and must not be answered.[74]

Nevertheless, it is difficult to understand how the two questions could have been
segregated in this way. Whether Article 4(1) was exhaustive of the legal requirements for admission, or provided only threshold criteria, depended upon how it
was interpreted and applied in the practice of the General Assembly and the
Security Council. Thus, whether or not the Security Council was prepared to
accept a package deal would certainly have been a political decision, but one that
would inevitably have impacted on how Article 4(1) would, in the future, have
been interpreted. If the former was a political decision, then it would appear to follow that how Article 4(1) should be interpreted was more a matter of political than
of legal determination, and therefore equally outside the jurisdiction of the Court.

As to the more important issue for this paper, i.e. the extent to which account is
taken of the two reference points, the time at which the treaty was made and the
time at which it is applied, the emphasis is still on the latter even if the application
is, as we have seen, 'abstract' rather than related to the specific issues in dispute.
Certainly matters that have occurred with regard to the treaty since its inception

---

[73] For a consideration of the subsequent history of this issue in the Court's jurisprudence, see S.
Rosenne, *The Law and Practice of the International Court 1920–1996*, vol. II (3rd edition, 1997) 1003–11.

[74] *Supra* note 64, 93.

and which are relevant to the issues, even in an abstract form, would be taken into account. Not that the principal case in which account was taken of practice under the treaty, the UN Charter, can be regarded as altogether 'abstract'. In the *Namibia* case,[75] although couched in fairly general terms, the question posed to the Court could hardly be described as 'abstract':

> What are the legal consequences for States of the continued presence of South Africa in Namibia, notwithstanding Security Council resolution 276 (1970)?

South Africa's objection to the validity of the resolution on the ground that two permanent members had abstained in the vote on its adoption, whereas Article 27(3) of the Charter required the affirmative vote of all the permanent members, was dismissed. As the Court pointed out, 'the proceedings of the Security Council extending over a long period supply abundant evidence that presidential rulings and the positions taken by members of the Council, in particular its permanent members, have consistently and uniformly interpreted the practice of voluntary abstention by a permanent member as not constituting a bar to the adoption of resolutions.'[76] It would have been possible for the Court to have expressed such a view even if the request for its Opinion had been expressed in more abstract terms.

The less than abstract nature of the question posed made it impossible for the Court to rely upon its excuse in the *Admission* case that its duty was 'to envisage the question submitted to it only in the abstract form which has been given to it; nothing which is said in the present opinion refers, either directly or indirectly, to concrete cases or to particular circumstances.'[77] This opened the way for South Africa to raise a series of arguments related to its claim that the question concerned a dispute involving South Africa.

The first contention was that, as the matter encompassed by the question asked of the Court concerned a dispute between South Africa and other members of the United Nations, the Court should have declined to give an Opinion on the basis of the *Eastern Carelia* case in which the Permanent Court had similarly declined to give an Opinion because 'the opinion which the Court had been requested to give bears on an actual dispute between Finland and Russia',[78] so that answering the question 'would be substantially equivalent to deciding the dispute between the parties'.[79] This was not something the Court could do in the absence of their consent. Russia had not consented to the proceedings, nor was it a member of the League of Nations so that it was not subject to the obligations of the Covenant with regard to the pacific settlement of disputes.

---

[75] *Namibia* case, *supra* note 22.
[76] *Ibid*, 22.
[77] *Supra* note 53, 61.
[78] *Supra* note 66, 27.
[79] *Ibid*, 29.

This latter ground would have been reason enough for the present Court to have held the *Eastern Carelia* case as not applicable to the circumstances of the *Namibia* case. Unlike Russia in relation to the League of Nations, South Africa was a member of the United Nations and therefore 'bound by Article 96 of the Charter, which empowers the Security Council to request advisory opinions on any legal question'.[80] However, the Court gave the additional justification that the case did not relate 'to a legal dispute actually pending between two or more States', nor to 'a dispute between South Africa and the United Nations'.[81] The reason given for the first part of the pronouncement, though it would seem to be equally applicable to the second part, was that the request had been 'put forward by a United Nations organ with reference to its decisions [in which it had sought] legal advice from the Court on the consequences and implications of these decisions'.[82]

While this explanation could justify the Court in answering questions concerning the powers of the United Nations, on which matters divergent views were held by South Africa and other States, it provided no reason why the issues did not constitute a dispute involving South Africa. On this latter point, the Court had placed itself in a position of logical difficulty. It had decided to reject South Africa's request to appoint a Judge *ad hoc* for the hearing of the case, initially giving no reasons for its decision.[83] When it came to the Advisory Opinion, the majority felt obliged to give some justification for their decision beyond the initial determination in which it decided, 'by ten votes to five, to reject the application' by South Africa to appoint an *ad hoc* Judge.[84] However, as pointed out above, the fact that the request 'sought legal advice from the Court on the consequences and implications' of various decisions of the General Assembly and Security Council was not inconsistent with those decisions also relating to a legal dispute between South Africa and other international persons.

The Court had to deal with two other contentions centred upon whether or not a dispute existed. These concerned the application of Articles 32 and 27(3) of the Charter. Under the former, South Africa claimed that it had been entitled to have participated, without a vote, in the Security Council's deliberations, as it was a party to the dispute but was not a member of the Council.[85] As for Article 27(3), in

---

[80] *Namibia* case, *supra* note 22, 23.
[81] *Ibid*, 24.
[82] *Ibid*.
[83] Order of 29 January 1971, *ibid*, 12.
[84] *Ibid*, 13.
[85] According to the first part of Article 32 of the UN Charter: 'Any Member of the United Nations which is not a member of the Security Council ... if it is a party to a dispute under consideration by the Security Council, shall be invited to participate, without vote, in the discussion relating to the dispute.' As South Africa argued: 'the fundamental rule of *audi alteram partem* was ignored by the Council. It did not at any time invite South Africa to participate in the discussions preceding the adoption of its relevant resolutions, notwithstanding that in terms of Article 32 of the Charter it was bound to do so', Written Statement of South Africa, *Namibia* case, ICJ Pleadings, Vol. I, 519.

decisions made under Chapter VI of the Charter it is required that 'a party to a dispute shall abstain from voting'. According to South Africa, there was a dispute between 'South Africa and a number of member States consisting probably of all of those which voted in favour of the General Assembly resolution 2145(XXI)' which had purported to terminate the mandate.[86] With regard to the relevant Council resolutions,[87] had 'these States abstained, the Council could not . . . have adopted the resolutions, since the requisite nine affirmative votes would have been lacking, and it is accordingly contended that their failure to abstain rendered the adoption of the resolutions concerned invalid and of no legal effect.'[88]

The avenue chosen by the Court to bypass this objection to the non-application of Articles 32 and 27(3) of the Charter amounted to an abdication by the Court of any role as an objective assessor of the conduct of the Security Council. The Court was content to accept that whether or not there was a dispute, this was subject to Council determination and that such a determination could be affected by the way in which the matter was designated on the Council's agenda:

> The language of Article 32 of the Charter is mandatory, but the question whether the Security Council must extend an invitation in accordance with that provision depends on whether it has made a determination that the matter under its consideration is in the nature of a dispute. In the absence of such a determination Article 32 of the Charter does not apply. The question of Namibia was placed on the agenda of the Security Council as a "situation" and not as a "dispute". No member State made any suggestion or proposal that the matter should be examined as a dispute, although due notice was given of the placing of the question on the Security Council's agenda under the title "Situation in Namibia". Had the Government of South Africa considered that the question should have been treated in the Security Council as a dispute, it should have drawn the Council's attention to that aspect of the matter. Having failed to raise the question at the appropriate time in the proper forum, it is not open to it to raise it before the Court at this stage. A similar answer must be given to the related objection based on the proviso to paragraph 3 of Article 27 of the Charter. This proviso also requires for its application the prior determination by the Security Council that a dispute exists and that certain members of the Council are involved as parties to such a dispute. [89]

The *Namibia* case presents a writer on the role of the Court in judicial review of the actions of UN bodies with conflicting signals. On the one hand, it did examine and endorse the legality of General Assembly Resolution 2145(XXI).[90] Moreover, with regard to the Security Council, it 'reached the conclusion that the decisions made by the Security Council in paragraphs 2 and 5 of resolution 276(1970), as

---

[86] *Ibid*, 417.
[87] These were Resolutions 264 (1969), *United Nations Yearbook* (1969) 696; Resolution 269 (1969), *ibid*, 697; Resolution 276 (1970), *United Nations Yearbook* (1970) 752–753.
[88] Written Statement of South Africa, *Namibia* case, *supra* note 85, 418.
[89] *Namibia* case, *supra* note 22, 22–23.
[90] *Ibid*, 45–50.

related to paragraph 3 of resolution 264(1969) and paragraph 5 of resolution 269(1969), were adopted in conformity with the purposes and principles of the Charter and in accordance with its Articles 24 and 25.'[91]

This contrasts sharply with the Court's lame acceptance of the inapplicability of Article 32 and the proviso to Article 27(3) of the UN Charter. To an extent, the difference might be justified by reference to the Court's earlier pronouncement in the *Certain Expenses* case that, 'when the Organisation takes action which warrants the assertion that it was appropriate for the fulfilment of one of the stated purposes of the United Nations, the presumption is that such action is not *ultra vires*.'[92] However, it would be a curious principle to cover for procedural irregularity. It was a surprising outcome that the way the matter was inscribed as an agenda item, which was purely a matter of internal procedure, should have been regarded as having binding consequences with regard to the external effects of the resolutions adopted in pursuance of that inscription. In particular, although South Africa had been denied access to the Council by virtue of a determination of the Council, it could hardly be bound by measures taken in its absence on the ground that it had accepted the determination. South Africa had no choice in the matter.

The approach adopted by the Court to resolving whether a dispute existed by reference to the way it was listed on the Council's agenda has something in common with the 'abstract' question issue. They are both means of avoiding the reality of having to consider the existence or substance of a dispute. Moreover it is undoubtedly an avoidance of the normal meaning of the 'application' of a treaty in the real world. The approach also disregards the Court's own definitions of a dispute.[93]

To some extent the difficulties and the contorted means of resolving them were of the Court's own making. They stemmed from the rejection of South Africa's

---

[91] *Ibid*, 53.

[92] *Certain Expenses of the United Nations (Article 17, paragraph 2 of the Charter)*, Advisory Opinion, ICJ Rep 1962, 168.

[93] As the majority of the Court said in the *South West Africa* case (Ethiopia v. South Africa; Liberia v. South Africa), *Preliminary Objections*, ICJ Rep 1962, 328: 'In the case of the *Mavrommatis Palestine Concessions*, PCIJ Ser A, (1924), No 2, 11), the Permanent Court defines a dispute as "a disagreement on a point of law or fact, a conflict of legal views or interests between two persons". The said Judgment, in proceeding to examine the nature of the dispute, enunciates this definition, only after establishing that the conditions for the existence of a dispute are fulfilled. In other words it is not sufficient for one party to a contentious case to assert that a dispute exists with the other party. A mere assertion is not sufficient to prove the existence of a dispute any more than a mere denial of the existence of a dispute proves its non-existence. Nor is it adequate to show that the interests of the two parties to such a case are in conflict. It must be shown that the claim of one party is positively opposed by the other. Tested by this criterion there can be no doubt about the existence of a dispute between the Parties before the Court, since it is clearly constituted by their opposing attitudes relating to the performance of the obligations of the Mandate by the Respondent as Mandatory.' See also the Dissenting Opinion of Judge Fitzmaurice in the *Namibia* case, *supra* note 22, 314.

request to appoint an *ad hoc* Judge, a decision made initially without giving reasons. When the Opinion was eventually delivered, as mentioned above, the Court relied upon the absence of a dispute to which South Africa was a party as justification for that rejection. In that respect the dissenters' views were the more persuasive. But, if the Court had admitted to the existence of a dispute, how could it have dealt with Article 32 and the proviso to Article 27(3)? With regard to Article 32, it would have been acceptable enough for the Court to have simply registered its preference for South Africa being allowed to present its case to the Council, while denying that its absence in any way affected the validity of the resolutions then adopted.

But what of the proviso to Article 27(3)? It would be an unreasonable interpretation of that provision if, in a multi-party dispute involving a significant number of the members of the Security Council, the compulsory abstention requirement concerning the use of the Council's powers under Chapter VI of the Charter meant that the Council could only adopt a valid resolution if it were acting under Chapter VII of the Charter. It would be possible to avoid this dilemma by accepting South Africa's alternative description of the dispute as being one between itself and the United Nations as an institution. In circumstances where, in what might originally have been a purely inter-state dispute, the Organisation, through bodies like the General Assembly and the Security Council, takes over the running of the dispute and where it is the actions of those bodies which is called in question, the dispute moves on to a different plane. As the dispute has become one between the United Nations and one of its members, there is no denying the existence of the dispute, but it is not one to which the proviso to Article 27(3) has any application.

The Court seemed prepared to take a different course in the *Lockerbie* case,[94] though this may be attributable to the fact that the Court was asked by Libya to exercise its contentious jurisdiction under the Montreal Convention for the Suppression of Unlawful Acts against the Safety of Civil Aviation 1971. The case arose out of the destruction of Pan-American Flight 103 over the Scottish village of Lockerbie on 21 December 1998, with considerable loss of life.[95] Charges were laid by the Scottish authorities against two Libyan nationals alleged to have been responsible for organising the placing of a bomb on board the airliner. Libya did not respond to British and American demands that the two individuals should be surrendered for trial in Britain or the United States. By Resolution 731 (1992), the

---

[94] *Questions of Interpretation and Application of the 1971 Montreal Convention arising from the Aerial Incident at Lockerbie,* (hereinafter *Lockerbie* case), (Libya v. United Kingdom), *Provisional Measures,* ICJ Rep 1992, 3; *Lockerbie* case (Libya v. USA), *Provisional Measures,* ICJ Rep 1992, 114; *Lockerbie* case (Libya v United Kingdom), *Preliminary Objections,* ICJ Rep 1998, 9; *Lockerbie* case (Libya v USA), *Preliminary Objections,* ICJ Rep 1998, 115.

[95] The figures are given in Judge Oda's Dissenting Opinion in the *Lockerbie* case, *Preliminary Objections, supra* note 94, 82 and 173.

Security Council urged 'the Libyan Government immediately to provide a full and effective response to those requests so as to contribute to an elimination of international terrorism'.[96] Three days after the close of hearings in Libya's request for the granting of provisional measures in the cases Libya commenced against the United Kingdom and the United States, the Council adopted Resolutions 748 (1992) in which it asserted that it was acting under Chapter VII of the Charter and decided that 'the Libyan Government must now comply without any further delay' with the requests referred to in the previous resolution.[97] By the time the Court heard the Preliminary Objections submitted by the two Respondent States, the Council had passed Resolution 883 (1993), setting out a further range of sanctions to be imposed on Libya should it not comply with the Council's demands.[98]

While deferring to the Security Council's first decision under Chapter VII at the provisional measures stage, holding that 'whatever the situation previous to the adoption of that resolution, the rights claimed by Libya under the Montreal Convention cannot now be regarded as appropriate for protection by the indication of provisional measures',[99] the Court adopted a more interventionist stance with regard to the preliminary objections of the United Kingdom and the United States. In the first place, unlike the attempt to pretend a dispute did not exist as in the *Namibia* case, in a contentious case like the present, the Court had no doubt as to the existence of a dispute between Libya and the United Kingdom and the United States with regard to 'the interpretation or application of the Montreal Convention'.[100] On the more contentious issue of whether the effect of the Council resolutions under Chapter VII was to render the claims of Libya 'without object', a reduced majority of the Court held that the objection did not have an exclusively preliminary character so should be considered at the merits stage of the proceedings.[101]

Being a contentious case, *Lockerbie* is not necessarily a portent of a change of attitude on the part of the Court as to how it might deal with an advisory case. Suppose the same issues had been submitted by the General Assembly to the Court in a request for an advisory opinion at the culmination of debates in the Assembly in which it had been claimed that the Council, and notably its permanent members, had abused their position in promoting, and voting in favour of the Chapter VII resolutions concerning Libya. The Assembly made it clear in a preambular paragraph that it wished to receive such advice as part of its policy to uphold the sanctity of such an important international regime as that created by the Montreal Convention, and that, in this action, it had the support of the ICAO.

---

[96] The text of the resolution appears in ICJ Rep 1992, 12 and 123.
[97] *Ibid*, 13–14; 124–125.
[98] Text in *United Nations Yearbook* (1993), 101–102.
[99] *Lockerbie* case, Provisional Measures, *supra* note 94, 15.
[100] *Lockerbie* case, Preliminary Objections, *supra* note 94, 30, 135.
[101] *Ibid*, 31, 136.

In order to resist the attempt by the Court to exercise its advisory function in such circumstances, the existence of a dispute would be a means of demonstrating that this would not be an appropriate case in which the Court should give an opinion. To argue this point successfully, the protagonists would have to show that the fact that the matter was listed on the Council's agenda as a 'question' should not be regarded as conclusive, even for an advisory opinion. At least this would be to introduce a measure of realism into the Court's consideration of the matter. Whether the Court would then give an opinion would depend upon the more difficult issue of whether the Court regarded it as appropriate for the General Assembly to receive advice on such a matter. Discussion of that issue would be too much of a diversion from the substance of this paper.

As to the interpretation and application of the Montreal Convention and their relevance to the *Lockerbie* case, it depends very much on how one classifies the dispute. The view of the United Kingdom and the United States was that the dispute related entirely to the effect of the two Security Council mandatory resolutions, which had nothing to do with the Montreal Convention. On the other side, it could be argued that the Council had adopted an adjudicatory role in determining that Libya's conduct had taken the situation outside the scope of the Convention. As this was entirely a matter of law, the Court, as the judicial arm of the United Nations, had priority in such matters and so could review the correctness in law of such a determination.

Considering the issue from the perspective of the three interpretative schools, one would not necessarily come up with differing conclusions. One would have to be of an extreme textualist persuasion to contend that the words of the Convention were sufficiently clear so that in all cases falling within Article 1,[102] Libya was entitled, and required, if it was not prepared to extradite the accused, to try the person or persons concerned in its own courts under Article 5(2) if the Convention.[103] But would this entitlement extend to persons who, it was alleged, had acted on the instructions of the very same State that wished to try them? Even the quasi-textual provisions of the Vienna Convention do enable supplementary means of interpretation under Article 32(b) if the meaning according to Article 31 'leads to a result which is manifestly absurd or unreasonable'.

---

[102] According to Article 1(1) of the Convention:
'Any person commits and offence if he unlawfully and intentionally:
...(c) places or causes to be placed on an aircraft in service, by any means whatsoever, a device or substance which is likely to destroy that aircraft, or to cause damage to it which renders it incapable of flight, or to cause damage to it which is likely to endanger its safety in flight'.
Article 1(2) stipulates that:
'Any person also commits an offence if he: (a) attempts to commit any of the offences mentioned in paragraph 1 of this Article; or
(b) is an accomplice of a person who commits or attempts to commit any such offence.'
[103] Article 5(2) requires each contracting State to establish its jurisdiction over such offences 'in the case where the alleged offender is present in its territory and it does not extradite him pursuant to Article 8'.

It may be doubted, however, whether, in negotiating the Convention, the representatives of the States concerned would have discussed the scarcely mentionable possibility that they might themselves be the instigators of terrorist acts against the aircraft of other States. In other words, the supplementary means might not be at all helpful. Recourse should therefore be had to the presumption, underlying Article 32(b), that a treaty should be interpreted in a manner that avoids a result which is absurd or unreasonable. Despite the textualist garb of Articles 31 and 32 of the 1969 Vienna Convention on the Law of Treaties, this reasonable implication is tantamount to attributing an intention to the parties of wishing to avoid such an outcome.

Whereas the intention of the parties can operate at the level of individual provisions, the position with regard to the object and purpose of a treaty may, as already pointed out, be less capable of applying to individual provisions. The difficulty with an object and purpose approach, which applies equally to its appearance in the general rule of interpretation in Article 31 of the Vienna Convention, is that a treaty's object and purpose may be stated at different degrees of generality some of which might be more helpful to a particular contention in a dispute than others. In this case, however, the Convention indicated that the parties recognised 'that, for the purpose of deterring... acts [against the safety of civil aviation], there is an urgent need to provide appropriate measures for punishment of offenders'. It is at least arguable that this purpose would not be served in an appropriate way by the State responsible for instigating the acts in question being entitled to try the perpetrators who acted at its instigation.

4. The Context of a Treaty

It has already been suggested that the term 'context' is capable of bearing at least two principal meanings. In its narrower form, it concerns the meaning to be attributed to a specific word or passage taking into consideration other words or passages in a document. Hence, to consider a part of a treaty in its context requires examining its relationship to other parts of the instrument. More broadly, the term 'context' may refer to events surrounding the making of the document in question. This second possibility can be extended in the case of a treaty to include events surrounding its application in contemporary circumstances.

As far as the Vienna Convention is concerned, it is no surprise, in light of its essentially textualist view of interpretation, that it adopted the first of the possible meanings. Thus, according to Article 31(1), the 'ordinary meaning' is to be given to the terms of a treaty 'in their context'. By Article 31(2), it is made clear that 'context' refers solely to the treaty itself and related instruments:

> The context for the purpose of the interpretation of a treaty shall comprise, in addition to the text, including its preamble and annexes:
>
> (a) any agreement relating to the treaty which was made between all the parties in connexion with the conclusion of the treaty;

(b) any instrument which was made by one or more parties in connection with the conclusion of the treaty and accepted by the other parties as an instrument related to the treaty.[104]

In addition to adopting the first of the possible meanings of the term 'context,' it also seems to exclude the employment of a broader version. The only possibility of the second meaning coming into play would be if recourse to the circumstances surrounding the making of the treaty was necessary to establish or clarify the object and purpose of the treaty to which Article 31(1) also refers. To that extent at least, the surrounding circumstances, including the *travaux préparatoires*, might be admissible in circumstances other than those referred to in Article 32.

The law as set out in Articles 31 and 32 has a resemblance to the Anglo-Australian law relating to the construction of written contracts. The prevailing view was that evidence of surrounding circumstances to the making of the agreement was only admissible 'to assist in the interpretation of the contract if the language is ambiguous or susceptible of more than one meaning'.[105] On the other hand there was recognition of the fact that some knowledge of background circumstances was probably necessary in order to begin the process of interpretation. As one judge explained, the words used must 'be construed with reference to the facts known to the parties and in contemplation of which the parties must be deemed to have used them'.[106]

As to how a judge was to choose between the two approaches, various possibilities were canvassed. For example, it may be that the explanation for employing the latter alternative has something in common with the need to identify the object and purpose of a treaty in accordance with Article 31(1) of the Vienna Convention. In the view of Lord Wilberforce:

> No contracts are made in a vacuum: there is always a setting in which they have to be placed. The nature of what is legitimate to have regard to is usually described as 'the surrounding circumstances' but this phrase is imprecise: it can be illustrated but hardly defined. In a commercial contract it is certainly right that the court should know the commercial purpose of the contract and this in turn presupposes knowledge of the genesis of the transaction, the background, the context, the matter in which the parties are operating.[107]

---

[104] Amongst the cases cited by the ILC, see *Vienna Conference, supra* note 18, 'Final Report on the Law of Treaties', 41 para (12), where in support of this interpretation of the term 'context' the following passage was quoted from the PCIJ's *Competence of the ILO to Regulate Agricultural Labour, Advisory Opinion*, PCIJ Ser B, (1922) Nos 2 and 3, 23: 'In considering the question before the Court upon the language of the Treaty, it is obvious that the Treaty must be read as a whole, and that its meaning is not to be determined merely upon particular phrases which, if detached from the context, may be interpreted in more than one sense'.

[105] *Codelfa Construction Pty Ltd v State Rly Authority of NSW* (1982) 149 CLR 337 at 352 per Mason J.

[106] *Inland Revenue Commissioners v Raphael* [1935] AC 96 at 143 *per* Lord Wright.

[107] *Reardon Smith Line Ltd v Yngvar Hansen-Tangen*, [1976] 1 WLR 995–996.

There is a further similarity between the international law position with regard to treaties and the Anglo-Australian approach to written contracts. Background circumstances, which might include evidence of the negotiations leading to the conclusion of the contract, are only admissible for the purpose of placing the Court in the position of the parties in order to be better able to assess their intentions. However, it is their objective or apparent intention drawn from the terms of the contract which is all important.[108] Thus, to quote the words of Lord Wilberforce, when 'one speaks of the intention of the parties, one is speaking objectively – the parties cannot themselves give direct evidence of what that intention was – and what must be ascertained is what is to be taken as the intention which reasonable people would have had if placed in the situation of the parties'.[109] Certainly, therefore, one of them could not introduce evidence of the negotiations in order to establish that party's subjective intention in the matter.

There are also similarities between the common law and international law when it comes to dealing with such issues as the intended operation or the validity of contracts or of treaties. With regard to the former matter, the classic English case of *Pym v Campbell*[110] concerned a written document which appeared to constitute a binding contract for the purchase of a share in an invention. However, it was held that the apparent purchaser was entitled to introduce evidence to show that the contract was only to become binding on him if a certain third party should approve the invention, but that the person concerned had not given his approval. As Erle J explained, 'evidence to vary the terms of an agreement in writing is not admissible, but evidence to show that there is no agreement at all is admissible'.[111]

This decision bears some resemblance to the *Aegean Sea* case.[112] There has been a continuing dispute between Greece and Turkey concerning their continental shelf rights in the Aegean Sea, claimed by Greece on the basis that all islands in the Sea, except those less than three miles from the Turkish coast, were Greek territory. In bringing this case to the International Court, Greece relied on two alleged bases of jurisdiction, one of which was the so-called Brussels Communiqué, issued by the two Prime Ministers at the end of a meeting in Brussels on 31 May 1975, which contained the following:

> They decided that those problems [as regards relations between their countries] should be resolved peacefully by means of negotiations and as regards the continental shelf of the Aegean Sea by the International Court at the Hague.

---

[108] Greig and Davis, *The Law of Contract* (1987) 410–411.
[109] [1976] 1 WLR 996.
[110] [1856] 119 Eng Rep 903.
[111] *Ibid*, 905.
[112] *Aegean Sea* case, *supra* note 17.

They also 'decided to bring forward the meeting of experts concerning the question of the continental shelf of the Aegean Sea'.[113]

In order to determine what was intended by the Communiqué, the Court examined in some detail the course of the negotiations, both prior, and subsequent, to the meeting in Brussels, between the two States on the issue of the continental shelf rights. It is possible to regard this approach from two different standpoints. It could be categorised as the equivalent of the *Pym v Campbell case* in which the Court had to determine whether the parties had entered into a binding contract to submit the case to the Court. Alternatively, it could be perceived as an example of an ambiguous instrument in which the background to it had to be examined to ascertain its true meaning. Both versions are compatible with the Court's judgment. The Court pointed out that the 'divergence of views as to the interpretation of the Brussels Communiqué makes it necessary for the Court to consider what light is thrown on its meaning by the context in which the meeting on 31 May 1975 took place and the Communiqué was drawn up'.[114] Then, having considered the earlier meetings and the subsequent negotiations between the parties, the Court observed that:

> Accordingly having regard to the terms of the Joint Communiqué . . . and to the context in which it was agreed and issued, the Court can only conclude that it was not intended to, and did not, constitute an immediate commitment by the Greek and Turkish Prime Ministers, on behalf of their respective Governments, to accept unconditionally the unilateral submission of the present dispute to the Court.[115]

It can hardly be claimed that either the Anglo-Australian law on these matters, or international law as depicted in Articles 31 and 32 of the Vienna Convention, is logically satisfying. With regard to the former at least, context, in the sense of background circumstances, is generally available in the construction of written commercial contracts as a basis for ascertaining the (objective) meaning of the document. For a similar purpose in the case of a treaty, the context as revealed in Article 31 and implied from Article 32 has a much narrower significance. However, in the legal doctrine of both, the course of negotiations is available in limited circumstances, one being to help determine whether an agreement has been reached. In the *Aegean Sea* case, the Court's extensive references to the negotiating context undoubtedly resolved the issue of whether the Brussels Communiqué did constitute an agreement entitling a party unilaterally to commence proceedings before the Court, while avoiding providing any answer to the question of the scope of any agreement that it might have constituted. As the Court explained:

> Having concluded that the Joint Communiqué issued in Brussels . . . does not furnish a basis for establishing the Court's jurisdiction in the present proceedings, the Court

---

[113] *Ibid,* 39–40.
[114] *Ibid,* 41.
[115] *Ibid,* 44.

is not concerned, nor is it competent, to pronounce upon any other implications which that Communiqué may have in the context of the present dispute. It is for the two Governments themselves to consider those implications and what effect, if any, is to be given the Joint Communiqué in their further efforts to arrive at an amicable settlement of their dispute.[116]

A similar dispute arose over the Court's jurisdiction in the *Qatar and Bahrain* case.[117] Negotiations concerning their contested territorial claims took place between the two States with the good offices of the King of Saudi Arabia over a period of some years. The first document to be produced in the course of the discussions was entitled the 'principles for the Framework of Reaching a Settlement' of 1983. This was in the nature of a 'how to proceed' set of guidelines which envisaged the settlement of all disputed matters 'relating to sovereignty over the islands, maritime boundaries and territorial waters . . . comprehensively together'. The principles also provided for the setting up of a Tripartite Committee which was to find solutions acceptable to the two States. In this task the Committee was unsuccessful.[118] In 1987 a further arrangement was agreed to on the basis of identical letters sent by the King to the two sides. While setting out the point that all 'the disputed matters shall be referred to the International Court', the document also provided for another Tripartite Committee to be established, this time 'for the purpose of approaching the . . . Court, and satisfying the necessary requirements to have the dispute submitted to the Court'.[119]

This version of the Committee was no more successful than its predecessor, though it did produce a list of the disputed matters in 1987. The disagreement between the two parties over one item on the list was subsequently settled by Qatar agreeing to the formula in question, that agreement being included in the so called Doha Minutes of 1990. The Minutes reaffirmed 'what was agreed previously between the two parties' and provided for the King's good offices to continue until May 1991. The parties were in disagreement as to whether the next part of the document referred to either of the parties being entitled to submit the matter to the Court at the end of that period (position of Qatar), or the *two* parties being entitled to do so jointly (position of Bahrain).[120]

A majority of the Court held that the combined effect of the 1987 and 1990 documents was to establish an international agreement which entitled Qatar to seise the Court of the case by unilateral application. It was true that the parties had

---

[116] *Id.*
[117] *Qatar and Bahrain* case, *Jurisdiction and Admissibility*, ICJ Rep 1994, 112; ICJ Rep 1995, 6.
[118] *Qatar and Bahrain* case, *Jurisdiction and Admissibility*, ICJ Rep 1994, 116.
[119] *Ibid*, 117.
[120] *Ibid*, 118–119.

resolved their differences over what territorial and maritime matters were in dispute between them in Qatar agreeing to the Bahraini formula. However, the documents could still be regarded as defective in that they were no more than an agreement to agree in the future.[121]

There is a good deal of case law in municipal courts concerning the issue of incompleteness of a contract and whether a court is entitled to fill the gap which the parties left. In the notorious English case of *May and Butcher Ltd v R*,[122] the appellants had agreed to take all supplies of tentage made available in a given year by a Board acting on behalf of a disposals commission. The contract contained a renewal clause and the contract was renewed. Subsequent negotiations for a further renewal broke down. The issue of whether the appellants had a contractual right of renewal depended upon how the part of the clause would be interpreted which stipulated that the 'price or prices to be paid ... for such old tentage shall be agreed upon from time to time between the Commission and the purchasers'. The House of Lords held that, as no such agreement had been reached, there was no contract for renewal on which the appellants could rely.

This is, on the face of it, rather an extreme case and, almost immediately, the House of Lords gave warning that a court should avoid being regarded as a 'destroyer of bargains'.[123] Thus, in more recent times, a court will seek to fill the gap by relying upon some formula, provided by the parties,[124] or to be implied in the circumstances,[125] or upon machinery, such as an arbitration clause, which it can claim as justifying a role for itself.

It is possible to draw a parallel with the situation confronting the International Court of Justice in the *Qatar and Bahrain* case, except with regard to the onus of proof. A municipal court would see its role as one of trying to give effect to the apparent intention of the parties to enter into an effective contract. The position with regard to a treaty or declaration accepting the jurisdiction of the International Court would seem to be that the burden of proving that it covered the dispute to which the application to the Court related is not entirely clear. There are a number of pronouncements by the Permanent Court and by the present Court in which the standard set was that of preponderance, that the arguments in favour of jurisdiction must be 'preponderant'.[126]

---

[121] *Ibid*, 120.

[122] (1929) reported in [1934] 2 KB 17n.

[123] *Hillas & Co Ltd v Arcos Ltd* (1932) 147 LT 503, 512 *per* Lord Tomlin.

[124] *Upper Hunter County District Council v Australian Chilling & Freezing Co Ltd* (1968) 118 CLR 429; *Brown v Gould* [1972] Ch 53.

[125] *Sudbrook Trading Estate Ltd v Eggleston* [1983] 1 AC 444.

[126] *Case Concerning the Factory at Chorzow*, (Germany *v.* Poland), *Jurisdiction*, PCIJ Series A, (1927), No. 9, 32; *Border and Transborder Armed Actions*, (Nicaragua *v.* Honduras), (hereinafter *Border and Transborder Armed Actions* case) *Jurisdiction and Admissibility*, ICJ Rep 1988, 76; *Fisheries Jurisdiction* (Spain v Canada), (hereinafter *Fisheries Jurisdiction* case), *Jurisdiction*, ICJ Rep 1998, 450.

Though the word 'preponderant' signifies something that is heavier or weightier, it is not easy to determine how much heavier or weightier the proof of submission to the jurisdiction has to be compared with the objections to the jurisdiction.[127] In the Oxford English Dictionary, the various examples of use of the word 'preponderance' include a number where degrees of that quality were obtained by the use of a qualifying adjective such as 'least' on one side and 'vast', 'overwhelming' or 'immense' on the other side of the scales.[128] With regard to the Court's jurisdiction, there are certainly examples of pronouncements which seem to be based on the supposition that the word 'preponderant' itself possesses the meaning of greatly outweighing the arguments for the contrary view. Thus, Judge Lauterpacht referred to what he regarded as 'the established practice of the Court . . . that the Court will not uphold its jurisdiction unless the intention to confer it has been proved beyond reasonable doubt'.[129] In a similar vein are expressions such as requiring 'an unequivocal indication of the desire of a State to obtain a decision on the merits of a suit',[130] or a 'voluntary and indisputable acceptance of the Court's jurisdiction',[131] or even a combination of both these tests.[132]

We shall come in a moment to the Court's decision in the *Qatar and Bahrain* case that the 1987 and 1990 documents established an international agreement which entitled Qatar to make a unilateral application to the Court. However, a number of the Judges dissented from the Court's conclusion. It was Judge Shahabudeen who surveyed the Court's jurisprudence on the necessary standard of proof required of a State seeking to establish the Court's jurisdiction before concluding that, in this case, 'the attempt to establish jurisdiction . . . does not meet the requisite standard of proof'.[133] Judge Schwebel saw the negotiations between the parties as having been conducted all along on the basis of trying to finalise a special agreement whereby the disputed issues could be brought to the Court and that no agreement had been reached that would have entitled Qatar to make a unilateral application to the Court. It was in this context that Judge Schwebel made his observation about the

---

[127] See the Dissenting Opinion of Judge Shahabuddeen in the *Qatar and Bahrain* case, *supra* note 36, 63.

[128] See the Dissenting Opinion of Judge Shahabuddeen in the *Qatar and Bahrain* case, *supra* note 36, 63.

[129] *Case of Certain Norwegian Loans*, (France *v.* Norway), *Merits*, ICJ Rep (1957), 58.

[130] *Rights of Minorities in Upper Silesia*, (Germany *v.* Poland), PCIJ Series A, (1928), No. 12, 23, 24.

[131] *Corfu Channel* case, (UK v Albania), *Preliminary Objection*, ICJ Rep 1948, 27.

[132] *Application of the Convention on the Prevention and Punishment of the Crime of Genocide* case, (Bosnia and Herzegovina *v.* Yugoslavia (Serbia and Montenegro)), *Further Request for the Indication of Provisional Measures*, ICJ Rep 1993, 342.

[133] Dissenting Opinion of Judge Shahabuddeen in the *Qatar and Bahrain* case, *supra* note 36, 65. Or as Judge Koroma stated in his Dissenting Opinion to the same case: 'to establish the Court's jurisdiction, 'the evidence must be clear and preponderant. Here the evidence is not of such quality', *ibid*, 72.

problem under Article 32 of the Vienna Convention of what to do if the *travaux* contradict the meaning which the Court wishes to apply to the alleged agreement between the parties.[134] The aspect of the *travaux* to which Judge Schwebel was referring was Bahrain's rejection of the original draft of the Doha Minutes put forward by Qatar which had made it clear that 'either of the two parties' could have made application to the Court, and insistence that the final text should be in the form of 'the two parties'.[135]

In assessing whether the Court was correct in upholding its jurisdiction, the municipal law analogy is helpful. The issue of whether the wording contained in the Doha minutes denoted that only a joint approach was possible or left open the alternative of a joint approach or a unilateral application was not conclusively established even by the *travaux*. The wording used could simply have represented a compromise between the conflicting positions.

This leads into the question of why a joint application was said to be necessary. The protracted negotiations had concerned two matters, both commencing from the need to identify what areas of maritime and land territory were in dispute. The first concerned whether the parties could resolve the dispute with regard to a particular area. The second was what mechanism was to be employed to decide a dispute which could not be resolved by negotiation. From a very early stage, the parties seemed to be agreed that the Court should be the arbiter. As it seemed to be impossible to negotiate a solution to the various disputed areas, all that was necessary for the parties was to agree on the areas in dispute and what aspects of those areas were in issue between them. Once this was achieved by the adoption of the Bahraini formula, the significance of who could initiate the proceedings (either one of the parties acting unilaterally, or the two of them acting jointly) was greatly diminished.

The parallel with the contract cases lies in Bahrain's contention that the alleged agreement, comprised by the 1987 letter, which both parties had accepted, and the Doha minutes, was incomplete in that it needed a special agreement between the two parties, or at least their joint approach to the Court, to perfect the Court's jurisdiction. Seen from this perspective, the evidence of the change made to the Minutes at Bahrain's insistence was admissible in order to test the reality of the agreement. For the purposes of this assessment, as the *Aegean Sea* case demonstrated, the restrictions in Article 32 of the Vienna Convention were irrelevant. While the change to the agreed Minutes undoubtedly supported Bahrain's contention as to the incompleteness

---

[134] Dissenting Opinion of Vice-President Schwebel, *ibid*, 31.

[135] The text reading in part: 'Once the period [of Saudi mediation] has elapsed, the [two] parties may submit the matter to the International Court of Justice in accordance with the Bahraini formula, which has been accepted by Qatar', *ibid*, 33. The bracket around the 'two' is because it was contested whether the Arabic word used meant simply 'the parties' or 'the two parties', *ibid*, 18. Judge Oda also took the view in his Dissenting Opinion that no agreement had been achieved on the right to proceed by unilateral application, *ibid*, 49. There were also doubts as to whether the parties had really agreed as to the scope of their dispute over Zubarah, see the Dissenting Opinion of Judge *ad hoc* Valticos, *ibid*, 75.

of the arrangements, it was an incompleteness without real substance. The critical issue had always been that of identifying what territorial and maritime matters were in dispute between the parties. With the adoption of the 'Bahraini formula', the parties had established their own formula to be applied in determining those matters. As the machinery to settle any dispute as to the meaning of the formula and how it was to be applied in the circumstances had already been decided by the parties in the form of submission to the Court, the only outstanding issue was the form the submission should take. However, given the crucial importance of the decisions as to the formula and the machinery, the form of the submission was of minor importance. It had only assumed importance to the definition of the scope of the dispute, but this had been settled by the adoption of the formula.

As far as the standard of proof is concerned, the outcome in the *Qatar and Bahrain* case, though plausible enough in light of the above analysis, is not compatible with the various statements dealt with above, which seem to suggest some higher standard than simply one based on a balance of probabilities. In this context, the Court's continued use of such statements as the need for 'the arguments militating in favour of jurisdiction' to be 'preponderant'[136] tends to conceal a degree of variability in the standard required. However, what should be rejected is the view that preponderant is designed to show a relatively high level of proof. The assertion of jurisdiction in the *Nicaragua*[137] and *Qatar and Bahrain* cases in no way supports such a standard. This is also clear from the *Chorzow Factory* case, where the preponderant requirement was first articulated:

> The fact that weighty arguments can be advanced to support the contention that it has no jurisdiction cannot itself create a doubt calculated to upset its jurisdiction.[138]

Indeed, in the *Fisheries Jurisdiction* case between Spain and Canada, the Court denied that the burden of proof had any role to play with regard to its jurisdiction:

> The Court points out that the establishment or otherwise of jurisdiction is not a matter for the parties but for the Court itself. Although a party seeking to assert a fact must bear the burden of proving it . . . , this has no relevance for the establishment of the Court's jurisdiction, which is a 'question of law to be resolved in the light of the relevant facts' . . . That being so, there is no burden of proof to be discharged in the matter of jurisdiction. Rather it is for the Court to determine from all the facts and taking into account all the arguments advanced by the Parties, 'whether the force of the arguments militating in favour of jurisdiction is preponderant'.[139]

---

[136] *Border and Transborder Armed Actions* case, *supra* note 126, 76; *Fisheries Jurisdiction* case, *supra* note 126, 450–451.

[137] *Military and Paramilitary Activities in and Against Nicaragua* (Nicaragua *v.* United States of America), (hereinafter *Nicaragua* case), Jurisdiction and Admissibility, ICJ Rep 1984, 392.

[138] *Factory at Chorzow, supra* note 126, 32; *Border and Transborder Armed Actions* case, *supra* note 126, 76.

[139] *Fisheries Jurisdiction* case, *supra* note 126, 450, quoting from the *Border and Transborder Armed Actions* case, *supra* note 126, 76.

As words like 'preponderant', or its dictionary equivalent 'predominant', are usually employed to signify some degree of outweighing beyond a bare minimum, one is left with the suspicion that the word is used for what might be termed 'cosmetic purposes'. That is to say that the word was selected for the impression it thus created to protect the Court from the criticism that it does not pay due deference to limitations placed by States on their acceptances of the Court's jurisdiction in order to promote its unexpressed agenda favouring the judicial settlement of disputes.

5. *The Significance of the Original Intentions of the Party or Parties*

From the discussion so far, it appears that the tendency is to regard the interpretation and application of treaty provisions as a one stage process whatever the impression created by Articles 31 and 32 of the Vienna Convention. Moreover, the longer a treaty remains in force, the less likely will this one stage approach be undermined by considerations of what the treaty may originally have intended to be its consequences. Just how far this trend has gone will be examined in the final section of this paper. However, in one specific area there does seem to be a contrary current flowing and that concerns the Court's attitude towards declarations accepting its jurisdiction under Article 36(2) of its Statute.

(a) *Declarations Accepting the Court's Jurisdiction*

The development of a potentially subjective approach to such declarations, in which the original intention of the declarant State is emphasised, can be traced back to the *Anglo-Iranian Oil Company* case.[140] The crucial question was whether the Iranian declaration of 2 October 1930, ratified by Iran on 19 September 1932, applied only to treaties and conventions to which Iran subsequently became a party. In accepting that this was the effect of the Iranian declaration, the Court made reference to a passage in the law by which the Iranian Parliament had approved the ratification of the declaration. The legislation stipulated that the declaration would operate with regard to 'all disputes arising out of the situations or facts relating, directly or indirectly, to the execution of treaties or conventions which the Government will have accepted after the ratification of the Declaration'.[141]

In adopting this position the Court stressed the importance in assessing a unilateral act accepting the Court's jurisdiction of the intention of the declarant State in making its declaration. In doing so it rejected the totally objective view maintained

---

[140] *Anglo-Iranian Oil Company* case, (United Kingdom *v.* Iran), *Preliminary Objections*, ICJ Rep 1952, 93.
[141] *Ibid,* 106.

by the textualist school that the intention was to be deduced solely from the instrument itself and expressed by Judge Hackworth as follows:

> When a State deposits with an international organ a document, such as a declaration accepting the compulsory jurisdiction of the Court, upon which other States are expected to rely, those States are entitled to accept that document at face value; they are not required to go back to the municipal law for explanations of the meaning or significance of the international instrument.[142]

In order to justify its view, it was necessary for the Court to provide some satisfactory explanation for the reception of evidence of the declarant State's 'real' intention. In allowing Iran to rely upon the law passed by the Iranian Parliament to enable the Government to ratify its declaration, the Court responded to the British objection to such evidence as follows:

> The Court is unable to see why it should be prevented from taking this piece of evidence into consideration. The law was published in the Corpus of Iranian laws voted and ratified during the period from 15 January 1931 to 15 January 1933. It has thus been available for the examination of other governments during a period of about twenty years.[143]

It cannot be claimed that this was a particularly helpful decision by the Court, as it would be beyond the resources of many States to acquaint themselves with the preparatory work of legislation passed to enable ratification of a State's acceptance of the Court's jurisdiction. In so far as such a ruling can be justified, it would be on the ground that, if a State was contemplating bringing proceedings before the Court against another declarant State, it would at that stage be necessary for the applicant State to familiarize itself with such background evidence that was available of the declarant State's intention in formulating its declaration.

At least in adopting this position the International Court had not strayed far from an objective approach to the interpretation of the Iranian declaration, in that the evidence being relied upon to establish Iran's intention was objectively available on the public record. However, unlike the one stage approach adopted towards the interpretation of treaties, this was a clear preference for a two stage approach with regard to declarations accepting the Court's jurisdiction under the Optional Clause. How such a declaration was to be interpreted depended upon the original intention of the declarant State and it was in light of an interpretation based upon that intention that the declaration was to be applied to the facts of the case.

Although the evidence employed by the Government of Iran to prove its intention at the time of ratifying the declaration retained a semblance of objectivity, the description of why it could be so employed was more open ended. In the words of the Court, the Iranian law 'was filed for the sole purpose of throwing light on a

---

[142] *Ibid*, 106.
[143] *Ibid*, 107.

disputed question of fact, namely, the intention of the Government of Iran at the time when it signed the Declaration'.[144] If this pronouncement was meant to signify that any evidence of that intention was admissible, it was subversive of the normal approach to the interpretation of unilateral statements having binding consequences,[145] and even in other cases concerning declarations accepting the Court's jurisdiction,[146] in which the principle of good faith had been regarded as imposing an objective approach.

The danger in the Court's potentially open ended test for the admissibility of evidence of intention in the *Anglo-Iranian Oil Company* case can be seen from what occurred in the *Aegean Sea* case.[147] Greece attempted to submit its dispute with Turkey over the continental shelf to the Court, relying *inter alia* on the fact that both States were parties to the General Act for the Pacific Settlement of Disputes 1928, Article 17 of which bestowed jurisdiction on the Permanent Court.[148] Even if the General Act was still in force,[149] Greece had to show that the dispute was not excluded by the reservation it had made to its accession to the General Act exempting from its acceptance 'disputes concerning questions which by international law are solely within the domestic jurisdiction of States, and in particular disputes relating to the territorial status of Greece, including disputes relating to its rights of sovereignty over its ports and lines of communication'.[150]

In attempting to show why this reservation had no application to the present dispute, Greece advanced two arguments to which its intention in making the reservation was of importance. First, it contended that the reservation was a single whole, in which the territorial status and rights over its ports and lines of communication were given as particular examples of matters of domestic jurisdiction. Secondly, it was the intention of Greece, as of other States which had been affected by the post-war settlements following 1918, to preserve their position under those settlements against revision through the Permanent Court. Hence the reference to territorial status related solely to such matters and had nothing to do with continental shelf rights which had been unknown in 1931 when Greece became a party to the General Act.

The contention about the reservation concerning territorial status being included solely to eliminate the jurisdiction of the Permanent Court with regard to matters concerning the post 1918 settlements was supported by the introduction into evidence of a letter dated 9 September 1928. In that letter a prominent Greek

---

[144] *Ibid.*

[145] *Nuclear Tests* cases, *supra* note 44, 267–268; 472–473.

[146] *Case concerning the Temple of Preah Vihear* (Cambodia v Thailand), *Preliminary Objections*, ICJ Rep 1961, 32; *Nicaragua* case, *supra* note 137, 418.

[147] *Aegean Sea* case, *supra* note 17.

[148] And therefore, on the International Court of Justice by virtue of Article 37 of its Statute.

[149] For doubts on this point, see ICJ Rep 1978, 16.

[150] *Ibid*, 20–21.

jurist and diplomat, Politis, who at the time had been Rapporteur for the group which had nearly completed drafting the General Act, had advised the Greek Foreign Minister as follows:

> I think it would be wise to safeguard ourselves against an eventual application of Bulgaria [to the Court] on matters related to our territorial status, to the access (of Bulgaria) to the Aegean and to the protection of Bulgarian-speaking minorities in Greece.[151]

That it was the purpose of this evidence to limit the reservation to matters arising out of the peace settlement is clear from the context in which it was employed in the Greek Memorial in the case.[152] Moreover, it was accepted as relevant and admissible for this purpose by the Court.[153] Indeed, not only did the Court refrain from expressing any doubts about the use of such evidence, but it also 'asked the Greek Government to furnish it with any available evidence of explanations of the instrument of accession given at the time'.[154]

This approach was an emphatic endorsement of the wider view on admissibility culled from the *Anglo-Iranian* case. The Court in the *Aegean Sea* case obviously regarded the cautionary requirement of the narrower version of the evidence having to be 'available for the examination of other governments',[155] and therefore available on a quasi objective basis, as irrelevant. There was no way in which the communication between Politis and the Greek Foreign Minister could have been regarded as available to outside scrutiny as its existence could not have been known to other governments. The Court preferred instead to concentrate exclusively on the intention of the State accepting the compulsory jurisdiction of the Court at the time when it did so, referring[156] solely to the page in the Court's judgment in the *Anglo-Iranian* case where this point was made.[157]

Before leaving this enthusiastic approval of a subjective approach to the original intention of the declarant State, the Court has more recently demonstrated the readiness with which it has been prepared to slide from an objective view represented by the text and its content (objective evidence) to a more subjective perception of the intention based upon other evidence which the declarant State might produce. This comes out from the following passage from its decision in the *Fisheries Jurisdiction* case between Spain and Canada:

> The intention of the reserving State may be deduced not only from the text of the relevant clause, but also from the context in which the clause is to be read, and an

---

[151] *Ibid*, 26.
[152] *Aegean Sea* case, ICJ Pleadings, para 235, 253.
[153] *Aegean Sea* case, *supra* note 17, 29.
[154] *Ibid.*
[155] *Anglo-Iranian Oil Company* case, *supra* note 140, 107.
[156] *Aegean Sea* case, *supra* note 17, 29.
[157] *Anglo-Iranian Oil Company* case, *supra* note 140, 104.

examination of evidence regarding the circumstances of its preparation and the purposes intended to be served.[158]

The evidence employed by the Court which it described as 'Canadian ministerial statements, parliamentary debates, legislative proposals and press communiqués', was part of the public record and therefore admissible under the narrower view of evidence of intention in the *Anglo-Iranian Oil Company* case. However, the last part of the above passage is potentially of wider application. That this was the Court's purpose appears from the fact that the Court adopted the passage in the *Aegean Sea* judgment in which the Court had asked the Greek Government 'to furnish it with any available evidence of explanations of the instrument of accession given at that time.'[159]

One can but conclude that, whatever may be the position with regard to the interpretation and application of treaty provisions, the Court sees nothing wrong with employing the most subjective evidence of the original intention of a declarant State as governing how a declaration accepting the Court's jurisdiction is to be interpreted. In adopting this stance, the Court is of course very much favouring a two stage approach to the interpretation and application of declarations accepting the Court's compulsory jurisdiction.

(b) The Evaluation of Treaty Provisions

It has already been explained how the Mandate Agreement between the League of Nations and Great Britain on behalf of South Africa was interpreted in light of the changed perceptions of the 'sacred trust of civilisation' in Article 22 of the League Covenant. It will be recalled that this was made possible, in the Court's view, by the fact that the parties to the Covenant had accepted 'the concepts embodied in Article 22' as not being 'static' but as being 'evolutionary':

> That is why, viewing the institutions of 1919, the Court must take into consideration the changes which have occurred in the supervening half-century, and its interpretation cannot remain unaffected by the subsequent development of law, through the Charter of the United Nations and by way of customary law. Moreover, an international instrument has to be interpreted and applied within the framework of the entire legal system prevailing at the time of the interpretation. In the domain to which the present proceedings relate, the last fifty years . . . have brought important developments. These developments leave little doubt that the ultimate objective of the sacred trust was the self-determination and independence of the peoples concerned.[160]

The question arises whether it is something of a fiction to ascribe the introduction of 'changing community values' into the interpretative process to the intention of

---

[158] *Fisheries Jurisdiction* case, *supra* note 126, 454.
[159] *Aegean Sea* case, *supra* note 17, 29; *Fisheries Jurisdiction* case, *supra* note 126, 454.
[160] *Namibia* case, *supra* note 22, 31.

the parties. Even if this is so, one can but assume that the Court regarded this explanation as preferable to acknowledging its adoption of a teleological approach to a
treaty by interpreting and applying it in accordance with what might be regarded as
its emergent purpose.

The Court's dilemma is well illustrated in the *Gabčikovo-Nagymaros Project*
case.[161] The 1977 Treaty between Hungary and Czechoslovakia concerning the
construction and operation of the Gabčikovo-Nagymaros System of Locks on
the River Danube included undertakings to ensure that the quality of water was
not impaired[162] and to secure 'compliance with the obligations for the protection of nature arising in connection with the construction and operation of the
System of Locks'.[163] The Court certainly expressed the view that the application
of contemporary environmental standards stemmed from the nature of the obligations themselves:

> These articles do not contain specific obligations of performance but require the
> parties . . . to take new environmental norms into consideration when agreeing upon
> the means to be specified in the Joint Contractual Plan. By inserting these evolving
> provisions in the Treaty, the parties recognized the potential necessity to adapt the
> Project. Consequently, the Treaty is not static, and is open to adapt to emerging norms
> of international law. [164]

This was reiterated in the Judgment:

> In order to evaluate the environmental risks, current standards must be taken into con-
> sideration. This is not only allowed by the wording of Articles 15 and 19, but even pre-
> scribed, to the extent that these articles impose a continuing – and thus necessarily
> evolving – obligation on the parties to maintain the quality of water of the Danube
> and to protect nature.[165]

However, the Court concluded its consideration of this aspect of the case with a
much broader basis for its application of contemporary environmental values,
whether in the form of new norms or standards:

> Throughout the ages, mankind has, for economic and other reasons, constantly inter-
> fered with nature. In the past, this was often done without consideration of the effects
> upon the environment. Owing to new scientific insights and to a growing awareness of
> the risks for mankind – for present and future generations – of pursuit of such inter-
> ventions at an unconsidered and unabated pace, new norms and standards have been
> developed, set forth in a great number of instruments during the last two decades.
> Such new norms have to be taken into consideration, and such new standards given

---

[161] *Case Concerning the Gabčikovo-Nagymaros Project*, (Hungary/Slovakia), (hereinafter the
Gabčikovo-Nagymaros case), ICJ Rep 1997, 7.
[162] Article 15 of the 1977 Treaty, *ibid*, 22.
[163] Article 19, of the 1977 Treaty, *ibid*, 23.
[164] *Ibid*, 67–68.
[165] *Ibid*, 77–78.

proper weight, not only when States contemplate new activities but also when continuing with activities begun in the past.[166]

While the first two extracts from the Court's judgment were reaffirmations of the
original intent approach to the interpretation of (particular classes of) treaties, the
third passage comes close to an acceptance of such factors as part of an environmental treaty's emergent purpose, to the interpretation of which such new norms or
standards are directly relevant.

The differences between the first two passages and the third passage have all the
hallmarks of a compromise between competing views on how the 1977 treaty might
be interpreted. The first issue concerned the range of treaties which might be
regarded as evolutionary in character and therefore affected by changes in community
values. According to Judge Weeramantry, environmental treaties constituted such a
category whenever they were made:

> Environmental concerns are live and continuing concerns whenever the project under
> which they arise may have been inaugurated. It matters little that an undertaking has
> been commenced under a treaty of 1950, if in fact that undertaking continues in oper-
> ation in the year 2000. The relevant environmental standards that will be applicable
> will be those of the year 2000.[167]

In contrast, Judge Bedjaoui was adamant that the primary point of reference for the
interpretation of any treaty was 'the intentions of the parties at the time of its conclusion',[168] intentions which 'are presumed to have been influenced by the law in
force at the time the Treaty was concluded, the law which they were supposed to
know, and not by future law, as yet unknown'.[169] In his view, therefore, 'the essential
basis for the interpretation of a treaty remains the *"fixed reference"* to contemporary
international law at the time of its conclusion. The *"mobile reference"* to the law
which will subsequently have developed can be recommended only in exceptional
cases'.[170] In the *Namibia* case,[171] 'the situation was special . . . the definition of the
"sacred trust" [was] evolutionary',[172] but the 1977 Treaty was quite different and
was, therefore, subject to the normal rules of interpretation:

> In general, it is noteworthy that the classical rules of interpretation do not require a
> treaty to be interpreted *in all circumstances* in the context of the entire legal system pre-
> vailing at the time of interpretation, in other words, in the present case, that the 1977
> Treaty should be interpreted *"in the context"* and in the light of the new contemporary
> law of the environment or of international watercourses. Indeed, it is quite the opposite

---

[166] *Ibid*, 78.
[167] Separate Opinion of Judge Weeramantry in the *Gabčikovo-Nagymaros* case, *ibid*, 114.
[168] Words taken from the *Namibia* case, *supra* note 22, 31.
[169] Separate Opinion of Judge Bedjaoui, *Gabčikovo-Nagymaros* case, *supra* note 161, 121.
[170] *Ibid*, 122.
[171] *Namibia* case, *supra* note 22.
[172] Separate Opinion of Judge Bedjaoui, *Gabčikovo-Nagymaros* case, *supra* note 161, 122.

that these rules of interpretation prescribe, seeking as they do to recommend an interpretation consonant with the intentions of the parties at the time the Treaty was concluded. [173]

Accordingly, it was only in 'very special situations' that the subsequent law could be taken into account 'as an element of interpretation or modification of the obligations of a treaty'.[174]

The view of the Court in the *Gabčikovo-Nagymaros Project* case is symptomatic of a trend towards allowing the time of application to cast an inordinate influence over how a treaty is to be interpreted. The Court's acknowledgment of the need to take account of developments in the law when identifying the original intentions of the parties to a treaty disguises two relevant issues: first the range of treaties to which this evolutionary nature can be ascribed and secondly the extent to which the Court is in reality adopting a treaty's emergent purpose as a guide to its interpretation.

The second issue may be of no more than theoretical significance. Where a teleological interpretation of a treaty may be necessary, it does not matter much, in practical terms, whether this is ascribed to some emergent purpose or the same outcome is achieved by attributing it to the parties' original intentions. As far as the first matter is concerned, despite Judge Bedjaoui's objections, the tenor of the Court's judgment is much closer to Judge Weeramantry's broader view of what types of treaties were intended to contain evolutionary provisions:

> Environment rights are human rights. Treaties that affect human rights cannot be applied in such a manner as to constitute a denial of human rights at the time of their application. A Court cannot endorse actions which are a violation of human rights by the standards of their time merely because they are taken under a treaty which dates back to a period when such action was not a violation of human rights.[175]

6. The Backward Reach of Articles 31 and 32 of the Vienna Convention

Article 4 of the Vienna Convention deals with its 'non retroactivity' by providing:

> Without prejudice to the application of any rules set forth in the present Convention to which treaties would be subject under international law independently of the Convention, the Convention applies only to treaties which are concluded by States after the entry into force of the present Convention with regard to such States.

---

[173] *Ibid*, 123. As Judge Bedjaoui added: 'In general, in a treaty, a State incurs specific obligations contained in a body of law as it existed on the conclusion of the treaty and *in no wise incurs evolutionary and indeterminate duties*.'

[174] *Ibid*, 124 (heading D).

[175] *Ibid*, 114.

It is now well accepted that some of the rules in the Vienna Convention apply to present day treaties concluded among non-parties to the Convention on the ground that the particular rules represent customary international law. It would be pedantic to object to the Court's application of Articles 31 and 32 of the Convention in such circumstances. However, the tendency of the Court to employ the same justification in applying those provisions to treaties that predate the Convention is an entirely different matter. There should have been at least an examination of the historical record before adopting such a course.

In the *Territorial Dispute* between Libya and Chad, the substance of the case concerned the binding nature and application of the 1955 Treaty of Friendship and Good Neighbourliness between France and Libya, Article 3 of which provided:

> The two High Contracting Parties recognise that the frontiers between the territories of Tunisia, Algeria, French West Africa and French Equatorial Africa on the one hand and the territory of Libya on the other, are those that result from international instruments in force at the date of the constitution of the United Kingdom of Libya as listed in the attached Exchange of Letters (Annex I). [176]

Annex I listed a series of instruments, commencing with a Franco-British Convention of June 1898 and culminating with a Franco-British Convention of September 1919 and a Franco-Italian Arrangement of four days later in that same month.

The rules of interpretation contained in Articles 31 and 32 of the Vienna Convention were relied upon primarily in the context of the initial question of whether the recognition of the frontiers in Article 3 of the 1955 Treaty constituted a legal obligation. In the view of the Court, the 'word "recognise" used in the Treaty indicates that a legal obligation is undertaken. To recognise a frontier is essentially to "accept" that frontier, that is, to draw legal consequences from its existence, to respect it and to renounce the right to contest it in future.'[177] Hence, by 'entering

---

[176] *Territorial Dispute* case, (Libyan Arab Jamahiriya/Chad), ICJ Rep 1994, 20–21. The material part of the paper is taken from the present author's *Intertemporality and the Law of Treaties* (2002) 100 *et seq*.

[177] *Territorial Dispute* case, *ibid*, 22. As the Court continued: "In the contention of Libya, the parties to the 1955 Treaty intended only to recognise the frontiers that had previously been fixed by the international instruments: where frontiers already existed (as between Tunisia and Libya), they were confirmed by the 1955 Treaty, but where there was no frontier (as in the south), the treaty did not create one. The Court is unable to accept this view; it has no difficulty either in ascertaining the natural and ordinary meaning of the relevant terms of the 1955 Treaty, or in giving effect to them. In the view of the Court, the terms of the Treaty signified that the parties thereby recognised complete frontiers between their respective territories as resulting from the combined effect of all the instruments listed in Annex I; no relevant frontier was to be left undefined and no instrument listed in Annex I was superfluous. It would be incompatible with a recognition couched in such terms to contend that only some of the specified instruments contributed to the definition of the frontier, or that a particular frontier remained unsettled. So to contend would deprive Article 3 of the Treaty and Annex I of their ordinary meaning.' Subsequently (*ibid*, 27) the Court observed that it was 'not necessary to refer to the *travaux préparatoires* to elucidate the content of the 1955 Treaty; but, as in previous cases, it finds it possible by reference to the *travaux* to confirm its reading of the text, namely, that the Treaty constitutes an agreement between the parties which, *inter alia*, defines the frontiers.'

into the Treaty, the parties recognised the frontiers to which the text of the Treaty referred; the task of the Court is thus to determine the exact content of the undertaking entered into'.[178]

When it turned to the task of determining the frontier in accordance with the instruments listed in Annex I of the 1955 Treaty, which instruments spanned a period between 1898 and 1919, the Court made no reference to any particular rules of treaty interpretation, thus avoiding any problem of intertemporality.[179] Recourse to the rules of interpretation set out in the Vienna Convention in order to ascertain whether the meaning of Article 3 of the 1955 Treaty was to lay down a fixed frontier, was justifiable on the ground that those rules were based substantially on analyses of the law dating from the period of the 1955 Treaty. The interpretation of treaties was first dealt with by the International Law Commission in Waldock's Third Report of 1964,[180] the draft articles of which took 'their inspiration from the 1956 resolution of the Institute of International Law and from Sir G. Fitzmaurice's formulation of the "major principles" of interpretation in an article . . . published in 1957.'[181] There was, therefore, nothing anachronistic in the Court's use of Articles 31 and 32 of the Vienna Convention.[182]

More remarkable from the standpoint of what might be described as temporal dislocation was the *Kasikili/Sedudu Island* case between Botswana and Namibia.[183] By a Treaty of 1890, Britain and Germany had defined their respective spheres of influence along a river which, in time, became the boundary between the two parties to the case. According to Article III of the Treaty, the line 'in which the exercise of influence is reserved to Germany . . . runs eastward along [the 18th parallel of south latitude] till it reaches the river Chobe, and descends the centre of the main channel of that river to its junction with the Zambesi, where it terminates'.[184] At that time, neither party had a very clear idea of the topography of the area,[185] and

---

[178] *Ibid,* 22.

[179] The Court did point out that a number of aspects of the law relating to territorial acquisition, including 'the rules of intertemporal law', did not 'come within the ambit of the Court's enquiry', *ibid,* 38, 40.

[180] Waldock, 'Third Report on the Law of Treaties', Doc.A/CN.4/167 and Adds.1-3, *YBILC* (1964), vol. II, 52.

[181] *Ibid,* 55 para. 10. The texts quoted appear in *Annuaire de l'Institut de Droit International,* (1956) 364–365 and Fitzmaurice, 'The Law and Procedure of the International Court of Justice 1951–1954: Treaty Interpretation and Other Treaty Points', 33 *British Yearbook of International Law* (1957) 211–212 and are reproduced in *YBILC* (1964) vol. I, 55–56.

[182] See also the Court's use of Articles 31 and 32 of the Vienna Convention to interpret the Treaty of Amity, Economic Relations and Consular Rights of 1955 between the United States of America and Iran in the *Oil Platforms* case, (Islamic Republic of Iran v. United States of America), *Preliminary Objection,* ICJ Rep 1996, 812.

[183] *Kasikili/Sedudu Island* case (Botswana/Namibia), ICJ Rep 1999, 1045.

[184] *Ibid,* 1060.

[185] As Lord Salisbury informed the British Ambassador in Berlin in a letter of 14 June 1890: 'The character of this country is very imperfectly known, and the very position of Lake Ngami has been the

recognised therefore that the situation on the ground might require some adjustment to the line established by the treaty.[186] They were also aware that population
movements and activities might affect the extent of the influence which they might
be able to exercise. Hence the Treaty also contained provisions designed to protect
their rights from such events.[187]

As to how the Court should deal with the interpretation of the 1890 Treaty, the
Court had no doubt as to the relevance of the provisions of the Vienna Convention:

> As regards the interpretation of that Treaty, the Court notes that neither Botswana nor
> Namibia are parties to the Vienna Convention on the Law of Treaties of 1969, but that
> both of them consider that Article 31 . . . is applicable inasmuch as it reflects customary
> international law . . . Article 4 of the Convention, which provides that it "applies only
> to treaties which are concluded by States after the entry into force of the . . . Convention
> with regard to such States" does not, therefore, prevent the Court from interpreting the
> 1890 Treaty in accordance with the rules reflected in Article 31 of the Convention.[188]

This pronouncement is open to two obvious objections. In the first place, it is for
the Court and not for the parties, to determine what rules it will apply to the particular dispute, as the Court made clear in the *Nicaragua* case.[189]

---

subject of considerable uncertainty', quoted by Judge Parra-Aranguren in his Dissenting Opinion,
ibid, 1209; and as Lord Salisbury said of this lake in a speech in the House of Lords: 'We have had a
fierce conflict over the possession of . . . Lake Ngami . . . our only difficulty being that we do not know
where it is. We cannot determine its position within 100 miles, certainly not within 60 miles, and
there are great doubts whether it is a lake at all, or only a bed of rushes' (*id*).

[186] By Article VI of the Treaty (*ibid*, 1210): 'All the lines of demarcation traced in Articles I to IV shall
be subject to rectification by agreement between the two Powers, in accordance with local requirements'.

[187] By Article VII (*id*): "The two powers engage that neither will interfere with any sphere of influence assigned to the other by Articles I to IV. One Power will not in the sphere of the other make
acquisitions, conclude Treaties, accept sovereign rights or Protectorates, nor hinder the extension of
influence of the other. It is understood that no Companies or individuals subject to one Power can
exercise sovereign rights in a sphere assigned to the other, except with the assent of the other."

[188] *Ibid*, 1059. At least in the *Beagle Channel Arbitration*, 52 *International Law Reports* (1977) 93,
the arbitrators, all of whom were at the time or had formerly been Judges of the International Court
of Justice, justified the invocation of Article 31 of the Vienna Convention with regard to the
Boundary Treaty of 1881 between Argentina and Chile on the basis, not just of the parties' wishes (at
124), but also of the fact that it enshrined 'the traditional canons of treaty interpretation' (at 127).

[189] *Nicaragua* case, *Merits*, ICJ Rep 1986, 97–98: 'The Court notes that there is in fact evidence . . . of
a considerable degree of agreement between the Parties as to the content of the customary international
law relating to the non-use of force and non-intervention. This concurrence of their views does not however dispense the Court from having itself to ascertain what rules of customary international law are applicable. The mere fact that States declare their recognition of certain rules is not sufficient for the Court to
consider these as being part of customary international law, and as applicable as such to those States.
Bound as it is by Article 38 of its Statute to apply, *inter alia*, international custom "as evidence of a general
practice accepted as law", the Court may not disregard the essential role played by general practice. Where
two States agree to incorporate a particular rule in a treaty, their agreement suffices to make that rule a
legal one binding upon them, but in the field of customary international law, the shared view of the Parties
as to the content of what they regard as the rule is not enough. The Court must satisfy itself that the existence of the rule of the *opinio juris* of States is confirmed by practice'.

The second objection is an intertemporal one. The only evidence that Articles 31 and 32 constituted customary international law was drawn from the Court's own acceptance of them as having that status on the basis of their adoption in the Convention. While, as already suggested, there is evidence to indicate that a formulation along the lines of those provisions represented the law in the mid-1950s, the position in the period of the Permanent Court was less clear,[190] and no reason was given by the Court as to why the law set out in Articles 31 and 32 of the Vienna Convention should be regarded as applicable to a treaty from an even earlier time. As Judge Oda observed:

> It appears to me that the Judgment places excessive reliance upon the Vienna Convention . . . for the purpose of the Court's interpretation of the 1890 Anglo-German Treaty . . . Although I am fully aware that the Vienna Convention reflects customary international law, it should, however, be noted, as the Judgment correctly points out in its paragraph 18, that this Convention "applies only to treaties which are concluded by States after the entry into force of the present Convention with regard to such States" (Art 4). In fact, the Convention came into force in 1980. This case does not appear to me to be one related to the application of the Vienna Convention.[191]

It has already been acknowledged that it is difficult for an interpreter, whether an adviser or a tribunal, to avoid looking at a treaty from the perspective of the time of its application. Nevertheless, the Court's approach and the decision it rendered seem to have paid insufficient attention to the terms of the treaty in light of the circumstances existing at the time it was made.

There were various attempts to reconcile the overemphasis on subsequent events up to and including the time of application with whatever might have been the

---

[190] See, for example, Article 19(a) of the 'Harvard Draft Convention of the Law of Treaties', 29 *American Journal of International Law* (1935) Supp. 657 at 937: 'A treaty is to be interpreted in the light of the general purpose which it is intended to serve. The historical background of the treaty, *travaux préparatoires*, the circumstances of the parties at the time the treaty was entered into, the change in these circumstances sought to be effected, the subsequent conduct of the parties in applying the provisions of the treaty, and the conditions prevailing at the time the interpretation is being made, are to be considered in connection with the general purpose which the treaty is intended to serve.' This provision may be disregarded on the ground that it is similar to the US amendment to what became Articles 31 and 32 of the Vienna Convention, (*Vienna Conference, supra* note 18, 149), which was rejected by 66 votes to eight with 10 abstentions (*ibid*, 150), though much of the material relied upon by the Harvard project was taken from decisions and pronouncements of the Permanent Court. As already pointed out, in the *Advisory Opinion on the Interpretation of the 1919 Convention Concerning Employment of Women at Night*, PCIJ Ser A/B, (1932), No 50, 364, ready use was made of many of the factors referred to in Article 19, though their use was explained by the (bare) majority along the lines later adopted in Articles 31 and 32. A principal difference lay in how the use of subsequent conduct was justified, the Permanent Court allowing it if 'there were any ambiguity' (*Advisory Opinion on the Competence of the ILO to Regulate Agricultural Labour*, PCIJ Ser B, (1922), No 2, 39); the International Law Commission ostensibly limiting it to conduct establishing the parties' agreement regarding a treaty's interpretation (though in fact relying upon the latter pronouncement for this purpose, see *Vienna Conference, supra* note 18, 41, para (15)).

[191] Separate Opinion of Judge Oda in the *Kasikili/Sedudu Island* case, *supra* note 183, 1118.

parties' intentions in 1890 when the treaty was made. For example, Judge Higgins made the point that there was an inevitable balancing between geographical data now available and the task of employing the terms in a way that coincided with the parties' intentions in 1890:

> At the same time, we must never lose sight of the fact that we are seeking to give flesh to the intention of the parties expressed in generalised terms in 1890. We must trace a thread back to this point of departure. We should not, as the Court appears at times to be doing, decide what *in abstracto* the term "the main channel" might today mean, by a mechanistic appreciation of relevant indicia. Rather, our task is to decide what general idea the parties had in mind, and then make reality of that general idea through the use of contemporary knowledge.[192]

However, the more crucial issue concerned the way in which the Court made use of the parties' subsequent conduct in relation to the Treaty. The Court regarded the relevant time span as running from the date of the making of the treaty until the present, a period which included the disagreements between the Botswana authorities (even prior to independence) and the South African administration of Namibia. As the Court dealt with subsequent conduct in the context of Article 31(3)(b) of the Vienna Convention to the exclusion of Article 32, the evidence from the end of the colonial period demonstrated conclusively that no agreement or understanding had been reached establishing an interpretation of the Treaty in Namibia's favour as to its occupation and use of the disputed island.

This view is open to objection because it pays insufficient attention to a number of matters, including the time factor. Judge Parra-Aranguren was able to place an appropriate emphasis on the conduct of the parties in the quarter of a century following the Treaty by selecting 1914 as the critical date and thereby discounting events in more recent times. This is a plausible analysis because, during and after the 1914–18 War, the territory had been occupied by the British army and had then become a Mandate under South African stewardship. Indeed, until Namibia attained independence, it is probably true to say that no conduct on the part of South Africa could have altered the boundaries of the territory.[193] On this approach, the years from 1890 to 1914 constituted a critical period during which the disputed island had been subject to regular occupation and use by residents of German South West Africa, a use which was, in the Judge's view, regulated by its colonial administration, and therefore constituted more than the acts of private individuals.

---

[192] Declaration of Judge Higgins, *ibid*, 1113.

[193] Dissenting Opinion of Judge Parra-Aranguren, *ibid*, 1216–20; see also Judge Fleischhauer's, Dissenting Opinion, *ibid*, 1205. It could of course be argued that whereas South Africa could not have granted territory to any other State, there is no reason why it could not have acquired territory on behalf of the people of the territory. This was not the view of Judge Fleischhauer, but the position was so unclear that the British declined to enter into an agreement with South Africa to confirm the entitlement of the Namibians to use and occupy the island, (see the text of the Judgment, *ibid*, 1080–6).

Judge Weeramantry reached a similar conclusion by a different route, stressing in particular the significance of the time factor, which he referred to as 'contemporaneity'. As he explained:

> This principle of contemporaneity is one of the most important principles of treaty interpretation, and is not . . . given its proper effect by taking into account, as the Court has done, the attitude of the Parties more than 50 years later, when political and other circumstances may well have necessitated a change of administrative policy from that which had been evidenced for the half century immediately following the Treaty.[194]

Taking account of the fact that the presence of the persons on the island would have to be 'considered in the context of the particular geographical characteristics of the region and contemporary modes of human use and occupation of such territory'[195] and the absence of protest by the British authorities, the Judge concluded that by 1947, when differences first arose between those authorities and the South African administration, there was already a common understanding that the island was part of South West Africa and that the main channel of the river therefore lay to the south of the Island. Despite his recognition of the importance of the requirements of intertemporality that a treaty should be viewed in the context of the circumstances, including the rules of international law, surrounding its making, even Judge Weeramantry saw nothing wrong in relying upon Article 31 of the Vienna Convention without demanding proof that Article 31 had a contemporary relevance to the 1890 Treaty.

On the simple issue of the evaluation of the conduct of the parties relating to how Article III of the 1890 Treaty should be interpreted, the approach of the dissenters appears to be more convincing. However, that evidence raised a distinct issue of the significance those geographical uncertainties surrounding the drafting of the Treaty had for its application, in light of the provisions of Article VI.

It is not suggested that the Court ignored the fact that the representatives of the two States had no clear idea of the situation on the ground. What is suggested is that

---

[194] Dissenting Opinion of Judge Weeramantry, *ibid*, 1162. As he also observed in *ibid*, 1158: 'contemporaneous conduct in relation to the Treaty is especially important in this case in the light of the fact that observations regarding the various qualities of the river – whether they be breadth or depth or volume of flow – can vary considerably over a period of a hundred years, and could depend very much on the time of observation, be it in the wet season, the dry season or any other. The sense in which the Treaty was understood contemporaneously is the best index to what was actually intended, and any search for clarification of the terms used must focus intensely on this aspect.'

[195] *Ibid*, 1163. As the Judge went on to explain: 'we must not look for indicia of occupation in terms of settled housing or ordered agriculture, burial sites or schools, for the very nature of this terrain prevented settled habitation in the manner known to Western jurisprudence and tradition. At the best there would have been temporary occupation in makeshift huts from time to time as the rains and climate determined. Such mud huts as there were would tend to be washed away during flood time, for they were not constructed for permanent occupation. Even agricultural holdings could have been at best a rather haphazard variety as compared with the holdings one is accustomed to in settled societies.'

its implications for the interpretation of the Treaty were not fully examined. From the lack of knowledge of the parties to the Treaty, and the context of Article III within the Treaty, it can be said that that instrument did not constitute a boundary treaty designed to determine an international frontier for all time.[196] It is curious, therefore, that Namibia should have been prepared to recognise it 'as the treaty determining the boundary between their territories'.[197] Article III constituted no more than a provisional dividing line between the spheres of influence of the two colonial powers. To preserve the benefits of the Treaty in lessening or preventing possible territorial rivalries between them (the object and purpose of the treaty), they agreed, in Article VII, 'not to interfere with any sphere of influence assigned to the other by Articles I to IV', nor 'in the sphere of the other make acquisitions, conclude Treaties, accept sovereign rights or Protectorates, not hinder the extensions of influence of the other'.[198] It is clear from the wording of the last part of the provision that the boundary did not relate to an existing, but to a future sphere of influence in large areas allocated to the State concerned. Indeed, it was because of the geographical and demographic uncertainties of the region that Articles I to IV were qualified by Article VI whereby '[a]ll the lines of demarcation traced in Articles I to IV shall be subject to rectification by agreement between the two Powers, in accordance with local requirements'.[199] It would have made more sense from Namibia's point of view, therefore, to have contended that the line drawn in accordance with Article III of the Treaty was only the *de facto* boundary that could be converted into a *de jure* frontier with the due performance by Botswana of its inherited obligation under Article VI.

Given the prohibition in Article VII on subsequent changes affecting the operation of Article III, the 'local requirements' would seem to constitute primarily those

---

[196] As Judge Oda asserted in his Separate Opinion, *ibid,* 1128: 'The 1890 Treaty is an instrument which determined the respective spheres of influence of the Parties in this region of Africa but which certainly did *not* fix national boundaries there between the territories of Germany and Great Britain. The limit of the German sphere of influence was fixed as the "centre of the main channel of the Chobe River", but in that Treaty no concrete *boundary line* was indicated in this geographically complex area. The determination of the *boundary,* which would certainly have had the effect of determining the *legal status* of Kasikili/Sedudu Island, was at that time a matter far removed from the actual purpose of the Treaty'. On the same point see also Judge Weeramantry's, Dissenting Opinion, *ibid,* 1185–8.

[197] *Kasikili/Sedudu Island* case, *ibid,* 1073.

[198] *Id.*

[199] *Supra* note 186. The notion that 'rectification of a boundary denoted its realignment to take account of, and settle, claims conflicting with its previous delineation was current at the time of the 1890 Treaty. The Treaty of Fontainebleau of 1785 prevented a war between the Hapsburg Empire and the Netherlands over the extent of Austrian rights in the Austrian Netherlands. In addition to settling issues relating to the River Scheldt, the Emperor relinquished any claim to Maastricht and its surrounding territory in return for an indemnity of 10 mission guilders. W.E.H. Lecky, after dealing with these matters, in *A History of England in the Eighteenth Century,* vol V (1893), 335, concluded his descriptions of the 1785 Treaty as follows: 'A few slight rectifications of territory were made, a few small fortresses were dismantled, and the contracting parties formally renounced all further pretensions that either might have against the other.'

existing at the time of the treaty, or perhaps those circumstances becoming subject to regulation by the States concerned in assumed conformity with the Treaty. The evidence would appear to show that the Masubia people from the Caprivi Strip of South West Africa had intermittently been using and occupying the Island from at least as far back as 1907,[200] and probably even before the Treaty was made.[201] Moreover, as the Court admitted, the majority of maps from the earlier period 'placed the boundary around Kasikili/Sedudu Island in the channel of the Chobe'.[202] Because the thrust of Namibia's case was to demonstrate that the activities constituted either subsequent practice in performance of the Treaty or a basis for acquisitive prescription, the Court was able to determine the case on the ground that these activities had no 'official status'. It rejected the Namibian contention that 'Germany from 1909, then its successors after 1915, incorporated the local institutions of the Masubia into the structure of colonial governance, using them as instruments for exercising their authority'.[203] It was the Court's view that, 'as far as Bechuanaland, and subsequently Botswana, were concerned, the intermittent presence of the Masubia on the Island did not trouble anyone and was tolerated, not least because it did not appear to be connected with interpretation of the terms of the 1890 Treaty'.[204]

This evidence should not have been so readily dismissed as it did show the situation on the ground. As the Court said of those maps, 'the evidence would tend . . . to suggest that the boundary line was shown as following the southern channel as a result of the intermittent presence on the Island of people from the Caprivi Strip'.[205] It was that very evidence which established the need to rectify Article III of the Treaty. There was, accordingly, an obligation, imposed upon Britain (and its successors) by virtue of Article VI, to rectify the frontier established by Article III for that stretch of the river Chobe.

7. Conclusions

This paper has not examined the relationship between the understanding of a treaty's text at the time when it was adopted compared with how it is perceived in its contemporary setting with regard to the constitutional texts of various interna-

---

[200] There was, of course, a difference between the Court and the dissenters in the way in which the evidence was interpreted as to whether the Trollope-Redman Report of 1948 should be interpreted as signifying only use of the Island by the Caprivi tribesmen or 'use and occupation', the expression used by Judge Weeramantry in his Dissenting Opinion in the *Kasikili/Sedudu Island* case, *supra* note 194, 1164. For the report see *ibid,* 1168.

[201] As Namibia argued, see Dissenting Opinion of Judge Weeeamantry, *ibid.*

[202] *Ibid,* 1094.

[203] The argument as explained by the Court, *ibid,* 1093.

[204] *Ibid,* 1095.

[205] *Ibid,* 1094.

tional organisations. In the case of such instruments one would expect the time of application to assume primary importance because of their essentially evolutionary nature. It is curious, therefore, to notice how much attention is paid to the original intent of the framers of the UN Charter as revealed in the *travaux* in discussions of the powers of the International Court of Justice to examine the validity of the acts of other UN organs.[206] The only rational answer that can be given concerning such an issue is that ultimately it will depend upon how far the Court is prepared to assert such powers and the extent to which such assertions prove acceptable to the organs involved and, in the case of an organ of limited membership like the Security Council, to the wider international community.

Articles 31 and 32 of the Vienna Convention give rise to a number of issues of relevance to this paper. They were based upon the notion that treaty interpretation is a two stage process, i.e. of determining what interpretation arises from the application of the general rule in Article 31 before deciding whether that interpretation is unsatisfactory because it: (a) leaves the meaning ambiguous or obscure; or (b) leads to a result which is manifestly absurd or unreasonable, so that supplementary means of interpretation can be resorted to. This is hardly reconcilable with the practice of treaty interpretation in which the question of how the treaty can be applied in the circumstances of a particular dispute is the task of both of the legal advisers to the parties and of the ultimate adjudicator, so that interpretation and application constitute a unified whole.

A second matter is that, although the two provisions represent a primarily textual approach in which the words employed are supposed to constitute the sole or principal determinant of the parties' intentions in making a treaty, the International Court has been prepared to adopt a much more subjective approach to unilateral declarations accepting its jurisdiction. This subjectivity has taken two forms, the first is evident in the fact that the Court has sought to discover the 'real' intention of the declarant State outside the terms of its declaration, and the second in the Court's preparedness to consider evidence of this intention beyond that which is objectively available as part of the public record. This is a peculiar anomaly in view of the Court's proclaimed objective approach to the interpretation of unilateral declarations in general and even, on other occasions, to declarations accepting its jurisdiction.

A third aspect of Articles 31 and 32 is the way in which their textual origins, involving as they did a rejection of anything resembling an intentions perception of treaty interpretation, have been preserved against the possible incursions of a teleological approach. As interpretation depends very much upon the personal reactions and attitudes of the interpreter,[207] it is certainly possible for supporters of a

---

[206] See for example, the *Lockerbie* case, *Preliminary Objections, supra* note 94, 77–80, 169–171.

[207] One only has to consider the views of Judge Anzilotti in the days of the Permanent Court to be made aware of this factor. See his Dissenting Opinion in the *Advisory Opinion on the Interpretation of the Convention of 1919 Concerning Employment of Women at Night, supra* note 190, 383, and the fact that the Court reached its conclusions by a mere 6 votes to 5, with Judge Anzilotti in the minority.

more teleological approach to live within the confines of Article 31 as the object and purpose of a treaty may well be regarded differently over time. Rather than admit to this possibility, the Court, in the *Namibia* case,[208] preferred to regard the evolutionary nature of the Mandates system as built into Article 22 of the League Covenant by virtue of the intention of the States when they drafted the provisions and subsequently became parties to the Covenant. Just how extensive this approach might become was presaged in the *Gabčikovo-Nagymaros Project* case.[209]

However one seeks to justify this aspect of the *Namibia* opinion, as teleological or textual with the assistance of an intentions approach, it was an emphatic endorsement of the critical importance for the interpretation of a treaty of the circumstances as they changed to those existing at the time of application. It is possible to justify the importance of the date of application in terms of the constitutive nature of the instrument in question. The real explanation lies not so much in the nature of the treaty but in its longevity. The inevitable consequences of the long life of a treaty is that it becomes almost impossible for the interpreter of today to view the treaty from the perspective of the time when it was made, even when the circumstances of its conclusion are available from the historical record. The failure of the Court to regard Article VI of the 1890 Treaty between Britain and Germany as essential to the proper application of the treaty in the *Kasikili/Seduku* case[210] demonstrates how little attention can be paid to the time when a treaty is made as a guide to how it should be interpreted in the contemporary world.

---

[208] *Namibia* case, *supra* note 22.
[209] *Gabčikovo-Nagymaros* case, *supra* note 161.
[210] *Kasikili/Sedudu Island* case, *supra* note 183.

PIRACY AND THE ORIGINS OF ENMITY

Gerry Simpson*

1. You'll Never Guess to Who You're Talking

Piracy is regularly invoked as the first international crime, or the first offence to give rise to universal jurisdiction or the precursor to contemporary offences against the dignity of mankind.[1] Pirates, on this view, were the original terrorists.[2] They disrupted international commerce, they were an irritant to Empire, they acted in pursuit of disqualified ends (greed, anarchy), they were *res nullius* (having allegiance to no state) and, in doing all this, they behaved abominably showing no regard at all for the 'laws of war' or the principles of maritime civility or the *ius ad bellum*.[3] Neutrals, enemies and friends all belonged to an elaborate patchwork of other-regarding norms. The treatment to be afforded to such legal persons very much depended on the context in which they were found. With piracy, the matter was simpler. These were enemies of all men – the identity of the pirate was bound up with the idea of universal antipathy.[4] One could have mixed feelings about the French or about revolutionaries, but general agreement prevailed in relation to these ocean-going plunderers. It was simply a case of naming them and eliminating them.[5]

---

* Reader in Public International Law, London School of Economics.

[1] See, e.g., Kaufman J. in *Filartiga v Pena-Irala*, 630 F.2d. 876 (2d Cir. 1980), 890; Randall, 'Universal Jurisdiction under International Law', 66 *Texas Law Review* (1988) 785, 792.

[2] This idea cannot be explored fully here but forms part of the argument contained in a larger research project on piracy. For an explicit analogy see Halberstam, 'Terrorism on the High Seas: The Achille Lauro, Piracy and the IMO Convention on Maritime Safety', 82 *American Journal of International Law* (1988) 269.

[3] On the idea of pirates as *res nullius* see Schwarzenberger, 'The Problem of an International Criminal Law', 3 *Current Legal Problems* (1950) 269; on piracy and empire see C. Schmitt, *The Nomos of the Earth* (2003) 65; on the lack of allegiance to sovereigns, see W.E. Hall, *A Treatise on International Law* (5th ed. 1904) 262.

[4] There is, scattered throughout the jurisprudence of war crimes, the idea that the war criminal, like the pirate, is an enemy of mankind – "*hostis humanis generis*" – operating outside the bounds of law and outside the jurisdiction of national law. He is engaged in *a form* of killing or plundering that is unacceptable. War criminals became the successor to pirates (and slave traders). They threatened international society because the particular form of violence they indulged in was a departure from legitimate violence. This gives rise to a class of universal jurisdiction (see e.g. *Filartiga, supra* note 1; *Prosecutor v Furundzija*, Case No. IT-95-17, Judgement of 10 December 1998; *Eichmann v Attorney-General*, 36 *International Law Reports* (1962) 277).

[5] See L. Oppenheim, *International Law: A Treatise* (1928) 278.

In the cultural life of the West, though, there is another tradition in which pirates occupy a borderland position between respectability and deviance. In Thucydides' *History of the Peloponnesian Wars*, there is a passage in which piracy is discussed:

> For in early times, the Hellenes . . . were tempted to turn pirates . . . indeed this came to be their main source of livelihood, no disgrace being yet attached to such an achievement, but even some glory . . . Old poets ask – 'Are they pirates?' as if those who are asked the question would have no idea of disclaiming the imputation.[6]

The literary figure of the pirate is quite often sympathetic, sometimes transgressive, rebellious, communitarian and often opaque. Frederic, the apprentice pirate, in Gilbert and Sullivan's operetta, *The Pirates of Penzance*, would have been an apprentice *pilot* but for a mistake made by his nursemaid. He loves the pirate band he has joined but at the end of his apprenticeship, he regrets that duty will require him to kill them all as enemies of the Crown. The other pirates, meanwhile, are revealed first as 'orphans' and then as 'noblemen'. The identity of the pirates is at all times in question.[7] In Brecht's song, *Pirate Jenny*, a cleaner on board ship is, unknown to the crew who treat her badly, a pirate sympathiser and spy ('you'll never guess to who you're talking'). How could this mere cleaner be a pirate, how could this *woman* be a pirate? Pirate society, meanwhile, has been mythologised as a socialistic, brotherhood or alternative society. Pirates are not simply enemies of mankind because they attack the interests of the ruling classes but also because they offer ideological opposition by living a counter-life (Byron contributed greatly to this view of piracy). On the other hand, pirates often were the ruling elite or, at least, in the pay of this elite. In 16th Century England, pirates were sometimes hanged, but not all of them could be disposed of in this way because with the uniform application of nominal anti-piracy laws, 'the south coast of England would have been virtually depopulated and the Spanish Armada would have met with little opposition.'[8]

In this essay, I begin an exploration of piracy in international law that situates it in the latter tradition or, at least, opposes this understanding to the discipline's more conventional renderings of the pirate figure.

2. *The Certainties of Empire*

Three months after the invasion of Iraq by US-UK-led forces in March 2003, Iraqis and allied troops began to uncover mass graves; sites of atrocities committed by the

---

[6] R.B. Stassler (ed.), *Landmark Thucididyes* (1996) 1.5.

[7] In the first production of *The Pirates of Penzance*, the actors were in the middle of a season of *H.M.S. Pinafore*. They transformed themselves from sailors in the King's Navy to pirates by tying handkerchiefs around their heads, online: D'Oyly Carte Opera Company, <http://www.doylycarte.org.uk/Operas/Pirates_Of_Penzance.htm.>

[8] D. Mitchell, *Pirates* (1976) 12.

Iraqi regime. The relatives of victims called for some form of punishment of those responsible. One relative spoke bluntly: 'Either the people who did this must be brought to court or we should ask for the authority to kill them'.[9] To some extent, this mirrored the views of many within the Bush Administration and Blair Cabinet about the decision to go to war in the first place. While the neo-conservatives within the Bush Administration were willing (reluctantly) to tolerate Security Council debate and involvement in the decision-making process (they were happy for Iraq to be 'brought to court' as it were), they also were very prepared to take political action to eliminate the regime outside the parameters of legality. As Jack Straw put it prior to the intervention: 'We are completely committed to the United Nations route, if that is successful. If, for example, we end up being vetoed . . . then of course we are in a different situation'.[10]

The movement between law and politics in the field of war and crime is also, then, a movement between the use of judicial processes to punish enemies on one hand, and resort to non-judicial methods to remove these enemies from the political scene on the other. But the relationship between law and politics in this regard is not straightforward. In a forthcoming book I argue that war crimes trials are political trials (in a very particular sense). Equally, though, political action directed at defeated enemies turns out to be, very often, grounded in legal forms.[11] In 1943, as the Allies began to contemplate war crimes trials, there was inevitably resistance among those of a more punitive inclination. Anthony Eden took the position, shared by Churchill, that Nazi guilt fell outside the framework of law.[12] He was in favour of summary execution or political action, arguing that there was simply no international law capable of confronting the sort of evil seen in the 1930s and 40s. But, of course, this was not quite political action. Summary execution, after all, required some legal authority. The Lord Chancellor, Lord Simon, suggested that Nazi fugitives be treated like the outlaws of mediaeval Britain. This pseudo-legal procedure permitted any citizen to kill an outlaw declared such by the Grand Jury: '. . . the Sheriff did not try the outlaw or bring him before any court for trial; he merely hanged him'.[13]

This idea of outlawry was taking hold, too, among prominent academics. Georg Schwarzenberger shared the Eden view that the Nazis fell outside the ambit of international law. In his book, *Totalitarian Lawlessness and International Law*, he called for the Nazi Regime to be designated an outlaw regime or pirate state, one that could no longer avail itself of the protections of international law, and one, in relation to whom, the term neutrality could have no meaning.[14] Henry Morgenthau, Roosevelt's

---

[9] McCarthy, 'They Must be Brought to Court', *The Guardian*, 20 June 2003.
[10] Borger, 'Straw Threat to Bypass UN over Attack on Iraq', *The Guardian*, 19 October 2002.
[11] G. Simpson, *Law, War and Crime* (Polity, forthcoming 2007).
[12] R. Overy, *Interrogations*, (2001) 7.
[13] *Ibid*, 4.
[14] G. Schwarzenberger, *International Law and Totalitarian Lawlessness* (1943).

Treasury Secretary, meanwhile, was busy working on a plan that would combine the two ideas of state piracy and individual outlawry in one overarching scheme for an emasculated post-war Germany.[15]

In contemporary international society, too, the idea of piracy has enjoyed a renaissance on a number of fronts. The pirate state, for example, is a readily identifiable figure in the practices of the international community and in the rhetoric of the Great Powers.[16] In addition, terrorism often is regarded as the new 'piracy'. Arguments are being increasingly made for placing terrorists in a parallel legal regime subject to universal jurisdiction or relatively unfettered enforcement action.[17] Recalling Anthony Eden's language, President Bush has called the Guantanamo Bay detainees, the 'evil of the evil'. And, of course, there is the revival of old-fashioned free-market piracy itself in the South-east Asian shipping lanes and enclaves, and elsewhere.[18]

But how ought we to understand the identity of our enemies, now, and in history? Take the use of the term 'criminal' to describe the state of Afghanistan or the Taliban or Osama Bin-Laden. To describe an adversary as 'criminal' might be a useful rhetorical ploy: creating the impression of an enemy to be destroyed and without mercy. I think this is what the Bush administration was getting at when it used this term. Indeed, President Bush's deployment of the mythic imagery of the Wild West plays well in this regard. The chief characteristic of the Wild West was that it was wild and lawless; criminals got smoked out dead or alive. So, the use of this language seemed to me to be a way of positing retribution as an alternative to trial.

But in liberal legal traditions criminals are tried and convicted not killed or liquidated by Special Forces. Inevitably, then, in characterising Bin Laden as 'criminal', U.S. officials were signalling or bringing into play two contradictory images: the image of lawlessness and vigilantism on one hand, and the image of trial and conviction on the other. The President might think that calling Bin Laden a criminal means that he must be killed more ruthlessly than if he were just an enemy (after all we accord honour and respect to our enemies, criminals should be denied that respect), amongst international lawyers (and not just international lawyers), though, it means that we should set up a court and try Bin Laden offering him the privileges and immunities of criminal suspects (after all, he is no longer an enemy to be killed but a criminal to be defended in court).

---

[15] G. Bass, *Stay the Hand of Vengeance* (2000) 166; M. Beschloss, *The Conquerors* (2002).

[16] G. Simpson, *Great Powers and Outlaw States: Unequal Sovereigns in the International Legal Order*, (2004) passim. For a discussion of the pirate state see Shawcross, 'Opening Speeches of Prosecutors', *Trial of the Major War Criminals before the International Military Tribunal, Nuremberg, November 14th, 1945 to October 1st, 1947* (1947) 57–58.

[17] See Halberstam, *supra* note 2.

[18] E.g. J. Clayton, "Warlords take piracy to new extremes", *The Times*, 14 October 2005; International Maritime Organisation, *Reports of Piracy and Armed Robbery against Ships*, MSC.4/Circ.75, (2005) also available at: <http://www.imo.org/includes/blastDataOnly.asp/data_id%3D13502/78.pdf>

But what we are really conjuring into existence is a figure, or identity, who sits outside these two categories: not quite an enemy (entitled, after all, to certain protections under the Geneva Conventions and Protocols) nor quite criminal (entitled to due process and civil rights) (nor of course friend). The illegal combatant, the terrorist and the Islamic "fanatic" all seem to fall between these stools. What are they? If a criminal is at war with a particular society, and an enemy is at war with a particular state, then we might suggest that this new (or revivified) character is at war with everyone or international society or the international community. This, in turn, invokes 'the enemy of mankind' but in invoking this term, we inevitably call up another figure, that of the pirate.

This then, we might say, is the age of outlawry with the pirate as our defining motif. Pirates were, of course, international law's original enemies of humankind. Indeed, piracy is a founding metaphor for a whole sub-discipline of public international law: international criminal law or the law of war crimes. Piracy is international law's foundational *bête noire*. It may be that the international legal order's own imperial ambitions rest on the presence of outsiders like pirates. But piracy also seems to belong to law's past or international society's past. The category has the ring of obsolescence about it. The modernisation of the international legal order has surely rendered piracy an old-fashioned category, and pirates no longer a threat to the state system?

Bert Roling, the Dutch judge at the Tokyo War Crimes Trials, in his famous interview with Nino Cassese, worried that the piracy metaphor could not extend to war crimes or terrorism precisely because of the lack of solidarity in the international system, because the 'international community' did not exist.[19] But Roling came at this the wrong way surely. The pirate category is precisely how international community is made. The presence of mere 'enemies', in the old Geneva Convention sense of the word (enemy personnel entitled to certain protections under the laws of war), is evidence of a lack of community, and the continued presence of legitimate ideological or political disputation and conflict, or pluralism. In order to *construct* international community, adversaries must be transmuted into pirates. Enemies become outlaws, criminals become pirates. *Our* enemies become enemies of humankind. Pirates are enemies of particular political projects that happen to have been universalised: Empire, globalisation, Christianity, America. We could go further and suggest that Empire needs pirates. This contains a literal truth about empire: pirates (transformed into privateers) are agents of imperial ambition and regulation and, at the same time, subject to it. Osama bin Laden, after all, was once 'licensed' as one of our privateers or terrorists just as the High Court of Admiralty issued licenses to pirates to become privateers. But at a deeper level, enemies of humankind are one way of ensuring the continued purchase of 'humankind' as a category capable of waging perpetual war. So,

---

[19] B. Roling, *The Tokyo Trial and Beyond* (1991) 97.

when the particular is universalised, particular enemies must become enemies of humankind. In this sense, piracy might also be characterised as international law's future. The concept of piracy, applied widely enough, anticipates a future deepening or homogenisation (forced or otherwise) of international society.

All of this recalls Carl Schmitt's distinction between foes and enemies.[20] The revival of piracy (initially, the pirate state at the end of the Great War) signals, for him, the beginning of a post-duellist international order marked by police action rather than war. In this international order, the international community fights humanitarian wars against outlaws and pirates. Old wars, between equal sovereigns, are abolished. The pirate, then, represents the passing of a tradition in warfare between equal combat to police actions or, in Schmitt's chilling phrase, "pest control". The transformation of the Iraqi resistance from legitimate military adversaries to terrorist brigands is a perfect example of this. Almost at every instance where the US met serious resistance, this opposition was instantly converted into piracy or terror. This is the second story of new wars, alongside the idea of them as predominantly internal and chaotic affairs.[21] When the US and its allies fight wars, these wars will tend to be labelled 'wars' but the war will be the war against pirates or terror or disorder – never the old-style war between two states with conflicting political projects or territorial ambitions. Pirate states will be subject to territorial intrusion as part of an enforcement action on the part of the legally-empowered Great Powers acting in a policing capacity; not the 'war between' but the 'war against'. These will not be wars between sovereigns but enforcement actions against some transcendent evil, represented by a particular sovereign. Imperial projections are publicised as wars *against*, say, terror but at the same time not as wars *with* (this is not a war with Iraq or with the Iraqi people but a war against the regime or the pirates using the state's territory as a base). In the occupation phase, a similar process occurs. The police action, very temporarily an invasion in the case of Iraq, is converted back to counter-piracy policing or vigilantism within days of occupation. There can be no legitimate resistance (implying the possibility of politics and disagreement) only the pathology of counter-imperialist piracy.

This points to a paradox and a danger in the construction of new international law. Initially, piracy may appear to be international law's saving grace. If the problem of international law is a problem of social solidarity then piracy will have its uses. The completion of international law, for some, would be marked by the final consummation of the 'international community', marking a movement from the pluralistic, competitive society where international law has sought to ameliorate the effects of war to the idea of international law as a sort of moral community defined in part by the presence of outsiders. But these outsiders are configured as *beyond* international law, too. These are not enemies of society whose prosecution,

---

[20] See, e.g., C. Schmitt, *The Concept of the Political* (1996); *idem, supra* note 3.
[21] See M. Kaldor, *New and Old Wars* (1999).

conviction and incarceration confirms the majesty of law, but rather radically estranged outlaws whose lack of law also becomes a lack for international law. And there is a deeper problem, still, relating to the character of piracy. The ongoing attempts at the international level to define enemies of humankind whether they be terrorists or aggressors has met with failure precisely because these always have the potential to become self-definitions. We, too, are pirates and aggressors. This ambiguity is not simply an accident of contemporary politics or late-modern indeterminacy, but is found in the very origins of the original enemy.

3. The Ambiguities of Piracy

It is important here to do more than simply make an argument about the return of the pirate or, indeed, produce a Schmittian salvo in the direction of Empire. What I want to suggest is that the pirate is a deeply ambiguous figure, and therefore entirely appropriate as a motif for the age. This ambiguity emerges precisely because of efforts to inject clear moral distinctions into our dealings with enemies while at the same time erasing some of international law's most enduring demarcations.

One feature of the modernisation of international law has been the effort to distinguish between different categories of identity e.g. neutrals/non-neutrals, combatants/non-combatants, war/peace, pirates/enemies and so on (it is also a feature of this process that the identity of sovereignty itself is fixed as neither good nor bad but simply sovereign). Now, a counter-trend appears to have emerged in which more and more actors are assimilated to pirates and in which these various distinctions are being eroded, and sovereigns are unequal.[22] We need think only of 'infinite justice' or the assault on neutrality or the shift in risk from combatants to non-combatants during humanitarian wars or, as I have already noted, the way in which members of the Iraqi resistance, were repositioned as 'terrorists' even as the initial stage of the war was being fought, or of the rise of the pirate state to be contrasted with the decent sovereign.[23] Yet this counter-trend perhaps returns us to our foundations in the regulation of piracy. If the pirate is our foundational figure here – the original enemy of humankind to whom all others are to be assimilated – then it is little wonder that categories are blurring as this figure resurfaces. Indeed, the return of the pirate is a return to ambiguity.

---

[22] G. Simpson, *supra* note 16.

[23] The language is from J. Rawls, *The Law of Peoples* (1999). See, too, John Kerry's comment that, 'In dealing with states that are outright criminal, the United States may, at times, need to take unilateral action to protect its citizens, its interests, its integrity' (J. Kerry, *The New War: The Web of Crime that Threatens America's Security* (1997) 182, cited in Cockburn, 'Surrendering Quietly', 29 *New Left Review* (2004) 17).

But what are (or were) pirates? Piracy was defined by King James as 'depredations committed on the seas by certain lewd and ill-disposed persons'.[24] In the English common law, for example, piracy has been characterised as, '. . . acts of robbery on the high seas'.[25] These are, of course, over-inclusive definitions and most international law definitions focus on the presence of a private motive or purpose. The UN Law of the Sea Convention defines piracy as an illegal act of '. . . violence or detention, or any act of depredation committed for private ends by the crew or the passengers of a private ship . . .'.[26]

States and state actors cannot, on the conventional definition, commit acts of piracy (except when they mutiny and cease to be publicly authorised) but nor, seemingly, can private actors acting for public or political ends (e.g., insurgents or belligerents) commit acts of piracy.

What, then, are private ends? In another set of definitions, the emphasis is on the absence of authorisation rather than the presence of pecuniary motives on the part of the individuals involved.[27] So, while in the earlier cases, private acts are assimilated to selfish motives or intent to plunder, the later definitions begin to emphasise the absence of an official mandate. In this way, the sailor is reduced to the status of pirate in the act of mutiny. The pirate, then, is not marked by his or her plundering psychology but rather by the absence of public authority. It is very much who they are as well as what they do.

Elsewhere, in case law and literature on piracy, there are further complications: In one case, failure to act within the laws of warfare or beyond the law on the use of force becomes a defining feature of piracy.[28] In an early US case, piracy is defined as an absence of public authority including a 'lawless appetite for mischief' or 'plunder' or 'not commissioned and engaged in lawful warfare'.[29] Pirates, then, are not those acting from selfish motives (or not just that) but also those who engage in illegal warfare. They are, perhaps, illegal combatants.

This distinction between private and public was explored in greater detail in a case called *The Republic of Bolivia v Indemnity Mutual Marine Assurance*.[30] Here, an English court was obliged to determine the status of a group of rebels operating on the Bolivian-Brazilian border. The case required consideration of some exclusions in an insurance policy in the aftermath of losses incurred after an attack on the insured

---

[24] H.A. Ormerod, *Piracy in the Ancient World* (1921) 1.

[25] *Russell on Crimes* (6th Ed.), vol I. at 260 quoted in *Republic of Bolivia v. Indemnity Mutual Marine Assurance Co.*, [1909] 1 K.B. 785.

[26] *United Nations Convention on the Law of the Sea*, (1982) 1833 UNTS 3, Articles 100–107; *Convention on the High Seas*, (1958) 450 UNTS 11, Article 15.

[27] See, e.g. J. Brierly, *Law of Nations* (1928) 154; L. Oppenheim, *International Law* (1955) 608.

[28] *In Re Piracy Jure Gentium*, [1934] AC 598.

[29] See Story J.'s opinion in *U.S. v. Brig Malek Adhel* 43 U.S. (2 How.) 232 (1844).

[30] *Republic of Bolivia v Indemnity Mutual Marine Assurance Co.*, *supra* note 25.

shipping by Bolivian rebels representing the 'Free Republic of Acre'. Acts of piracy were indemnified but not acts of rebellion. The key definition in the insurance schedule referred to piracy as 'plunder for private gain . . . not for a public, political end'. Despite the presence of some private motives these motives, were not enough to deprive the Bolivian insurgents of the privilege of public action. The activities of the Acre 'Privateers' were essentially political. The Acre Rebels were dedicated to the overthrow of a particular state authority in a particular place. Theirs was not plunder for personal greed and gain, but plunder for political change.

It is clear, then, from *Republic of Bolivia*, and much of the writing around piracy, that private greed is not the controlling feature of what it means to be a pirate. It is a lack of politics that is the distinguishing mark. Pirates are not our enemies, with that term's implication of political contestation, but rather the enemies of all. The El Acre rebels were enemies of one particular state not of all states. So, though the activities of the El Acre insurgents may have been, in form, almost exactly that of pirates, their plunder had a public purpose. It was lawless but only in relation to the laws and sovereign authority of Bolivia. Theirs was behaviour lacking the '. . . spirit and intention of universal hostility'.[31] But this raises a question about groups who are neither insurgents nor plunderers. Is the political actor whose actions are indiscriminate, a pirate? Can we assimilate the idea of universal hostility to the concept of piracy? Are terrorists enemies of humankind? Are there different sorts of terrorists?

There is a problem with the attempt to analogise terrorists to pirates. Despite the inevitable parallels between some terrorists and the conventional imagery associated with piracy, terrorists, most often, *are* acting for political ends. Yet there has been an effort among some international lawyers to see Al Queda, or the PLO at the time of the Achillo Lauro Affair, as fundamentally pirates.[32]

These international lawyers have argued that Al Queda, say, is not acting in a private capacity for private gain but nor is it, so the characterisation goes, acting against one state. Doing the latter would constitute a political project along the same lines as the insurgents in *Republic of Bolivia* or the rebels in the *Santa Clara* incident (where naval officers took over a Portuguese vessel in an act of rebellion in 1960 against the Salazar regime).[33] Instead, they are configured, like pirates, as existing outside the realm of politics, acting in the name of inhumanity. The political project is *disallowed*, converted into an act of private madness directed at international society generally. This is probably what a League of Nations committee was suggesting in 1926 when it concluded that for the purposes of piracy, 'private ends' could encompass 'anarchistic vengeful motivations'. The contrast, then, is between international

---

[31] *In Re Piracy Jure Gentium, supra* note 28.
[32] Halberstam, *supra* note 2; Reisman, 'In Defence of Public Order', 95 *American Journal of International Law* (2001) 833.
[33] Green, 'The Santa Maria: Rebels or Pirates', 37 *British Yearbook of International Law* (1961) 496.

terrorism and activities of the El Acre rebels who were, as the court put it: 'Not only not the enemy of the human race but the enemy of a particular state' and therefore not pirates.[34]

So, one might say a pirate is either acting in a private capacity or is acting publicly against the whole world. Pirates are either individuals acting for private ends or political actors acting indiscriminately.

Here it is not the quality of the act that is decisive but rather the personality of the actor. Is this terrorist, an enemy of humankind and of all states or simply an enemy of one state? Michael Reisman, has pursued this line in distinguishing previous 'crimes' of terrorism (by, for example, the IRA or Basque separatists) from the attack on the Twin Towers. The activities of the IRA were directed at particular political ends whereas, according to Reisman, the terrorist attack on the United States was an 'aggression' against the 'values of the system of world public order.' As a result of the attack, 'all peoples who value freedom and human rights' have been forced into a war of self-defence.[35] Thus the attack on the United States was not simply a hideous breach of international law and an attack on a particular set of values (say, capitalism or US foreign policy in the Middle-East), but an assault on international society by those outside this society, aimed at the destruction of that society. The key attribute of piracy was an animus against the whole world.

So, the conflation of certain forms of terrorism with the idea of piracy results in a combination of universal jurisdiction over pirate-terrorists (anyone can try them) with their increasing vulnerability to unilateral, discretionary political action (pirates could simply be executed without trial in the 17th Century). In the words of Judge Moore, in the *Lotus Case*, the pirate is to be treated as: 'outlaw, as the enemy of mankind . . . whom any nation may in the interest of all capture and punish.'[36]

This return to piracy comes with some baggage, though. There is a rigid demarcation between good and evil and, paradoxically at the same time, a blurring of categories. There seems to be a search for the clarity of categories: If they are pirates, they must be bad. If they are assimilable to pirates, they must be enemies of mankind. But, at the same time, there is a lack of (jurisprudential) certainty about the nature and identity of pirates themselves. Maybe this failure to achieve the requisite level of certainty can be traced back to piracy's origins. Indeed, were pirates, enemies of (hu)mankind? Were they acting in their private capacity or with an animus against the world? Were they the 'worst of the worst'?

There are passages in *The History of the Peloponnesian Wars* in which Thucididyes describes a transition from a pirate class to a more static, civilised life usually adopted

---

[34] *Republic of Bolivia, supra* note 25, 4.

[35] Reisman, *supra* note 32, 833.

[36] Dissenting Opinion of Judge Moore in *The Lotus Case* (France v. Turkey), PCIJ, Ser. A., No. 9 (1927) 70.

by the most successful pirates or by those colonisers who had expelled the pirates. The pirates, then, begin as romantic heroes, a respectable job for a young Hellene. At some point, these pirates must have ceased to be respectable. This occurs at the very point when their power becomes a threat to the state (or the state system). But this is the point at which pirates are on the cusp of constituting the city states of international society. So, we have the spectre of pirates becoming states or the state system finding its violent foundations in the successes of piracy. And of course there are states that become pirate states. Again, the history of piracy is dotted with examples of states that simply pursue their economic and political interests through piracy. These pirate states may be forerunners to the contemporary outlaw states: partially demonised, partially tolerated. Illyria, for example, was regarded as a 'predatory state' by the Romans.[37]

Indeed, the whole distinction between pirates and a multiplicity of other agents was often very obscure. This is reflected best in the transformation of the Barbary pirates, through association with the Great Powers, from pirate to privateer. Here the pirate becomes a confident, land-based actor capable of generating acts of recognition on the parts of others. The Barbary States in Tunis and Algiers, for example acquired such recognition after years of piracy, and the US began paying tribute to the Barbary pirates at the turn of 18th century.[38] So here we see a transformation from private greed to public respectability (all the while engaging in the *actus* of piracy). But as one of the textbooks on piracy puts it: 'At different stages of their history, most of the maritime peoples have belonged to first one class, then another'.[39]

Indeed, it is not always clear that piracy was at all times criminal. Piracy was often a mode of production supported by the Great Powers and Empires (akin to today's narco-terrorism, perhaps) and there is great uncertainty surrounding the legitimacy of piracy in, say, the ancient Mediterranean where it was, at various times, regarded as a form of production, a cheap way of getting slaves to market and a method of harassing competitors. The pirate, rather like the 'contemporary enemy of humankind', was simply the enemy of particular political projects. It is clear that in the Ancient Mediterranean, for example, pirates are enemies of humankind subject to policing action only where there is Empire. At other times they find themselves in a melting pot of rebellions, wars and revolutions.

So, the counter-trend towards moralising clarities in the international system (good and evil) perhaps returns us to our foundations in the regulation of piracy. If

---

[37] H.A. Ormerod, *supra* note 24, 19.

[38] J. Braithwaite & P. Drahos, *Global Business Regulation* (2000) 419.

[39] H.A. Ormerod, *supra* note 24, 13: Individuals, too, underwent these transformations: Sextus Pompeius, a Roman legend, begins as a brigand in Spain, then is cast as a pirate before being appointed commander of the Roman naval forces, a position he uses to engage in more acts of plunder until the challenge from another Roman force obliges him to return again to piracy.

the pirate is our foundational figure here, the original enemy of humankind to whom all others are to be assimilated, then it is little wonder that categories are blurring as we recover this figure. This is because the return of the pirate is a return to ambiguity and because the identity and identification of pirates has always raised difficult questions about war and peace, about sovereigns and non-sovereigns, and about policing and warfare. Pirates turn out to be not enemies of humankind but humankind in it plural guises.

DISTANCE AND CONTEMPORANEITY IN EXPLORING THE PRACTICE OF STATES: THE BRITISH ARCHIVES IN RELATION TO THE 1957 OMAN AND MUSCAT INCIDENT

Anthony Carty[*]

Introduction

The international lawyer needs, as much as the diplomatic historian, to understand State conduct and this means having reliable access to State intentions. These remain, in principle, State secrets except in so far as the State itself chooses to disclose them, or when recalcitrant officials leak them, or journalists otherwise come improperly or irregularly on State intentions. There is a second equally important problem, especially concerning the analysis of contemporary events, and that is to know whether one can be sure of the factual circumstances which are supposed to justify the invocation of a norm. Based on archival records in the UK Foreign Office (FO) which are here revealed for the first time, the present article focuses on the active FO discussions in July and August 1957 about the best way to present the UK's relations with Oman and Muscat internationally, when an Arab block of States, led by Egypt, tried to place (what it called) UK armed aggression against Oman on the agenda of the Security Council. The legal advice of Francis Vallat and Sir Gerald Fitzmaurice played a considerable part in these discussions which reveal a vision of governmental structures for dealing with international relations which appear very much a hangover from the period of the High Renaissance. Secrecy is prized as the most reasonable option when it comes to providing public explanations of State conduct. Without consistent and comprehensive access to the governmental policy-making process in which government international lawyers may also have a significant input, it is impossible to assess the process of decision-making in such a way as to determine exactly how international law is being interpreted, applied, followed or ignored.

This Chapter appeared initially as an article in vol. 9 of the Singapore Yearbook of International Law. The editors would like to thank the Singapore Yearbook of International Law for its kind permission to reprint this chapter.

* Professor of Law, University of Aberdeen; Visiting Professor, School of Law, City University of Hong Kong. This article is the result of a Foreign Office archival research project on Sir Gerald Fitzmaurice funded by the United Kingdom Arts and Humanities Research Board. I acknowledge the assistance of the AHRD Research Assistant, Dr. R.A. Smith, in the retrieval of much of the archival materials on the Oman and Muscat Incident.

1. State Practice

It is very difficult to discuss contemporaneous events for a number of reasons. The main one is the fact that those involved are usually still alive and may continue to be engaged in the very same events that are ongoing. Perspectives and opinions about the best course of action will remain openly contested. Furthermore, there will not usually be agreed objective and detached sources from which one can draw to determine the nature of the events. There will be much fresh, first-hand testimony, but it will be conflicting. Where official events are concerned, and State practice falls under this rubric, there will not be direct access to primary source material, and, indeed it may be wondered whether the very idea of primary source material itself is becoming archaic in the post-modern age of political spin. Contemporary events will be important to those still engaged and passions will run high in attempting to discuss them. At the same time the objective, detached, perhaps officially agreed records for the description of the events will not be available and there will be no final authority to adjudicate contesting versions of the events.

All of this impinges directly on the practice of the international lawyer in at least two respects. The international lawyer needs, as much as the diplomatic historian, to understand State conduct and this means having reliable access to State intentions. These remain, in principle, State secrets except in so far as the State itself chooses to disclose them, or when recalcitrant officials leak them, or journalists otherwise come improperly or irregularly on State intentions. Such well-known problems pose for the theory of State practice the temptation to avoid the psychological or intentional element of State practice when collecting and analysing it. I suggest that it is a remedy a lot worse than the disease.

There is a second equally important problem with the analysis of contemporary events in which States participate, and that is to know whether one can be sure of the factual circumstances which are supposed to justify the invocation of a norm. Perhaps the most usual example is where a State alleges that it has intelligence information (which it cannot disclose for fear of endangering sources, etc) that another country constitutes an imminent threat justifying pre-emptive actions.

International Law is supposedly based upon the practice of states. Whether this is simply a matter of assessing the development of a new rule of general customary law or more specifically a matter of assessing the attitude of a particular state to the application of the evolving law to itself, orthodox doctrine still supposes that the practice will have two elements, the material practice of the state and a psychological element which evidences the intention of the state and the way in which it makes clear whether it is following a rule, or somehow, creating a rule as a matter of legal obligation. Therefore, in principle, the international legal practitioner should expect to become embroiled in all the problems of contemporary history writing.[1]

An authoritative recent representation of the debates about the two elements which make up customary law, material practice and the subjective element, is Mendelson's article "The Subjective Element in Customary International Law".[2] He raises the important question of whether, in order to assess the subjective element of custom, it is necessary to know the inner workings of a state bureaucracy. States do not have minds of their own, ". . . and in any case, since much of the decision making within government bureaucracies takes place in secret, we cannot know what States (or those who direct or speak for them) really think, but only what they say they think. There may be something of an exaggeration here. In some instances we can discover their views because the opinions of their legal advisers or governments are published. [Footnote: Though admittedly this is done only on a partial and selective basis and often only long after the event; and though it must also be conceded that the opinion of a government legal adviser does not invariably become that of the government . . .]" After these important deliberations, Mendelson writes that it is better to speak of the subjective rather than the psychological element of custom ". . . for it is more a question of the positions taken by the organs of States about international law, in their internal processes [Footnote: Including the communications of governments to national legislatures and courts, and the express or implicit prise de position about rules of international law by national courts and legislatures in the exercise of their functions] and in their interaction with other States, than of their beliefs."[3]

The United Kingdom Materials on International Law (until recently, edited by the late Geoffrey Marston) have been available in the British Yearbook annually since 1978. Marston has followed what is called the Model Plan for the Classification of Documents concerning State Practice in the Field of Public International Law, adopted by the Committee of Ministers of the Council of Europe in its Resolution (68)17 of 28 June 1968. This was amended by Recommendation (97)11 of 12 June 1997, following General Assembly Resolution 2099(XX) on technical assistance to promote the teaching, study, dissemination, etc of international law. The changes are not significant, and the essence of Marston's approach is that he sets out, as Mendelson has put it ". . . positions taken by organs of States about international law, in their internal processes and in their interaction with other States . . ."[4]

---

[1] A. Carty & R. Smith (eds.) *Sir Gerald Fitzmaurice and the World Crisis: A Legal Adviser in the Foreign Office (1932–1945)* (2000) 23–27.

[2] Mendelson, 'The Subjective Element in Customary International Law', 66 *British Yearbook of International Law* (1995) 177.

[3] *Ibid* 195–196.

[4] *Ibid.* See further, Marston, 'The Evidences of British State Practice in the Field of International Law' in A. Carty & G. Danilenko (eds.) *Perestroika and International Law, Current Anglo-Soviet Approaches to International Law* (1990) 35, saying that parliamentary sources predominate in the UK

What will be attempted here is to analyse further the implications of these activities with respect to a single significant issue, the use of force by Britain in international relations, with respect to one incident as offering a pivotal precedent, the Oman and Muscat Incident of 1957 and the rule of international law with respect to intervention in a country at the request of its government. However, before considering the case-study in some detail, some general remarks can be made about the significance of penetrating the bowels of the State. In strict legal terms, the issue can arise in distinct ways. It may be a matter of determining whether Britain is observing or violating a rule of law. Alternatively this may be a matter of assessing what contribution Britain is making to the development or clarification of the law, where it is taken to be uncertain. In either case, it is not enough simply to know what verbal positions British state organs take up. It is necessary to know what Britain has actually done. The discrepancy will arise where the British positions are either not true or not the whole truth. But it need not even be so black and white morally. It may simply be that without the full picture, the actions of a State, such as the UK, may be unintelligible.

2. The Practical Requirement of Secrecy

In an article published in 1986, a Foreign and Commonwealth Office (FCO) Legal Adviser drew attention to the fact that "informal agreements" played a large part in British foreign relations.[5] The basic principle is that a state is free to deny itself the advantages of concluding a legally binding treaty in order to benefit from the advantages of concluding informal instruments. Security and defence issues are not the only issues covered, but it is clear that the advantage here is the flexibility which comes from secrecy. This background will usually be relevant to cases involving the use of force, as there will be agreements between the UK and its allies that are not public knowledge, or there may be relevant agreements even if the UK is not itself formally a party to them. This was the case with Oman and Muscat in 1957.

To present the issue in a wider context, one might take a well-known and still uncertain case, the US bombing of Libya in 1986 from bases within the UK. The terms under which the US enjoys the use of military bases within the UK are known only to be the subject of informal agreements or even understandings. With the US bombing of Libya from British territory, one question was whether the UK had the full legal power to permit the US action. The UK did not try to claim that the US had acted independently of it, but supported US action, again relying upon undisclosable intelligence information that there were very specific Libyan targets

---

Materials on International Law, i.e. positions taken by Ministers before Parliament. He points out that only rarely is material made available here which has not already been released to the public.

[5] Aust, 'The Theory and Practice of Informal International Instruments', 35 *International and Comparative Law Quarterly* (1986) 787.

engaged in terrorist activity. The information could not be disclosed for fear of jeopardising sources. The Prime Minister, in an emergency debate in the House of Commons on 16 April 1986, affirmed that her legal advice was that the bombing targets chosen were permitted by Article 51 of the UN Charter, as a matter of an inherent right of self-defence against armed attack.[6]

It was argued, however, in the House of Commons debate, that she should be obliged to demonstrate, with relevant evidence before the Security Council, that Article 51 had been observed. This would mean producing concrete evidence that, at the least, without an air strike there would be planned raids from specific camps, putting British citizens at risk. The Foreign Secretary, Sir Geoffrey Howe, himself a Q.C., argued in reply that the right of self defence includes the right to destroy or weaken one's assailants, to reduce his resources and to weaken his will so as to discourage and prevent further violence.

The argument by the Foreign Secretary was, to repeat the point, presented in a context where the information which was supposed to ground the threat or risk and the justification for military action could not be disclosed because it would jeopardise sources of intelligence information. There was effectively a claim to determine unilaterally the scope of international obligations with respect to restraint on the use of force, not only with respect to the extent of the norm but also the factual context of its application.

Such resort to arguments about the necessity of State secrets leaves the UK open to the types of charges levied against it in works such as Curtis' The Ambiguities of Power and the successor volume, The Great Deception, Anglo-American Power and World Order.[7] Curtis' view is that Britain has a clear foreign policy aim, which it follows in concert wit the United States. This aim is to preserve as much as it can the economic, political and military advantages which it possessed at the time of the Empire. In his analysis, Britain continues to be largely successful in the pursuit of this policy in the Middle East, especially in the Gulf, and in Southeast Asia. Military interventions, whether covert or open, and support for friendly regimes, particularly military and other security training, will be attuned to the need to preserve these interests. Obviously, the language of international law is a potentially useful propaganda weapon in the hands of opponents and so no useful purpose is served by an explicit and provocative disregard of it.

Therefore the British rhetoric is one of continued commitment to the principles of the UN Charter, viz., above all, non-intervention in the internal affairs of other countries, respect for human rights and democracy, and priority to the peaceful settlement

---

[6] See Carty, 'The UK, the Compulsory Jurisdiction of the ICJ and the Peaceful Settlement of Disputes' in A. Carty & G. Danilenko (eds.) *Perestroika and International Law*, 131–3. Aust's 1986 International and Comparative Law Quarterly article is discussed here.

[7] M. Curtis, *The Ambiguities of Power, British Foreign Policy since 1945* (1995); *idem, The Great Deception, Anglo-American Power and World Order* (1998).

of disputes. Positions in accordance with these principles will be declared in international fora and even in public debates within national fora. The actual practice is difficult to put together because it remains largely secret and one obtains only sporadic glimpses of it.

3. Implications for the Development of Customary Law on the Use of Force: The Example of Oman and Muscat (1957)

What are the implications of these polemics for attempts to assess what contribution Britain is making to the development of international customary law on the law relating to the use of force and the right of intervention at the behest of a friendly government? For instance, the 1986 United Kingdom Materials on International Law contain a document produced by the Planning Staff of the FCO in July 1984, entitled "Is Intervention Ever Justified?"[8] The question is how, or even whether, such a document is to be read critically, i.e. how to assess the relationship of the document to an inevitably largely hidden practice. For instance, in paragraph II.6, intervention under a treaty with, or at the invitation of, another state is mentioned. If one state requests assistance from another, then clearly that intervention cannot be dictatorial and is therefore not unlawful. In 1976, the Security Council recalled that it is the inherent right of every state, in the exercise of its sovereignty, to request assistance from any other state or group of states. An example of such lawful intervention at the request of states might be the British aid to Muscat and Oman.

Curtis comments on this incident as follows. Oman requested British military aid to quell a revolt in the north of the territory in the summer of 1957. In fact, in Curtis' view, Oman was a de facto client state controlled by Britain as much as any former colony. Its armed forces were commanded by British officers under the overall control of a British general. The Ministries of Finance and Petroleum respectively and the Director of the intelligence service were British. Banking and the oil company management were controlled by the British. The country was desperately poor, with infant mortality at 75%. The Royal Air Force and the Special Air Service together struggled until 1959 to put down a revolt against these conditions. Oman continued after its suppression to serve British financial and other interests very well. Extensive bombing of villages was an integral part of this campaign. At one point, the British Political Resident recommended that the villages should be warned that unless they surrendered ring leaders, they would be destroyed one by one, etc.[9]

---

[8] G. Marston, (ed.), 'United Kingdom Materials on International Law', 57 *British Yearbook of International Law* (1986) 614–620.

[9] M. Curtis, *The Ambiguities of Power, British Foreign Policy since 1945, supra* note 7, 98–99.

The FCO paper fully recognises the complexity and controversy surrounding this area of law. It continues, on mentioning Oman in 1957, to say in paragraph II.7 that international law does prohibit interference (except maybe humanitarian) when a civil war is taking place and control of the state's territory is divided between warring parties. At the same time the paper claims that it is widely accepted that outside interference in favour of one party to the struggle permits counter-intervention on behalf of the other, as happened recently in Angola.

Before considering what a closer examination of the Archives might reveal about the Oman Incident, it might be interesting to consider some reactions in the academic community to Curtis' work. The reception of The Great Deception in a review in International Affairs is pointed. The review begins: "This book does not explain, so much as to seek to condemn . . ." Curtis supposedly implores his readers to extricate themselves from the view of establishment scholarship which includes the vast majority of academics. One might imagine Curtis scouring the archives looking for evidence to incriminate British and American policy makers. He often refers back to his earlier book The Ambiguities of Power where the sources are often personal recollections or references to other secondary works. If his sources are so accessible, why then have only a tiny minority of other scholars been able to see the story this way. The reviewer concludes by exhorting Curtis to ". . . be more measured in his judgments, show more sensitivity to complexities and moral dilemmas that confront policy-makers, and offer some more viable alternatives to the policies he so roundly condemns . . ."[10]

There was a very full discussion within the Foreign Office in July and August 1957 about the best way to present the UK's relations with Oman and Muscat internationally, when an Arab block of States, led by Egypt, tried to have what it called UK armed aggression against Oman placed on the agenda of the Security Council. Legal advice by Sir Gerald Fitzmaurice and Francis Vallat played a considerable part. The Foreign Office was reacting to arguments put forward in a particular context, a UN forum. Arab States, backed by the Soviet Union, wanted to have British military action in the Sultanate characterised in UN Charter language as constituting aggression against the independent State of Oman, coming from British forces in Muscat.

4. Fitmzaurice's and Vallat's Legal Advice

The advice from Vallat for the benefit of the Secretary of State was that intervention, at the request of the Sultan of Muscat, to put down an insurrection by tribes in Oman was legal. Intervention is wrongful but that only refers to dictatorial interference, not assistance or cooperation. Oppenheim gives numerous examples of

---

[10] Dobson, 'The Great Deception (Book Review)', 74 *International Affairs* (1998) 923–924.

military assistance to maintain internal order, including Portugal in 1826, Austria in 1849, Cuba in 1917 and Nicaragua in 1926–1927.[11]

Fitzmaurice is more explicit about the importance of the status of Muscat and Oman. Oman is not an independent State. In the international legal sense, it is not a State at all, but merely part of Muscat and Oman. The Imam of Oman exercised no territorial sovereignty. There are no frontiers between Oman and any other State or between Oman and Muscat. An agreement, known as the Sib Agreement, was reached in 1920. During the negotiations in 1920, a request for independence was completely rejected. The Agreement worked well until 1954. The Sultan's sovereignty was recognised by the Imam, in that external affairs remained in the hands of the Sultan, i.e. concerning individuals and their lawsuits with foreign administrations. The Imam's adherents relied upon passports issued by the Sultanate. Judgments of the Muscat Appellate Court were accepted in the interior. An attempt to assert independence in 1954 failed. No State had regarded "Oman" as a sovereign State independent of Muscat until the Saudi and Egyptian intrigues which followed a Saudi incursion into neighbouring Buraimi in 1952.[12]

This presentation of the situation was successful when the UK argued it before the Security Council. Sir Pierson Dixon mirrored the legal advice closely. There could be no aggression against the independent State of Oman because none existed. The Sultan of Muscat and Oman had his sovereignty over both recognised since the 19th century. Egypt and other countries claim that the independence of Oman was reaffirmed in the 1920 Treaty of Sib. This Treaty granted the tribes of the interior a certain autonomy but did not recognise Oman as an independent State. This request was refused by the Sultan. Also the agreement was not a treaty, but merely an agreement between the Sultan and his subjects. Sir Pierson Dixon followed Fitzmaurice's line very closely about the later marks of sovereignty. He concluded by saying the UK's action in supporting the legitimate Government of Muscat and Oman had been in the interests of stability of this area. If the subversion there had not been checked, the consequences might have been felt beyond the Sultanate and would not have been to the advantage of any of the countries in the region that signed the letter to place this issue on the agenda of the Security Council.[13]

The vote against putting the matter on the agenda was five to four, with two abstentions.[14] Only the Philippines denied the legality of an intervention at a request of a government. The Soviet Union confined itself to generalities about the oppression of the national liberation movement of the Oman people. There was little stress on the argument about outside intervention in Oman, except from France, which led the vote against adopting the Arab item on the Security Council agenda.

---

[11] UK, Foreign Office, FO/371/126877/EA1015/89.
[12] UK, Foreign Office, FO/371/126887/EA1015/365.
[13] UK, Foreign Office, FO/371/126884/EA1015/282(A), 20 August 1957.
[14] UK, Foreign Office, FO/371/126884/EA1015/283, 20 August 1957.

The UK itself played it down because it did not want to exacerbate its relations with Saudi Arabia.[15] An item to this effect was circulated to all the British embassies in the Middle East. Although the UK knew of the Saudi involvement, a higher priority had to be given to drawing Saudi Arabia out of the Soviet and Egyptian sphere of political influence.[16] This goal would have been lost if one had entered into specific detail about Saudi subversive activities. Instead the legality of a response to an invitation for assistance was stressed.

At the same time Ehili Lauterpacht gave a full account of the events in the International and Comparative Law Quarterly.[17] The account reproduced a statement by the Foreign Secretary in the House of Commons in July 1957. It followed the same lines as Sir Pierson Dixon's UN presentation, stressing the invitation from the Sultan. He emphasised the importance for Britain's reputation in the region, that it responded to its implicit obligation to protect the rulers of sheikdoms under British protection from attack. There was a direct British interest and the House did not need to have stressed the importance of the Persian Gulf. The fact that dissidents had received assistance from outside the territories of the Sultan was briefly mentioned. The Joint Under-Secretary of State at the Foreign Office also made a statement concerning the right to send arms to support a ruler upon invitation. The UN had not been informed directly because it was an internal matter. Finally, a note was sent to the Soviet Government. The latter alleged Britain had recognised the independence of Oman in an agreement and had now invaded the territory of Oman and evaded responsibility for this aggression by blocking discussion at the UN. The British response was that the district of Oman had been an integral part of the dominions of the Sultan of Muscat and Oman since the middle of the 18th century and had been recognised as such in a number of treaties between the Sultan and foreign Powers. The UK's action was a response to a direct request on the occasion of an internal uprising stimulated from outside the country. There was no question of UK aggression against Oman and, of course, it had never recognised the independence of the Oman area in any treaty.

Lauterpacht himself offered an extensive note on the law on intervention, suggesting a limit to the right to intervene by invitation where a revolt had reached the point of intensity that recognition of belligerency would be permissible. He commented briefly from the answers in the House of Commons, that the insurgents did not represent any substantial dissentient proportion of the inhabitants of the area subject to the rule of the Sultan and that, in any event, they were stimulated and supported in their rebellion by foreign elements. Lauterpacht finally reiterated the international treaty practice evidencing the Sultanate's independence. However, he

---

[15] UK, Foreign Office, FO/371/126878/EA1015.
[16] See also G. Nolte, *Eingreifen auf Einladung* (1999) 86–89.
[17] Lauterpacht, 'Contemporary Practice of the United Kingdom', 7 *International and Comparative Law Quarterly* (1958) 99–109.

did add two points. In an agreement in 1891, the Sultan pledged not to alienate his dominions save to the British government, thereby giving the latter a direct interest in anything affecting the territorial integrity of the Sultanate. Lauterpacht concluded, further, that its independence was in no way compromised by the undertaking of the Sultan, given in 1923, that he would not grant permission for the exploitation of petroleum in his territory "without consulting the Political Agent at Muscat and without the approval of the High Government of India". In a footnote, Lauterpacht remarked that the rights under this agreement cannot properly be said to have lapsed with India's independence. Nor can it be said that India succeeded to these rights. The term "Government of India" was a mere administrative convenience.

5. Pressure for Public Disclosure: Sir Ronald Wingate's Counsel

However, further pressure came upon the Foreign Office from quite a different source: the domestic media, in particular an article in the Guardian of 7 August 1957. Pressure grew within the UK, in the media and through questions in Parliament, to uncover what the exact relationship between HMG and the Sultan of Muscat and Oman was. Here, the picture which emerged in Foreign Office discussions was quite different from the public face at the UN. A focus for discussion was whether to publish the Sib Agreement which appeared to define the relations within the Sultanate. This was thought not advisable, as the more the history and operation of the agreement was explored, the clearer it would become that the only coherence and stability that the Sultanate enjoyed came from British support at every level. The British Political Agent, now Sir Ronald Wingate, who had effectively written both sides of that Agreement, was still alive in 1957.

In September 1957, Sir Ronald came to see officials in the Foreign Office. He explained to Foreign Office officials, in particular a Mr. Walmsley, that the Western concept of sovereignty was meaningless in the region. The Walis, whom the Sultan maintained in Oman, did nothing and could not be said to constitute a token of government. The entire Sultanate of Muscat and Oman was, for all practical purposes, not administered. The situation there in 1954, as in 1920, could be compared to the Scottish Highlands before 1745. The Sultan was completely dependent on Britain and powerless outside a few coastal towns. Wingate commented upon a copy of Dixon's speech to the Security Council. He said that he could see nothing wrong with it, except that he would have expressed himself more frankly. The immediate comment of Walmsley was that while one might speak reasonably to reasonable people, it was impossible to concede any point unnecessarily in the UN.[18]

---

[18] UK, Foreign Office, FO/371/126887/EA1015/371.

Wingate made a further detailed comment on the Agreement of Sib and Sir Pierson Dixon's speech. Treaties concluded by the Sultan did not mean he had any effective sovereignty over an undefined area. His power had always extended only to a few coastal towns and it would be impossible to hold that the Sultan exercised any sovereignty over the interior between 1913 and 1955. Indeed the interior tribesmen, who hated the Sultan, could have driven him into the sea had it not been for a strong battalion of imperial troops. This policy cost the UK a lot and served no purpose. It had been there in the 19th century to keep the French out and to combat the slave trade. Both reasons were long defunct. In 1920, Wingate, as Political Agent, undertook to reorganise the Sultanate, putting Egyptian personnel in charge of administration. He, Wingate, and not the Sultan, refused to acknowledge the independence of Oman. He refused to recognise the Imam of Oman as Imam because of the religious significance of such an act. It would have given the Imam authority over the whole Sultanate. However, the Imam remained as head of the tribal confederation. The agreement recognised the facts of the situation in a way that permitted Muscat and the coastal Oman on the one side, and the tribes of the interior Oman on the other, to exist as separate self-governing units. No question of allegiance to the Sultan arose. What the Sultan did in 1955 was not to reassert his authority but to take over the interior by armed force. This could be justified as necessary for the security of the coastal regions. However, one also had to be careful about how to deal with the extraordinary rise in the Sultan's revenues, derived presumably from oil exploration rights which he had granted in the interior tribal areas, and which necessitated the provision of security for the drilling parties in the tribal territories.[19]

Wingate's comments were relevant to the advisability of publishing the Sib Agreement as a way of silencing British media controversy about the status of the Sultan, in particular the article in the Guardian of 7 August 1957. It was thought that, on balance, publication would merely show how uncertain the situation in Muscat and Oman was, although selected journalists were shown the agreement on a confidential basis. A further detailed internal FO reading of the Agreement of Sib revealed that it was difficult to use. The difficulty of the Agreement was that it made no mention of sovereignty for either side, so officials reasoned that they would have to elaborate a thesis that the Sultan's authority was implicitly assumed and that the burden of proof would be on Omanites to show they had any corresponding sovereignty. The whole question was that much more prickly because of a British Administration Report which appeared on a FO Confidential Print on the Buraimi. ". . . The Agreement of Sib virtually establishes two states, the coast under the Sultan, and the interior, that is Oman proper, under the rule of the Imam . . . The tribes and tribal leaders having attained in their own eyes complete

---

[19] UK, Foreign Office, FO/371/126829: FO Confidential Note on the Agreement of Sib, and Sir Pierson Dixon's Speech in the Security Council of 20/8/1957, prepared by Sir Ronald Wingate.

independence . . .".[20] The best one could make of this would be to stress the words "virtually" and "in their own eyes". The Sultan's interpretation of this agreement was equally valid. There was a consensus that this was also the direction of Wingate's commentary.[21]

A further difficulty is that while Wingate's report as Political Agent states categorically that the demand for the independence of Oman was refused, it also makes a number of uncomfortable points, if one had to rely upon it by publishing it. He denigrated the unparalleled degree of ineptitude of the Sultan and even worse, his despatch made the following "acid remarks" on British policy: ". . . Our influence has been entirely self-interested, has paid no regard to the peculiar political and social conditions of the country and its rulers and by bribing effete Sultans to enforce unpalatable measures which benefited none but ourselves, and permitting them to rule without protest, has done more to alienate the interior and to prevent the Sultans from re-establishing their authority than all the rest put together . . ."[22]

One might try to say that the Agreement had been violated, and ceased to exist by virtue of the subversion coming from Oman and so it was quite pointless to produce it. However, if one attempts to argue that the balance of the Agreement has been destroyed by the aggression of the Imam Ghalib and treats the Agreement as no longer valid, to do this ". . . we should have to explain how completely he was in the pocket of the Saudis, and this would conflict with the Secretary of State's decision that at present we must avoid attacking the Saudi Government over Oman . . ."[23]

Therefore, it can be argued that in 1957, the senior Foreign Office officials did not think that there was any realistic way in which they could present publicly what they understood to be happening in the Sultanate of Muscat and Oman, other than in the Charter language of friendly states and supporting internal order within them. In fact there was no State other than what Britain undertook to maintain, but the alternative would be for Saudi Arabia, Egypt and eventually the Soviet Union to occupy a space if Britain were to vacate it. Dorril explains at length that further insurgency against the Sultan in the late 1960s convinced the Wilson Government of the need for change, and the Conservative Government gave the goahead at the end of June 1970. It was agreed to replace the Sultan with his English-educated and more competent son. It still took until 1975 to defeat Chinese and Soviet-backed insurgency.[24]

It is ironical that assessments of Curtis and Dorril, that the Sultanate was so misgoverned in the years before the 1970 coup, are part of the implicitly official UK view of that period from the hindsight of post-coup developments. The two authors rely upon much secondary evidence, as the Chatham House reviewer complains, but

---

[20] UK, Foreign Office, FO Confidential Print on the Buraimi, 157.
[21] UK, Foreign Office, FO/371/26882/EA1015/235.
[22] UK, Foreign Office, FO/371/26882/EA1015/235(A).
[23] *Ibid.*
[24] S. Dorril, *MI6: Fifty Years of Special Operations* (2000) 729–735.

the secondary evidence is a book called Oman: The Making of a Modern State, by John Townsend and published in 1977.[25] Townsend was economic adviser to the Oman Government from 1972 to 1975. Curtis quotes him as arguing that, after the regime change, the Sultan's response to the rebels in the 1960s was not an alternative program with proposals for reform or economic assistance, but simply the use of even greater force.[26] By 1970, that policy promised to lose the Sultanate to communist-backed forces. This was not acceptable. Furthermore, with the Shell-owned Petroleum Development (Oman) oil company producing oil in commercial quantities by 1967, there was plenty of domestic revenue to allow scope for a more pragmatic social policy.

6. *The International Lawyers Perplexity*

For the perplexed international lawyer, the question that is most pressing is whether and how the Charter paradigm and language for the analysis and understanding of international society can retain not merely formal validity but also a significant impact upon the forces at work in that society. Perhaps the least that one can say as an international lawyer is that positions taken up by the UK, or for that matter any other government, cannot be taken at face value, or even be treated with anything other than complete scepticism. Without consistent and comprehensive access to the governmental policy-making process in which government international lawyers may also have a significant input, it is impossible to assess the process of decision-making in such a way as to determine exactly how international law is being interpreted, applied, followed or ignored.

The difficulty has already been seen to lie in part with the continuing and presumably inevitable secrecy of diplomacy where strategic interests are engaged. This is, in effect, to acquiesce to the vision that governmental structures for dealing with international relations remain a hangover from the period of the High Renaissance. A typology of this world is provided by Jens Bartelson in his A Genealogy of Sovereignty.[27] The so-called modern state arising out of the wars of religion of the 16th and 17th centuries is traumatised by its bloody foundation and hence silent about its origins. It becomes the subject of Descartes' distinction between the immaterial subject and the material reality which it observes, classifies and analyses. Knowledge supposes a subject and this subject, for international relations, is the Hobbesian sovereign who is not named, but names, not observed, but observes, a mystery for whom everything must be transparent. The problem of knowledge is

---

[25] J. Townsend, *Oman: The Making of a Modern State* (1977).
[26] M. Curtis, *Web of Deceit: Britain's Real Role in the World* (2003) 279.
[27] J. Bartelson, *A Genealogy of Sovereignty* (1995), especially Chapter 5.

the problem of security, which is attained through rational control and analysis. Self-understanding is limited to an analysis of the extent of the power of the sovereign, measured geo-politically. Other sovereigns are not unknown "others" in the anthropological sense, but simply "enemies", opponents with conflicting interests whose behaviour can and should be calculated.

So, mutual recognition by sovereigns does not imply acceptance of a common international order, but merely a limited measure of mutual construction of identity resting upon an awareness of sameness, an analytical recognition of factual, territorial separation. The primary definition of state interest is not a search for resemblances or affinities, but a matter of knowing how to conduct one's own affairs, while hindering those of others. Interest is a concept of a collection of primary, unknowable, self-defining subjects, whose powers of detached, analytical empirical observation take absolute precedence over any place for knowledge based on passion or empathy.

However, a more precise paradigm suitable for a situation which may be peculiar to North-South relations is suggested by Robert Cooper's The Breaking of Nations.

7. Concluding Remarks: Towards a More Precise Paradigm

Cooper denies the universality of international society and divides it into three parts, the pre-modern, the modern and the post-modern. The United Nations is an expression of the modern, while failed States come largely within the ambit of the pre-modern. This means, on a practical level, that the language of the modern UN does not apply to pre-modern States. This is not to say the Charter is violated in that context. It is simply conceptually inapplicable.[28]

The pre-modern refers to the pre-modern, post-imperial chaos of Somalia, Afghanistan and Liberia. The State no longer fulfils Max Weber's criterion of having a legitimate monopoly on the use of force. Cooper elaborates upon this with respect to Sierra Leone.[29] This country's collapse teaches three lessons. Chaos spreads (in this case, to Liberia, as the chaos in Rwanda spread to the Congo). Secondly, crime takes over when the State collapses. As the law loses force, privatised violence enters the picture. It then spreads to the West, where the profits are to be made. The third lesson is that chaos as such will spread, so that it cannot go unwatched in critical parts of the world. An aspect of this crisis is that the state structures themselves, which are the basis of the UN language of law, are a last imperial imposition of the process of decolonisation.

---

[28] R. Cooper, *The Breaking of Nations, Order and Chaos in the Twenty-First Century* (2003), especially 16–37.
[29] *Ibid* 66–69.

The modernity of the UN is that it rests upon State sovereignty and that in turn rests upon the separation of domestic and foreign affairs.[30] Cooper's words are that this is still a world in which the ultimate guarantor of security is force. This is as true for realist conceptions of international society as governed by clashes of interest, as it is for idealist theories that the anarchy of States can be replaced by the hegemony of a world government or a collective security system. I quote: "The UN Charter emphasizes State sovereignty on the one hand and aims to maintain order by force."[31]

It is because the world is divided into three parts that three different security policies will be followed.[32] Europe is a zone of security beyond which there are zones of chaos which it cannot ignore. While the imperial urge may be dead, some form of defensive imperialism is inevitable. All that the UN is made to do is to throw its overwhelming power on the side of a State that is the victim of aggression.[33] Cooper generally counsels against foreign forays. European humanitarian intervention abroad is to intervene in another continent with another history and to invite a greater risk of humanitarian catastrophe.[34] However, the three lessons of recent State collapse in Sierra Leone and other places cannot be ignored. Empire does not work in the post-imperial age, i.e. the acquisition of territory and population. Voluntary imperialism, a UN trusteeship, may give the people of a failed State a breathing space and it is the only legitimate form possible, but the coherence and persistence of purpose to achieve this will usually be absent. There is also no clear way of resolving the humanitarian aim of intervening to save lives and the imperial aim of establishing the control necessary to do this.[35] While Cooper concludes by saying that goals should be expressed in relatives rather than absolutes, his argument is really that the pre-modern and the modern give us incommensurate orders of international society.

This brings one back to the conversation between Walmsley and Wingate in the Foreign Office in 1957. After reading Dixon's address to the Security Council, Wingate said he would have expressed himself more frankly. Walmsley replied that one could speak reasonably to reasonable people, but that at the UN it is better not to make unnecessary admissions. I think that is where Britain still remains, except that the world in which Britain operates today has become infinitely more dangerous. Is it not time for a rethink of the nature of reasonableness?

---

[30] *Ibid* 22–26.
[31] *Ibid* 23.
[32] Unfortunately, time does not permit further discussion of post-modern Europe.
[33] *Ibid* 58.
[34] *Ibid* 61.
[35] *Ibid* 65–75.

INDEX